The Psychology of Prejudice:
The Ontario Symposium, Volume 7

ONTARIO SYMPOSIUM ON PERSONALITY AND SOCIAL PSYCHOLOGY

THE PSYCHOLOGY OF PREJUDICE:

The Ontario Symposium, Volume 7

Edited by

MARK P. ZANNA
University of Waterloo

JAMES M. OLSON
University of Western Ontario

LEA LAWRENCE ERLBAUM ASSOCIATES, PUBLISHERS
1994   Hillsdale, New Jersey   Hove and London

Lawrence Erlbaum Associates, Inc., Publishers
365 Broadway
Hillsdale, New Jersey 07642

Library of Congress Cataloging-in-Publication Data

The Psychology of prejudice / edited by Mark P. Zanna, James M. Olson.
        p.   cm. -- (The Ontario symposium ; v. 7)
    Includes bibliographical references and index.
    ISBN 0-8058-1119-2 (cloth). -- 0-8058-1355-1 (paper)
    1. Prejudice--Congresses. 2. Stereotype (Psychology)-
-congresses. I. Zanna, Mark P. II. Olson, James M., 1953-
III. Series.
BF575.P9P78   1994
303.3'85--dc20   93-32412
                                                                      CIP

Printed in the United States of America
10 9 8 7 6 5 4 3 2

Books published by Lawrence Erlbaum Associates are printed on acid-free paper,
and their bindings are chosen for strength and durability.

Contents

Preface

The Seventh Ontario Symposium on Personality and Social Psychology was held at the University of Waterloo, June 22–23, 1991. The topic of the symposium was the psychology of prejudice, and the presentations covered a wide variety of issues in this area. As has become the fortunate custom of Ontario Symposia, the papers generated many interesting discussions among participants, as well as many productive interchanges with the approximately 80 additional audience members (25 faculty and 55 graduate students) from 15 Canadian universities.

The current volume consists of the expanded and updated versions of papers presented initially at the conference. The span of time between the conference and the publication of the book is the result of the practice of giving the authors an opportunity to revise their papers based on, among other things, feedback obtained from other participants and audience members at the conference. Also, as has become customary, contributors provided comments on preliminary drafts of other participants' chapters—an undertaking for which we, as editors, are grateful.

The chapters in this volume are very loosely organized in the following sequence of topics: The determinants and consequences of stereotypes (Chapters 1 to 5); individual differences in prejudicial attitudes (Chapters 6 and 7); inter-group relations (Chapters 8 and 9); the responses of victims to prejudice and discrimination (Chapters 10 to 12); and, finally, an integrative summary/commentary (Chapter 13). Specifically, in Chapter 1, Gardner examines various definitions of stereotypes and argues that more attention be paid to stereotypes as consensual beliefs. In Chapter 2, Snyder and Miene provide a functional analysis of stereotypes (and prejudice). In Chapter 3, Banaji and Greenwald propose (and provide evidence for) the existence of implicit or unconscious stereotyping (and prejudice). In Chapter 4, Esses, Haddock, and Zanna demonstrate the influence of negative mood states on stereotypes. In Chapter 5, Neuberg proposes a model of the effects of stereotypes on expectancy confirmation. In Chapter 6, Altemeyer discusses his program of research on Right-Wing Authoritarianism (RWA) and suggests methods for reducing the prejudice of RWAs. In Chapter 7, Batson and Burris review (and organize) the very interesting literature on the religiosity-prejudice relation. In Chapter 8, Bourhis discusses research on the effect of power on discrimination in the minimal group paradigm. In Chapter 9, Bourhis, Sachdev, and Gagnon provide (for the first time in North America) a detailed description of the various measures of discrimination that can be derived from the Tajfel Matrices. In Chapter 10, Taylor, Wright, and Porter attempt to account for the fact that members of minority groups typically believe that they personally experience less discrimination than a typical member of their group. In Chapter 11, Lalonde and Cameron analyze the dimensions underlying victims' responses to discrimination. In Chapter 12, Crocker and Major propose (and provide evidence) that perceived justifiability moderates victims' reactions to discrimination. In Chapter 13, Brewer organizes the field (and the book!) in an insightful commentary chapter. (As editors, we are especially grateful to Marilynn Brewer for agreeing to play the role of discussant at the symposium and for writing a commentary chapter. We would like to take full credit for asking the right person to do these jobs, however!)

We believe that these chapters illustrate both the diversity and vitality of research on the psychology of prejudice. Our hope is that this volume will stimulate further research and theorizing in this area.

Six previous Ontario Symposia on Personality and Social Psychology have been held. The series is designed to bring together scholars from across North America who work in the same substantive area, with the goals of identifying common concerns and integrating research findings. Participation by Canadian faculty and graduate students in the symposia has been gratifying. We hope that the symposia have contributed to (and will continue to stimulate) the growth of personality and social psychology in Ontario and Canada. The first Ontario Symposium, held at the University of Western Ontario in August 1978, dealt with social cognition (see Higgins, E. T., Herman, C. P., and Zanna, M. P. (Eds.) (1981). *Social Cognition: The Ontario Symposium*. Vol. 1. Hillsdale, NJ: Lawrence Erlbaum Associates); the second, held at the University of Waterloo in October 1979, had the theme of variability and consistency in social behavior (see Zanna, M. P., Higgins, E. T., and Herman, C. P. (Eds.) (1982). *Consistency in Social Behavior: The Ontario Symposium*. Vol. 2. Hillsdale, NJ: Lawrence Erlbaum Associates); the third, held at the University of Toronto in May 1981, addressed the social psychology of physical appearance (see Herman, C. P., Zanna, M. P., and Higgins, E. T. (Eds.) (1986). *Physical Appearance, Stigma, and Social Behavior: The Ontario Symposium*. Vol. 3. Hillsdale, NJ: Lawrence Erlbaum Associates); the fourth, held at the University of Western Ontario in

October 1983, was concerned with relative deprivation and social comparison processes (see Olson, J. M., Herman, C. P., and Zanna, M. P. (Eds.) (1986). *Relative Deprivation and Social Comparison: The Ontario Symposium.* Vol. 4. Hillsdale, NJ: Lawrence Erlbaum Associates); the fifth, held at the University of Waterloo in August 1984, dealt with social influence processes (see Zanna, M. P., Olson, J. M., and Herman, C. P. (Eds.) (1987). *Social Influence: The Ontario Symposium.* Vol. 5. Hillsdale, NJ: Lawrence Erlbaum Associates); and the sixth, held at the University of Western Ontario in June 1988, focused on self-inference processes (see Olson, J. M., and Zanna, M. P. (Eds.) (1990). *Self-Inference Processes: The Ontario Symposium.* Vol. 6. Hillsdale, NJ: Lawrence Erlbaum Associates).

Once again, primary financial support for the Seventh Ontario Symposium was provided by the Social Sciences and Humanities Research Council of Canada, whose continuing support has been the backbone of the series. We are also deeply indebted to the Department of Psychology and the Faculty of Arts of the University of Waterloo for their financial and administrative support. In particular, we would like to thank Anne Harris and Yvonne Weppler for paying the bills, David Reynolds for helping coordinate the conference facilities, and the social psychology graduate students at the University of Waterloo, especially Rebecca Filyer and Hillary Allen, for organizing a most delicious barbecue for 100! Finally, we would like to thank Larry Erlbaum for his continuing support and editorial guidance.

Mark P. Zanna
James M. Olson

The Psychology of Prejudice:
The Ontario Symposium, Volume 7

1 Stereotypes as Consensual Beliefs

R. C. Gardner
University of Western Ontario

PREJUDICE AND STEREOTYPES—GENERAL OBSERVATIONS

Prejudice is bad! To declare that someone is prejudiced is to make a critical comment about them. Stereotypes, too, are bad! They are perceived to be so by many researchers because they are seen as comprising "a set of beliefs that is incorrectly learned, overgeneralized, factually incorrect, or rigid" (Ashmore & Del Boca, 1981, p. 16). To accuse someone of stereotyping is a serious condemnation. Often, stereotypes and prejudice are seen to coexist (cf. Ashmore & Del Boca, 1981). They are both bad. As Stroebe and Insko (1989) stated: "It will be argued that the concepts of 'stereotype' and 'prejudice' are closely related and that prejudice as a negative attitude towards an outgroup or the members of that group is usually based on a negative stereotype, that is, on beliefs that associate that group with predominantly negative attributes" (p. 4).

The argument put forth in this chapter is that the terms *prejudice* and *stereotypes* are bad in a different sense, namely, their scientific utility: Both terms have acquired such a great deal of excess meaning (often in the absence of any empirical justification) that when researchers gather to discuss them, they often talk at cross purposes. Theorists use the same terms to refer to very different phenomena, often referring to the same previous research, and then are surprised to find that they disagree on very basic conclusions.

The difficulty can be seen by considering the concept of prejudice. At one level, the term prejudice refers simply to a judgment about something before the fact (a prejudgment). It represents a preconceived notion about something, often a social object or class of objects. Conceptually, therefore, it is identical to many uses of the concept stereotype. At another level, a prejudice may have an evalua-tive component, and the evaluation may be positive or negative. Thus, one speaks of someone as being prejudiced for or against a particular social object or class of objects. Viewed in this way, prejudice is restricted to evaluative prejudg-ments. At a third level, the definition of prejudice may be restricted even more to refer to negative judgments. This type of definition is often used in the context of ethnic relations (cf. Stephan, 1985). For example, Stroebe and Insko (1989) cited Harding, Kutner, Proshansky and Chein (1954) and Harding, Proshansky, Kutner, and Chein (1969) and defined *prejudice* as an attitude toward members of some outgroup and in which the evaluative tendencies are predominantly negative (p. 8). Note, with this definition, prejudice cannot be positive, nor can one have a prejudice about an ingroup. That is, ingroup favoritism (Brewer, 1979), by definition, is not a form of prejudice!

This example highlights a major problem with research in the context of prejudice, stereotypes, and ethnic relations. Often researchers start off with underlying definitions of various concepts, and these definitions help to deter-mine the results obtained. If, for example, one defines prejudice as a negatively evaluative prejudgment about a category and stereotypes as negatively evaluative judgments about a category, then obviously they are interconnected. If, however, either or both concepts are defined somewhat differently, different results might emerge. With relatively slight alterations in meaning, a rather simple concept can be changed quite dramatically. You can well imagine the argument that would ensue if three researchers attempted to discuss prejudice but each held a different one of the three meanings discussed previously.

Overview

In this chapter, I consider various conceptualizations of stereotypes and show that each reflects one of three basic notions. Stereotypes are seen as consensual beliefs, unjustified beliefs, or beliefs that distinguish one category from another. I show how one's characterization of the concept of stereotype colors one's views of various issues such as the consequences of stereotyping, the relation of stereo-types to prejudice, or the personal and social relevance of stereotypes. I show too that often the measurement operations associated with stereotype assessment confuse levels of analysis. Sometimes, generalizations based on data at one level are applied to another level. Considering all of these issues, I argue that the most meaningful conceptualization of stereotypes is to be found in their consensual nature and that there are many important implications from this perspective. I review studies relevant to a number of issues that highlight both the individual and societal role played by stereotypes.

Definitions of Stereotype

The concept of stereotype is even more plagued with excess meanings than is that of prejudice. Over the years, stereotypes have been characterized as rigid, illogi-

TABLE 1.1
Representative Definitions of Stereotypes

Allport (1954) p. 191	A stereotype is an exaggerated belief associated with a category. Its function is to justify (rationalize) our conduct in relation to that category.
Vinacke (1957) p. 229	For experimental purposes, a stereotype has, in effect, been defined statistically as a collection of trait-names upon which a large percentage of people agree as appropriate for describing some class of individuals.
Brigham (1971) p. 31	An ethnic stereotype is a generalization made about an ethnic group, concerning a trait attribution, which is considered to be unjustified by an observer.
McCauley and Stitt (1978) p. 935	...Stereotypes are best understood as predictions that distinguish the stereotyped group from others...stereotypes are best measured as diagnostic ratios.
Taylor (1981) p. 155	Stereotype is defined as "consensus among members of one group regarding the attributes of another."
Stroebe and Insko (1989) p. 5	...we will define (1989) stereotype as a set of beliefs about the personal attributes of a group of people.

cal, oversimplified. exaggerated, negative, and so forth (Ashmore & Del Boca, 1981; Brigham, 1971; Lippman, 1922; Taylor, 1981; Taylor & Lalonde, 1987). Table 1.1 presents a representative sample of these definitions. As the definitions in Table 1.1 demonstrate, there are some differences in the excess meanings attached to stereotypes, but there is general agreement that stereotypes are beliefs.

Some researchers argue that the term stereotype should not be restricted only to consensual beliefs. Ashmore and Del Boca (1981) proposed that the term "stereotype should be reserved for the set of beliefs held by an individual regarding a social group and the term 'cultural stereotype" should be used to describe shared or community-wide patterns of beliefs" (p. 19); such sentiments are shared by others (e.g., Karlins, Coffman & Walters, 1969; Vinacke, 1957). This distinction may or may not have value, but the simple truth is that it is not consistently made in the literature, and it sometimes takes a careful reading of an article to ascertain which stereotype is under investigation. A major focus of this chapter is to raise the possibility that stereotypes as consensual beliefs do have behavioral implications and that, at a minimum, researchers should determine the extent to which the beliefs they are investigating are consensual.

Regardless of the excess meanings associated with the term, the actual assessment of stereotypes is relatively straightforward. When one studies ethnic stereotypes, one asks individuals to give their views of the attributes of a particular ethnic group. Thus, the basic information obtained comprises individuals' beliefs about a category. Viewed in this light, stereotypes about ethnic groups become just another set of cognitions. An individual can be said to have beliefs about Blacks, Germans, Canadians, and so forth, in much the same way as she or he has beliefs about old people, dill pickles, professors, and dogs. Alternatively, I suppose, one could speak about stereotypes of Blacks, professors, old people, dogs and/or dill pickles.

This type of framework eliminates much of the confusion and disagreement that permeates the literature on stereotypes, prejudice, and ethnic relations. Moreover, this particular framework provides an added bonus because it permits a researcher to study both individual differences in such beliefs and correlates of these differences. Thus, one might study whether there is any relation between an individual's attitude toward a group and the degree to which that person ascribes evaluative attributes to that group. Based on the research by Ajzen and Fishbein (1977), one would certainly expect there to be such a correlation (see also Esses, Haddock, & Zanna, in press). Or, one could investigate the factor structure of beliefs about a particular group or about a number of groups. Or one could study the relationship between individuals' beliefs about various groups and their behavior toward those groups. Or one could determine whether some individuals had exaggerated beliefs about a group, or whether these beliefs were rigidly held. Thus, this approach to the concept of ethnic stereotypes, or any type of stereotypes for that matter, permits one to determine where, or if, the excess meanings associated with stereotypes apply.

The problem with this perspective is that it no longer permits reference to the concept of the stereotype about a specific group, such as, for example, Germans. One can speak about an individual's beliefs (stereotypes) about Germans, but this is not "the stereotype" about Germans. This is where the notion of social stereotypes or consensual beliefs becomes useful. This is a particular class of beliefs, and it is an important one in the context of ethnic relations. Consensual stereotypes tell not only something about an individual's beliefs, but also something about the beliefs that tend to be shared within a particular group. This distinction is important, because often it is the set of consensual beliefs that people are referring to when they talk about stereotypes leading to prejudice.

These also are the types of beliefs investigated in many studies of ethnic stereotypes. Often researchers summarize the beliefs held by the sample by identifying those attributes selected most frequently (Katz & Braly, 1933), presenting mean percentage endorsements about a group (Brigham, 1971), or identifying those attributes that distinguish an ethnic group from the general class of people (McCauley & Stitt, 1978). In such situations, one can then consider the statistics computed on the sample to be reasonable estimates of the corresponding population parameters. The important point to note, however, is that these are estimates of the general beliefs in the population. Not all members of the population, nor all members of the sample for that matter, necessarily subscribe to these beliefs. But these are the beliefs represented in the sample data.

Consider, for example, the stereotypes identified by Katz and Braly (1933) and investigated in follow-up studies by Gilbert (1951) and Karlins et al. (1969). These investigators asked individuals to select, from a list of 84 adjectives, those

TABLE 1.2
Stereotypes About the Chinese Obtained From Three Classic Studies

Attributes	Katz and Braly	Gilbert	Karlins, Coffman, and Walters
	%	%	%
Superstitious	34	18	8
Sly	29	4	6
Conservative	29	14	15
Traditional loving	26	26	32
Loyal to family ties	22	35	50
Industrious	18	18	23
Meditative	19	–	21
Reserved	17	18	15
Very religious	15	–	6
Ignorant	15	–	7
Deceitful	14	–	5
Quiet	13	19	23
Courteous	–	–	20
Extremely nationalistic	–	–	19
Humorless	–	–	17
Artistic	–	–	15

Adapted from Karlins, Coffman, and Walters (1969).

that best characterized a number of ethnic groups. Table 1.2 presents an example of the stereotype of the Chinese as summarized by Karlins et al. (1969). These three studies are often cited as evidence for the stability of stereotypes. Their major data are in terms of the percentage of the samples that selected various attributes to characterize the different groups. These studies are also cited as ones that investigated the consensual nature of stereotypes. What is seldom emphasized is the generally low levels of endorsement of the various attributes. Although one speaks of consensual beliefs, in point of fact there is relatively little consensus. Of the 120 attributes listed in the Katz and Braly (1933) study as being in the stereotypes, only 7 attributes were selected by more than 50% of the subjects. These were *sportsmanlike* (53%) for the English, *scientifically minded* (78%) and *industrious* (65%) for Germans, *artistic* (53%) for Italians, *shrewd* (79%) for Jews, and *superstitious* (84%) and *lazy* (75%) for "Negroes" In fact the mean percentages for the 12 consensual attributes for each group were generally quite low: 27.92% (Americans), 20.92% (Chinese), 28.67% (English), 29.67% (Germans), 24.67% (Irish), 27.17% (Italians), 22.00% (Japanese), 28.75% (Jews), 32.42% ("Negroes"), and 18.00% (Turks).

Comparable values were reported by Gilbert (1951) and Karlins et al. (1969). In the former case, only 2 attributes were selected by more than 50% of the subjects, and in the latter case, the number of such attributes was only 5. It is not as if there was a great deal of agreement as to the nature of the various groups. That is, the majority of the students in all three studies did not subscribe to the stereotypes listed. Whether these low percentages reflect relatively little consensus in the stereotypes or a limitation of this methodology (see the following section) cannot be ascertained from these data. What is clear is that little true consensus is demonstrated in these studies!

THE UNIT OF ANALYSIS

When attention is directed to stereotypes as consensual beliefs, it is necessary to differentiate between two units of analysis. First, because stereotype refers to those beliefs that are held by a group of individuals, an obvious unit of analysis is the group. When Katz and Braly (1933) stated that the stereotype about "Negroes" is that they are superstitious, lazy, happy go lucky, and so on, they are using the group as the unit of analysis. Similarly, when they stated that "The manner in which public and private attitudes are bound up together is shown in the order of the ten racial and national groups as determined by the definiteness with which students assigned characteristics to them," (p. 289) they again are making a generalization based on the group as the unit of analysis. Obviously, this generalization might be applicable to some of the subjects, but not to all of them. It is reasonable to conclude that if the stereotype about an ethnic group is evaluatively negative, then quite likely the group has negative attitudes toward that group (i.e., Katz and Braly's "public attitude"). It doesn't follow necessarily that all members of the group have negative attitudes toward the ethnic group, if for no other reason than not all members of the group necessarily share that stereotype.

The second unit of analysis is the individual. Although, stereotypes are viewed as consensual beliefs, one can still focus attention on the individual and ask whether she or he shares these beliefs. Moreover, one can ask other questions, still focusing on stereotypes as consensual beliefs. Is the individual's attitude related to the extent to which he or she adopts the stereotype? Are stereotypes evoked relatively automatically in any given situation, or do they require some cognitive activity? Are some individuals stereotypers in that, if they adopt the stereotype about one group, they adopt the stereotype about other groups? Are individuals from the same group able to communicate about other ethnic groups through the stereotype alone? Do stereotypes influence person perception? These questions are addressed in this chapter, and the answers obtained help to clarify the social implications of the stereotype when viewed as a consensual belief. These answers indicate that stereotypes, as consensual beliefs, have considerable social relevance to the individual in that they influence many aspects of social behavior.

The Measurement of Stereotypes

As indicated in the definitions provided in Table 1.1, there are many ways of conceptualizing ethnic stereotypes, and it stands to reason that there are consequently many ways of measuring them. This section focuses attention on four procedures for assessing stereotypes and summarizes advantages and shortcomings of each (cf. Gardner, Lalonde, Nero, & Young, 1988).

The Katz and Braly (1933) Method.   This approach focuses on stereotypes as consensual beliefs. Subjects are presented with a list of adjectives (Katz and Braly used 84 adjectives) and are asked to read through the list and select those 10 that they feel best characterize a particular ethnic or national group. Once they have done this for all groups, they are asked to go back through their lists and select for each group the 5 attributes that they feel are the most characteristic. The stereotype about each group is defined in terms of those attributes (Katz and Braly listed 12 for each ethnic group) chosen most frequently to characterize each group.

The obvious advantage of this technique is its simplicity. It is easy to administer and easy to interpret, at least at the group level. But the shortcomings are many.

1. There is no guarantee that an individual truly considers the applicability of an attribute to each group. With so many adjectives, some may be overlooked. There is no way of knowing if an individual fails to select an adjective whether that individual feels that the adjective definitely isn't applicable or simply whether it isn't as appropriate as others.

2. Subjects often find the task distasteful. They object to selecting attributes to characterize an ethnic group, feeling that it represents an unfair generalization or some form of prejudice.

3. There really isn't any good individual difference measure of the extent to which the individual adopts the consensually defined stereotype. One could, after the fact, go back and count for each subject the number of adjectives he or she selected that were in the final list of 12 adjectives for any one group, but because each individual selects only 5 adjectives, such an individual difference score would vary from only 0 to 5. This provides a score of limited value and reliability for studying individual differences in stereotyping.

The Brigham (1971) Method.   Brigham (1971) proposed that stereotypes are best conceived as unjustified generalizations. The methodology he proposed asks subjects to indicate the percentage of individuals of an ethnic group that possess a given attribute (about 25 to 30 are presented). A scale of percentages varying from 0 to 100 in units of 10 is provided, and subjects circle the value they feel is most applicable. This technique is used to provide a group level measure of stereotypes in terms of the mean of the percentage judgments of a group on any one attribute (cf., Eagly & Kite, 1987). Brigham (1971), however, defined the stereotype as an unjustified generalization and suggested that what constitutes unjustified is up to the investigator. He suggested two possible operational definitions. First, "unjustified" refers to any extreme judgment. He suggested that any estimate of 80% or more or 20% or less be considered as unjustified. The second measure of unjustified he suggested is in terms of some departure from the mean. He suggested that any individual who makes a judgment that varies more than some difference from the mean (e.g., .50 standard deviation units) be considered as having made an unjustified generalization.

There are many advantages to this approach: (a) It is a task that most subjects find acceptable and easy to understand, (b) The researcher knows that any given subject has considered each attribute, and (c) It provides for both group and individual assessments of the stereotype process, though the two different ways of conceptualizing unjustified provide two measures that can be quite different.

The shortcomings of this procedure rest primarily on the ambiguity of what constitutes the stereotype. At the group level, the stereotype is identified simply in terms of the mean percentage judgment assigned to each trait for each group. Attributes with very high percentages are considered to make up the stereotypes (e.g., Eagly & Kite, 1987). Attributes with very low percentages are a bit ambiguous. For example, if the mean percentage for some group were 15% on the attribute *serious*, would this imply that the stereotype includes the attribute *humorous* or simply that serious is not characteristic of the group? In the Eagly and Kite (1987) study, only the high percentages were considered, but one might reasonably ask whether it is meaningful to reject particularly low percentages as indicating stereotypical judgments. In any event, a measure of stereotypes based on mean judgments does not reflect the unjustified nature of stereotypes that Brigham (1971) felt was their significant feature.

When attention is directed to the assessment of unjustified generalizations at the group level, this technique defines the stereotype in terms of those attributes for which the mean percentage was equal to or greater than 80% or equal to or less than 20%. Thus, with the attribute *serious*, the stereotype could include serious or alternatively *humorous* (or at least not serious). One could then characterize the stereotype of a group in terms of those K attributes that satisfy these criteria. To refer to the complexity of the stereotype of a particular group, one could assign a score of K to that group. At the individual level, one could similarly assign a stereotyping score to an individual that is a count of the number of scales for which his or her percentage judgments meet the criterion of extremity. This measure is expected to reflect consensual judgments in that with a high mean percentage for an attribute, many individuals would assign high percentages to it. However, it is also possible that individuals might obtain a count on any particular attribute, because their judgment was made at the opposite end of the scale. Thus, a count of extreme judgments is ambigious as to content at the individual level.

If extremity of judgment were alternatively defined in terms of some departure from the mean judgment, different assessments could result. Attributes with very high (or low) mean percentages would contribute very little to the count, and those that did count would be derived from judgments from the opposite end of the scale. It is conceivable, therefore, that scores from these two measures of unjustifiability could correlate negatively with each other.

The McCauley and Stitt (1978) Method. The method proposed by McCauley and Stitt (1978) and McCauley, Stitt, and Segal (1980) focused on stereotypes as distinctive attributes. These are assessed by asking two questions. The first assesses the probability of possessing a trait given membership in a particular ethnic group. Subjects are asked to write in the percentage of a particular group that possesses various attributes (McCauley and Stitt presented 9 attributes). The second question assesses the probability of having a given trait. Subjects are asked for the percentage of all the world's people who have these attributes. The ratio of these two probabilities is referred to as a *diagnostic ratio,* and stereotyping is indicated to the extent that the ratio differs from 1.0. The diagnostic ratio is defined formally as:

$$DR = \frac{P(\text{Trait/Ethnicity})}{P(\text{Trait})}$$

It is reported (cf. Jonas & Hewstone, 1986) that subjects sometimes find the assessment of probabilities confusing or distasteful. However, such probabilities can be estimated using the Brigham (1971) percentage procedure that is generally found to be more socially acceptable. Jonas and Hewstone (1986) found substantial correlations between the two estimates, thus confirming their equivalence. Using this approach, subjects are asked to make the estimates for both the ethnic group in question and also for people in general. The ratios of the two percentages are a reasonable estimate of the diagnostic ratio.

McCauley and Stitt (1978) focused on ratios greater than 1.0; however, the ratios could vary from 0 to infinity, particularly when they are computed on individual data as opposed to group means. Gardner et al. (1988) pointed out that ratios less than 1.0 are as indicative of distinctiveness as are ratios greater than 1.0. Consequently, they recommended that it is often necessary to compute reciprocals when the ratios are less than 1.0 (As a cautionary note, this application should not permit a judgment of 0%, otherwise a diagnostic ratio could be indeterminate if the denominator were ever 0.)

The advantages of this procedure (particularly using the Brigham method to estimate the probabilities) rest in the ease of administration and the fact that the task is readily understood by subjects. At the group level an attribute might be considered stereotypical if the diagnostic ratio differs from 1.0. Thus, for the attribute *serious,* a diagnostic ratio greater than 1.0 indicates that more members of the group are perceived as serious than are people in general, whereas a ratio less than 1.0 means that less are. Both the content of the stereotype and a measure of the number of traits on which the group is stereotyped can be determined. They are most readily understood when the estimates of the percentages for the target group are high (greater than 50%) but are somewhat ambiguous when the percentage is low (because the meaning of a low percentage for an attribute is ambiguous). Diagnostic ratios less than 1.0 are also difficult to interpret. At the individual level, an individual can be said to be stereotyping a group on an attribute if his or her diagnostic ratio departs from 1.0 (but again the same queries remain as those just raised), and a stereotyping score can be determined as a count of the number of attributes where the diagnostic ratio is not 1.0. Alternatively, the score might be computed as the mean of diagnostic scores once the reciprocal of all values less than 1.0 has been taken. In this way, the larger the value, the more the individual can be said to be stereotyping.

There are a number of shortcomings of this procedure. As already indicated in the previous paragraph, interpretation is difficult when estimates involve low percentages and/or diagnostic ratios less than 1.0.

The logic of the base statistic actually defines stereotyping in terms of an evaluative judgment. That is, when subjects distinguish between members of some group and people in general, it seems likely that they really are making a discriminatory judgment. Ashmore and Del Boca (1981) suggested that this conceptualization is comparable to that used in the study of gender stereotypes, but this is definitely not the case. A gender stereotype is based on the difference between males and females—two clearly identifiable groups. In the diagnostic ratio, the base term *people in general* is too diffuse. One might argue that if someone sees a difference between members of a group and people in general, that they are making a very evaluative judgment. Perhaps one way around this is to make the base group the individual's own group. Thus, for Canadians the base group would be Canadians. Quite likely such a formulation would result in stereotypes being defined in terms of ingroup favoritism. Note, from this perspective there is considerable similarity between the McCauley and Stitt approach and the matched guise procedure proposed by Lambert, Hodgson, Gardner, and Fillenbaum (1960). In the latter technique, subjects rate bilingual speakers on a series of attributes once when speaking each language, and then comparisons are made of the same speakers when they are using the two languages. Differences are assumed to reflect reactions to the two different linguistic groups involved.

The Gardner Method.   Gardner (1973) proposed that stereotypes, defined as consensual beliefs, be identified using the *stereotype differential*. This procedure presents subjects with the name of the ethnic group in question and a series (usually 25 to 30) of semantic differential scales comprised of bipolar trait descriptive adjectives. Subjects rate each group on each 7-point scale, where 1 represents the adjective on the left, 7 the adjective on the right, and 4 a neutral position. A stereotype is defined in terms of significant polarity on a scale, and this is assessed in terms of Student's single sample t statistic $[t = (\bar{x} - \mu)/S/\sqrt{n}]$. The mean rating on each scale is tested for its deviation from an assumed neutral value of $\mu = 4.0$. Scales for which the mean is significantly greater than 4.0 indicate stereotyping involving the adjective on the right. If the t statistic is significantly less than 0,0. this indicates that the group is stereotyped in terms of the trait on the left. Type I error rate can be controlled using the Bonferroni inequality, requiring a t statistic to be significant at the .05/K level, where K equals the number of scales. At the group level, the stereotype is defined in terms of those attributes toward which polarity is significant (or greatest). An individual difference measure of stereotyping can be determined by summing an individual's score on those scales for which polarity was significant, once those scales with negative t statistics have been reflected. In this way, the higher the score, the more the individual subscribes to the stereotype.

The advantages of this approach are the following:

1. The task is relatively easy to understand.
2. Subjects generally do not object to rating groups on scales.
3. Ratings are obtained with respect to all dimensions presented.
4. The definition of the attributes comprising the stereotype is objective and straightforward, and both group and individual indices of the stereotype are provided.
5. The procedure can be applied as easily to target individuals as to groups. This permits a direct measure of the relation between reactions to groups and reactions to individual people that is useful in studies of stereotypes and person perception. This advantage is unique to the stereotype differential.

The shortcomings of the approach have to do with the need to compute t statistics for each scale and the potential ambiguity of consensus if the majority of subjects rated the group on the neutral value on the scale (4). This would produce a t value of 0 (or a very low value), yet obviously there is consensus.

Measures of Stereotypes, Meaning, and Excess Meaning

One thing that stands out in all of these assessment techniques is that the task facing the subjects is relatively straightforward. Subjects are asked to give their impressions of a particular group in much the same way that they might be asked to give their impressions of any other category from dill pickles to professors. Assigning attributes to a class of objects is a normal cognitive activity. Virtually the only way that subjects could escape from stereotyping is by refusing to do the task. This is literally true with respect to the Katz and Braly technique, and more or less so with the other procedures, depending on how stereotyping is operationally defined. To the extent that subjects make anything other than a bland judgment, they can be characterized as stereotyping.

The measurement procedures have definite operational definitions of stereotypes associated with them. The Katz and Braly and the Gardner procedures operationally define stereotypes in terms of consensus. They do not ask subjects to estimate consensus or to make all-inclusive judgments, but, at the group level, the scoring procedures identify attributes that subjects tend to agree are applicable to the group in question. At the individual level, the tendency to endorse the consensual stereotype can also be assessed, though variability with the Katz and Braly method would be low. The Brigham procedure, as intended, assesses stereotypes in terms of unjustified generalizations, but as indicated previously, the term *unjustified* is equivocal and can be defined in different ways at both the group and individual level. The McCauley and Stitt method operationally defines the stereotype in terms of distinctiveness of the group in question. Like the Brigham method, it too is ambiguous (see earlier discussion). Nonetheless, all four methods have clearly identifiable meanings applied to the notion of stereotype.

The excess meanings that are associated with stereotypes are not part of the measurement operations. Though stereotypes are sometimes characterized as incorrectly learned, overgeneralized, incorrect, rigid, illogical, or exaggerated, these attributes are not part of any of the standard assessment procedures. To be sure, when using percentage endorsement scales, a judgment that 100% or 0% of a group has a particular attribute is extreme, but even that is not prima facie evidence that a subject has made an illogical overgeneralization, is factually incorrect, or is rigid. Nor is it proof that the subject uses the belief to rationalize his or her behavior toward that group. Such excess meanings must first be demonstrated to apply before they are accepted as part of the construct of stereotypes.

If individuals are illogical in their reliance on stereotypes, if they overgeneralize to the extent that they permit no exceptions, if they use them to justify hatred and the like, such individuals are displaying socially unacceptable behavior. But none of this is necessarily demonstrated in the judgment itself. These excess meanings that have sometimes been attached to the concept of stereotypes have yet to be demonstrated to exist in anything but the definitions themselves.

Relations Among Various Measures of Stereotypes

Group Level of Analysis. Some research has been conducted comparing stereotypes defined by these various methods. Gardner et al. (1988) contrasted the stereotypes about French Canadians identified by the methods proposed by Brigham (1971), McCauley and Stitt (1978), and Gardner (1973). In making this contrast, they noted that various indices could be computed using the group as the unit of analysis and computing scores for each attribute. For the Brigham method, there was the mean percentage of the target group on each attribute and the number of times subjects made extreme ratings on the scale. For the Mc-Cauley and Stitt measure, there was the diagnostic ratio based on the mean rating for the target group divided by the mean rating for people in general and the mean of diagnostic ratios computed individually for subjects (first, inverting all ratios less than 1.0, so that the mean value was always greater than 1.0). For the stereotype differential method, there was the t statistic for that scale. These scores were correlated using the 30 scales as the unit of analysis (i.e., $N = 30$). The results demonstrate that the stereotype differential provided similar assessments to those obtained with the mean percentage based on the Brigham procedure ($r = .91$) and on the diagnostic ratio of McCauley and Stitt based on mean judgments ($r = .63$), whereas it provided an index that was negatively related to that based on the mean of individually based diagnostic ratios ($r = -.61$). This pattern also characterizes the relationship between the two types of diagnostic ratios and the Brigham mean percentage assessment ($r = .55$ and $-.51$ for the diagnostic ratio based on mean judgments and the mean of individual diagnostic ratios respectively). The Brigham measure of the number of unjustified generalizations did not correlate highly with any of the measures (all correlations less than .34). Some of these correlations would be expected, whereas others are counterintuitive. The point is, however, that oftentimes the measures provide very different pictures of the stereotype, thus, it is important to know which measurement operation is used to define a stereotype.

Other studies contrast pairs of procedures and yield results that are comparable to those reported previously. Gardner, Kirby, Gorospe, and Villamin (1972) found that the stereotype differential procedure yields a stereotype that is very similar to that identified by the Katz and Braly procedure, particularly when the stereotype is highly consensual. They assessed the stereotypes of nine national groups in two comparable samples of potential school teachers in the Philippines, one using the stereotype differential and the other the Katz and Braly procedure. Percentage of agreement between the two procedures varied from 20% for Canadians (a group relatively unknown to the subjects) to 80% for Americans (a group with considerable presence in the country). The rank order correlation between an index of consensus (the mean percentage for the 10 stereotype traits defined by the Katz and Braly procedure) and the degree of similarity between the two sets of stereotypes was .73 ($df = 7$, $p < .05$).

Comparable stereotypes are also obtained when the Katz and Braly procedure is compared with the other techniques, though the results are less clearcut. Stapf, Stroebe, and Jonas (1986 [as reported in Stroebe & Insko, 1989]) found that the stereotypes they obtained with a percentage rating procedure are comparable to those obtained by Karlins et al. (1969), as well as other researchers using the Katz and Braly procedure. On the other hand, McCauley and Stitt (1978) found that when they based their analysis on the group as the unit of analysis, the diagnostic ratio provided a better assessment of the (German) stereotype defined by the Katz and Braly procedure than the Brigham mean percentage measure. Using the individual as the unit of analysis, McCauley and Stitt (1978, Study 2) found that both the diagnostic ratio and the percentage assessment correlated similarly with ratings of typicality that they interpreted as equivalent to a Katz and Braly assessment.

In his research Brigham (1971) argued that there is a flaw with the Katz and Braly assessment because of discrepancies between mean percentages obtained with his technique and the degree of consensus obtained with the Katz and Braly procedure. He reported that "in many cases, subjects saw *all five* of the 'most typical' traits as being characteristic of *less than half* of the members of the ethnic group" (p. 30). This point has been made again by other researchers (McCauley & Stitt, 1978; Stroebe & Insko, 1989), but it simply isn't meaningful. The data points are not at all comparable, and there is no reason to expect them to be related. One set consists of the percentage of subjects that select an attribute to characterize a group, whereas the other is the mean percentage of the group that subjects perceive as having the attribute. They refer to very different things. Moreover, in the Katz and Braly procedure, subjects are asked to select those attributes that characterize a given ethnic group, not those attributes that characterize every member or even a great number of the group.

Individual Level of Analysis.   One can also consider stereotypes using the individual as the unit of analysis and again the various measures of stereotype can produce very different interpretations. Gardner et al. (1988) found, for example, that when individual difference measures from the various methods were factor analyzed along with a number of other measures, four factors were obtained, three of which involved the different measures of stereotyping. One factor was defined primarily by the diagnostic ratio measure and indices of attitudes toward the target group and attitudes toward multiculturalism. The factor suggests that one component of variation in the diagnostic ratio is associated with unfavorable attitudes toward the group in question, as well as other groups. That is, individuals with unfavorable attitudes toward outgroups tended to evidence high diagnostic ratios.

Another factor obtained high loadings from the Brigham measure of unjustified generalizations, the diagnostic ratio and an index of social desirability. This factor suggests that social desirability responding is a source of variation associated with these two measures of stereotyping. It suggests that subjects who make many extreme judgments and who have high diagnostic ratios tend also to give socially desirable impressions of themselves. This unexpected pattern of relationships can be understood when attention is directed to the nature of the extreme judgments. Most of these are positive in evaluative tone, thus the factor structure suggests that subjects who wish to portray themselves positively make individual generalizations about another group that are positively evaluative in nature.

A third factor is defined by the stereotype differential measure of stereotypes and Brigham's measure of unjustified generalizations. Both loadings were positive, indicating that many of Brigham's unjustified generalizations are in fact consensual in that many subjects see them as characterizing a large number of the target group. In the Gardner et al. (1988) study, these traits were all positively evaluative, however, and generally not the type that Brigham considered as unjustified.

The results of studies concerned with contrasting the various ways of assessing ethnic stereotypes demonstrate at both the group and individual level of analysis that the different stereotypes are at times very different and have very different implications. Thus, researchers should pay careful attention to the way in which the stereotypes have been assessed when discussing stereotyping. In the next section, I focus on the notion of stereotypes as consensual beliefs. It is quite probable that the processes underlying the adoption of consensual beliefs about an ethnic group are very different from those underlying adoption of relatively idiosyncratic beliefs (sometimes referred to as nonstereotype attributes in the discussion to follow).

IMPLICATIONS OF CONSIDERING STEREOTYPES AS CONSENSUAL BELIEFS

One could speculate that consensually defined stereotypes have a more cognitive basis than relatively idiosyncratic beliefs. This is because, to the extent that they are consensual, such beliefs have social support and a common source. Phenomenologically, they might well be seen not so much as beliefs but as facts. As a consequence, one would expect them to be relatively automatic and less related to attitudinal/motivational characteristics. Research to be discussed later supports this type of speculation. Relatively idiosyncratic beliefs, on the other hand, might be expected to have a more motivational basis. Lacking social support, they may be seen as factual by the individual holding them, but there would be little opportunity for consensual validation. One might expect them to be less automatic, more tentative, and more related to attitudinal/motivational characteristics of the individual. Research to be discussed later supports this speculation as well.

Such considerations suggest that, at a minimum, researchers should consider whether the beliefs they are investigating are relatively consensual or relatively idiosyncratic. It is possible that phenomena such as ingroup favoritism (Brewer, 1979), outgroup homogeneity (Quattrone & Jones, 1980), differential accessibility (Cohen, 1983), and the like might be expressed differently depending upon whether they are being considered in the context of consensual or relatively idiosyncratic beliefs.

When attention is directed to consensual beliefs about ethnic groups, some of the findings with respect to stereotypes are somewhat at odds with preconceptions. Moreover, some other findings tend to highlight the implications of their consensual nature. This section considers these implications with respect to four issues: (a) the relation of stereotypes to attitudes, (b) the generality of stereotyping, (c) the informational content of stereotypes, and (d) the role of stereotypes in person perception. In these sections, the term stereotype is used to refer to consensual beliefs about the group concerned.

The Relation of Stereotypes to Attitudes

Stereotypes are often considered the language of prejudice. Some researchers (cf. Stroebe & Insko, 1989) argue that stereotypes are the basis for prejudice; however, the foundation for such conjecture is shaky at best. Katz and Braly (1935) also linked stereotypes and prejudice. They stated, for example, "Racial prejudice is thus a generalized set of stereotypes of a high degree of consistency which includes emotional responses to race names, a belief in typical characteristics associated with race names, and evaluation of such traits" (pp. 191–192). This is a very strong statement that loses much of its impact in light of the findings.

To begin with, the statement can be interpreted as referring to an individual's beliefs; however, considering the earlier comments concerning the unit of analysis, attention must be directed to the precise nature of the data. All of the data presented by Katz and Braly (1933, 1935) are based on the group as the unit of analysis. The stereotypes are presented in terms of the percentage of individuals in the sample that selected a given attribute as describing a particular group. And, as already seen, the percentages were generally quite low. For only one group was the mean percentage greater than 30% (range from 18% to 32.42%), and the mean of the mean percentages was only 26.02%. Similarly, generalizations concerning the uniformity and evaluation of the stereotypes were based on group data. The replication factors were either the groups themselves (10) or the attributes associated with each group (12).

If one directs attention to the content of the stereotypes, there is evidence of some evaluative component, though it is not overwhelmingly negative. Of the (10 × 12 =) 120 entries listed as stereotypical by Katz and Braly (1933), only 50 are in the bottom 50% in evaluation based on norms provided by Karlins et al. (1969). Each group has at least one negative attribute (for Americans, it is *materialistic*, which ranks 49 in the list of 84 attributes).

In analyzing their data, Katz and Braly (1933) concluded that the uniformity of the stereotype (i.e., degree of consensus) has little relation to prejudice, because the greatest degree of prejudice was expressed toward "Negroes" and Turks, and the stereotype of "Negroes" was the most uniform whereas that for Turks was the least. Karlins et al. (1969) correlated mean evaluative ratings of the stereotypes over the 10 groups with uniformity in the stereotype for the data provided by Katz and Braly (1933), Gilbert (1951), and themselves. They obtained a nonsignificant correlation ($r = .164$) for the Katz and Braly study, thus confirming Katz and Braly's conclusion. However, the correlations for both the Gilbert data and their own were positive (.677 and .770, respectively) suggesting that there was more uniformity in the stereotypes for those groups that were seen positively. They concluded, with respect to their own data, that "overall, the verbal norms in 1967 more nearly approach a vocabulary for friendly attitudes—a "language of tolerance," so to speak" (Karlins et al., 1969, p. 13).

This is not meant to suggest that stereotypes cannot have a strong (positive or negative) evaluative component. They most certainly can. Moreover, the evaluative tone reflected in the stereotype reflects the attitudes, held by the community, toward the group in question. This is most clearly evident in studies that investigate the influence of war on the nature of the stereotype. Two studies (Meenes, 1943; Seago, 1947) investigated the effects of World War II on the stereotypes about the Germans and Japanese. The Meenes' study was conducted with two samples of Black university students, one tested in 1935 and the other in 1942. The Seago study was conducted on five samples of women university students, tested in the years 1941, 1942, 1943, 1944, and 1945. Both studies show a great deal of stability in the stereotypes obtained in the different years. In both, however, there is an introduction of negative elements in the stereotypes that the authors attributed to the international situation and the resulting media coverage. The stereotypes of both the Japanese and the Germans became more negative as a function of the war, but the effects were more pronounced for the Japanese than for the Germans.

Similar results were reported by Sinha and Upadhyaya (1960) in the context of the Chinese–Indian border dispute. They investigated changes over a 1-year period in the stereotypes of university students in India of nine ethnic groups, one of which was Chinese. The stereotypes of eight of the groups were very similar over this period, but that of the Chinese showed an increase in the use of negative attributes. Although the three most consensual attributes before the dispute were retained in the later stereotype (artistic, religious, and industrious), there was the addition of some very negative attributes (aggressive, cheat, selfish, etc.). When the dispute was ongoing; therefore, the consensual nature of the beliefs about the Chinese clearly includes an increased attitudinal component, precipitated undoubtedly by information provided at the time.

These data dealing with stereotypes at the group level suggest then that there can be an evaluative component in the content of the stereotype. The data are silent, however, on the question as to whether these stereotypes reflect individuals' attitudes. Thus, it is meaningful to ask whether an individual who subscribes to a consensually defined evaluative stereotypic attribute actually reflects a corresponding attitude or whether that individual is merely expressing a belief that is extant in his or her community. Stated another way, one could ask whether there is any correlation at the individual level of analysis between attitudes and stereotypes.

Some research has been conducted on this question. Gardner, Wonnacott, and Taylor (1968) assessed the stereotype of French Canadians using the stereotype differential and then conducted a factor analysis of the correlations among reactions to the various attributes and measures of attitudes. The major finding is that one factor, defined primarily by the stereotype attributes, was independent of the measure of attitudes, whereas another factor was defined by a measure of attitudes toward French Canadians and a number of attributes not contained in the stereotype. This led them to conclude that, in fact, attitudes are independent of stereotypes. Subsequent research was conducted in the Philippines where the target group was the Chinese (Gardner, Kirby, & Arboleda 1973). This group has some negative attributes in the stereotype (e.g., extravagant, secretive), but again the same phenomenon occurred. The stereotype factor is independent of an evaluative factor and also a social distance dimension.

Other research (Lalonde & Gardner, 1989) examines the correlation between stereotype scores (based on the stereotype differential) and attitude scores (based on a Likert assessment) in two different studies. In the first study, a significant correlation with the relevant attitude measures was found for the stereotype involving the ingroup (English Canadians, $r(89) = .40$) but not for two outgroups (Americans and French Canadians, $r = -.05$ and $r = .11$ respectively). The second study involves two samples of students, English Canadian and Chinese, and three labels, American, Canadian, and Chinese. Significant correlations were obtained in both samples between attitudes and stereotypes for the ingroup labels [$r(38) = .54$ for the Canadian sample and $r(38) = .55$ for the Chinese sample], replicating the previous study. The only other significant correlation was for the label Americans used for the Canadian sample [$r(38) = .43$]. This latter finding is inconsistent with the previous study, though the lack of significant correlations for the other labels tends to reinforce the conclusion that in general attitudes and stereotypes about outgroups tend to be independent.

This relative independence of attitudes and stereotypes has also been demonstrated with both the Katz and Braly and the Brigham formats. Brigham (1971) reported that he computed biserial correlations between a measure of attitudes toward Negroes and whether or not individuals subscribed to each of the 15 attributes contained in the stereotype (as assessed by the Katz and Braly procedure). Only 5 of the correlations were significant, and interestingly enough these were the ones for which consensus was relatively low (i.e., percentages of 11, 16.5, 24, 13.5, and 18.5 when the mean percentage was 27.3). Eight of the correlations between attitudes and percentage attributions using the Brigham procedure were significant, but again these tended to involve the attributes for which percentage attribution (based on the Katz and Braly procedure) was low. The mean percentage for those attributes for which the correlations were significant was 20.2, whereas it was 35.4 for those where the correlations were not significant. Such results suggest that to the extent that consensus is high, the tendency to subscribe to the stereotype is relatively independent of attitudes. It is worthwhile to extend this analysis to other settings and other groups, because there may be exceptions to this generalization. Nonetheless, there is little in these data to suggest a correlation between the tendency to subscribe to the stereotypes and attitudes toward the group in question.

The finding that stereotypes about outgroups are unrelated to attitudes toward these groups suggests that motivational factors do not underlie these stereotypes. Instead other factors are important, and a prime candidate is societal information. The very consensual nature of these stereotypes suggests common sources of information. This is not meant to imply any "kernel of truth" in the stereotypes but rather a "shell of information." As noted earlier, such stereotypes, because of their consensual validation, are quite likely seen more as facts than beliefs. That is, cognitive factors rather than motivational ones underlie stereotypes about outgroups. Such does not seem to be the case with ingroup stereotypes, however. The tendency to adopt them is correlated with attitudes. The same is true with respect to ratings of outgroups on nonstereotype attributes that tend also to be related to attitudes (cf. Gardner et al., 1968, Gardner, Kirby, & Arboleda, 1973). Thus, ingroup stereotypes are seen to have a motivational basis, as do outgroup nonstereotypes (i.e., relatively idiosyncratic beliefs).

This is not meant to imply that individuals' attitudes are not reflected in the attributes they ascribe to groups. To the extent that individuals vary in their attitudes toward an ethnic group, it is reasonable to expect them to perceive the group in a different way evaluatively. Thus, an individual with a favorable attitude toward French Canadians might say that what is so nice about them is that they are religious. An individual with a negative attitude might state that the problem with them is that they are too religious. Both individuals, however, might ascribe the attribute of religious to French Canadians. This type of generalization is supported by Esses et al. (in press). They found significant correlations between attitudes toward a group and the individual's ratings of the evaluativeness of attributes they assigned to the group. That is, individuals with different attitudes perceive different evaluative connotations in the attributes they assign to a group.

Generality in Stereotyping

Two points stand out when one considers stereotypes as consensual beliefs. First, in the majority of cases, consensus isn't all that great. On average, the percentage endorsement, using the Katz and Braly technique, of any one trait for a group is only about 20%. Second, it is not clear what this 20% represents. Does it mean that roughly 20% of the sample accounts for most of these consensual judgements? If this were the case, one could speak of an individual difference characteristic of stereotyping, where some individuals tend to be more susceptible to stereotyping than others. On the other hand, it might mean that different individuals contribute to the stereotypes of different groups or that different individuals focus on some common attributes for reasons that are unknown. It would be difficult to postulate anything other than pockets of information that different subjects draw on when asked to characterize groups, but the nature and the reasons for such pockets are not easy to explain. Despite the possible implications, no research appears to have been done using the Katz and Braly paradigm to determine the generality of stereotyping. It has merely been assumed that it is a general phenomenon.

Such research has, however, been conducted using the stereotype differential. As discussed previously, Gardner et al. (1968) factor analyzed English Canadians' ratings of French Canadians, and obtained three factors, one of which was defined primarily by attributes contained in the stereotype. Similarly, Gardner, Kirby, and Arboleda (1973) found that one factor was defined primarily by stereotypic attributes in Filipinos' ratings of the Chinese. Such findings demonstrate that to the extent that an individual subscribes to one aspect of the stereotype she or he subscribes to most. This suggests that stereotyping does generalize at least across the traits associated with one group.

Other research demonstrates that the tendency to stereotype also generalizes across ethnic groups. In one study, Gardner et al. (1972) studied the stereotypes of nine groups held by subjects in the Philippines. They computed stereotype scores for each group, then computed the correlations among these scores. All but 3 of the 28 correlations among the eight outgroups were significant (range = .14 to .51; median $r = .36$, $df = 98$), suggesting that to the extent that an individual stereotyped one outgroup, he or she would stereotype all outgroups. This leads to the conclusion that stereotyping is a generalized trait across target groups as well as within a target group. On the other hand, only 2 of the 8 correlations between stereotyping of Filipinos and stereotyping the outgroups were significant (range = $-.02$ to .34, median $r = .09$, $df = 98$), suggesting that the tendency to stereotype the ingroup is relatively independent of the tendency to stereotype outgroups. This differential pattern indicates again that ingroup stereotyping and outgroup stereotyping reflect different processes. As suggested earlier, it is quite meaningful to argue that outgroup stereotyping has a cognitive basis, whereas ingroup stereotyping is more motivationally based.

Stereotypes and Communication

If stereotypes represent cultural beliefs that are shared by many individuals, it is meaningful to argue that it should be possible to communicate through the stereotypes alone. Thus, one individual could simply describe an ethnic group by listing the stereotype attributes, and another individual should be able to identify the group in question. In fact, this technique was first used by Meenes (1943) to assess stability in stereotypes over time. He felt that such a communicational paradigm could be used and that "the extent to which such groups are correctly identified may be taken as an indication of stability of the stereotypes, while a high percentage of incorrect identifications may be assumed to indicate that the earlier stereotype has changed, or that there is much individual difference of attitude toward the race in question" (pp. 334–335). He tested 18 subjects in 1942 presenting them in counterbalanced random order the lists from his 1935 and 1942 testings. He found that the number of correct identifications was fairly substantial. For the 1935 stereotype, the number of correct identifications was 63% overall. The lowest was for the Japanese (22%), whereas the highest was for the Germans, Jews, and Italians (83% in each case). When the identifications were based on the 1942 stereotypes, the figures were somewhat better—72% overall. As before, identification was poorest for Japanese (50%) and best for Jews (89%).

Centers (1951) conducted a similar study. He presented students with the 10 groups investigated by Katz and Braly (1933) and read the 12 stereotypes associated with each group in that study. A subject's task was to identify the group referred to in each case. The number of correct identifications varied from a low of 73% for the Japanese to a high of 95% for the English. Such results suggested that at least when considering the stereotype as an entire unit, there is considerable information value in it, even after a relatively long period of time (18 years in the Centers study).

A study by Gardner, Kirby, and Finlay (1973) investigated the extent to which the degree of consensus of the stereotypes, the number of attributes, and the age of the subjects influenced the degree to which groups could be recognized and how difficult the task was perceived by the subjects. Subjects were Grade 9 and Grade 12 high school students. They were presented with the stereotypes obtained by Karlins et al. (1969) and the names of the 10 groups. At each grade level, one half of the subjects were presented with lists consisting of 4 attributes, and the other with lists of 2 attributes. Each subject received 30 such lists. Each list consisted of attributes from the 4 most consensual attributes, the next 4 most consensual, or the 4 least consensual from the 12 attributes associated with each group. (Obviously, for the four-attribute list, all 4 attributes were used at each level; for the 2-attribute condition, 2 of the four were chosen at random.) Subjects read each set and indicated the group he or she felt was being described, then rated how difficult it was to decide on the group.

The results indicate that identification is better for high consensual items than for medium or low consensual ones and that older subjects are more successful at identification than the younger ones. Moreover, this difference is greater when subjects were presented with only 2 as opposed to 4 attributes. In addition, subjects found the task to decrease in difficulty as consensus increased. That is, they rated the task as much less difficult when the items were highly consensual. This effect is much more pronounced for the 2-element condition than the 4-element one.

These data emphasize the informational value of consensually defined stereotypes. It is not even necessary to provide a large number of the attributes. As few as two can be enough to promote communication, particularly if the level of consensus of the attributes is relatively high. With fewer attributes, communication is not as good as it is with more (note, in this study that the level of identification averages only about 26% compared to figures of about 70% in the studies by Meenes and Centers reported previously), but it is appreciably above chance. To the extent stereotypes are consensual, individuals can understand them, regardless of whether or not they subscribe to them. Note, too, that these results again support the proposition that stereotypes about outgroups have a cognitive foundation in that they serve an information function.

Stereotypes and Person Perception

One criticism of ethnic stereotypes is that they color people's perceptions so that when they encounter an individual from another group concerned, they perceive him or her in terms of the stereotype of that group. In general, the research certainly supports this generalization. Many of the original studies present subjects with only minimal information in the form of photographs (Gregory, 1941; Razran, 1950), written descriptions (Bruner & Perlmutter, 1957), speech samples (Lambert et al., 1960), or actual individuals (Tajfel, Sheikh, & Gardner, 1964). Generally, it was found that subjects responded to these stimuli in ways that would be expected on the basis of consensual stereotypes. One possible criticism of these studies, however, is that because the stimuli provided very little information other than group membership, it is perhaps reasonable to expect that the results would mirror group judgments.

Other later studies attempt to overcome this criticism (Aboud & Taylor, 1971; Gardner & Taylor, 1968; Grant & Holmes, 1981; Taylor & Gardner, 1969). In one study, for example, Gardner and Taylor (1968) used specially constructed tape-recorded messages to investigate the effects of message content on the extent to which stereotypes about the group influenced perception of the individual. They also varied social pressure. Subjects heard a French Canadian speaker describing himself in a manner that either conformed to the stereotype of French Canadians, was contrary to the stereotype, or was neutral with respect to content—the prostereotype, antistereotype, and neutral message conditions, respectively. Each subject heard only one message and rated the speakers on a number of scales. Before each rating, they also heard four compatriots rate the speaker. Six of the scales involved attributes that were stereotypical of French Canadians, and on these scales they heard their compatriots rate the speaker in a way that either conformed with, was contrary to, or was neutral with respect to

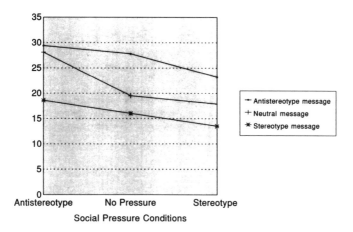

FIG. 1.1.   Effect of message content and social pressure on ratings of a French Canadian speaker. Adapted from Gardner and Taylor (1968).

the stereotype. The major analysis consisted of an analysis of variance of the aggregate of these six ratings reflected such that a high score indicated ratings of an antistereotypical nature.

Figure 1.1 presents the results of this analysis. It demonstrates clearly that both message and social pressure have the predicted effects, even though the stereotype is still influential. Bonferonni post hoc analyses performed for this chapter demonstrate that all means except the one for the antistereotypical message heard under the stereotype social pressure condition deviate significantly from the neutral value of 24. Thus, it is clear that when the only source of information was the ethnicity of the speaker, subjects tended to see him having the traits of a French Canadian. However, when he described himself in a manner that contradicted this impression or when he said nothing about himself that was relevant to the stereotype dimension but peers rated him as contrary to the stereotype, he was perceived in a way that was antistereotypical. That is, the message and the social pressure could operate to counter the effects of the stereotype on person perception. Note, further that a self-description that confirmed the stereotype tended to withstand the effects of social pressure to perceive the speaker in an antistereotype fashion whereas social pressure to perceive him in a way that conformed to the stereotype neutralized an antistereotype message.

Other researchers have similarly shown that information can influence subjects' reactions to ethnic group members even though ethnicity continues to influence person perception. Grant and Holmes (1981) found, for example, that Chinese and Irish ethnicity influenced the perception of individuals but that other information that was unrelated to the stereotype was also incorporated into the impression of the individuals. That is, these individuals were perceived as having traits typically associated with the Chinese and the Irish, even though they were also seen as having traits consistent with information provided about the relevance of the other traits to them. In a different context, Taylor and Gardner (1969) found that the conditions under which a target person described himself influenced the effects of the stereotype on person perception. Under a private condition where the speaker could be viewed as being candid, the effects of stereotypes on person perception were neutralized.

Recently we have begun research directed at uncovering processes involved in outgroup and ingroup stereotyping and person perception. In one such study, Gardner, MacIntyre, & Lalonde (1991) presented 60 subjects with the six categories (men, women, 20-year-olds, 70-year-olds, French Canadians, and English Canadians) and had them rate each one on 12 stereotype differential scales. Following this they were "introduced" to eight "individuals" on three different occasions, and each time they rated them on 4 stereotype differential scales. The individuals were referred to simply as Person 1 (a male 20-year-old French Canadian), Person 2 (a 70-year-old English Canadian female), etc. That is, each individual represented a cell in the $2 \times 2 \times 2$ block comprising gender, age, and ethnicity. Lastly, they were asked to recall the age, gender, and ethnicity of the eight individuals. All testing was done by computer so that both judgments and the latency of the judgments were recorded.

The first set of data permitted the identification of the stereotypes of males, females, 20-year-olds, 70-year-olds, French Canadians, and English Canadians using the t tests of polarity. For each of these categories, a distinction was made between stereotype and nonstereotype scales. The stereotype scales were defined in terms of those six scales for which polarity was greatest, and the stereotype was identified in terms of those attributes toward which ratings were polarized. The nonstereotype scales comprised the remaining six scales. Thus, the distinction between stereotype and nonstereotype scales is relative. Although polarity was significant for all stereotype scales, it may also have been (though not so extreme) for some of the nonstereotype scales.

Analysis of the latency of judgments on the stereotype and nonstereotype scales for each category confirmed findings obtained by other researchers. In their first study, for example, Lalonde and Gardner (1989) found that English Canadian subjects made faster judgments of stereotype traits than nonstereotype traits when rating the outgroups, Americans and French Canadians, but not the ingroup English Canadians. In their second study, they found that Canadian subjects made faster judgments on stereotype as opposed to nonstereotype traits for Americans, Chinese, and Canadians and that Chinese subjects made faster stereotypical judgments for Canadians and Americans. The Chinese subjects, however, were significantly slower on stereotypical judgments of the ingroup Chinese.

Similar analyses were conducted by Gardner et al. (1991) for judgments concerning the ethnic, age, and gender categories. Significant effects were obtained for stereotypicality of traits, category, and the interaction between the two factors. Contrasts of the means for stereotypical versus nonstereotypical traits for each category demonstrated that for all but the category French Canadians, stereotypical traits had shorter latencies than nonstereotypical traits. (The means for French Canadians were very similar to each other.) Obviously there are some exceptions, but the results of these studies suggest that in general, stereotypical information is processed more quickly than nonstereotypical information. A similar generalization follows from the research conducted by Cohen (1983), Dovidio, Evans, and Tyler (1986), and Gaertner and McLaughlin (1983).

As indicated earlier, use of the stereotype differential permits a researcher to make direct comparisons of judgments of categories and individuals. In this study, Osgood D scores were used to assess the comparability of ratings of the eight individuals with each of the six categories. These D scores are the square root of the mean of the squared deviations between the ratings of the individuals and the ratings of the categories. D scores were computed separately for stereotype and nonstereotype scales. Thus, the smaller the D score, the more the individuals are seen as similar to the categories on the scales in question.

Attention here is directed to the results obtained with respect to judgments regarding the ethnicity of the target (i.e., English Canadian and French Canadian). Table 1.3 presents the mean D scores and the mean latency scores for the judgments of the individuals on traits that were stereotypical and not stereotypical for French Canadians and English Canadians respectively. Significant effects for the D score measures were obtained for both ethnicity of target and stereotypicality of trait for the French Canadian stereotype [$Fs(1, 59) = 65.65$ and

TABLE 1.3
Mean D Scores for Judgments and Mean Latency of Judgments for Stereotype Versus Nonstereotype Scales for French Canadians and English Canadian Targets

French Canadian Stereotypes

| | Judgment Targets | | | Latency Targets | |
	English	French		English	French
Stereotype	1.955	1.589	Stereotype	117.631	121.075
Nonstereotype	1.707	1.435	Nonstereotype	120.304	128.617

English Canadian Stereotypes

| | Judgment Targets | | | Latency Targets | |
	English	French		English	French
Stereotype	1.659	1.740	Stereotype	109.846	117.671
Nonstereotype	1.657	1.656	Nonstereotype	128.089	132.021

16.35 respectively, $p < .001$] but not the English Canadian stereotype [Fs 1, 59) = 2.12 and .85 respectively]. The interactions were marginally significant for both the French Canadian [$F(1, 59) = 3.80, p < .10$] and English Canadian stereotypes [$F(1, 59) = 3.46, p < .10$]. Comparisons of the English and French targets on the scales demonstrate that the appropriate targets are seen as much more similar to the categories. That is, French Canadian individuals in comparison to English Canadian individuals are seen as much more similar to French Canadians on the French Canadian stereotype scales [$t(103)^1 = -7.86, p < .001$] as well as the nonstereotype scales [$t(103) = -5.84, p < .001$]. When compared to French Canadians, English Canadian individuals are seen as more similar to English Canadians on the English Canadian stereotype scales [$t(111) = -2.22, p < .05$] but not on the nonstereotype scales [$t(111) = -.03$].

The analysis of the latency of judgments shows that individuals respond faster to English Canadian individuals than French Canadian ones [$F(1, 59) = 12.74, p < .001$]. When contrasts are made based on the stereotypicality of the traits, judgments are significantly faster on stereotype scales in comparison with nonstereotype scales for the French Canadian stereotype [$F(1, 59) = 11.65, p < .001$] and for the English Canadian one [$F(1, 59) = 111.78, p < .001$]. The interactions are not significant in either case. Nonetheless, post hoc contrasts between stereotype and nonstereotype scales reveal that the difference is significant for French targets when the stereotype involved French Canadians [$t(118) = -3.65, p < .001$] but not for English Canadian targets [$t(118) = -1.29$]. For the English Canadian stereotype, however, judgments were faster on the stereotype scales for both the English Canadian [$t(117) = -8.65, p < .001$] and French Canadian targets [$t(117) = -6.80, p < .001$].

When attention is directed to the memory for these individuals, the results demonstrate that although subjects were able to remember the ethnicity of French Canadians and English Canadians virtually equally [means = 3.20 and 3.16 out of 4, respectively; $t(59) = .60$], they took significantly longer to recall the French Canadians (mean = 20.76 seconds) than the English Canadians [mean = 17.46; $t(59) = 2.93, p < .01$].

The research with respect to person perception demonstrates that stereotypes, defined as consensual beliefs, influence the way individuals perceive members of an ethnic group. Again, however, it is clear that the excess meaning attached to stereotypes is not supported by the research evidence. Although they influence person perception, there are situations in which their influence can be attenuated. Subjects do not adhere to stereotypes rigidly; instead they use them to reduce ambiguity. Stereotypes, like message content, social pressure, and perceived intention, provide information to individuals to enable them to make judgments.

---

[1]The t tests presented in this section were based on contrasts following analyses of variance. The degrees of freedom reported are derived from Satterthwaite adjustments required by the pooling of error terms.

Individuals process such information efficiently, probably because the consensus associated with stereotypes causes them to be interpreted more as social reality than as personal beliefs. More idiosyncratic beliefs, on the other hand, are processed less efficiently. The findings with person perception, as with the other topics reviewed here, point to the necessity of determining whether the beliefs under investigation in any stereotype investigation are consensual or relatively idiosyncratic.

SUMMARY AND CONCLUDING REMARKS

In this discussion, I outline a number of issues associated with studying and theorizing about ethnic stereotypes. To begin, I demonstrate that whereas the concept of the stereotype has many excess meanings, measurement operations consider only three actual meanings. That is, ethnic stereotypes are traditionally assessed in terms of: (a) consensual beliefs, (b) unjustified generalizations, or (c) distinctive attributes. Such stereotypes can be considered from the point of view of the individual or the group, and care must be taken to limit generalizations to the unit of analysis in which the measures are taken. This hasn't always been the case!

Second, discussion of *the stereotype* by definition involves a group level of analysis and thus implies some degree of consensus. Regardless of whether one considers stereotypes as consensual, unjustified, or distinctive, a summary state-ment about the stereotype is based on a statistic derived from the sample and is consequently a statement of consensus. It describes those attributes that the greater number of individuals agree characterize a group, those attributes on which a greater part of the sample make unjustified generalizations, or those attributes for which the greater number of individuals in the sample distinguish the group in question. Different measurement procedures lead to the identifica-tion of different attributes in the stereotype.

When attention is directed toward the individual, the level of analysis must be taken into account to ensure that generalizations are accurate. I demonstrate, for example, that individuals can well make unjustified generalizations on attributes that are not part of, or are even opposite to, the attributes on which the sample is described as making unjustified generalizations. The same can be said about stereotypes viewed as distinctive attributes but not about stereotypes as consen-sual judgments. As a consequence, considering stereotypes as either unjustified generalizations or distinctive characterizations precludes easy reference to the stereotype when discussing data focusing on the individual as the unit of analy-sis. Moreover, the characterization as unjustified or distinctive remains simply in the operational definition. Research is needed to determine whether this general-izes to other aspects of behavior.

Such considerations argue for viewing stereotypes as consensual beliefs and directing attention to the functions they serve for the individual. The measurement procedure most suitable to such research is the stereotype differential, because it provides an objective way of assessing stereotypes at the group level of analysis and a direct individual difference measure of the extent to which subjects subscribe to the stereotype. The Katz and Braly technique can also be used, of course, but for some purposes the distribution of scores is restricted and of limited value in statistical analyses.

Research focusing on the individual, but still considering stereotypes as consensual beliefs, points to some interesting generalizations. First, the tendency to stereotype outgroups is relatively independent of attitudes. This suggests that, for the individual, such stereotyping is not motivationally based but rather has a cognitive foundation. Individual differences in reactions to outgroups on nonstereotypical attributes, on the other hand, tend to be motivationally based (i.e, related to attitudes). Second, there is evidence to suggest that stereotyping, in the sense of attributing consensually defined attributes to a group, is a relatively generalized phenomenon both within and between outgroups. To date, possible correlates of such stereotyping have not been determined, but it is likely given the independence of stereotyping and attitudes that cognitive rather than motivational factors are found to be involved. Moreover, the greater efficiency in terms of latency of judgments on stereotypic as opposed to nonstereotypic traits again points to the cognitive basis of stereotypes. On the other hand, stereotypical reactions to ingroups tend to be unrelated to stereotyping of outgroups.

A third line of research also suggests that outgroup stereotypes have cognitive as opposed to motivational influences. Individuals are able to communicate with other individuals through stereotypic content. As indicated previously, some individuals subscribe to stereotypes more than others, but it is clear that most individuals recognize them and can process such information accordingly.

A fourth area of research similarly emphasizes the cognitive aspects of ethnic stereotypes. Research on person perception demonstrates that individuals respond to members of an ethnic group in terms of ethnic stereotypes, but that information from other sources tends to moderate this process under certain circumstances. This again indicates a more cognitive than motivational role of ethnic stereotypes. Moreover, although individuals react more quickly (and thus efficiently) when making stereotypic as opposed to nonstereotypic judgments about both ingroup and outgroup members, their recall concerning ethnicity takes more time for outgroup than ingroup members. Thus, cognitive processing of stereotypic information about outgroups is different in some respects from the processing of ingroup information.

Given these generalizations, it is prudent to suggest that researchers and theorists concerned with ethnic stereotypes consider carefully the manner in which their stereotypes are assessed. It is clear that conclusions derived from group-level data may or may not apply at the individual level. Similarly, stereotypes that researchers and theorists have about stereotypes may not withstand close empirical scrutiny. Finally, it is evident that processes underlying judgments that individuals make on traits that are consensually attributed to an ethnic group may be very different from those underlying relatively idiosyncratic beliefs. More research is clearly required to better understand the nature and causes of ethnic stereotypes and stereotyping; this research should consider carefully the distinction between consensual beliefs and relatively idiosyncratic ones.

ACKNOWLEDGMENTS

Preparation of this chapter was facilitated by Grant no. 410-90-0195 from the Social Sciences and Humanities Research Council of Canada for research on attitudes, motivation, and anxiety in second-language learning. I would like to thank Vicki Galbraith for her assistance in the preparation of this manuscript.

REFERENCES

Aboud, F. E., & Taylor, D. M. (1971). Ethnic and role stereotypes: Their relative role in person perception. *Journal of Social Psychology, 85,* 17–27.

Ajzen, I., & Fishbein, M. (1977). Attitude–behavior relations: A theoretical analysis and review of empirical research. Psychological Bulletin, 84, 889–918.

Allport, G. W. (1954). *The nature of prejudice.* Cambridge, MA: Addison-Wesley.

Ashmore, R. D., & Del Boca, F. K. (1981). Conceptual approaches to stereotypes and stereotyping. In D. L. Hamilton (Ed.), *Cognitive processes in stereotyping and intergroup behavior* (pp. 1–35). Hillsdale, NJ: Lawrence Erlbaum Associates.

Brewer, M. B. (1979). Ingroup bias in the minimal intergroup paradigm: A cognitive–motivational analysis. *Psychological Bulletin, 86,* 307–324.

Brigham, J. C. (1971). Ethnic stereotypes. *Psychological Bulletin, 76,* 15–38.

Bruner, J. S., & Perlmutter, H. V. (1957). Compatriot and foreigner: A study of impression formation in three countries. *Journal of Abnormal and Social Psychology, 55,* 253–260.

Centers, R. (1951). An effective classroom demonstration of stereotypes. *Social Psychology, 34,* 41–46.

Cohen, C. E. (1983). Inferring the characteristics of other people: Categories and attribute accessibility. *Journal of Personality and Social Psychology, 44,* 34–44.

Dovidio, J. F., Evans, N., & Tyler, R. B. (1986). Racial stereotypes: The contents of their cognitive representations. *Journal of Experimental Social Psychology, 22,* 22–37.

Eagly, A. H., & Kite, M. E. (1987). Are stereotypes of nationalities applied to both women and men? *Journal of Personality and Social Psychology, 53,* 451–462.

Esses, V. M., Haddock, G., & Zanna, M. P. (1993). Values, stereotypes, and emotions as determinants of intergroup attitudes. In D. M. Mackie & D. L. Hamilton (Eds.), *Affect, cognition, and stereotyping: Interactive processes in group perception.* New York: Academic Press.

Gaertner, S. L., & McLaughlin, J. P. (1983). Racial stereotypes: Associations and ascriptions of positive and negative characteristics. *Social Psychology Quarterly, 46,* 23–30.

Gardner, R. C. (1973). Ethnic stereotypes: The traditional approach, a new look. *The Canadian Psychologist, 14,* 133–148.

Gardner, R. C., Kirby, D. M., & Arboleda, A. (1973). Ethnic stereotypes: A cross-cultural replication of their unitary dimensionality. *The Journal of Social Psychology, 91,* 189–195.

Gardner, R. C., Kirby, D. M., & Finlay, J. C. (1973). Ethnic stereotypes: The significance of consensus. *Canadian Journal of Behavioural Science, 5,* 4–12.

Gardner, R. C., Kirby, D. M., Gorospe, F. H., & Villamin, A. C. (1972). Ethnic stereotypes: An alternative assessment technique, the stereotype differential. *The Journal of Social Psychology, 87,* 259–267.

Gardner, R. C., Lalonde, R. N., Nero, A. M., & Young, M. Y. (1988). Ethnic stereotypes: Implications of measurement strategy. *Social Cognition, 6,* 40–60.

Gardner, R. C., MacIntyre, P. D., & Lalonde, R. N. (1991). *The effects of ethnic, gender, and age stereotypes on "person perception."* Unpublished manuscript, University of Western Ontario, London, Canada.

Gardner, R. C., & Taylor, D. M. (1968). Ethnic stereotypes: Their effects on person perception. *Canadian Journal of Psychology, 22,* 267–276.

Gardner, R. C., Wonnacott, E. J., & Taylor, D. M. (1968). Ethnic stereotypes: A factor analytic investigation. *Canadian Journal of Psychology, 22,* 35–44.

Gilbert, G. M. (1951). Stereotype persistence and change among college students. *Journal of Abnormal and Social Psychology, 46,* 245–254.

Grant, P. R., & Holmes, J. G. (1981). The integration of implicit personality theory schemas and stereotype images. *Social Psychology Quarterly, 44,* 107–115.

Gregory, W. S. (1941). A study of stereotyped thinking: Affective reactions to persons as the basis for judging their nationality. *Journal of Social Psychology, 13,* 89–102.

Harding, J., Kutner, B., Proshansky, N., & Chein, I. (1954). Prejudice and ethnic relations. In G. Lindzey (Ed.), *The handbook of social psychology* (Vol. II, pp. 1021–1061. Cambridge, MA: Addison-Wesley.

Harding, J., Proshansky, H., Kutner, B., & Chein, I. (1969). Prejudice and ethnic relations. In G. Lindzey & W. Aronson (Eds.), *The handbook of social psychology* (2nd ed.), Vol. V., pp. 1–76. Reading, MA: Addison-Wesley.

Jonas, K., & Hewstone, M. (1986). The assessment of national stereotypes: A methodological study. *The Journal of Social Psychology, 126,* 745–754.

Karlins, M., Coffman, T. L., & Walters, G. (1969). On the fading of social stereotypes: Studies in three generations of college students. *Journal of Personality and Social Psychology, 13,* 1–16.

Katz, D., & Braly, K. (1933). Racial stereotypes of one hundred undergraduates. *Journal of Abnormal and Social Psychology, 28,* 280–290.

Katz, D., & Braly, K. W. (1935). Racial prejudice and racial stereotypes. *Journal of Abnormal and Social Psychology, 30,* 175–193.

Lalonde, R. N., & Gardner, R. C. (1989). An intergroup perspective on stereotype organization and processing. *British Journal of Social Psychology, 28,* 289–303.

Lambert, W. E., Hodgson, R. C., Gardner, R. C., & Fillenbaum, S. (1960). Evaluational reactions to spoken languages. *Journal of Abnormal and Social Psychology, 60,* 44–51.

Lippman, W. (1922). *Public opinion.* New York: Macmillan.

McCauley, C., & Stitt, C. L. (1978). An individual and quantitative measure of stereotypes. *Journal of Personality and Social Psychology, 36,* 929–940.

McCauley, C., Stitt, C. L., & Segal, M. (1980). Stereotyping: From prejudice to prediction. *Psychological Bulletin, 87,* 195–208.

Meenes, M. (1943). A comparison of racial stereotypes of 1935 and 1942. *Journal of Social Psychology, 17,* 327–336.

Quattrone, G. A., & Jones, E. E. (1980). The perception of variability within ingroups and outgroups: Implications for the law of small numbers. *Journal of Personality and Social Psychology, 38,* 141–152.

Razran, G. (1950). Ethnic dislikes and stereotypes: A laboratory study. *Journal of Abnormal and Social Psychology, 45,* 7–27.

Seago, D. W. (1947). Stereotypes: Before Pearl Harbor and after. *The Journal of Psychology, 23,* 55–63.

Sinha, A..K.P., & Upadhyaya, O. P. (1960). Change and persistence in the stereotype of university students toward different ethnic groups during the Sino-Indian border dispute. *Journal of Social Psychology, 52,* 31–39.

Stapf, K. H., Stroebe, W., & Jonas, K. (1986). *Amerikaner uber Deutschland und die Deutschen: Urteile und Vorurteile.* Koln: Westdeutscher Verlag.

Stephan, W. G. (1985). Intergroup relations. In G. Lindzey & E. Aronson (Eds.), *The handbook of social psychology* (Vol. 2), pp. 599–658. New York: Random House.

Stroebe, W., & Insko, C. A. (1989). Stereotype, prejudice, and discrimination: Changing conceptions in theory and research. In D. Bar-Tal, C. F. Graumann, A. W. Kruglanski, & W. Stroebe (Eds.), *Stereotype and prejudice: Changing conceptions* (pp. 3–34). New York: Springer-Verlag.

Tajfel, H., Sheikh, A. A., & Gardner, R. C. (1964). Content of stereotypes and the inference of similarity between members of stereotyped groups. *Acta Psychologica, 22,* 191–201.

Taylor, D. M. (1981). Stereotypes and intergroup relations. In R. C. Gardner & R. Kalin (Eds.), *A Canadian social psychology of ethnic relations* (pp. 151–171). Toronto: Methuen.

Taylor, D. M., & Gardner, R. C. (1969). Ethnic stereotypes: Their effects on the perception of communicators of varying credibility. *Canadian Journal of Psychology, 23,* 161–173.

Taylor, D. M., & Lalonde, R. N. (1987). Ethnic stereotypes: A psychological analysis. In L. Driedger (Ed.), *Ethnic Canada: Identities and inequalities* (pp. 347–373). Toronto: Copp Clark.

Vinacke, W. E. (1957). Stereotypes as social concepts. *Journal of Social Psychology, 46,* 229–243.

2 On the Functions of Stereotypes and Prejudice

Mark Snyder
Peter Miene
University of Minnesota

In January 1991, students and faculty at the University of Minnesota returned from their holiday break to begin the winter term with a rare event—a university-wide convocation. By order of the president of the university, all classes were canceled, and all members of the university community were invited to attend this convocation. In addition, all faculty received materials to help them lead discussions on their first day of class. The subject of this convocation and of the classroom discussions? Racism on campus. A number of shocking racial incidents had taken place on campus during the preceding few months, including threatening and harassing phone calls made to students of color, as well as the appearance of extremely offensive and threatening graffiti messages in several locations around campus.

Sad to say, incidents such as these are far from isolated on college campuses these days. For, it isn't just this university that has been visited by racism; the University of Michigan and many other schools have also been the sites of numerous racial incidents in recent years. Moreover, acts of overt racism have not been restricted to institutions of higher learning, although their goal of fostering an understanding of cultural diversity makes these incidents all the more shocking when they occur in academic settings. Racial tensions have been running high in many locations around the country, even prior to the events in Los Angeles in the wake of the acquittal of the four White police on trial for the beating of a Black motorist, Rodney King. Consider, too, the situation in Dubuque, Iowa. Unlike Los Angeles, where minorities represent 35% of the total population, Dubuque is a city so predominantly White that Blacks make up a minority of the membership of the local NAACP chapter. Dubuque city officials proposed a financial incentive package to attract minority families to the area,

33

and the response to this proposal included racial fights and student walkouts at the high school, cross burnings, and a visit by national Ku Klux Klan members. A White resident wrote a letter to the paper questioning why Blacks would move to Dubuque because "everyone knows Blacks don't like cold weather" (Wilkerson, 1991).

But acts of prejudice need not be so dramatic or blatant to be offensive. In a magazine article on racism in the Twin Cities, a district court judge, who happens to be Black, tells of the difficulties she encountered when paying for her purchases by check (Robson, 1990). An African-American man reports that he no longer goes to convenience stores at night, because store clerks regard him as a likely robber. Currently, the Black community in the Twin Cities is organizing a boycott of a major department-store chain, after a recent investigative report on a local news program revealed highly racist security procedures. American society is clearly far from winning the war on prejudice, intolerance, and bigotry.

Prejudice and discrimination are not restricted to matters of race. Every day, in ways blatant and subtle, people find themselves the targets of prejudice and discrimination simply because they are somehow different—by way of race, sex, sexual orientation, religion, ethnicity, nationality, lifestyle, ideology, and the list goes on. The costs of prejudice and discrimination—the psychological pain, the physical suffering, the economic costs, the lost opportunities, the denial of the (supposedly inalienable) rights to life, liberty, and the pursuit of happiness—are beyond calculation. Much as one might like to believe otherwise, this is simply not a kind and gentle world.

Closely associated with prejudice and discrimination, and intricately interwoven in their fabric, are the stereotypes that pervade people's views of their social worlds. There is no denying their existence. Stereotypes are usually simple, overgeneralized assertions about what "they" are like, "they" being the members of social categories who are robbed of their individuality by having applied to them a set of beliefs that ascribe to them, one and all, a set of shared attributes of character and propensities of behavior. In so many cases, stereotypes are decidedly negative in character and have as their targets social groups who are also the victims of prejudice and discrimination. Even though they are held with little or no foundation in fact, many of these stereotypes have a pernicious way of persisting over time, both within individuals and across generations. The belief that Jews are miserly and materialistic, for one, is centuries old (one need only read Shakespeare's *Merchant of Venice*), and despite all disconfirming evidence, this belief lives on in nearly all parts of the world. Likewise, it is simply not true that all Blacks are musical and athletic, that all women are passive and conforming, that all lesbians are mannish in personality and demeanor, or that all old people are feeble of mind and crabby of temperament, to name but a few stereotypes. People cling to their stereotyped beliefs and assumptions, and the fundamental question is: Why?

THE STRATEGY OF FUNCTIONAL ANALYSIS

Why, despite the fact that stereotypes are so often grossly inaccurate, do people hold on to them? What purposes are served by stereotypes? The question of "Why?" is fundamentally a question of motivation. It is this question of motivation that we address in our program of research. Although much is known about the mechanics of stereotyping—about the ways that stereotypes influence how people think, feel, and act—comparatively little is known about the motivational foundations of stereotypes.

One approach to addressing motivational concerns is to employ the strategy of *functional analysis*. In general terms, a functional analysis is concerned with the reasons and purposes, needs and goals, plans and motives that underlie and generate psychological phenomena (see Snyder, 1988). In the specific case of stereotypes, a functional analysis is concerned with the needs being met and the motives being served by social stereotypes and the involvement of stereotypes in executing plans and fulfilling purposes, both personal and social ones. That is, in functional terms, the question of motivation is framed as: What are the psychological functions being served by social stereotypes?

Functional analysis is a versatile strategy that can be employed productively to investigate a wide variety of psychological phenomena. In fact, this strategy has been applied to understand diverse domains of individual and social functioning. We are all familiar with the functional approaches to attitudes and persuasion, the classic theories of a few decades ago, the frustrations of early attempts to test them that stumbled on a persistent inability to separately measure attitudes and their functions, and the contemporary research that, by employing new approaches to identifying functions, has breathed new life into functional approaches to attitudes and persuasion (Herek, 1987; Katz, 1960; Katz, Sarnoff, & McClintock, 1956; Shavitt, 1989; Smith, Bruner, & White, 1956; Snyder & DeBono, 1989). Less familiar perhaps, but nonetheless offering testimony on behalf of functionalist perspectives, are theoretical and empirical applications of the functional approach to the domains of personality and social behavior, attribution and person perception, social interaction and interpersonal relationships, membership in groups and organizations, and participation in volunteerism and other forms of social activism (for elaboration, see Snyder, 1988, 1992).

A central tenet of the functional approach is the proposition that psychological phenomena that share the same surface features may serve quite different underlying motivational functions. In the case of stereotypes, the functional approach alerts one to the possibility that the same stereotypes may serve quite different underlying functions for different people. Moreover, stereotypes about different target groups, although they may share the same mechanical workings, may actually operate in the service of dramatically different motivational functions.

Identifying the Functions of Stereotypes

Just what are the functions of stereotypes? As historians of theories of stereotypes, Ashmore and Del Boca (1981) outlined three general approaches to the
study of stereotypes: (a) the cognitive, (b) the psychodynamic, and (c) the
sociocultural. These three orientations provide a convenient point of departure,
because each orientation focuses on one particular function of stereotypes.

The Cognitive Orientation.   The cognitive orientation is more than a little
familiar to those conversant with the literature on the cognitive structures and
processes involved in stereotyping (e.g., Hamilton & Trolier, 1986). According
to Ashmore and Del Boca (1981), the most distinctive feature of the cognitive
perspective is its view of stereotypes as "'nothing special', as not essentially
different from other cognitive structures and processes" (p. 28). The cognitive
orientation assumes that humans are limited in the amount of incoming information that they can process, and hence form stereotypes as one way to reduce the
cognitive burden of dealing with a complex world. From a functional perspective, then, stereotypes can be construed as serving the function of _cognitive
economy_ by helping their holders to reduce incoming information to a manage-
able size, thereby lending a sense of predictability to the social world.

The Psychodynamic Orientation.   Stereotypes viewed from the dynamic perspective of this orientation are vehicles for providing a variety of ego-defensive
services. These protective services include, but are not limited to, the classic
defense mechanisms of psychoanalytic theory. More generally, they include the
derogation of others, particularly those who are perceived to be competitors for
limited resources (Taylor & Moriarty, 1987), and the building of self-esteem
especially by engaging in downward social comparison (Wills, 1981). Stereotypes about members of other groups are thus seen as useful tools for making
people feel better about themselves and less threatened by other groups of people. From this perspective, stereotypes can be said, in functional terms, to serve
the function of ego protection.

The Sociocultural Orientation.   As a third perspective, the sociocultural orientation focuses on how stereotypes emerge from social and cultural factors.
This tradition includes studies of stereotypes in the context of community norms,
such as those reported by Minard (1952) and Pettigrew (1959). The sociocultural
orientation suggests that stereotypes serve the social function of helping people
fit in and identify with their own social and cultural ingroups. Through their
socialization, people acquire stereotyped beliefs and expectations about other
groups of people. To the extent that these stereotypes facilitate interaction with
other members of their referent groups, people may never question the veracity
of their stereotypes. Such stereotypes, in the words of Sherif and Sherif (1953),

are "functionally related to becoming a group member—to adopting the group and its values (norms) as the main anchorage in regulating experience and behavior" (p. 218). As such, stereotypes rooted in people's social relations may be said to serve a *social* function.

Empirical Evidence for the Functions of Stereotypes

Thus, a consideration of three general orientations to stereotyping leads to propositions about three specific functions that stereotypes serve. But, can the same stereotype plausibly serve a cognitive economy, an ego protective, or a social function? Take the case of the elderly, a group about whom negative stereotypes are widely held. Consider what young people believe about old people (that is, the contents of their stereotypes) and what motivational functions such stereotyped convictions serve for young people.

Stereotypes of the Elderly.   Brewer and her colleagues (Brewer, Dull, & Lui, 1981; Brewer & Lui, 1984; Lui & Brewer, 1982) used cluster analyses of photographs and trait adjectives to examine three hypothesized subtypes of the elderly stereotype. These subtypes are the *grandmother,* characterized by the traits old-fashioned, traditional, and helpful; the *elder statesman,* characterized as authoritarian, conservative, and dignified; and the *senior citizen,* described by traits such as lonely, worried, and weak. More recently, Schmidt and Boland (1986) assessed the contents of stereotypes of the elderly using exploratory cluster analyses with no a priori subtype structure. The results of this analysis provide clear evidence of multiple subtypes, a total of 12 in fact, 8 of which were rated as negative (e.g., despondent, mildly impaired, vulnerable, severely impaired, shrew/curmudgeon, recluse, nosy neighbor, and bag lady/vagrant); only 4 were rated positive (e.g., John Wayne conservative, liberal matriarch/patriarch, perfect grandparent, and sage).

Thus, the evidence suggests that both positive and negative components contribute to an overall stereotype of the elderly, although Schmidt and Boland (1986) found twice as many negative as positive subtypes. In addition, even the positive subtypes contain attributes that have negative components, such as, "lives life through their children" and "frustrated about mandatory retirement." And, as flattering as some of the labels for these subtypes may sound on first hearing, the facts of the matter are quite the opposite. The grandmother is, after all, an old-fashioned woman; the elder statesman, an authoritarian one; and the senior citizen, worried and weak. In addition, stereotypes of the elderly include a set of negative beliefs regarding the difficulties associated with old age (Aaronson, 1966; Branco & Williamson, 1982; McTavish, 1971). These negative beliefs emphasize the decline in daily functioning and the diminishing of physical abilities (e.g., loss of hearing), mental capabilities (e.g., forgetfulness), and physical appearance (e.g., wrinkled skin) associated with old age. Thus, although the subtypes may vary in the evaluative content of their associated traits, the superordinate category of the elderly represents a group about whom negative beliefs are generally held.

Stereotypes about the elderly are particularly intriguing to contemplate from a psychological perspective and especially from an explicitly motivational vantage point. Why? As a group about whom stereotypes are held, the elderly differ from just about all other outgroups in an important respect: Everyone will eventually become a member of this outgroup, assuming one lives long enough to grow old. The aging process in effect transforms a person from an ingroup (the young) to what was once an outgroup (the old). Although this is not necessarily a unique state of affairs (e.g., a person can switch political or religious affiliations and, in effect, join a former outgroup), it is perhaps the only transformation that is beyond the person's control and that is inevitable for all people in the normal course of events. The way in which people view older people now is, in a very real sense, a view of their own future selves. Therefore, it becomes all the more intriguing to consider why people hold negative stereotypes about their own future selves.

Consider now the possible functions of stereotypes about the elderly. The cognitive perspective assumes that the underlying cognitive processes are essentially the same for all stereotypes and that all stereotypes exert essentially the same influence on the processing of information (e.g., Hamilton & Trolier, 1986). Stereotypes of the elderly are thus assumed to function like stereotypes of any group, as reducers of the complexity of the information-processing task, that is, as a mechanism simplifying the processing of information about old people. When an elderly person is encountered by a holder of the stereotype, he or she is categorized as belonging to a group of people who share specific characteristic attributes. The process of categorizing this person as old, which occurs to reduce the complexity of the information-processing task, produces a number of predictable effects on judgments and behaviors. Thus, members of an outgroup like the elderly are perceived to be similar to each other (Linville, Fischer, & Salovey, 1989) and are likely to be rated more extremely on various psychological dimensions (Linville, 1982; Linville & Jones, 1980). Memory for negative outgroup behaviors is better than memory for negative ingroup behaviors (e.g., Howard & Rothbart, 1980), and attributions about the behavior of outgroups are generally less favorable than attributions about the ingroup (e.g., Pettigrew, 1979). In this sense, stereotypes about the elderly serve the function of cognitive economy.

But, stereotypes about the elderly also serve the ego-protection function of defending the holder against threats to the self. According to this logic, the elderly present a threat to the young, because thoughts of aging and the elderly remind young people that they too will grow old someday. Thoughts about the elderly remind the young of the transience of youth, the nonpermanent nature of their physical appearance and abilities, and even their own mortality. Elderly people serve as examples of the changes in store for the young; because these changes are not necessarily pleasant or desirable, the elderly represent a negative possible self (Markus & Nurius, 1986). They constitute an outgroup who present a threat to the ingroup of the young. To the extent that the elderly do pose a threat to the young, a stereotype about the elderly might serve an ego-protecting function in the following manner. A young person sees old people as having highly undesirable mental and physical deficiencies. To attribute these deficiencies to the aging process implies that as young people age, they too will inevitably acquire such deficiencies, a threatening prospect no doubt. An alternate attribution, one that localizes the problem within old people, minimizes the perceived threats of growing old. By believing that some people are deficient in old age because they always have had deficiencies, that is, they have always been physically and mentally frail, young people who are not now physically or mentally deficient can believe that they will not necessarily become sickly, frail, or forgetful in old age. By blaming the elderly themselves instead of the aging process itself, the young are protected from the frightening truth that they are likely to end up with these same deficiencies. Thus, according to this logic, stereotypes of the elderly serve an ego-protection function.

As for the social function, American society is certainly age segregated, with people spending time and engaging in activities with others of a similar age. Students socialize with other students, young professionals associate with other young professionals, and retired persons spend their time with others who are retired. It is quite common for young people to have little direct contact with older persons, except perhaps their own grandparents (if they happen to live nearby). To the extent that direct experience with the elderly is minimal, the beliefs that young people hold are likely to be greatly influenced by what others (e.g., their friends, the media) say about old people. Thus, young people, through their socialization, may absorb a stereotype of the elderly, the sharing of which is very much a part of their relationships with their peers. In this sense, stereotypes of the elderly serve a social function.

Just what function or functions do stereotypes of the elderly actually serve? Do they serve the function of cognitive economy? Or is it the function of ego protection? Or do they serve a social function? Our theoretical analysis suggests that a stereotype of the elderly may be served by any or all of these functions. It may be that not only does this stereotype serve different functions for different people, but the same stereotype may serve more than one psychological function for the same individual. One way to determine which function or functions is being served is to employ a research strategy suggested by a functional analysis, the strategy of *intervention.* The logic of this strategy is one of attempting to change stereotypes by interventions designed to address the functions thought to be served by stereotypes. Such interventions are designed to demonstrate to those who hold a particular stereotype that the stereotype at issue does not in fact serve its hypothesized function. In addition, interventions are designed to prevent the stereotype from continuing to serve that function or to allow that function to be served by means other than the stereotype. To the extent that such an intervention succeeds in changing the stereotype, it suggests that the functional purpose underlying the stereotype has been identified. The intervention research strategy, not incidentally, is one that has its precedent in research on attitudes and persuasion, in which it has been demonstrated that people are most likely to be persuaded by appeals that engage the functions characteristically served by their own attitudes (e.g., DeBono, 1987; Katz et al., 1956; Snyder & DeBono, 1989).

To demonstrate the utility of the functional approach, we examine the motivational foundations of stereotypes of the elderly by employing the strategy of intervention (Snyder & Miene, in prep.). In our research, we have assumed, on the basis of previous research (e.g., Brewer et al., 1981; Kite & Johnson, 1988; Schmidt & Boland, 1986), that college-age men and women possess stereotypes of the elderly and that, in the absence of any intervention designed to eliminate them, they use their stereotypes. Based on our analysis of the functions of stereotypes, we designed three interventions to reduce their use of these stereotypes. These interventions occurred in the form of stories, which described a same-sex character (named "Bob" for men and "Julie" for women) who has had little contact with elderly people apart from his or her grandmother, who, according to the story, had died after a long illness. The character joins a Friends of the Elderly volunteer program and begins to spend time visiting and talking with older people. Eventually, the character realizes that he or she has been thinking about old people in stereotypic ways. The character then begins to think through the motivations behind those beliefs and subsequently gains insight into the function underlying his or her stereotyped beliefs about old people.

Three Interventions.   Based on the hypothesized cognitive economy function, one intervention addresses the possible cognitive foundations of stereotypes. The cognitive intervention focuses on the character's belief that old people all share the many undesirable traits of his or her grandmother. In this intervention, a key ingredient of the scenario is: [The character] Bob knew that he and his friends were always busy doing something—going to class, working, going out, studying—and it just seemed like old people sat around all day. He saw all the ways in which he and his friends were different from each other and how varied their interests were, but he realized he had pretty much assumed that all old people were the same. And, not only did he think they were all the same, he thought they were all like his sickly grandmother. The insight in this story is based on the character's realization that the elderly are as diverse as people his or her own age.

Based on the hypothesized ego-protection function, another intervention set its sights on motivational underpinnings of a more defensive nature. This intervention focuses on the fear and apprehension of aging, highlighted by the character's belief that becoming severely incapacitated in old age is inevitable. Critical to this intervention is that:

Bob had felt sorry for [his grandmother], but at the same time had been sort of repulsed by her. He felt that somehow it was his grandmother's own fault that she had ended up this way. It was frightening to see her in that condition. . . . He realized that he was afraid that he would end up like her when he got older. He didn't really like to think about getting older because he thought becoming so sickly and lonely was inevitable.

The insight here is based on the realization that he blamed the elderly for the difficulties of old age.

Based on the hypothesized social function, a third intervention plays on social considerations. The narrative in the social intervention focuses on the character's limited contact with old people and subsequent reliance on his or her friends' beliefs. Of particular importance is that

They talked about being old themselves and what they would be like, and his friends all believed that old people must be unhappy. Bob wasn't sure he truly believed that, but he ended up agreeing with his friends. After all, they seemed to know more old people than he did.

The insight gained here comes through the character's realization that he or she had enough of a basis for forming independent beliefs about old people.

Participants randomly assigned to a control condition did not read a story. To assure that the intervention stories did not vary in terms of quality, believability, or persuasiveness, an independent group of 60 participants (30 women and 30 men) rated the stories on a number of dimensions related to the story, the character, and the character's insight process. An analysis of variance revealed no significant main effects or interactions on any dimension. Thus, men and women did not differ in their perceptions or of the stories of the characters, and the stories did not differ in terms of their quality, persuasiveness, or believability (which, had there been differences, might have constituted alternate interpretations of any differential effectiveness of the interventions).

Assessing Stereotyping. To assess stereotyping of the elderly, we employed a task modeled after one used extensively in research on the role of illusory correlation in stereotyping (e.g., Hamilton & Gifford, 1976; Hamilton & Rose, 1980; Sanbonmatsu, Sherman, & Hamilton, 1987). This task presented a variety of trait adjectives that were positive, negative, or neutral in meaning and either relevant or irrelevant to a stereotype of the elderly. Each trait was paired a number of times with a person's name (male and female names were used an equal number of times) and either the age 20 or the age 74. After reading through a series of these trait–age pairings, participants received a surprise recall test that asked them to indicate the number of times each trait appeared with each age. To the extent that stereotypes about the elderly are accessible, they ought to influence the frequency estimations offered in this task, such that participants relying on stereotypes about the elderly should overestimate the number of times traits relevant to stereotypes of the elderly appeared with the age 74 but should not offer biased estimates for traits irrelevant to stereotypes of the elderly. We emphasize that participants in our study were not expecting a recall test while they were reading the trait–age presentation sentences; nor did they recognize the recall test as a measure of stereotyping as they were completing it. Therefore, because it was not clear to participants that we were in fact measuring stereotyping, we believe that social desirability and demand concerns are largely eliminated in this task. However, to the extent that the typical illusory correlation finding is due to cognitive processes of which the individual is unaware, the same features of our task that inoculate it against problems of demand and social desirability also make it a rather conservative test of the effectiveness of our interventions in reducing stereotyping.

Critical to the assessment of stereotyping, therefore, is the assurance that the trait presentation task did, in fact, contain traits that were relevant and irrelevant to stereotypes about the elderly. To identify a set of stereotype-relevant traits, we first selected, based on previous research (Brewer et al., 1981), nine adjectives believed to be relevant to a stereotype of the elderly: (a) lonely, (b) forgetful, (c) traditional, (d) neat, (e) old-fashioned, (f) trustworthy, (g) dignified, (h) conservative, and (i) strong-willed. All traits except strong-willed and neat were recalled significantly more often with age 74 than with age 20, providing evidence of age-based stereotyping; because the participants did not consider strong-willed and neat a part of the stereotype of the elderly, we dropped them from further analyses. The recall task also included seven trait adjectives thought to be irrelevant to stereotypes about the elderly: (a) unfair, (b) selfish, (c) perfectionistic, (d) meddlesome, (e) outspoken, (f) smart, and (g) likable. Participants did not recall any of these irrelevant traits as occurring more often with age 74 than with age 20. The stereotyping task used in this study, then, discriminated between traits considered relevant or irrelevant to stereotypes about the elderly.

Stereotyping Reduced for Women.   Are any of the interventions effective in reducing stereotyping of the elderly? Our analysis of the seven stereotype-relevant adjectives revealed that for the women, the interventions tended to reduce the amount of stereotyping compared to the no-intervention control condition (see Fig. 2.1). As expected, women in the control condition demonstrated a strong tendency to stereotype. They recalled stereotype relevant traits as being paired with the age 74 with a frequency of, on average, over six more occurrences than was actually the case. (All estimates were adjusted for the actual number of presentations, so that a score of zero reflects an accurate response and negative and positive scores represent underestimations and overestimations, respectively.) Women in the social and cognitive-economy intervention conditions provided frequency estimates that were less inflated than the women in the

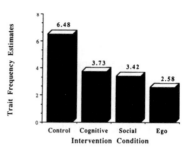

FIG. 2.1. Intervention effects on stereotyping for women.

control condition, but neither of these interventions produced significantly lower scores than the control condition.

The ego-protection intervention alone significantly reduced the amount of stereotyping compared to the no-intervention control condition. Women in the ego-protection condition estimated that the stereotype-relevant words were paired with age 74 an average of four occurrences fewer than the women in the control condition. Thus, although all three interventions produced lower stereotyping scores than the control condition, only the ego-protection intervention produced a statistically significant reduction in stereotyping of the elderly.

Stereotyping Increased for Men. The data for the men, on the other hand, showed the reverse pattern (see Fig. 2.2). The men did not demonstrate the overestimation bias indicative of stereotyping in the no-intervention condition. They were, in fact, quite accurate in estimating the number of times stereotypically relevant traits were paired with the age category 74; they overestimated the number of stereotype relevant pairings with the age 74 by only one presentation, which suggests that they were hardly relying on a stereotype of the elderly to guide them in the recall task. Similarly, men in the social and cognitive-economy intervention conditions were quite accurate in their frequency estimates, producing scores that were not significantly different from the control condition. However, when men read the ego-protection intervention stories, they demonstrated significantly increased degrees of recall bias consistent with reliance on stereotypes of the elderly. These men recalled the relevant words as

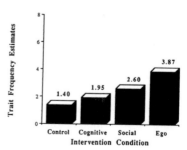

FIG. 2.2. Intervention effects on stereotyping for men.

having been presented over two occurrences more frequently than men in the control condition. That is, for the men, our attempt to reduce stereotyping with an ego-protective functional intervention seems to have actually induced them to engage in stereotyping of the elderly.

Thus, in our experiment, the interventions designed to reduce stereotyping of the elderly had their intended effects for women but not for men. That the ego-protection intervention significantly reduced stereotyping suggests that, at least among women, stereotypes of the elderly work to serve an ego-protection function.

Why Did the Men and Women Differ?   The critical question to be addressed, then, is why the men and women differed, both in their reliance on stereotypes about the elderly and in their reactions to interventions targeted at the possible functions of such stereotypes. One explanation may be found in their responses to measures of beliefs, attitudes, and life experiences. In addition to being more likely to rely on stereotypes of the elderly, women were significantly more "afraid of growing old" than men. This fear of aging is consistent with the idea that images of the elderly present threats to current, younger selves. Not only did the men not report being afraid of growing old, but in the control condition they reported believing their skills and abilities to be far above average and actually improving with age. Quite possibly, in their minds at least, the elderly did not represent their future selves and thus did not present a threat to their current selves. That is, it appears that the women in our experiment, more so than the men, met the theoretical prerequisites of the ego-protection account of stereotypes.

Alternatively, differences in the fear of aging may reflect the thoughts and images that come to mind when people consider the elderly. Our society has different expectations of women and men as they age. For example, our society holds women to strict standards of physical appearance that cause women to focus to a great extent on the physical changes (e.g., gray hair, wrinkled skin) associated with old age. Because 72% of the residents of the nation's nursing homes are women, according to a National Health Survey (Hing, 1989), the image of the weak and isolated nursing home resident is more likely to be a woman than a man. Men, on the other hand, are told by society that their appearance becomes "distinguished" in old age. Role models of the high-status elder statesman abound, and far less media attention is devoted to the physical difficulties associated with aging in men. It is possible, then, that women are fearful of aging because they are taught to worry about the negative aspects of aging, whereas men are not fearful because they are encouraged to see the positive side of growing old.

Whatever the reasons, it is clear that the intervention that addressed itself to ego-protective motivations had the unintended effect of prompting men to display a stereotype that they did not manifest in the absence of any intervention.

That it succeeded in promoting stereotyping may nevertheless attest to the power of this intervention to engage motivations relevant to stereotyped thinking about the elderly, and in this sense provides further evidence that stereotypes of the elderly serve the function of ego protection. This outcome, however, does suggest some caution in using functionally oriented interventions. An intervention designed to reduce stereotyping, even though it is aimed at functionally relevant motivations, may actually backfire and create a stereotype or encourage its use by those not previously relying on it.

THE SCOPE OF THE FUNCTIONAL ANALYSIS

With this study of stereotypes about the elderly, we illustrate the theoretical and empirical logic of the functional approach to stereotyping. However, although our study implicates the function of ego protection for stereotypes of the elderly, we in no way assume that this is the case for any and all stereotypes. After all, not all targets of stereotypes pose threats to the self, as aging and the elderly do (at least for women in our study). There is no reason to believe that all stereotypes serve an ego-protection function or that the same stereotype necessarily serves the same function for all people and in all circumstances.

But, how can we know which functions underlie specific stereotypes held by particular individuals? One productive avenue for answering this question is provided by a strategy for studying personality and social behavior outlined by Snyder and Ickes (1985). Their analysis suggested that the functions served by stereotypes can be addressed by inquiring about: (a) the person holding the stereotype, (b) the target of the stereotype, and (c) the situation in which the person forms and uses the stereotype.

Thus, there are some people who, by features of their identities and personalities, hold stereotypes serving particular functions. For example, persons for whom reference groups are an important source of information about appropriate beliefs may be especially likely to hold stereotypes serving a social function. Research on self-monitoring (e.g., Snyder, 1987; Snyder & DeBono, 1989) identified high self-monitors as one category of people for whom social and interpersonal specifications of behavioral appropriateness are particularly important; these people may be especially likely to hold stereotypes serving a social function. In addition, research on the authoritarian personality (Adorno, Frenkel-Brunswik, Levinson, & Sanford, 1950) indicated that authoritarians, who have little tolerance for social and ethnic groups other than their own, are especially likely to hold ego-protecting stereotypes. Moreover, some people, such as those with a high need for cognitive structure or predictability (e.g., Jackson, 1974; Rehfisch, 1958) may prefer to regard others not as individuals but as members of social groups. These people are likely to rely on stereotypes serving the function of cognitive economy.

Similarly, some targets may be conducive to stereotypes serving particular functions. In addition to the elderly, groups such as the physically disabled, who remind one of one's own vulnerabilities, may be targets of ego-protecting stereotypes. However, other groups may be the targets of stereotypes serving other functions. Any stereotype shared by large segments of society is likely to be serving a social function. For example, people living on the East coast may share a stereotype of people living on the West coast and vice versa, and people living in the country's midsection are likely to hold stereotypes about people living on both coasts. These stereotypes, which may be perpetuated by jokes and stories about the residents of particular regions of the country, are likely to serve a social function. Similarly, any group with whom one has little direct experience or for whom there is little need to see diversity may be the subject of stereotypes serving a cognitive economy function. Examples include inhabitants of foreign countries, especially those perceived to pose little threat to our own country.

Finally, some situations are predisposed to encourage stereotypes serving particular functions. For example, people who join exclusive social clubs whose doors are closed to minorities may find themselves in situations where stereotypes about minorities abound; these stereotypes, to the extent that they reflect and promote club ties, are likely to serve social functions. On the other hand, competitive situations, especially those pitting members of different groups against one another, encourage stereotypes serving an ego-protection function. For example, athletic events between schools or cities, companies bidding for the same contract, or gangs defending their turf may prompt stereotyping of an ego-protective nature. Finally, situations in which there is insufficient time or need to see persons as individuals rather than as members of a group may promote stereotypes serving cognitive-economy functions. Such situations include encounters with others fulfilling their occupational roles (e.g., waiters, librarians, police officers) or other brief social encounters (e.g., deciding whether to offer your seat to a person on a crowded bus or judging another's driving abilities on the freeway).

Taken together, consideration of the role of the persons who hold stereotypes, the targets of those stereotypes, and the circumstances in which stereotypes operate contribute to an emerging functional account of stereotyping. Although we have limited our discussion to three functions underlying stereotypes— chosen because they capture the themes of three historically significant orientations to understanding the nature of stereotypes—by no means do we assert that these are the only functions served by stereotypes. Quite possibly, other functions underlie stereotypes; these may yet be identified by further theoretical analysis and empirical investigation.

Matters of Prejudice and Discrimination

Our next task is to bring the functional approach to bear on the phenomena of prejudice and discrimination in society. Clearly, much of the theoretical and practical importance of understanding stereotypes derives from the fact that the targets of so many stereotypes are groups that are also the targets of prejudicial attitudes and discriminatory behaviors. Thus, some consideration of matters of prejudice and discrimination, in particular those cases in which negative stereotypes are expressed in prejudice and discrimination, contributes meaningfully to the further articulation of the functional theory and its practical application.

One clue to the functions of prejudice is provided by a careful reading of theory and research on modern or *symbolic racism* (e.g., McConahay, 1986; Kinder & Sears, 1981). Symbolic racism is described as:

> a blend of anti-black affect and the kind of traditional American moral values embodied in the Protestant Ethic . . . a form of resistance to change in the racial status quo based on feelings that blacks violate such traditional American values as individualism and self-reliance, the work ethic, obedience, and discipline. (Kinder & Sears, 1981, p. 416)

Translated into functional terms, the construct of symbolic racism suggests that some prejudice serves as an expression of underlying value systems. In this particular case, it suggests that people who value individualism, self-reliance, obedience, hard work, and discipline (the so-called Protestant Ethic) may harbor prejudicial attitudes and direct discriminatory behaviors toward segments of society that they regard as lazy, rebellious, undisciplined, welfare abusers (which just happen to be attributes common to many "majority" stereotypes about racial, ethnic, and immigrant minorities). In functional terms, these instances of prejudice and discrimination (and the stereotypes associated with them) provide expressions of the values of the individualism, self-reliance, obedience, and discipline. They also help foster and solidify those values as defining features of the identities of those people who hold stereotypes, harbor prejudices, and engage in discriminatory actions expressive of those values.

There is, in fact, empirical evidence that suggests that the expression of values can be related to prejudicial attitudes toward an out group. Katz and Hass (1988, Study 2) had White college students complete a scale that permitted them to express their adherence to the values inherent in the Protestant Ethic. These participants then displayed significantly more anti-Black attitudes than participants for whom no values were made salient. This finding is certainly consistent with the notion of an expressive function that may be served by some prejudicial attitudes.

However, the more we thought about matters of prejudice and discrimination, the more we have been sensitized to the operation of a motivational dynamic that we refer to as the *function of detachment*, a motivation that helps understand the linkages between stereotypes and the prejudice and discrimination associated with them. Prejudicial attitudes and discriminatory actions serving a detachment function allow their holders to dismiss, ignore, or otherwise detach themselves from the targets of these attitudes and actions. This detachment function is especially likely in the case of the prejudice and discrimination that members of advantaged ingroups direct toward disadvantaged outgroups. Attitudes and actions serving this function allow ingroup members to justify inequitable relationships with outgroups, to ignore the misfortunes of outgroups, or to lessen ingroup members' own sense of personal responsibility for the adverse fortunes and harsh treatment of outgroups.

Such a detachment function is reflected in wartime images of the enemy and in acts of war as well. Throughout history, nations have constructed stereotyped images that allow them to see and treat their enemies as somehow less than human, and therefore deserving of the inhumane acts of war. Enemy soldiers are seen as "fighting machines," and their leaders are portrayed as maniacal monsters. Over the years, the United States has fought wars with "gooks," "commies," "japs," and "krauts." Although it is never easy to hate or kill another person, it may be easier to hate or kill a "gook" or another dehumanized creature.

In like manner, much of the prejudice and discrimination that pervades contemporary life may also serve a detachment function. Relations between members of different social classes typically involve differences in power, and the attitudes and beliefs held by those in positions of power may be used to justify these existing relationships. Consider the problem of homelessness. Along with society's increasing awareness of the large and growing numbers of homeless people has come a belief that all homeless people somehow deserve (or even desire) their present condition. In this country at least, all too many people have detached themselves from the plight of the homeless. To some extent, this detachment is supported by the belief that the homeless deserve or desire their fate, that is, by an invocation of a "just world" explanation for homelessness (Lerner & Miller, 1978). If people can be seen as somehow deserving their misfortune, the need for individual or collective action to address the plight of the homeless is eliminated. This belief is captured in the words of Thomas Monaghan, the Domino's Pizza founder, whose personal wealth is estimated to exceed $500 million; he told a group of business executives, "To me one of the most exciting things in the world is being poor. Survival is such an exciting challenge" ("Thrill of Poverty," 1990, p. 22). Clearly, the plight of the poor and homeless is easier to accept when their lives are viewed as exciting adventures.

Whites' prejudices toward Blacks serve a detachment function in a slightly different way. Although one may blame the poor for their misfortune, one does not typically "blame" a racial or ethnic minority for their group membership; yet the need to justify the existing social order is equally strong whenever one group is at a disadvantage vis à vis another. Prejudice toward Blacks may serve a detachment function for Whites by regulating opportunity and controlling role assignments in the social, economic, and political worlds. Historically, a principal component of stereotyped conceptions of Blacks has been that they possess animalistic qualities, a belief prominent among slave owners in the United States, who placed great emphasis on the physical strength of the Black people they bought and sold (Jordan, 1977). Sad to say, remnants of this belief are still prevalent. A White South African woman recalls a White doctor explaining to her that Black miners did not need anesthesia when having their lacerations stitched closed because "they don't feel pain the way we [Whites] do" (Tatge & Lasseur, 1990). In the United States, the success of Black athletes is often attributed to their "natural abilities" of strength, endurance, and physical prowess. These abilities, not incidentally, are ones that are cited in support of assertions that Blacks are better suited to being players than managers (recall the claim by Al Campanis, former general manager of the Los Angeles Dodgers, that "Blacks lack the necessities" to be good managers). These abilities, also not incidentally, are ones that sports commentator Jimmy the Greek attributed to the selective breeding practices of slave owners. These natural abilities are, of course, precisely the abilities sought after in the selective breeding of animals, whether to produce race horses or beasts of burden. It may be only one small step from thinking of some people as animals to treating them as such, as centuries of racial discrimination and denial of opportunity prove.

A similar justification for inequitable social relationships is the perception of childlike qualities in the members of particular groups who are on the short end of the equity stick. After all, if some people are really just children, then they can be treated like children, who after all are believed to be limited in their intellectual capacities, unable to make decisions for themselves, incapable of performing complex tasks, and in need of control by adults. Repeatedly, Blacks are portrayed as childlike, from *Uncle Tom's Cabin* to the carefree, happy-go-lucky singers and dancers on the stage and screen. In addition, perceptions of women as childlike abound. In Ibsen's 1978 *A Doll House,* the heroine Nora leaves her husband Torvald because he regards her and treats her exactly as her father did— as a child. Says Torvald, quite pointedly: "Oh, you think and talk like a silly child" (p. 194). Empirical research reveals that stereotypes of women include traits such as immature, naive, emotional, irrational, nonobjective, gullible, and—you guessed it—childlike (e.g., Broverman, Vogel, Broverman, Clarkson, & Rosenkrantz, 1972).

Children, of course, occupy positions of less power and status than adults. Prejudicial treatment of women as if they were children, portrayed in stereotyped images of women, may perpetuate sex-based differences in power, status, and influence. Two recent events serve as reminders that women, even in the upper professional strata of our society, are not treated as the equals of men. One example, noted by Goodman (1990, p. 18A) of *The Boston Globe* occurred during the confirmation hearings for Judge David Souter's nomination to the Supreme Court of the United States. Leaders of women's rights groups testifying before the (all male) Senate Judiciary Committee were greeted as a "group of lovely ladies" by Senator Strom Thurmond. But when Molly Yard of NOW noted, "You don't say to the men, 'Gentlemen, you all look lovely,'" Senator Alan Simpson accused them of "a tiresome arrogance." Goodman quoted linguistics scholar Deborah Tannen, who noted, "The way our culture talks to women and to people of high status are at odds," and if women "talk in ways that get us the floor, we will be seen as bitches." And if women don't, according to Goodman, "We will, like children, be seen and not heard" (p. 18A).

In so many ways, the detachment function, by regulating and constraining social interactions and interpersonal relationships, works to preserve the existing social order (see also Sidanius, in press, for a related discussion of the dynamics of oppression). Consider the case of Ann Hopkins, an extremely productive accountant for the (then) Big Eight accounting firm Price Waterhouse, who was denied promotion to the level of partner despite the fact that she had more billable hours than any other candidate and had generated $25 million in business for her firm. Hopkins alleged that she was denied partnership because of her sex, but Price Waterhouse argued that the problem rested with her "interpersonal skills." The promotion committee believed she was too "macho," "overcompensated for being a woman," and needed a "course at charm school." A sympathetic male colleague told her she could improve her chances of promotion if she would just "walk more femininely, talk more femininely, dress more femininely, wear make-up, have her hair styled, and wear jewelry" (Hopkins v. Price Waterhouse, 1985, p. 1117, as quoted by Fiske, Bersoff, Borgida, Deaux, & Heilman, 1991, p. 1050). Rather than following this advice, she took the firm to court. After a series of appeals, the Supreme Court ruled in 1989 that she had been denied partnership on the basis of sex discrimination. Hopkins provides an example of a woman who refused to "like a child, be seen and not heard," but when she shunned her stereotypic role and generated massive income for Price Waterhouse, she most likely was seen (as Goodman and/or Tannen might put it) as a bitch. In functional terms, this discriminatory treatment can be seen in terms of the detachment function. The male partners at Price Waterhouse acted on their stereotypes and tried to keep her out of the male partners' "club" and hence preserve and perpetuate the existing social order.

Thus, the function of detachment may allow people to blame the victim, as in the case of the homeless, or it may justify keeping people of lower status in their place, as in the case of relations between the races and the sexes. The net result is the same: The existing social order is maintained, and the boundaries between groups (e.g., the "haves" and the "have nots") are defined and reinforced. In addition, the solidification of this boundary may bolster the stereotype holder's sense of positive ingroup identity. These considerations of detachment underscore the intimate involvement of stereotypes in the dynamics of prejudice and discrimination, as well as the ways in which they are tightly woven into the very fabric of social interaction and interpersonal relationships, at both the individual and the societal levels.

CONCLUSION

What, then, does a functional approach offer to the study of stereotypes, prejudice, and discrimination? First, the functional approach offers a framework for examining the motivational foundations of stereotyping, prejudice, and discrimination. Specifically, it suggests that a variety of functions are served by possessing stereotyped beliefs, harboring prejudicial feelings, and engaging in discriminatory actions. Moreover, it is possible to identify or predict the function underlying specific stereotypes and held by particular categories of individuals. Finally, the functional approach suggests techniques or interventions that may reduce reliance on stereotypes, as well as the prejudice and discrimination associated with them.

Lest we appear to end on too optimistic a note, let us underscore just how difficult the task of rooting out prejudice and discrimination is, especially when we are confronting long-standing and firmly entrenched patterns of thoughts, feelings, and actions. We are reminded of a tale told by Allport (1954) in his classic work on the nature of prejudice. It is a tale of a child who had come to believe that people who lived in Minneapolis were called monopolists. From his father, moreover, he had learned that monopolists were evil folk. It wasn't until many years later, when he discovered his confusion, that his aversion to the residents of Minneapolis vanished.

Of course, Allport knew that it is not so easy to wipe out false stereotypes and the prejudices built on them. And, indeed it is not. In our own recent history, we were pleased to see that our campus convocation to address racism at the University of Minnesota had some of its intended effects. The threats stopped and the graffiti disappeared. But, no sooner did the new academic year begin than our campus bore witness to the formation of a White Student Union with avowedly White supremacist goals. In response, the Coalition Against White Supremacy was formed to battle its efforts. Moreover, the Vice President for Student Affairs announced that "a student organization whose goals are inherently racist will not be recognized as a University organization and therefore will not be supported . . . in any . . . way by the University" ("U Bans White Union," 1992, p. 1). This move triggered debates about the First Amendment, free speech, and civil rights (as well as concerns that a ban might actually help, rather than hurt, the efforts of groups such as the White Student Union). Although the last chapter in this drama is yet to be written, the University has modified its position, allowing the White Student Union to register as a student organization, but withholding its recognition or endorsement ("U Lifts White Union Ban," 1992).

Real prejudice, Allport argued, is buried deep in the human character, and only a restructuring of education could begin to ferret it out. Education, however, may not be as simple as exposing people to the diversity among the groups that make up society, and hoping that, with more experience with this diversity, people of good will can shed their stereotypes and abandon their prejudices. Life, when it comes to the eradication of prejudice and discrimination, may not follow the script of *Guess Who's Coming to Dinner,* the movie in which Joanna's parents' struggle to balance their long-held beliefs that racial prejudice is wrong with the shocking fact that their daughter is marrying a man of a different race. In the movie, Joanna's parents come to realize that their opposition to the marriage runs counter to their own attitudes and values and, being people of good will, they support Joanna's decision. The movie ends with the father's stirring speech about racial equality. In life, however, the kind of educational restructuring that can effectively address matters of deeply rooted prejudice and discrimination may be one whose goals are the designing and implementation of interventions that dig down to the underlying motivational functions. These are the interventions that could systematically harness the power of those motivations to free individuals and society from the shackles of false stereotypes, prejudice, and discrimination.

ACKNOWLEDGMENTS

This research and the preparation of this manuscript were supported by National Science Foundation Grants BNS 87-18558 and DBC 91-20973 to Mark Snyder. We thank Cynthia Thomsen, April Gresham, and Mark Zanna for their constructive commentary on an earlier version of the manuscript.

REFERENCES

Aaronson, B. W. (1966). Personality stereotypes of aging. *Journal of Gerontology, 21,* 458–462.
Adorno, T. W., Frenkel-Brunswik, E., Levinson, D. J., & Sanford, R. N. (1950). *The Authoritarian Personality.* New York: Harper.
Allport, G. W. (1954). *The nature of prejudice.* Reading, MA: Addison-Wesley.
Ashmore, R. D., & Del Boca, F. K. (1981). Conceptual approaches to stereotypes and stereotyping. In D. L. Hamilton (Ed.), *Cognitive processes in stereotyping and intergroup behavior* (pp. 1–35). Hillsdale, NJ: Lawrence Erlbaum Associates.
Branco, K. J. & Williamson, J. B. (1982). Stereotyping and the life cycle: Views of aging and the aged. In A. G. Miller (Ed.), *In the eye of the beholder: Contemporary issues in stereotyping* (pp. 364–410). New York: Praeger.
Brewer, M. B., Dull, V., & Lui, L. (1981). Perceptions of the elderly: Stereotypes as prototypes. *Journal of Personality and Social Psychology, 9,* 656–670.
Brewer, M. B., & Lui, L. (1984). Categorization of the elderly by the elderly: Effects of perceiver's category membership. *Personality and Social Psychology Bulletin, 10,* 585–595.
Broverman, I., Vogel, S., Broverman, D., Clarkson, F., & Rosenkrantz, P. (1972). Sex-role stereotypes: A current appraisal. *Journal of Social Issues, 28,* 59–78.
DeBono, K. G. (1987). Investigating the social adjustive and value expressive functions of attitudes: Implications for persuasion processes. *Journal of Personality and Social Psychology, 52,* 279–287.
Fiske, S. T., Bersoff, D. N., Borgida, E., Deaux, K., & Heilman, M. E. (1991). Social science research on trial: Use of sex stereotyping research in Price Waterhouse v. Hopkins. *American Psychologist, 46,* 1049–1060.
Goodman, E. (1990, September 28). Sexism in the inner sanctums [opinion]. *Minneapolis Star Tribune,* p. 18A.
Hamilton, D. L., & Gifford, R. K. (1976). Illusory correlation in interpersonal perception: A

cognitive basis of stereotypic judgments. *Journal of Experimental Social Psychology, 12,* 392–407.

Hamilton, D. L., & Rose, T. L. (1980). Illusory correlation and the maintenance of stereotypic beliefs. *Journal of Personality and Social Psychology, 39,* 832–845.

Hamilton, D. L., & Trolier, T. K. (1986). Stereotypes and stereotyping: An overview of the cognitive approach. In J. Dovidio & S. L. Gaertner (Eds.), *Prejudice, discrimination, and racism: Theory and research* (pp. 127–163). Orlando, FL: Academic Press.

Herek, G. M. (1987). Can functions be measured? A new perspective on the functional approach to attitudes. *Social Psychology Quarterly, 50,* 285–303.

Hing, E. (1989). Nursing home utilization by current residents: United States, 1985 (DHHS Publication No. PHS 89-1763). Hyattsville, MD: Public Health Service.

Howard, J. W., & Rothbart, M. (1980). Social categorization and memory for ingroup and outgroup behavior. *Journal of Personality and Social Psychology, 38,* 301–310.

Ibsen, H. (1978). A doll house. In R. Fjelde (Ed. and Trans.), *Ibsen: The complete major prose plays* (pp. 119–196). New York: Plume. (Original work published 1879)

Jackson, D. N. (1974). *Personality Research Form Manual.* Goshen, NY: Research Psychologists Press.

Jordan, W. D. (1977). *White over black: American attitudes toward the Negro, 1550–1812.* New York: Norton.

Katz, D. (1960). The functional approach to the study of attitudes. *Public Opinion Quarterly, 24,* 163–204.

Katz, D., Sarnoff, I., & McClintock, C. (1956). Ego-defense and attitude change. *Human Relations, 9,* 27–45.

Katz, I., & Hass, G. R. (1988). Racial ambivalence and American value conflict: Correlational and priming studies of dual cognitive structures. *Journal of Personality and Social Psychology, 55,* 893–905.

Kinder, D. R., & Sears, D. O. (1981). Prejudice and politics: Symbolic racism versus racial threats to the good life. *Journal of Personality and Social Psychology, 40,* 414–431.

Kite, M. E., & Johnson, B. T. (1988). Attitudes toward older and younger adults: A meta-analysis. *Psychology and Aging, 3,* 233–244.

Lerner, M. J., & Miller, D. T. (1978). Just world research and the attribution process: Looking back and looking ahead. *Psychological Bulletin, 85,* 1030–1051.

Linville, P. W. (1982). The complexity–extremity effect and age-based stereotyping. *Journal of Personality and Social Psychology, 42,* 193–211.

Linville, P. W., Fischer, G. W., & Salovey, P. (1989). Perceived distributions of the characteristics of ingroup and outgroup members: Empirical evidence and a computer simulation. *Journal of Personality and Social Psychology, 57,* 165–188.

Linville, P. W., & Jones, E. E. (1980). Polarized appraisals of outgroup members. *Journal of Personality and Social Psychology, 38,* 689–703.

Lui, L., & Brewer, M. B. (1982). Recognition accuracy as evidence of category-consistency effects in person memory. *Social Cognition, 2,* 89–107.

Markus, H., & Nurius, P. (1986). Possible selves. *American Psychologist, 41,* 954–969.

McConahay, J. B. (1986). Modern racism, ambivalence, and the modern racism scale. In J. Dovidio & S. L. Gaertner (Eds.), *Prejudice, discrimination, and racism: Theory and research* (pp. 91–126). Orlando, FL: Academic Press.

McTavish, D. G. (1971). Perceptions of old people: A review of research methodologies and findings. *The Gerontologist, 11,* 90–101.

Minard, R. D. (1952). Race relations in the Pocahontas coal field. *Journal of Social Issues, 8,* 29–44.

Pettigrew, T. F. (1959). Regional differences in anti-Negro prejudice. *Journal of Abnormal and Social Psychology, 59,* 28–36.

Pettigrew, T. F. (1979). The ultimate attribution error: Extending Allport's cognitive analysis of prejudice. *Personality and Social Psychology Bulletin, 5,* 461–476.

Rehfisch, J. M. (1958). A scale for personality rigidity. *Journal of Consulting Psychology, 22,* 10–15.

Robson, B. (1990, January). Pride and prejudice. *Mpls/St Paul,* pp. 42–51, 130–136.

Sanbonmatsu, D. M., Sherman, S. J., & Hamilton, D. L. (1987). Illusory correlation in the perception of groups and individuals. *Social Cognition, 5,* 461–476.

Schmidt, D. F., & Boland, S. M. (1986). Structure of perceptions of older adults: Evidence for multiple stereotypes. *Psychology and Aging, 1,* 255–260.

Shavitt, S. (1989). Functional imperative theory. In A. R. Pratkanis, S. J. Breckler, & A. G. Greenwald (Eds.), *Attitude structure and function* (pp. 311–337). Hillsdale, NJ: Lawrence Erlbaum Associates.

Sherif, M., & Sherif, C. W. (1953). *Groups in harmony and tension: An integration of studies on intergroup relations.* New York: Harper.

Sidanius, J. (in press). The psychology of group conflict and the dynamics of oppression: A social dominance perspective. In W. McGuire & S. Iyengar (Eds.), *Current approaches to political psychology.* Hillsdale, NJ: Lawrence Erlbaum Associates.

Smith, M. B., Bruner, J. S., & White, R. W. (1956). *Opinions and personality.* New York: Wiley.

Snyder, M. (1987). *Public appearances/private realities: The psychology of self-monitoring.* New York: Freeman.

Snyder, M. (1988, August). *Needs and goals, plans and motives: The new "new look" in personality and social psychology.* Address presented at the annual meeting of the American Psychological Association, Atlanta, GA.

Snyder, M. (1992). Motivational foundations of behavioral confirmation. In M. P. Zanna (Ed.), *Advances in Experimental Social Psychology* (Vol. 25, pp. 67–114). Orlando, FL: Academic Press.

Snyder, M., & DeBono, K. G. (1989). Understanding the functions of attitudes: Lessons from personality and social behavior. In A. R. Pratkanis, S. J. Breckler, & A. G. Greenwald (Eds.), *Attitude structure and function* (pp. 339–359). Hillsdale, NJ: Lawrence Erlbaum Associates.

Snyder, M., & Ickes, W. (1985). Personality and social behavior. In G. Lindzey & E. Aronson (Eds.), *The handbook of social psychology* (3rd ed., Vol. 2, pp. 883–947). New York: Random House.

Snyder, M., & Miene, P. K. (in prep.). *Stereotyping of the elderly: A functional approach.* University of Minnesota, Minneapolis.

Tatge, C., & Lasseur, D. (Producers & Directors). (1990). *Beyond Hate* with Bill Moyers [Documentary]. New York: Mystic Fire Video.

Taylor, D. A., & Moriarty, B. F. (1987). Intergroup bias as a function of competition and race. *Journal of Conflict Resolution, 31,* 192–199.

The thrill of poverty. (1990, August). *Harper's Magazine,* p. 22.

U bans White union. (1992, March 6). *Minnesota Daily,* p. 1.

U lifts White union ban. (1992, March 9). *Minnesota Daily,* p. 1.

Wilkerson, I. (1991, November 10). Dubuque confronts prejudice amid cross-burnings fear. *Minneapolis Star Tribune,* p. 6A.

Wills, T. A. (1981). Downward social comparison principles in social psychology. *Psychological Bulletin, 90,* 245–271.

3 Implicit Stereotyping and Prejudice

Mahzarin R. Banaji
Yale University
Anthony G. Greenwald
University of Washington

The world Gordon Allport wrote about in *The Nature of Prejudice* provided impressive illustrations of prejudice and discrimination—of lynchings and the KKK, of religious persecution and Nazism, of political repression and Mc-Carthyism. In contemporary American society, such overt expressions are vastly diminished, although even superficial analyses reveal that disturbing expressions of prejudice and resulting inequities are pervasive. All sciences of society recognize that inequities in access to human rights and justice significantly track demarcations of social categories (e.g., race/ethnicity, gender, socioeconomic class, religion), and conspicuous challenges to barriers that preserve systems of discrimination have recently been proposed (see, Galbraith, 1983; MacKinnon, 1989; Sen, 1985; Thompson, 1992).

In approaching the 21st century, it is timely for social psychology to define and, as necessary, refine the theoretical, empirical, and applied considerations of research on the nature of prejudice. One such refinement, we believe, is the exploration of the *unconscious*[1] operation of stereotyped beliefs, prejudicial attitudes, and discriminatory behavior. With greater ease than the social psychologist of Allport's time, contemporary social psychologists can identify and ap-

---

[1] Terminology. The term unconscious is used to refer to processes or events of which the actor is unaware. Two senses of the term unconscious have been identified to refer to (a) processes that occur outside of attention (preattentive) and (b) processes that are unreportable or not accurately reportable (see Bargh, 1989; Greenwald, 1992). In this chapter, it is largely the second sense of the term unconscious that is invoked in our discussions of *implicit* stereotyping and discrimination. We borrow the term implicit from recent research on memory in which that term describes effects attributed to unreportable residues of prior experiences (see Richardson-Klavehn & Bjork, 1988; Roediger, 1990; Schacter, 1987).

preciate the powerful influence of indirect, subtle, and seemingly innocuous expressions of stereotypes and prejudice (e.g., Bem & Bem, 1970; Brewer, 1988; Crosby, Bromley, & Saxe, 1980; Devine, 1989; Dovidio, Evans, & Tyler, 1986; Fiske, 1989a; Geis, in press; Perdue & Gurtman, 1988; Pratto & Bargh, 1991; Snyder, 1981; Word, Zanna, & Cooper, 1974). Yet, current theories and measurement techniques largely ignore the potential unconscious operation of this fundamental evaluation system (see the analysis of this point by Greenwald, 1990).

In this chapter, our concern lies chiefly with the unconscious operation of beliefs about social groups in judgments of individual members of the group, namely, unconscious stereotyping. We cannot deny the important advances in the understanding of stereotyping and attitudes that has resulted from the almost exclusive consideration of their conscious operation. Explicit theoretical attention to unconscious processes, however, is necessary if discoveries of their increasingly prominent role in cognition is to be integrated into theories of social judgment. The central goals of this chapter are to: (a) argue that examinations of stereotyping and prejudice can be profitably pursued by focusing on their unconscious operation, (b) identify recent empirical effects of unconscious stereotyping by locating their causal role in biases in perception and memory, and (c) propose that the pervasive nature of such unconscious influences calls for more radical corrective procedures than are generally acknowledged. If stereotyping and discrimination operate outside of conscious awareness, changing consciously held beliefs may be ineffective as a corrective strategy.

To accomplish these goals, we examine the involvement of unconscious cognition in stereotyping, discuss the role of implicit memory in revealing stereotypes, provide evidence from our recent research on implicit gender stereotypes and others' research on implicit race stereotypes, and speculate about the implications of implicit stereotyping for producing social change and the role of intention and responsibility in social action.

INVOLVEMENT OF UNCONSCIOUS COGNITION IN STEREOTYPING

Definitions of stereotypes and stereotyping offered by prominent theorists (see Tab. 3.1) reveal that the question of conscious versus unconscious operation is typically ignored in identifying the central features of the construct. Neglecting the possible unconscious operation of stereotypes and stereotyping appears to be true for selected definitions that emphasize the inaccuracy in such judgments as well as those that emphasize the categorization aspect of stereotyping. In attempting to determine the credit given to conscious versus unconscious cognition in analyses of stereotypes, we searched the subject indices of prominent social psychological texts on stereotyping and prejudice, looking for entries that would

TABLE 3.1
Definitions of Stereotypes and Stereotyping

A. Emphasis on Inaccuracy of Judgment

"A stereotype is a fixed impression, which conforms very little to the fact it pretends to represent, and results from our defining first and observing second" (Katz & Braly, 1935, p. 181).

"... a stereotype is an exaggerated belief associated with a category" (Allport, 1954, p. 191).

"An ethnic stereotype is a generalization made about an ethnic group, concerning a trait attribution, which is considered to be unjustified by an observer" (Brigham, 1971, p. 13).

"A generalization about a group of people that distinguishes those people from others. Stereotypes can be overgeneralized, inaccurate, and resistant to new information" (Myers, 1990, p. 332).

B. Emphasis on Categorization in Judgment

"... a categorical response, i.e., membership is sufficient to evoke the judgment that the stimulus person possesses all the attributes belonging to that category" (Secord, 1959, p. 309).

"A set of beliefs about the personal attributes of a group of people" (Ashmore & Del Boca, 1981, p. 16).

"In stereotyping, the individual: (1) categorizes other individuals, usually on the basis of highly visible characteristics such as sex or race; (2) attributes a set of characteristics to all members of that category; and (3) attributes that set of characteristics to any individual member of that category" (Snyder, 1981, p. 183).

"Stereotypes, the cognitive component of group antagonism, are beliefs about he personal attributes shared by people in a particular group or social category" (Sears, Peplau, Freedman, & Taylor, 1988, p. 415).

"... a collection of associations that link a target group to a set of descriptive characteristics" (Gaertner & Dovidio, 1986, p. 81).

"... a cognitive structure that contains the perceiver's knowledge, beliefs, and expectancies about some human group" (Hamilton & Trolier, 1986, p. 133).

"To stereotype is to assign identical characteristics to any person in a group, regardless of the actual variation among members of that group" (Aronson, 1988, p. 233).

---

reveal treatment of the role of consciousness (*conscious/unconscious, intentional/unintentional, aware/unaware, explicit/implicit, controlled/automatic, mindful/mindless, voluntary/involuntary, effortful/effortless*). This search included works by Allport (1954), Bettelheim and Janowitz (1964), Dovidio & Gaertner (1986), Hamilton (1981), Katz and Taylor (1988), and Miller (1982). It is revealing that only one volume (Dovidio & Gaertner, 1986) included a single entry for one of the terms (unintentional).

In modern social psychological thinking, however, some attention to unconscious processes is present even if investigators sometimes avoid use of the term *unconscious* (Bargh, 1989; Fazio, Sanbonmatsu, Powell, & Kardes, 1986; Higgins, 1989; Langer, 1978; Nisbett & Wilson, 1977; Wilson, Dunn, Kraft, &

Lisle, 1986). Postattentive unconscious processes (i.e., those based on unreportable residues of previously attended events—see Bargh, 1989; Greenwald, 1992) in stereotyping and prejudice can be observed in several important experimental demonstrations (Darley & Gross, 1983; Goldberg, 1968; Hamilton & Gifford, 1976; Snyder, Tanke, & Berscheid, 1977), although these investigators were not interested in unconscious processes per se. A renewed interest in unconscious cognitive processes (Brody, 1987; Greenwald, 1992; Jacoby & Kelley, 1987; Kihlstrom, 1987, 1990; Marcel, 1988; Uleman & Bargh, 1989) provides new opportunities for theoretical and methodological advances in experiments on the social psychology of stereotyping and prejudice.

We endorse Ashmore and Del Boca's (1981) synthesis of various definitions proposed by social psychologists that a stereotype is "a set of beliefs about the personal attributes of a group of people" (p. 16). Thus, stereotyping is the application of beliefs about the attributes of a group to judge an individual member of that group. Unlike other conceptions of stereotyping (Allport, 1954; Katz & Braly, 1935; Lippmann, 1922; Myers, 1990), this definition assumes that beliefs about the attributes of the group may be derived from accurate knowledge of a group or differences between two or more groups (e.g., the belief that "more men than women are famous"). Although stereotyping can involve the use of incorrect or distorted knowledge in the judgment of groups, we refer to it more generally as the unconscious or conscious application of (accurate or inaccurate) knowledge of a group in judging a member of the group.

It is in the theory underlying measurement and in the specific techniques used to measure stereotypes that the tacit assumption of their conscious operation is most obvious. In spite of well-publicized warnings about the limitations of introspective self-reports (Nisbett & Wilson, 1977) and appeals in favor of indirect methods of measuring attitudes (Campbell, 1950; Dovidio & Fazio, 1992; Gaertner, 1976; Webb, Campbell, Schwartz, & Sechrest, 1966), direct self-report measurement of stereotyping and prejudice remain dominant in practice. We partition measures that have been used to study stereotyping into three general classes to point out their varying reliance on the assumption of conscious operation.

Adjective Check List and Adjective-Rating Measures of Stereotypes and Stereotyping. As several reviews document, adjective check lists and rating scales have been used almost exclusively in the history of research on stereotyping and continue to be used (Brigham, 1971; Broverman, Vogel, Broverman, Clarkson, & Rosenkrantz, 1972; Ehrlich & Rinehart, 1965; Harding, Kutner, Proshansky, & Chein, 1954; Judd & Park, 1988; Judd & Park, 1993; Katz & Braly, 1933; Karlins, Coffman, & Walters, 1969; Linville, Fisher, & Salovey, 1989; Ruble & Ruble, 1982; Sherif & Sherif, 1969). In the paper credited as the first empirical demonstration of stereotypes, Katz and Braly (1933) noted, "Stereotyped pictures of racial and national groups can arise only so long as individuals accept *consciously or unconsciously* the group fallacy attitude toward place of birth and skin color" (pp. 288–289, italics added). This statement of the possible unconscious status of stereotypes is rare and particularly ironic because Katz and Braly's (1933) adjective check-list technique became the method of choice for the assessment of consciously available and socially acceptable expressions of stereotypes. That measurement tradition continues today, with rare explicit acknowledgment of the unconscious operation of stereotyping and prejudice. (e.g., Brown & Geis, 1984). Contemporary measures of stereotypes and stereotyping continue to place the target of evaluation (a group or a group member) at the conscious focus of the respondent's attention.

Attitude Scales as Measures of Stereotypes and Stereotyping. Arguably the oldest measure used in social psychology—the attitude scale—is routinely used in studies of stereotyping and intergroup relations. Some examples that focus on race/ethnicity, political ideology, and gender as attitude objects are the Modern Racism Scale (McConahay, 1986), the Right Wing Authoritarianism Scale (Altemeyer, 1988), the Attitudes Toward Feminism Scale (Smith, Ferree, & Miller, 1975), the Sex-Role Inventory (Bem, 1974), the Attitudes Toward Women Scale (Spence & Helmreich, 1972), and the Personal Attributes Questionnaire (Spence, Helmreich, & Stapp, 1974). All these instruments make the respondent explicitly aware of the object of the attitude or stereotype that is being assessed. It is of some interest that even those who are specifically interested in the shifting trends in white American racism from open bigotry to more symbolic forms of racism (McConahay, 1986; Kinder & Sears, 1981) adopt explicit measurement techniques such as the following items: "Blacks shouldn't push themselves where they're not wanted" or "Over the past few years, Blacks have got more economically than they deserve" (Sears, 1988).

Experimental Measures of Stereotyping. In some experimental investigations of stereotyping and prejudice, the stigmatizing feature of the stimulus object is often kept out of the respondent's awareness, by using unobtrusive measures (e.g., Jahoda, Deutsch, & Cook, 1951; Webb et al., 1966). These experiments stand in contrast to the vast majority of explicit measures of stereotyping, although again, the interest in implicit manipulations does not stem from a theoretical interest in unconscious processes themselves. For example, Goldberg (1968) asked subjects to judge an essay attributed to a female or male author. The finding, striking because it was obtained from female judges, was that male-attributed essays were rated as more competent than female-attributed essays. The name of the author (which conveyed knowledge of author's gender) was not at the focus of subjects' conscious attention. Nevertheless, author's gender influenced judgments in a way that indicated discrimination against females. In another experiment, subjects rated behaviors performed by Black targets as representing greater aggression than the same behaviors performed by White targets (Sagar & Schofield, 1980; see also, Duncan, 1976). Similarly, Darley and Gross (1983) manipulated cues denoting socioeconomic class and found that such knowledge, although it alone did not bias subjects' judgments of the target's future academic performance, dramatically influenced judgment if the target was observed in a test-taking situation. Here, identical test performance led to predictions of better future performance if subjects believed the target to be from a high rather than a low socioeconomic class. In each of these examples, a stigmatizing feature of the target (gender, race, or social class), even though not at the focus of conscious attention, led to a stereotype-influenced judgment.

IMPLICIT MEMORY REVEALS GENDER STEREOTYPES

Although interest in the role of memory in stereotyping and prejudice is not new (see Allport, 1954, pp. 483–499), a concerted effort to understand the role of memory in stereotyping has been undertaken only recently, as part of a general development of information-processing interpretations of social cognition (e.g., Bellezza & Bower, 1981; Cohen, 1981; Hamilton & Gifford, 1976; Hamilton & Trolier, 1986; Rothbart, Evans, & Fulero, 1979; Snyder & Uranowitz, 1978; Taylor, 1981). Using nearly exclusively explicit (conscious recollection) memory measures such as free recall, cued recall, and recognition, these investigations revealed errors at both encoding (initial exposure to information) and retrieval that result in stereotype-reflecting judgments.

Studies of implicit memory have produced surprising and exciting discoveries that may represent a paradigm shift in understanding the role of unconscious cognition in human memory (see Greenwald, 1992; Jacoby, Lindsay, & Toth, 1992; Kihlstrom, 1987). In a typical experiment to demonstrate implicit memory, subjects are exposed to a series of stimuli, such as a list of words, and are later asked to perform an ostensibly unrelated second task on a new stimulus set. The new stimuli contain, perhaps in modified form, both previously seen (old) and new items. Subjects' performances at the second task on the old versus new items are compared to reveal the effects of prior exposure (i.e., implicit memory). Performances that provide such implicit measures of memory include perceptual identification, lexical decisions, word-fragment completions, and evaluative judgments; these tasks often reveal data patterns that contrast with the traditional explicit measures of free recall, cued recall, and recognition (Graf & Schacter, 1985; Merikle & Reingold, 1991; Richardson-Klavehn & Bjork, 1988; Roediger, Weldon, & Challis, 1989; Schacter, 1987; Smith & Branscombe, 1988). Studies using these procedures regularly demonstrate striking dissociations (i.e., evidence for implicit [unconscious] memory in the absence of explicit [conscious] recollection.

An Implicit Memory Effect: "Becoming Famous Overnight"

Jacoby, Kelley, Brown, and Jasechko (1989; Jacoby & Kelley, 1987) reported a provocative demonstration of the operation of implicit memory in fame judgments. Their basic procedure involved a two-phase experiment. On Day 1, subjects read a list that contained names of both famous and nonfamous people. On Day 2, 24 hours later, the same subjects were presented with a list containing previously seen (old) and new (unseen on Day 1) nonfamous names, interspersed with old and new famous names. Subjects judged each name on the new list in response to the question: Is this person famous? (to be answered "*yes*" or "*no*"). Jacoby et al. (1989) hypothesized that although episodic (i.e, explicit) memory for the nonfamous names would fade over the 24-hour delay, some residual (perceptual) familiarity for the previously seen (but not explicitly remembered as seen) nonfamous names should lead to false judgments of fame. That is, subjects should mistakenly judge more old (than new) nonfamous names as famous. As predicted, Jacoby et al. found a higher false-alarm rate for old nonfamous names than for new nonfamous names. In this way, Jacoby et al. succeeded in making nonfamous names "become famous overnight," an effect that indicates a potent unconscious influence of memory.

Stereotypical Gender Bias in False-Fame Judgments

Some of our recent research has taken advantage of the ease of identifying the gender of names (even those of unknown people). Although names carry other social category information as well (e.g., race; ethnicity, age), we manipulated gender because of (a) the relative ease of varying gender through names, (b) the likelihood that subjects (even in a within-subjects design) would not be alerted to our use of this commonplace category as an independent variable, and (c) the pervasive and accurate association between gender and fame (i.e., greater male than female fame).

Procedure.   Adapting the Jacoby et al. (1989) procedure, we (Banaji & Greenwald, 1991; Banaji & Greenwald, 1992) varied the gender of nonfamous names by attaching a female or male first name to a common last name (e.g., Peter Walker, Susan Walker). Famous names were derived by generating names in three categories of fame (actors, musicians, and writers) and by selecting names in these categories thought to be known to most but not all undergraduates (Gladys Knight, Dave Brubeck, Doris Lessing, Thornton Wilder, Jane Wyman,

Rod Steiger). In the experiment we describe here, each of 49 subjects (23 male, 26 female) initially judged a list of 72 names for ease of pronunciation, the ostensible purpose being to estimate the difficulty that each name would pose to a person unfamiliar with the English language. The 72-name Day 1 list included 36 famous and 36 nonfamous names, with 18 female names and 18 male names in each of these sets of 36. After a 48-hour delay, subjects were shown a new list of 144 names, consisting of the 72 old (Day 1) names, randomly intermixed with 72 new names generated in the same fashion. Subjects judged each of the 144 Day 2 names simply as famous or not.

Data Analysis.   Data from each subject's judgments for each of the four within-subject conditions (old male, new male, old female, and new female) were reduced to a hit rate (proportion of famous names correctly judged famous) and a false-alarm rate (proportion of nonfamous names mistakenly judged famous). One can see in Table 3.2 that (a) hit rates were higher for male names than for female names, (b) false alarm rates were higher for old names than for new names, and (c) the false-alarm rate for old male names was higher than that for old female names.

Unfortunately, the hit and false-alarm data do not readily allow judgments of the extent to which findings reflect effects of the independent variables on sensitivity to the famous–nonfamous distinction versus their effects on readiness to judge that names are famous (independent of their actual fame). However, signal detection analysis can decompose hit and false-alarm data into measures of sensitivity to a stimulus variation (name fame in this case) and threshold or criterion for assigning the judgment. These measures are referred to, respectively, as d' (d prime) and β (beta) (Green & Swets, 1966). Our analyses used these measures, replacing β with its logarithm because of the superior distributional properties (greater approximation to normality) of this log transformation.

Mean values of d' and log β for the four conditions are given in Tab. 3.3. The results for d' indicate that subjects were more sensitive to the fame variation for

TABLE 3.2
Hit and False Alarm Rates for Old and New, Male and Female Names ($n = 49$)

	Old Names		New Names	
	Hit Rate	F-A Rate	Hit Rate	F-A Rate
Male names				
Mean	.78	.08	.73	.03
SD	.15	.10	.21	.06
Female names				
Mean	.64	.04	.61	.03
SD	.17	.06	.21	.06

TABLE 3.3
Mean Values of d' and log β for Old and New, Male and Female Names (n = 49)

	Old Names		New Names	
	d'	log β	d'	log β
Male names				
Mean	2.39	.71	2.63	1.17
SD	.61	1.09	.86	.94
Female names				
Mean	2.15	1.38	2.19	1.45
SD	.54	.81	.77	.82

male names than female names [$F(1,48) = 37.50$]. The results for log β show subjects more readily judged famousness for male than for female names [$F(1,48) = 28.02$] and for old than new names [$F(1,48) = 8.67$]. Further, there was a significant interaction such that the greater tendency to assign fame to male rather than to female names was greater for old than for new names [$F(1,48) = 6.07$]. These tendencies were displayed equally by male and female subjects.

The main findings are graphed in Fig. 3.1. These findings provide evidence for implicit stereotypes that associate maleness more than femaleness with fame. In our experiment, the stereotype apparently operates with greatest force for nonfamous names that are given a boost in familiarity by presentation on Day 1. When encountered on Day 2, such names' familiarity is more likely to be interpreted as fame when the name is male than when female. The findings shown in Fig. 3.1 have now been replicated in much the same form in three experiments (Banaji & Greenwald, 1992). These additional experiments show a reliable name gender difference in β even in the absence of a name gender difference in d' (i.e., when famous male and female names were equally famous).

Stereotypical Gender Bias in Judgments of Dependence and Aggression

Higgins, Rholes, and Jones (1977) demonstrated that the presentation of trait-category information in one context can influence judgments of an ambiguously described target person in an unrelated context. We (Banaji, Hardin, & Rothman, 1993) used a variant of their procedure to examine another form of implicit stereotyping (cf. Srull & Wyer, 1979). Based on two established gender stereotypes (see Broverman et al., 1972), we asked whether activating a trait category would lead to more extreme judgments, specifically of targets whose social category (male or female) was stereotypically consistent with the trait category (aggressiveness and dependence, respectively).

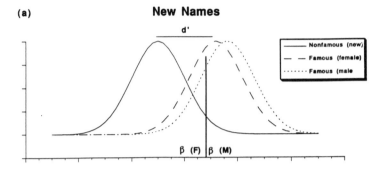

(a) **New Names**

(b) **Old Names**

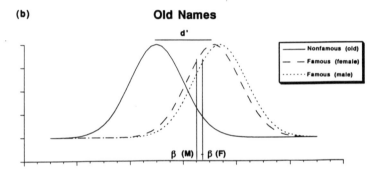

FIG. 3.1. Signal detection analysis of fame judgments. Noise distributions, to the left in each panel, indicate the distribution of strength of evidence for famousness provided by nonfamous names (solid line). The signal distributions, to the right, give the corresponding distributions for famous names, separately for male names (dotted line) and female names (dashed line). The separation between means of the noise and signal distributions measures subjects' sensitivity to the fame variation. This sensitivity (signal detection theory's d' measure) was significantly greater for male than female names. The vertical lines represent placements of criterion for subjects' judgments of fame for male and female names. Areas in the signal distributions to the right of criterion placement represent the hit rates shown in Table 2, and areas in the noise distributions to the right of the criterion represent Table 2's false alarm rates. The signal detection measure, beta, is the ratio of the height of the signal distribution to that of the noise distribution, at the point corresponding to criterion placement. Beta was lower for male names than female names (i.e., weaker evidence was required to judge a male name as famous), and this male-favoring bias occurred for names previously encountered on Day 1 (old names, Panel B) but not for names first encountered during the fame judgment task on Day 2 (new names, Panel A).

Procedure.   Banaji et al. (1993) assigned subjects to either a dependence or aggression experiment. Subjects in each experiment were assigned to a condition in a 2 (trait exposure vs. control) × 2 (target gender: male vs. female) between-subjects design. In each experiment, subjects believed they were participating in two separate experiments. In the "first" experiment, subjects unscrambled 45 four-word sentences that were either all neutral in meaning or included 30 sentences each of which described a behavior indicative of the target trait (dependence or aggression). Examples of unscrambled sentences for the target trait dependence are: *G. conforms to others, B. takes verbal abuse, T. has low self-esteem.* Examples of unscrambled sentences for the target trait aggression are: *C. threatens other people, R. cuts off drivers, T. abuses an animal.* Then, a new experimenter conducted the "second" experiment, in which subjects read a paragraph that described either a male (Donald) or female (Donna) target performing a series of weakly trait-relevant actions. For example, in the dependence experiment, embedded in a story containing several neutral statements were items such as: "I ordered only coffee, and so did she (he)," or ". . . but wanted to check with her (his) boyfriend (girlfriend) first." Likewise, in the aggression experiment, embedded in a story containing several neutral statements were items such as: "Noticed his (her) mug was dirty and asked the waitress for a new one," or ". . . wanted to take his (her) car, so we left mine at the cafe." After a short filler task, subjects rated Donald or Donna on the target trait and other traits, related and unrelated to the target trait.

Results.   Both experiments demonstrated implicit gender stereotyping. In the dependence experiment, subjects who were exposed to primes that described dependent behaviors judged the female target as more dependent than subjects who rated the same target after exposure to neutral primes. However, subjects exposed to the same dependence primes judged the male target as less dependent than subjects who rated the target after exposure to neutral primes. In the aggression experiment, subjects who were exposed to primes that described aggressive behaviors judged the male target as more aggressive than subjects who rated the same target after exposure to neutral primes. When judging a female target, previous exposure to the same aggression primes produced no change in judgment.

In summary, both experiments demonstrate the importance of a match between priming information and target's social category in producing the trait priming effect. Like the previous demonstration of gender bias in fame judgments, this result involves an implicit form of gender stereotyping. These are implicit effects because they occur without the subject being consciously aware of the influence of recent experience (name familiarity and trait activation, respectively). At the same time, these effects reveal gender stereotypes because they occur selectively when the information content of recent experience stereotypically fits with the gender category of the judgment target.

Commentary on the Goldberg Variations

Goldberg (1968) reported that female subjects underrated the quality of essays that were attributed to female-named rather than male-named authors. That result inspired a large replication literature, a recent review of which declared, in arriving at a conclusion opposed to Goldberg's, "[M]any authors . . . misrepresent the strength of the results Goldberg reported. . . . A quantitative meta-analysis of research using Goldberg's experimental paradigm shows that the average difference between ratings of men and women is negligible" (Swim, Borgida, Maruyama, & Myers, 1989, p. 409). Because Goldberg's finding is a prime example of implicit gender discrimination, Swim et al.'s questioning of its conclusion raises an issue about the generality of the implicit gender stereotyping results described in this chapter. We consider in turn the two main points of Swim et al.'s conclusion.

First, with regard to the strength of the original findings we note that, although reporting no statistical tests, Goldberg (1968) did provide enough data to permit effect size computations. Assuming that Goldberg used a two-tailed, alpha $= .05$ significance criterion, the mean effect size (across 6 topics) was between $d = .43$ and $d = 1.03$. These effect-size numbers are in a range conventionally described by Cohen (1988) as *moderate* to *large*. With topics (instead of subjects) used as the unit of observation, Goldberg's effect size was calculatable exactly as $d = .88$, which is conventionally a *large* effect.

Second, with regard to the strength of effects found in their meta-analytic review, Swim et al. reported an overall mean effect size of $d = .07$ (95% confidence interval between .04 and .10). This mean effect size is, indeed, below a conventional *small* level (Cohen, 1988). Nevertheless, as Rosenthal (1990) effectively argued, even effect sizes smaller than $d = .07$ can be very important and should therefore not be routinely dismissed as *negligible*. For example, translating a $d = .07$ sex-discrimination effect size finding into a large-scale hiring situation in which 50% of applicants are to be hired, 107 men would be hired for every 100 equally qualified women. That should not be "negligible" to the approximately 3.5% of deserving women who end up without jobs (nor to the 3.5% of undeserving men who end up with jobs!).

Perhaps more important than the overall mean effect size observed by Swim et al. was the highly significant heterogeneity in effect sizes that they reported (1989, p. 415, Table 1). As a consequence of this heterogeneity, it is inappropriate to accept the overall mean effect size as an adequate description of the literature reviewed by Swim et al. Rather, it is more proper to evaluate Goldberg's original conclusion by considering selectively, within the Goldberg Variations literature, those studies that had characteristics most similar to the original report. For example, studies that (like Goldberg's original) manipulated the target-person-sex independent variable minimally (by name only) showed larger effect sizes (mean $d > = .12$) than do other studies (Swim et al., 1989, Tables

17–19, pp. 420–422). This observation agrees with our assumption that Goldberg's original finding captured an implicit discrimination phenomenon and therefore might be undone by independent variable manipulations that brought the author's sex more into the subject's conscious focus of attention.

Implicit Race Stereotyping

Our studies focus on gender stereotypes, but there is no reason to believe that implicit stereotyping is confined to gender. In particular, some findings have already established that implicit stereotyping occurs for race categories. These findings were obtained chiefly within the social cognition tradition that has typically focused on conscious cognition. However, as will be apparent, the results reviewed here reflect the same implicit (unconscious) processes that are apparent in our studies of gender-related stereotyping.

Gaertner and McLaughlin (1983) presented subjects with pairs of letter strings, requesting a "*yes*" judgment if both were words and "*no*" otherwise. Hypothesizing that faster "*yes*" responses should reflect stronger existing associations between the two words in a pair, they found that White subjects responded reliably faster to White-positive word pairs than to Black-positive pairs (e.g., *White–smart vs. Black–smart*). This difference did not emerge on judgments of negative traits (e.g., *White–lazy vs. Black–lazy*). These findings were apparent both for subjects who scored high and those who scored low on an explicit measure of race prejudice. In a related study, Dovidio et al. (1986) used the procedure of presenting a prime (*Black* or *White*) followed by a target (a positive or negative trait) and asking subjects to judge if the target trait could *ever be true* or was *always false* of the prime category. Again, subjects responded reliably faster to positive traits that followed the prime *White* than *Black,* and in this study they also responded faster to negative traits that followed the prime *Black* than *White.*

The results just described were interpreted by Gaertner and Dovidio (1986) as evidence for *aversive racism,* which they define as a conflict "between feelings and beliefs associated with a sincerely egalitarian value system and unacknowledged negative feelings and beliefs about blacks" (p. 62). From our perspective, these findings can effectively be described as *implicit racism.*

Devine (1989) reported that white subjects who were subliminally exposed to a series of words, 80% of which were stereotypically associated with Black Americans (e.g., poor, jazz, slavery, Harlem, busing) judged a male target person to be more hostile than subjects for whom only 20% of the words had the stereotype association. Again, there was no difference in this result between subjects who scored high and low on an explicit measure of prejudice. Two aspects of the procedure and results render conclusions based on this finding tentative. First, the male target's race was unspecified, and we must therefore assume that subjects imagined a white American target, raising the question of whether the effect is due to activation of the stereotype of Black Americans or possibly to a hostility component of the priming procedure. Further, the dissociation result was obtained across separate experiments and between an implicitly measured stereotype and explicitly measured prejudice. However, the importance of Devine's study derives from its pioneer status in identifying this particular form of an implicit stereotyping effect.

Gilbert and Hixon (1991) showed that a race stereotype, presumably activated by including an Asian female in a videotaped sequence seen by subjects, influenced subsequent word-fragment completions, a type of measure often used in implicit memory research. Subjects who were in a condition that included a cognitive load (e.g., rehearsing an eight-digit number) during exposure to the Asian stimulus completed fewer fragments with stereotypic terms than subjects not given the additional cognitive task, suggesting that cognitive load interfered with stereotype activation. On the other hand, those who had no load during the stereotype activation stage (and for whom, therefore, it could be assumed that the stereotype was activated), gave more stereotype-consistent completions than those who had added mental load. Results were reversed when cognitive load was introduced after stereotype activation (i.e., when judging the target). Now, subjects in the cognitive load condition were more likely to display the activated stereotype than those in the no-load condition. These findings indicate that implicit stereotype expressions are less likely when subjects can devote greater conscious effort to their task.

SPECULATIONS ABOUT IMPLICIT STEREOTYPING
FOR SOCIAL CHANGE

Not surprisingly, interest in person-level and consciously operative psychological processes has led social psychologists to offer prescriptions for social change by transformations in (a) individual thought and behavior, and (b) the conscious expression of stereotypes and prejudice, by using conscious methods of change (but see Gaertner & Dovidio, 1986, p. 85). A clear example of both these features is Allport's (1954, p. 487) discussion of methods that focus on conscious change at the individual level.

We do not deny the importance of individual-based or conscious methods of change. To continue the argument made in this chapter, however, we recommend going beyond the almost exclusive reliance on such techniques. The enormity and complexity of intergroup behavior make methods that focus exclusively on individual change in conscious awareness ineffectual. Here, we speculate briefly about the relevance of implicit stereotyping for the endeavor of reducing prejudice and discrimination.

Change in Social Structure Will Change Cognitive Structure. It is plausible that influential stereotypes are derived from everyday experiences of reality, for example, that women as a social group are less famous than men or that men commit more crimes of aggression than women. Such knowledge is obtained without the distortion of facts or the accompaniment of strong feelings about the social groups in question. The focus of this chapter is on the unconscious application of such commonplace knowledge of groups in the judgment of individual members. Each act of implicit stereotyping can be seen as an implicit individual reproduction of beliefs about the collective. In other words, social structure (e.g., stratification of fame by gender) causes cognitive structure (e.g., a higher criterion of fame in judgments of an individual female). If implicit stereotyping is the unconscious application of knowledge about an existing relationship between an attribute (fame) and a social category (females, males), then the stratification of attributes by social categories fosters the potential for implicit stereotyping and prejudice. The unconscious mechanisms that transduce knowledge of the social world for use in individual judgment demonstrate the influence of socio-cultural realities on cognition. Future programs for social change in beliefs and attitudes can be facilitated by research that establishes links between the social conditions of the collective and the cognitive output of individuals.

Of the several ways in which social structure itself can be changed, a minority of social psychologists have argued for the need for legislation and social policy as a way to ensure relatively swift social change (e.g., Allport, 1954; Aronson, 1988; Clark, 1955; Katz & Taylor, 1988). Although it may be obvious that legislated social change creates individual belief change, this view is a relatively new one and has not always been endorsed with enthusiasm. For example, the United States Supreme Court defended its "equal but separate" decision in *Plessey v. Ferguson* (1896) by stating that the law was powerless to counter "racial instincts" (p. 537) and that "If one race be inferior to the other socially, the Constitution of the United States cannot put them upon the same plane" (p. 551). Likewise, in recent Supreme Court decisions on abortion rights, the court has transferred the decision making to states, and thereby to the individual voters in each state, presumably reflecting the position that stateways can't change folkways. To the contrary, we emphasize that legislated change can effectively transform social structure that can change cognitive structure. In particular, legislated social change has the benefit of potentially widespread influence without the involvement of conscious decisions by single individuals to adopt non-discriminatory behaviors.

Making the Unconscious Conscious Reduces the Incidence of Stereotyping and Prejudice. Recognition of implicit stereotyping and prejudice leads to a critical question: How can stereotyping and prejudice be reduced when their operation is concealed from the perpetrator and (perhaps) even the target of discrimination? One method is to alert subjects to the stigmatizing attribute that produces the stereotyped judgment. Data relevant to this issue suggest that individuals may show evidence of stereotyping on an implicit measure but not on an explicit measure (Baxter, 1973; Crosby et al., 1980; Devine, 1989; Dovidio et al., 1986). Drawing social category information into conscious awareness allows mental (cognitive and motivational) resources to overrule the consciously un-wanted but unconsciously operative response. The notion of highlighting aware-ness of the social category at the time of judgment may be controversial because other well-reasoned suggestions dictate minimizing awareness of social category distinctions (Brewer & Miller, 1988). Future research must address the task and goal conditions under which, and the methods by which, increasing the salience of category information decreases the expression of prejudice.

THE ROLE OF INTENTION AND RESPONSIBILITY IN SOCIAL ACTION

Social psychologists have avoided addressing issues concerning responsibility and intention in situations that produce stereotyping and prejudice (although see Bargh, in press; Fiske, 1989a). Such issues have historically been considered to be in the purview of social philosophy and legal discourse. In particular, the issue of "intention to harm" has been central to important decisions by the United States Supreme Court. Of central interest is the issue of the unfairness of assign-ing blame for an act committed without conscious intention to harm versus the damage that results to the victim. For example, in an important libel case, the court ruled that such acts of harm doing must be shown to have occurred with actual malice, with knowledge that it was false, and with reckless disregard of the truth (*The New York Times v. Sullivan*, see Lewis, 1991). Likewise, the Supreme Court gave a restrictive interpretation of the Voting Rights Act of 1965, ruling that district lines and other voting procedures did not violate the law unless it could be shown that they were adopted for the purpose of discriminating. That decision produced an immediate response from Congress, which passed an amendment clarifying that the Voting Rights Act applies to actions that have a discriminatory result even if intentional discrimination is not proven (see Green-house, 1991).

Social psychologists have been concerned with the implications of their re-search for legal action, albeit only rarely have their experimental data been offered as part of testimony in important legal decisions (e.g., Clark, 1955; Fiske, 1989b). However, empirical discoveries about the implicit nature of social judgments are indeed relevant to discussions about the legal consequences of such acts for the perpetrator as well as the survivor of stereotyping and prejudice. Specifically, if implicit stereotyping arises (a) from knowledge shared by a culture as a whole and is not uniquely possessed by the perpetrator alone, (b) from an accurate understanding of reality and not necessarily from misperception or distortion, and (c) without the conscious awareness of the perpetrator, such data would argue for removing responsibility from individual perpetrators of social crimes of stereotyping and prejudice. Such conditions surrounding discoveries of implicit stereotyping encourage consideration of the notion of *perpetratorless crimes* (as a parallel to the existing notion of *victimless crimes*). The notion of removing responsibility and blame from individual perpetrators differs vastly from conventional assumptions of most justice systems. Discussion of the implications of this construct for justice systems must be considered at length, without sacrificing attention to the consequences of perpetratorless crimes for the target of prejudice.

From the perspective of the victim of implicit stereotyping, the potential pervasiveness of such actions demand discussion of the status of victim remuneration. In particular, implicit stereotyping is, by its very nature, likely to be unnoticed by the target, and hence traditional methods of guaranteeing due process and so forth become irrelevant. However, if future research documents the extent of damage produced by implicit stereotyping and prejudice, alternative methods of recognizing the extent of discrimination and providing remuneration will need to be developed. For example, an important issue for consideration is the target's attribution of internal versus external location of the causes of negative outcomes. Specifically, if the (external) cause of a discriminatory act is hidden from the victims' view, an internal attribution of its cause may be produced. Judgments of internal causes of behavior that actually reside in the environment (i.e., in the perpetrator's implicit discrimination) can produce psychological damage in members of groups routinely targeted for implicit stereotyping and prejudice. The combination of an absence of a conscious perpetrator of stereotyping and prejudice and the presence of such acts themselves and their consequences suggests that new dialogue is needed about methods for recognizing implicit stereotyping and treating its symptoms.

CONCLUSIONS

Historically, implicit stereotyping and prejudice have been disregarded in considerations of social behavior. With increasing attention to unconscious processes in thought and judgment, their operation can now be effectively investigated. Research on implicit stereotyping and prejudice can: (a) question the currently dominant conception that such evaluations operate primarily within consciousness, (b) provide increased understanding of the subtle yet powerful mechanisms by which stereotyped judgments are produced, and (c) instigate discussion of potential new solutions to a major social problem.

ACKNOWLEDGMENT

Preparation of this chapter was supported in part by the National Science Foundation Grant DBC 9120987. We thank Richard Ashmore, R. Bhaskar, Anne Beall,

Irene Blair, Florence Geis, Curt Hardin, John Jost, Alex Rothman, and Mark Zanna for helpful comments on a previous draft.

REFERENCES

Allport, G. W. (1954). *The nature of prejudice.* Cambridge, MA: Addison-Wesley.

Altemeyer, R. (1988). *Enemies of freedom: Understanding right-wing authoritarianism.* San Francisco: Jossey-Bass.

Aronson, E. (1988). *The social animal.* New York: Freeman.

Ashmore, R. D., & Del Boca, F. K. (1981). Conceptual approaches to stereotypes and stereotyping. In D. L. Hamilton (Ed.), *Cognitive processes in stereotyping and intergroup behavior* (pp. 1–36). Hillsdale, NJ: Lawrence Erlbaum Associates.

Banaji, M. R., & Greenwald, A. G. (1991, June). *Measuring implicit attitudes.* Paper presented at meetings of the American Psychological Society, Washington, D.C.

Banaji, M. R., & Greenwald, A. G. (1992). *Implicit stereotyping in false fame judgments.* Unpublished manuscript, Yale University, New Haven, CT.

Banaji, M. R., Hardin, C., & Rothman, A. J. (in press). Implicit stereotyping in person judgment. *Journal of Social and Personality Psychology.*

Bargh, J. (1989). Conditional automaticity: Varieties of automatic influence in social perception and cognition. In J. S. Uleman & J. A. Bargh (Eds.), *Unintended thought* (pp. 3–51). New York: Guilford.

Bargh, J. A. (in press). Being unaware of the stimulus versus unaware of how it is interpreted: Why subliminality per se does not matter to social psychology. In R. F. Borenstein and T. S. Pittman (Eds.), *Perception without awareness.* New York: Guilford.

Baxter, G. W. (1973). Prejudiced liberals? Race and information effects in a two-person game. *Journal of Conflict Resolution, 17,* 131–161.

Bellezza, F., & Bower, G. H. (1981). Person stereotypes and memory for people. *Journal of Personality and Social Psychology, 41,* 856–865.

Bem, D., & Bem, S. (1970). Case study of a nonconscious ideology: Training the woman to know her place. In D. Bem, *Beliefs, attitudes, and human affairs* (pp. 89–99). Belmont, CA: Brooks/Cole.

Bem, S. L. (1974). The measurement of psychological androgyny. *Journal of Consulting and Clinical Psychology, 42,* 155–162.

Bettelheim, B., & Janowitz, M. (1964). *Social change and prejudice.* New York: The Free Press.

Brewer, M. B. (1988). A dual process model of impression formation. In R. S. Wyer & T. K. Srull (Eds.), *Advances in social cognition* (Vol. 1, pp. 1–36). Hillsdale, NJ: Lawrence Erlbaum Associates.

Brewer, M. B., & Miller, N. (1988). Contact and cooperation: When do they work? In P. A. Katz & D. A. Taylor (Eds.), *Eliminating racism: Profiles in controversy* (pp. 315–326). New York: Plenum.

Brigham, J. C. (1971). Ethnic stereotypes. *Psychological Bulletin, 76,* 15–33.

Brody, N.(Ed.). (1987). *Personality and Social Psychology Bulletin, 13,* 291–429.

Broverman, I., Vogel, S. R., Broverman, D. M., Clarkson, F., & Rosenkrantz, P. S. (1972). Sex role stereotypes: A current appraisal. *Journal of Sex Roles, 28,* 59–78.

Brown, V., & Geis, F. (1984). Turning lead into gold: Evaluations of men and women leaders and the alchemy of social consensus. *Journal of Social and Personality Psychology, 46,* 811–824.

Campbell, D. T. (1950). The indirect assessment of social attitudes. *Psychological Bulletin, 47,* 15–38.

Clark, K. B. (1955). *Prejudice and your child.* Boston: Beacon Press.

Cohen, C. E. (1981). Person categories and social perception: Testing some boundaries of the processing effects of prior knowledge. *Journal of Personality and Social Psychology, 40,* 441–452.

Cohen, J. (1988). *Statistical power analyses for the behavioral sciences.* Hillsdale, NJ: Lawrence Erlbaum Associates.

Crosby, F., Bromley, S., & Saxe, L. (1980). Recent unobtrusive studies of Black and White discrimination and prejudice: A literature review. *Psychological Bulletin, 87,* 546–563.

Darley, J. M., & Gross, P. H. (1983). A hypothesis-confirming bias in labeling effects. *Journal of Personality and Social Psychology, 44,* 20–33.

Devine, P. G. (1989). Stereotypes and prejudice: Their automatic and controlled components. *Journal of Personality and Social Psychology, 56,* 5–18.

Dovidio, J. F., Evans, N. E., & Tyler, R. B. (1986). Racial stereotypes: The contents of their cognitive representations. *Journal of Experimental Social Psychology, 22,* 22–37.

Dovidio, J. F., & Fazio, R. H. (1992). New technologies for the direct and indirect assessment of attitudes. In J. Tanur (Ed.), *Questions about questions: Meaning, memory, expression, and social interactions in surveys.* New York: Sage.

Dovidio, J. F., & Gaertner, S. L. (Eds.). (1986). *Prejudice, discrimination, and racism.* New York: Academic Press.

Duncan, B. L. (1976). Differential social perception and attribution of intergroup violence: Testing the lower limits of stereotyping of Blacks. *Journal of Personality and Social Psychology, 34,* 590–598.

Ehrlich, J. J., & Rinehart, J. W. (1965). A brief report on the methodology of stereotype research. *Social Forces, 43,* 564–575.

Fazio, R. H., Sanbonmatsu, D. M., Powell, M. C., & Kardes, F. R. (1986). On the automatic activation of attitudes. *Journal of personality and social psychology, 59,* 229–238.

Fiske, S. T. (1989a). Examining the role of intent: Toward understanding its role in stereotyping and prejudice. In J. S. Uleman & J. A. Bargh (Eds.), *Unintended thought* (pp. 253–283). New York: Guilford.

Fiske, S. T. (1989b, August). *Interdependence and stereotyping: From the laboratory to the Supreme Court (and back).* Paper presented at the meeting of the American Psychological Association, New Orleans, LA.

Gaertner, S. L. (1976). Nonreactive measures in racial attitude research: A focus on "liberals." In P. A. Katz (Ed.), *Towards the elimination of racism* (pp. 183–211). New York: Pergamon Press.

Gaertner, S. L., & Dovidio, J. F. (1986). The aversive form of racism. In S. L. Gaertner & J. F. Dovidio (Eds.), *Prejudice, discrimination, and racism* (pp. 61–89). New York: Academic Press.

Gaertner, S. L., & McLaughlin, J. P. (1983). Racial stereotypes: Associations and ascriptions of positive and negative characteristics. *Social Psychology Quarterly, 46,* 23–30.

Galbraith, J. K. (1983). *The role of the poor: Essays in economic and political persuasion.* Cambridge, MA: Harvard University Press.

Geis, F. L. (in press). Self-fulfilling prophecies: A social psychological view of gender. In A. E. Beall & R. J. Sternberg (Eds.), *Perspectives on the psychology of gender.* New York: Guilford.

Gilbert, D. T., & Hixon, J. G. (1991). The trouble of thinking: Activation and application of stereotypic beliefs. *Journal of Personality and Social Psychology, 60,* 509–517.

Goldberg, P. (1968). Are women prejudiced against women? *Transaction, 5,* 28–30.

Graf, P., & Schacter, D. (1985). Implicit and explicit memory for new associations in normal and amnesic subjects. *Journal of Experimental Psychology: Learning, Memory, & Cognition, 11,* 501–518.

Green, D. M., & Swets, J. A. (1966). *Signal detection theory and psychophysics.* New York: Wiley.

Greenhouse, L. (1991, November 3). Morality play's twist: Is new rights bill a liberal victory over conservative court? Not exactly. *The New York Times,* p. 26.

Greenwald, A. G. (1990). What cognitive representations underlie social attitudes. *Bulletin of the Psychonomic Society, 28,* 254–260.

Greenwald, A. G. (1992). New Look 3: Unconscious cognition reclaimed. *American Psychologist, 47,* 766–779.

Hamilton, D. L. (1981). *Cognitive processes in stereotyping and intergroup behavior.* Hillsdale, NJ: Lawrence Erlbaum Associates.

Hamilton, D. L., & Gifford, R. K. (1976). Illusory correlation in interpersonal perception: A cognitive basis of stereotype judgments. *Journal of Experimental Social Psychology, 12,* 392–407.

Hamilton, D. L, & Trolier, T. K. (1986). Stereotypes and stereotyping: An overview of the cognitive approach. In S. L. Gaertner & J. F. Dovidio (Eds.), *Prejudice, discrimination, and racism* (pp. 127–157). New York: Academic Press.

Harding, J., Kutner, B., Proshansky, H. & Chein, I. (1954). Prejudice and ethnic relations. In G. Lindzey (Ed.), *Handbook of social psychology* (Vol. 2, pp. 1021–1061). Cambridge, MA: Addison-Wesley.

Higgins, E. T. (1989). Knowledge accessibility and activation. In J. S. Uleman & J. A. Bargh (Eds.), *Unintended thought* (pp. 75–123). New York: Guilford.

Higgins, E. T., Rholes, W. S., & Jones, C. R. (1977). Category accessibility and impression formation. *Journal of Experimental Social Psychology, 13,* 141–154.

Jacoby, L. L., & Kelley, C. M. (1987). Unconscious influences of memory for a prior event. *Personality and Social Psychology Bulletin, 13,* 314–336.

Jacoby, L. L., Kelley, C. M., Brown, J., & Jasechko, J. (1989). Becoming famous overnight: Limits on the ability to avoid unconscious influences of the past. *Journal of Personality and Social Psychology, 56,* 326–338.

Jacoby, L. L., Lindsay, D. S., & Toth, J. P. (1992). Unconscious processes revealed: A question of control. *American Psychologist, 47,* 802–809.

Jahoda, M., Deutsch, M., & Cook, S. W. (1951). *Research methods in social relations.* New York: Dryden.

Judd, C. M., & Park, B. (1988). Out-group homogeneity: Judgments of variability at the individual and group levels. *Journal of Personality and Social Psychology, 54,* 778–788.

Judd, C. M., & Park, B. (1993). Definition and assessment of accuracy in social stereotypes. *Psychological Review, 100,* 109–128.

Karlins, M., Coffman, T. L., & Walters, G. (1969). On the fading of social stereotypes: Studies in three generations of college students. *Journal of Social and Personality Psychology, 13,* 1–16.

Katz, D., & Braly, K. (1933). Racial stereotypes of 10 college students. *Journal of Abnormal and Social Psychology, 28,* 280–290.

Katz, D., & Braly, K. (1935). Racial prejudice and racial stereotypes. *Journal of Abnormal and Social Psychology, 30,* 175–193.

Katz, P. A., & Taylor, D. A. (1988). *Eliminating racism: Profiles in controversy.* New York: Plenum.

Kihlstrom, J. F. (1987). The cognitive unconscious. *Science, 237,* 1445–1452.

Kihlstrom, J. F. (1990). The psychological unconscious. In L. A. Pervin (Ed.), *Handbook of personality: Theory and research.* New York: Guilford.

Kinder, D. R., & Sears, D. O. (1981). Prejudice and politics: Symbolic racism versus racial threats to the good life. *Journal of Personality and Social Psychology, 40,* 414–431.

Langer, E. (1978). Rethinking the role of thought in social interaction. In J. H. Harvey, W. J. Ickes, & R. F. Kidd (Eds.), *New directions in attribution research* (Vol. 2, pp. 35–58). Hillsdale, NJ: Lawrence Erlbaum Associates.

Lewis, A. (1991). *Make no law: The Sullivan case and the first amendment.* New York: Random House.

Linville, P., Fisher, G., & Salovey, P. (1989). Perceived distributions of the characteristics of ingroup and out-group members: Empirical evidence and a computer simulation. *Journal of Personality and Social Psychology, 57,* 165–188.

Lippmann, W. (1922). *Public Opinion.* New York: Harcourt Brace Jovanovitch.

MacKinnon, C. (1989). *Toward a feminist theory of the state.* Cambridge, MA: Harvard University Press.

Marcel, A. J. (1988). Phenomenal experience and functionalism. In A. J. Marcel & E. Bisiach (Eds.), *Consciousness in contemporary science* (pp. 121–158). Oxford University Press.

McConahay, J. B. (1986). Modern racism, ambivalence, and the modern racism scale. In J. F. Dovidio & S. L. Gaertner (Eds.), *Prejudice, discrimination, and racism* (pp. 35–60). New York: Academic Press.

Merikle, P. M., & Reingold, E. M. (1991). Comparing (direct) explicit and (indirect) implicit measures to study unconscious memory. *Journal of Experimental Psychology: Learning, Memory, & Cognition, 17,* 224–233.

Miller, A. G. (1982). *In the eye of the beholder: Contemporary issues in stereotyping.* New York: Praeger.

Myers, D. (1990). *Social psychology* (3rd ed.). New York: McGraw-Hill.

Nisbett, R. E., & Wilson, T. D. (1977). Telling more than we can know: Verbal reports on mental processes. *Psychological Review, 84,* 231–259.

Perdue, C. W., & Gurtman, M. B. (1988). Evidence for the automaticity of ageism. *Journal of Experimental Social Psychology, 26,* 199–216.

Plessey v. Ferguson, 163 U. S. 537 (1896).

Pratto, F., & Bargh, J. A. (1991). Stereotyping based on apparently individuating information: Trait and global components of sex-stereotypes under attention overload. *Journal of Experimental Social Psychology, 27,* 26–47.

Richardson-Klavehn, A., & Bjork, R. A. (1988). Measures of memory. *Annual Review of Psychology, 39,* 474–543.

Roediger, H. L. (1990). Implicit memory: Retention without awareness. *American psychologist, 45,* 1043–1056.

Roediger, H. L., Weldon, M. S., & Challis, B. H. (1989). Explaining dissociations between implicit and explicit measures of retention: A processing account. In H. L. Roediger & F.I.M. Craik (Eds.), *Varieties of memory and consciousness: Essays in honour of Endel Tulving* (pp. 3–41). Hillsdale, NJ: Lawrence Erlbaum Associates.

Rosenthal, R. (1990). How are we doing in soft psychology? *American Psychologist, 45,* 775–777.

Rothbart, M., Evans, M., & Fulero, S. (1979). Recall for confirming events: Memory processes and the maintenance of social stereotypes. *Journal of Experimental Social Psychology, 15,* 343–355.

Ruble, D. N., & Ruble, T. L. (1982). Sex stereotypes. In A. G. Miller (Ed.), *In the eye of the beholder: Contemporary issues in stereotyping* (pp. 188–252). New York: Praeger.

Sagar, H. A., & Schofield, J. W. (1980). Racial and behavioral cues in Black and White children's perceptions of ambiguously aggressive acts. *Journal of Personality and Social Psychology, 39,* 590–598.

Schacter, D. (1987). Implicit memory: History and current status. *Journal of Experimental Psychology: Learning, memory, and cognition, 12,* 432–444.

Sears, D. O. (1988). Symbolic racism. In P. A. Katz & D. A. Taylor (Eds.), *Eliminating racism: Profiles in controversy* (pp. 315–326). New York: Plenum.

Sears, D. O., Peplau, L. A., Freedman, J. L., & Taylor, S. E. (1988). *Social Psychology.* Englewood Cliffs, NJ: Prentice-Hall.

Secord, P. (1959). Stereotyping and favorableness in the perception of Negro faces. *Journal of Abnormal and Social Psychology, 59,* 309–315.

Sen, A. (1985). *Commodities and capabilities.* New York: North-Holland.

Sherif, M., & Sherif, C. W. (1969). *Social psychology.* New York: Harper & Row.

Smith, E. R., & Branscombe, N. R. (1988). Category accessibility as implicit memory. *Journal of Experimental Social Psychology, 24,* 490–504.

Smith, E. R., Ferree M. M., & Miller, F. D. (1975). A short scale of attitudes toward feminism. *Representative Research in Social Psychology, 6,* 51–56.

Snyder, M. (1981). On the self-perpetuating nature of social stereotypes. In D. Hamilton (Ed.), *Cognitive processes in stereotyping and intergroup behavior* (pp. 183–212). Hillsdale, NJ: Lawrence Erlbaum Associates.

Snyder, M., Tanke, E. D., & Berscheid, E. (1977). Social perception and interpersonal behavior: On the self-fulling nature of social stereotypes. *Journal of Personality and Social Psychology, 35,* 656–666.

Snyder, M., & Uranowitz, S. W. (1978). Reconstructing the past: Some cognitive consequences of person perception. *Journal of Personality and Social Psychology, 36,* 941–950.

Spence J. T., & Helmreich, R. (1972). The attitudes toward women scale: An objective instrument to measure attitudes toward the rights and roles of women in contemporary society. *JSAS Catalog of Selected Documents in Psychology, 2,* 66.

Spence, J. T., Helmreich, R., & Stapp, J. (1974). The personal attributes questionnaire: A measure of sex-stereotypes and masculinity–femininity. *JSAS Catalog of Selected Documents in Psychology, 4,* 43.

Srull, T. K., & Wyer, R. S. (1979). The role of category accessibility in the interpretation of information about persons: Some determinants and implications. *Journal of Personality and Social Psychology, 37,* 1660–1672.

Swim, J., Borgida, E., Maruyama, G., & Myers, D. G. (1989). Joan T. McKay versus John T. McKay: Do gender stereotypes bias evaluations? *Psychological Bulletin, 105,* 409–429.

Taylor, S. E. (1981). A categorization approach to stereotyping. In D. Hamilton (Ed.), *Cognitive processes in stereotyping and intergroup behavior* (pp. 83–114). Hillsdale, NJ: Lawrence Erlbaum Associates.

Thompson, L. (1992). *A history of South Africa.* New Haven, CT: Yale University Press.

Uleman, J. S., & Bargh, J. A. (Eds.). (1989). *Unintended thought.* New York: Guilford.

Webb, E. J., Campbell, D. T., Schwartz, R. D., & Sechrest, L. (1966). *Unobtrusive measures: Nonreactive research in the social sciences.* Chicago: Rand McNally.

Wilson, T. D., Dunn, D. S., Kraft, D., & Lisle, D. J. (1989). Introspection, attitude change, attitude-behavior consistency: The disruptive effects of explaining why we feel the way we do. *Advances in Experimental Social Psychology, 22,* 287–343.

Word, C. O., Zanna, M. P., & Cooper, J. (1974). The nonverbal mediation of self-fulfilling prophecies in interracial interaction. *Journal of Experimental Social Psychology, 10,* 109–120.

4

The Role of Mood in the Expression of Intergroup Stereotypes

Victoria M. Esses
University of Western Ontario

Geoffrey Haddock
Mark P. Zanna
University of Waterloo

We usually think of the stereotypes we hold as quite stable over time. In contrast, the stereotypes we express at different points in time may vary. Situational constraints, such as contextual cues regarding appropriateness, play a role in this regard (Dovidio & Gaertner, 1986). However, in addition to monitoring what we say, the stereotypes that come to mind for possible expression at various times may differ. That is, only a subset of our available pool of stereotypes may be accessible at any particular time. One factor that may influence which stereotypes come to mind, and thus the likelihood of their expression, is the mood in which we find ourselves. In particular, when we're in a bad mood, we may find that negative stereotypes are especially likely to come to mind and be expressed.

The focus of this chapter is on how mood influences the expression of intergroup stereotypes. We present a model that places the role of mood in the context of an information-processing system. We also describe a series of studies that examine the effect of mood on the expression of ethnic stereotypes. Our interest in this topic was piqued by a set of on-the-street interviews reported in the local newspaper of a small Ontario community (Boucher, 1987). The question to which residents responded was, "Do you agree with the federal government's new policy restricting the entry of refugees into Canada?" Some typical responses were as follows:

- Yes, I've been unemployed for 6 months now. Canada should be a lot stricter in everything. Crime is a real factor in this, too.
- Yes, they keep trying to put that juvenile delinquent shelter in our neighborhood. Refugees? We don't need them.

- Yes, these people aren't welcome in their own countries so they shouldn't be welcome in ours. Most of them are radicals so they shouldn't be allowed to take up residence in Canada. Our taxes keep going up, too. (p. 3)

These responses brought to our attention the juxtaposition of unpleasant experiences (such as being unemployed, the battle over putting a group home in a residential area, and tax increases) and the reporting of negative perceptions of members of other groups. What was particularly noteworthy was that the negative perceptions seemed to be quite unrelated to the unpleasant experiences described. That is, the respondents did not seem to be describing refugees in negative terms because of unpleasant experiences involving refugees. Rather, they seemed to be describing refugees in negative terms because of events that generally made them feel bad. This led us to wonder whether there is a causal relation between how one feels and what one has to say about members of other groups.

THE SCAPEGOAT THEORY OF PREJUDICE

Of course, we are not the first to wonder about the possible association between feeling bad and expressing negative attitudes toward members of other groups. In the 1940s, the scapegoat theory of prejudice was developed to account for an observed relation between frustrating experiences and prejudice. The theory was derived from the more general theory of frustration and aggression popular at the time (Dollard, Doob, Miller, Mowrer, & Sears, 1939). It stated that when hostility was aroused through frustration but could not be directed toward its source (because the source was absent, unidentifiable, or too powerful), the hostility would be displaced onto a noninstigating target (Zawadzki, 1948). The most common target, or scapegoat, would be a minority group that could not retaliate. Prejudice was seen as the fulfillment of the hostile drive and negative stereotypes as its rationalization. Empirical evidence to support this theory was difficult to obtain because it was based on the concept of the accumulation of a hostile drive that required an outlet for its pent-up energy. The existence of such a drive was difficult to substantiate, as was the notion of its build-up and discharge.

More recently, Berkowitz (1989, 1990) proposed a reformulation of the general frustration–aggression theory, which specifies negative affect as the mediator between aversive occurrences of any kind and aggression. This cognitive neo-associationistic model states that negative affect aroused by unpleasant events activates anger-related feelings, thoughts, and memories as well as aggressive action tendencies. At least part of this model is based on current work examining the role of mood in information processing (Bower, 1981; Clark & Isen, 1982; Isen, 1984). Similarly, our model of the effect of mood on the expression of stereotypes is built on an information-processing foundation.

A MOOD AND INFORMATION-PROCESSING MODEL
OF THE EXPRESSION OF NEGATIVE STEREOTYPES

Although the scapegoat theory of prejudice has proven difficult to validate, the phenomenon it sought to explain still remains. That is, it seems that one's feeling state influences one's expression of intergroup attitudes. In light of recent work on the role of mood in information processing and social judgments, we have developed an information-processing model to explain why being in a negative mood state, whether caused by frustration or any other unpleasant occurrence, increases the likelihood of expressing negative stereotypes of other groups. We first briefly describe the literature on the effect of mood on information processing and social judgments. Then, we apply the processes described to the expression of negative stereotypes.

When people use the term *mood,* they are usually referring to a generalized feeling state that is not directed toward any particular target (Clark & Isen, 1982; Isen, 1984; Schwarz & Clore, 1988). Mood tends to be thought of as a pervasive, low-level affective state. This relatively undifferentiated nature of mood is reflected in everyday language. People often talk about being in a bad mood or in a good mood, but they are seldom more specific. Similarly, researchers studying the effects of mood often classify mood along the dimension of negative to positive. This is in contrast to specific emotions, such as admiration and fear, that usually have clear targets and possess specific labels. The pervasive nature of mood makes it capable of influencing many different types of thoughts and behaviors.

Research examining the effect of mood on cognitive processes indicates that mood can influence both the encoding of new information and the retrieval of information from memory (for reviews, see Blaney, 1986; Singer & Salovey, 1988). In particular, people are more likely to learn new information when its affective tone matches their current mood state. They are also more likely to remember information previously stored in memory when their current mood state and the valence of the information are affectively congruent. In order to explain these mood-congruency effects,[1] it has been suggested that mood serves as an organizing unit for the storage of information in memory and as a cue for the retrieval of information from memory (Bower, 1981; Clark & Isen, 1982; Isen, 1984).

Mood-congruent memory may, in turn, influence social judgments. In the context of evaluations of real or hypothetical individuals, it has been found that people who are in a positive mood tend to express relatively favorable evalua-

---

[1]Mood-congruency differs from mood state-dependency in that the latter refers to the facilitation of recall of any information when mood at learning and at recall are the same. In contrast to mood-congruent memory effects, mood state-dependent memory effects have been difficult to replicate (Bower & Mayer, 1985, 1989).

tions of others and that people who are in a negative mood tend to express relatively unfavorable evaluations of others (for a review, see Forgas & Bower, 1988). Mood-congruent acceptance of interpersonal feedback has also been documented (Esses, 1989). That is, people who are in a positive mood are most likely to accept positive feedback, and people who are in a negative mood are most likely to accept negative feedback. These effects have been most commonly explained in terms of memory processes, that is, mood's effect on the accessibility of relevant information in memory, either specifically relevant information or relevant interpretive categories (Clark & Isen, 1982; Forgas & Bower, 1988; Isen, 1984). Indeed, the mediation of mood-congruent memory in social judgments has received some empirical support in the context of specific trait ratings in a person-perception paradigm (Forgas & Bower, 1987). However, alternative mechanisms have been proposed.

Mayer (1986) suggested that mood may exert its influence on social judgments through shifts in category boundary lines for the assignment of an evaluation. For example, those who are in a positive mood may perceive more concepts as positive. It is possible that the accessibility of relevant interpretive categories is related to this type of shift. In contrast, Schwarz and his colleagues (Schwarz, 1990; Schwarz & Clore, 1988) proposed a mood-as-information model that suggests that people consult their current feelings as a source of information when making a social judgment. Because it may be difficult to separate reactions to a target (if any) from background mood, one's feelings may be mistakenly attributed to the target and the judgment colored accordingly. We suggest that this type of mechanism is most likely to come into play when a general affective reaction (e.g., life happiness and satisfaction; Schwarz & Clore, 1983) is being elicited.

In the context of our model, mood's influence on information processing may affect the expression of stereotypes in a number of ways. Mood may influence the accessibility of specific stereotypes and supporting information in memory, it may influence attention to and encoding of new information about social groups, and it may influence how recalled and new information is interpreted. These potential influences form the basis of our model of the effect of negative mood on the expression of negative stereotypes (see Fig. 4.1).

First, when people are in a negative mood, they have enhanced access to previously held negative stereotypes and to supporting information in memory. In addition, the combination of negative mood and easily accessed negative stereotypes ensures that they pay attention to and encode new negative information about social groups. In turn, memory for negative stereotypes and supporting information is further enhanced. Finally, when people are in a negative mood, the increased accessibility of negative interpretive categories unfavorably colors the meaning attached to both the new and recalled information. As a result of these processes, there is an increased likelihood that negative stereotypes are expressed.

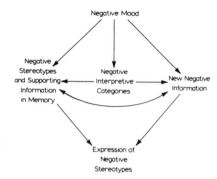

FIG. 4.1. How negative mood may increase the expression of negative stereotypes.

It is important to note that this model does not attempt to provide a comprehensive explanation of the origin and expression of negative stereotypes. There are certainly many motivational and social forces that are instrumental in the development and utilization of negative stereotypes (for reviews, see Brewer & Kramer, 1985; Stroebe & Insko, 1989). Parallel to these forces, our model suggests that negative mood increases the likelihood of expressing negative stereotypes through its influence on cognitive processes. This builds on previous cognitive models in that it specifies a central role for affective state.

It is also necessary to mention that, whereas previous studies have at times obtained weak effects of negative mood (Blaney, 1986; Forgas & Bower, 1988), in our research on the expression of stereotypes, we did not expect to encounter the controlled processes that seem to account for this finding. In contrast to the relatively automatic processes that we have applied in our model, two controlled processes have been proposed to explain inconsistent effects of negative mood. First, people who are in a salient mood state, whether positive or negative, may purposely focus on positive information in order to sustain or achieve a positive mood (mood maintenance and mood repair; Clark & Isen, 1982; Isen, 1984). Thus, although people who are in a negative mood may have easy access to negative information in memory, when mood is salient, they may purposely focus on positive information in an attempt to alleviate their aversive negative mood state. In addition, when making social judgments, there are norms about the inappropriateness of expressing negative evaluations of others that may at times prevent people who are in a negative mood from expressing their currently negative views (Berkowitz & Troccoli, 1990; Forgas & Bower, 1988).

In the case of the expression of stereotypes, neither of these controlled processes is likely to suppress the automatic effects of negative mood. First, if people try to purposely focus on positive information in order to achieve a positive mood state, this is likely to be restricted to positive characteristics of their own group. It is unlikely that people focus on the positive characteristics of members of other groups in order to make themselves feel better. In addition, there seem to be fewer norms inhibiting the expression of negative perceptions of out-groups than there are for evaluating specific individuals negatively. Therefore, we expected that negative mood effects on information processing would be evident in the expression of negative stereotypes.

THE RESEARCH PROGRAM

Research conducted to date has been aimed at determining whether experimentally induced mood states influence the expression of intergroup stereotypes. In particular, when people are placed in a negative mood, are negative stereotypes especially likely to come to mind and be expressed? The first three studies to be described address this issue. The final two studies examine more closely exactly what is being influenced by mood. But first, how do we go about measuring stereotypes?

The Measurement of Stereotypes

Although researchers generally agree that stereotypes are beliefs about the characteristics of members of a social group, several issues have been raised about the nature of these characteristics. Of central importance is the distinction between *consensual* stereotypes and *individual* stereotypes (Ashmore & Del Boca, 1981). Consensual stereotypes are shared beliefs about the characteristics of members of a social group, that is, ascribed characteristics for which there is considerable agreement. In contrast, individual stereotypes are those characteristics that an individual attributes to members of a social group, whether consensual or idiosyncratic. Perhaps due to the seminal work of Katz and Braly (1933), which looked at the degree of agreement of Princeton students in assigning traits to various racial groups, stereotypes have most commonly been assessed at the consensual level. For this purpose, measurement strategies have usually been based on the presentation to subjects of lists of characteristics or bipolar adjective scales. Researchers have primarily varied the type of responses that they have asked subjects to make on these measures and their technique for transforming responses into numerical values (for a review, see Gardner, this volume).

In examining the effect of mood on the expression of intergroup stereotypes, we wished to determine what type of characteristics come to mind in reference to social groups when people are in different mood states. In addressing this issue, we had several reasons for choosing not to utilize traditional measures of consensual stereotypes. First, we had no reason to limit ourselves to assessing consensual beliefs. In addition, the traditional checklist or rating scale techniques were likely to prime particular attributes or dimensions rather than to elicit spontaneous attributions. They were also bound to overlook many of the idiosyncratic stereotypes held by individuals. Therefore, we found it necessary to develop a new, open-ended procedure for assessing individual stereotypes (Esses & Zanna, 1989).

In developing an open-ended measure of individual stereotypes, we allowed definitional issues to determine our measurement strategy. First, although stereotypes have typically been operationalized as personality traits, there is no conceptual basis for this focus (Ashmore & Del Boca, 1981). Thus, in developing our measure, we attempted to elicit all characteristics that an individual attributes to members of a social group, irrespective of their nature. The type of characteristics that are most likely to be generated is an empirical issue. Second, although stereotypes are often considered to be part of the cognitive component of intergroup attitudes, they, like most other beliefs, have valences associated with them. That is, stereotypes usually involve an evaluative dimension ranging from negative to positive. To complicate matters further, the same stereotype can differ in valence depending on the individual making the attribution and the target group to which it is directed (e.g., Peabody, 1968; Saenger & Flowerman, 1954). For example, the characteristic *rich* can be considered positive, neutral, or negative depending on one's perspective and the group that is being described in this way. Therefore, in developing our individual stereotypes measure, we tried to take into account the meaning that an individual invests in characteristics when using them to describe particular groups. Finally, the notion of generalization has often been built into the definition of stereotypes, either implicitly or explicitly (Brigham, 1971a). Thus, our individual stereotypes measure determines perceived prevalence of each characteristic.

In our research program, subjects are asked to provide descriptions of various groups as follows. First, they are asked to list characteristics, using single adjectives or short phrases, that they would use to describe typical members of each group. They are told to provide as many characteristics as necessary to convey their impression of each group and to describe each group adequately. Then, they are asked to look at the characteristics that they have listed for each group and to assign a valence to each characteristic as they have used it to describe members of that particular group ($--$, $-$, 0, $+$, $++$; adapted from Karlins, Coffman, & Walters, 1969). Finally, they are asked to look once again at the characteristics that they provided for each group and to indicate the percentage of the group to which each characteristic applies (0% to 100%; adapted from Brigham, 1971b).[2] Anonymity and the need for honest responses are emphasized throughout.

In order to transform subjects' responses into numerical values, the valences and percentages they themselves provide are utilized. Valences (V) are transformed into numbers ranging from -2 ($--$) to $+2$ ($++$), and percentages (P) are divided by 100 so that they range from 0 to 1. A stereotype score is then

---

[2]Eagly and Mladinic (1989) have developed independently a similar measure to assess gender stereotypes.

computed for each subject for each group as $\Sigma_{i=1}^{n}(P_{ig} \times V_{ig})/n$, where n equals the number of characteristics attributed to the group.[3] As expected, these individual stereotype scores predict individuals' intergroup attitudes to a greater extent than do traditional measures of consensual stereotypes (Esses, Haddock, & Zanna, 1993).

Mood and the Expression of Ethnic Stereotypes: The Basic Effect

Once we had a measure in place to assess what stereotypes come to mind in response to different social groups, we conducted our first study to determine the effect of mood on the expression of these stereotypes (Esses & Zanna, 1989). Thirty male and 30 female university students were recruited to participate in two short studies, one on social expressiveness and one on social perception. In fact, one study was being performed. The "social expressiveness study" was used as our mood induction. A positive, neutral (baseline), or negative mood state was induced using a combination of the Velten mood induction procedure (Velten, 1968) and a recall of events procedure (Izard, 1972). Subjects were asked to read aloud 60 Velten mood induction statements that became increasingly positive, contained no emotional content, or became increasingly negative. They were instructed to make their voice sound as convincing as possible. Then, they were asked to describe an event in their life that had made them feel extremely happy, neither happy nor sad, or extremely sad. The "social perception study" constituted our individual stereotypes measure. Subjects were asked for their perceptions of six ethnic groups: Jewish, Pakistani, Chinese, English Canadian, Native Indian, and Arabic people. These groups were selected on the basis of a pilot study that indicated that our subject population understood these group labels, believed these groups to be distinct, and could provide descriptions of these groups. When subjects on occasion expressed concern about stereotyping, they were instructed to put down whatever came to mind when they thought about each of the groups. No further concerns were expressed.

Before we discuss the effect of mood on the complete stereotype scores, it is worth mentioning some of our preliminary findings. First, the average number of characteristics attributed to the groups ranged from approximately five characteristics used to describe Arabic people to approximately eight characteristics used to describe Chinese people. Of interest is that the number of characteristics

---

[3]There may be some issue as to whether an averaging or additive formula is most appropriate in this context. We chose to use an averaging formula because it corresponds best to the conceptual variable of interest, namely, the typical or average characteristic used to describe a group. In addition, in a related context, research on information integration in impression formation favors averaging models over additive models (Anderson, 1981). In an empirical sense the choice of one formula or the other makes little difference for our purposes because averaged scores and additive scores (where we don't divide by n) are very highly correlated ($>.80$ in all studies to date).

listed was not affected by mood state. Thus, negative mood did not seem to be disrupting subjects' ability to generate characteristics of the groups (cf. Ellis & Ashbrook, 1988), nor did positive mood seem to be connected to a more extensive array of information about the groups (cf. Clark & Isen, 1982). Second, although it was left to subjects to provide whatever type of characteristics came to mind, personality traits were most likely to be listed (approximately 76% of the characteristics), with physical characteristics (9%) and other characteristics, such as behaviors and circumstances (e.g., own corner stores, poor; 15%), playing secondary roles. Finally, subjects were indeed quite willing to generalize about members of the groups, attributing characteristics on average to 74% of group members. They were slightly less likely to generalize about members of the group to which most of them belonged, attributing characteristics on average to 69% of English Canadian people. The type of characteristics listed and the overall tendency to generalize were not affected by mood state.

On the basis of our mood and information-processing model, we predicted that when subjects were in a negative mood, negative stereotypes would be especially likely to come to mind. We expected this effect to be evident in our individual stereotypes measure for two reasons. First, there seem to be fewer norms inhibiting the expression of negative perceptions of groups (especially out-groups) than there are for evaluating specific individuals negatively. In addition, we tried to take advantage of this tendency by urging subjects to convey their true impressions of the groups. However, in asking subjects to provide characteristics of six different target groups, we did not expect negative mood to affect perceptions of all groups indiscriminately. Instead, we expected the effect to occur for groups for which negative information was most available to be accessed or to be interpreted in a particularly unfavorable light. We thought that we might be able to identify these groups by looking at the stereotypes provided when subjects were not in a negative mood state.

As is evident in Table 4.1, two target groups stood out as recipients of relatively unfavorable stereotypes by subjects in the positive and neutral mood conditions: Pakistani and Native Indian people.[4] These were the groups for which negative mood had an effect. In particular, when subjects were placed in a negative mood state, the expression of negative stereotypes toward these groups was accentuated.[5] Thus, we obtained initial support for our predictions. In addition, when subjects were placed in a positive or negative mood state, they provided especially favorable stereotypes of the group to which most subjects

---

[4]The type of characteristics attributed to these two groups by subjects who were not in a negative mood supports our contention that there are few norms inhibiting the expression of negative perceptions of certain groups. For example, Pakistani people were described as *dirty* and *stupid*, and Native Indian people were described as *lazy* and *alcoholics*.

[5]Subjects occasionally provided descriptions that seemed to reflect more on how a group is treated by others than on characteristics of the group (e.g., *mistreated, given many opportunities*). When these descriptions were eliminated from the stereotype scores, the effects were not appreciably altered.

TABLE 4.1
Mean Expression of Ethnic Stereotypes as a Function of Mood Condition and
Target Ethnic Group: Study 1

	Mood Condition		
Target Ethnic Group	Positive	Neutral	Negative
Jewish	0.27	0.28	0.18
Pakistani[#]	-0.04b	0.04b	-0.30a
Chinese	0.58	0.54	0.48
English Canadian[#]	0.51b	0.14a	0.46b
Native Indian[#]	-0.05b	0.02b	-0.40a
Arabic	0.08	0.14	0.13
Average	0.23	0.19	0.09

From Esses and Zanna (1989).
Note. $N = 60$. The numbers represent mean individual stereotype scores as determined by the formula $\Sigma_{i=1}^{n}$ $(P_{ig} \times V_{ig})/n$, where V = valence of characteristics, P = percentage of group to which characteristics are attributed divided by 100, and n = number of characteristics utilized (possible range = -2 to +2). The # indicates target groups for which post hoc comparisons revealed significant mood effects. For each of these target groups, means not sharing a common subscript differ from each other at the $p < .05$ level using Tukey's HSD test.

belonged, namely, English Canadian people. In line with the mood-maintenance and mood-repair processes described earlier, we explain this finding by suggesting that when mood was salient, subjects actively strove to feel good by describing their own group in favorable terms. All the effects were equally strong for males and females.

Two further issues were addressed in this study. First, having determined that mood affected perceptions of Pakistani, Native Indian, and English Canadian people, were the effects mediated primarily by mood's influence on the valence of characteristics attributed to the groups or by mood's influence on the percentage of the groups to which characteristics of different valences were attributed? In other words, which component or components of the stereotype scores were affected by mood? As we mentioned previously, the overall tendency to generalize was not affected by mood state. However, it was still possible that subjects in different mood states assigned percentages to the characteristics differentially, depending on the valence of each characteristic. In order to address this issue, we analyzed each component of the stereotype scores separately. We found that subjects' mood state did affect the valence of characteristics attributed to the groups but had no effect on the percentage of group members believed to possess characteristics of different valences.[6] In particular, mood's influence on the ste-

---

[6]This point is relevant to critiques of the use of multiplicative composites, which, in contrast to simple measures, can sometimes lead to differing findings depending on the scales used for each composite (Evans, 1991). This is not a problem in analyzing our data because findings do not change when we replace the composite measure with a simple measure of average valence, $\Sigma_{i=1}^{n} V_{ig}/n$.

reotype scores was predominantly mediated by the differential attribution of characteristics of a double negative valence—characteristics considered to be very unfavorable. Subjects who were in a negative mood used a higher proportion of these very unfavorable characteristics in describing Pakistani and Native Indian people, and subjects who were in a positive and negative mood used a lower proportion of these very unfavorable characteristics in describing English Canadian people.

The second issue we addressed was whether the effects would have occurred if we had examined only consensual stereotypes. In order to find out, we solicited the consensual stereotypes of the target groups from an independent pool of subjects and then went back and looked at the individual stereotypes generated by our original group of subjects.[7] We found that the consensual stereotypes made up a rather small proportion of the individual stereotypes provided. In addition, and perhaps as a consequence, there were no significant effects of mood on stereotype scores computed on the basis of consensual stereotypes alone. Thus, in order to detect mood effects on the expression of stereotypes, the stereotypes measure must be broad enough to include the idiosyncratic beliefs held by individuals.

Testing Alternative Explanations and Generalizability

Although the findings of the initial study were quite clear cut, the mood induction procedure that we utilized left us with some uncertainty about the interpretation of our findings. There has been a great deal of controversy in the mood induction literature concerning potential demand characteristics of the procedures used to induce mood and the self-referent nature of many of these procedures (Berkowitz & Troccoli, 1986; Kenealy, 1986; Riskind, 1989; Teasdale, 1983). It has been suggested that effects obtained are sometimes the result of subjects' awareness that the experimenter is interested in effects of mood or are the result of the priming of specific cognitions about the self, rather than of mood per se. In our study, demand effects seemed unlikely because the procedure was set up so that subjects were unaware that their mood was purposely being manipulated. However, the positive and negative Velten mood induction statements that subjects read were explicitly self-referent, and the life events that subjects recalled certainly had the potential to implicate self-evaluations. This use of self-referent cognitions to manipulate mood suggested an alternative explanation for our findings: downward comparison following a threat to self-esteem.

The theory of downward comparison states that a threat to self-esteem moti-

---

[7]Consensual stereotypes were elicited by asking the independent group of subjects to list characteristics that people often attribute to members of the groups. In other words, they were asked to provide the current stereotypes of each group. Those characteristics of a target group that were listed by at least 25% of the sample were considered to be consensual stereotypes.

vates people to enhance subjective well-being through comparison with less fortunate others (Wills, 1981). One possible manifestation of this motivation is the active derogation of out-groups, often low status groups who are seen as "safe" targets, along with enhancement of the in-group. Self-enhancement is achieved by maximizing the psychological distance between the self and targeted others. This is a viable explanation for our findings because, as suggested in the mood induction literature, our mood manipulation might have primed specific cognitions about the self. In particular, the negative mood manipulation, which involved the reading of negative self-referent statements and the recall of an unpleasant life event, might have been perceived as a threat to self-esteem. In addition, our findings can be seen as conforming to the predictions of downward comparison theory. Subjects who were in a negative mood provided especially favorable stereotypes of the group to which most of them belonged—English Canadian people—and provided especially unfavorable stereotypes of two out-groups—Pakistani and Native Indian people. Psychological distance between the self and less fortunate others might thus have been achieved. This type of downward comparison explanation received some support from studies that found that individuals whose self-concept had been threatened displayed enhancement of their own group (Crocker, Thompson, McGraw, & Ingerman, 1987). However, in those studies, the general negativity evident in subjects with low self-esteem did not fit with the predictions of downward comparison theory. Instead, it was most easily explainable in terms of the effect of negative mood (Crocker et al., 1987).

We conducted a second study to determine the generalizability of our findings with respect to the method of manipulating mood and the ethnicity of subjects (Esses & Zanna, 1993). At the same time, this study shed some light on the viability of downward comparison as an alternative explanation of the findings. Downward comparison theory specifies the crucial role of threat to self-esteem as a mediator of motivated derogation of out-groups. In the second study, we utilized a mood manipulation that almost definitely involved no threat to self-esteem: a musical mood induction procedure (Clark, 1983; Pignatiello, Camp, & Rasar, 1986).

The second study was similar to the initial study, with a few crucial modifications. The musical mood induction procedure was described to subjects as a pilot study examining the effect of music on imagery. In order to induce a positive, neutral (baseline), or negative mood state, subjects were asked to listen to four appropriate excerpts of music that lasted approximately 10 minutes and to record any imagery that came to mind. The music was classical and contained no lyrics. Subjects were also asked to rate the music and their imagery on a number of dimensions. In addition to this change in the mood induction procedure, we utilized three separate groups of subjects who differed in terms of their own ethnic identity: (a) English Canadian subjects, (b) Chinese subjects, and (c) other identity subjects who did not belong to any of the target ethnic groups (e.g., Italian, Greek, Portuguese). The Other identity subjects were of particular interest because they would not be making explicit comparisons to their own ethnic group when completing the stereotypes measure. The target ethnic groups and stereotypes measure remained the same as in the initial study.

Subjects frequently did report imagery in response to the music and, irrespective of ethnic identity, the themes that they described were remarkably consistent. In response to the negative mood music, they frequently reported images of death and tragedy; in response to the neutral mood music, they frequently reported images of concert performances and motion; in response to the positive mood music, they frequently reported images of children playing, cartoons, and ballroom dances. It is interesting to note that most of the images that subjects described did not involve themselves. That is, subjects seldom placed themselves in the situations described. This supports our contention that the mood induction procedure did not prime specific cognitions about the self and, more specifically, that the negative mood induction was not a threat to self-esteem.

Analyses of the stereotype scores were conducted separately for each of the three ethnic identity groups of subjects. However, as is evident in Tables 4.2 through 4.4, irrespective of ethnic identity, the pattern of findings is quite similar. Mood consistently had an effect on perceptions of Pakistani and Native Indian people, as in the initial study, and also influenced perceptions of Arabic people.[8] In particular, when subjects were placed in a negative mood state, they were especially likely to express unfavorable stereotypes of these target groups. These were the target groups for which stereotypes in the positive and neutral mood conditions were generally least favorable. For Chinese subjects, the negative mood effect also applied to the English Canadian target group. The effect demonstrated in the initial study for subjects' own ethnic group did not replicate for either the English Canadian subjects or the Chinese subjects.[9]

---

[8]Perceptions of Arabic people were not affected by negative mood in the initial study but were affected in the second study. This can most likely be attributed to an increase in availability of negative information about members of this group due to events occurring in the Middle East and the media coverage of these events (e.g., Ayatollah Khomeini's death threat to Salman Rushdie—Smith, 1989; Iraq's use of poison gas on Kurds—Wallace, 1988).

[9]Although this chapter focuses on the expression of negative stereotypes, there may be some question as to why the positive mood induction did not accentuate the expression of positive stereotypes. That is, overall, there were no differences between the stereotypes expressed by subjects in the positive mood condition and those expressed by subjects in the neutral mood condition. The explanation for this finding may have to do with what we mean when we use the term *neutral mood*. As in most other mood induction research (see Blaney, 1986), in the neutral mood condition we attempted to maintain subjects in the mood in which they came into the laboratory, rather than inducing a truly neutral state. In our manipulation checks, subjects in this condition did not rate themselves at the midpoint of a mood scale ranging from negative to positive. Instead, they generally provided mood ratings on the positive side of the scale (though not as positive as the ratings of subjects in the positive mood condition). Thus, the expression of stereotypes may not have differed between the neutral and positive mood conditions because, in both cases, subjects were in a relatively positive mood state. They merely differed in degree of positivity. This fits with previous evidence that, in general, people usually feel slightly positive (Clark & Isen, 1982).

TABLE 4.2
Mean Expression of Ethnic Stereotypes as a Function of Mood Condition and
Target Ethnic Group: English Canadian Subjects, Study 2

Target Ethnic Group	Mood Condition		
	Positive	Neutral	Negative
Jewish	0.29	0.25	0.38
Pakistani[#]	0.26_b	-0.07_{ab}	-0.42_a
Chinese	0.38	0.32	0.36
English Canadian	0.31	0.23	0.47
Native Indian[#]	-0.02_b	-0.11_b	-0.67_a
Arabic[#]	0.20_b	-0.03_{ab}	-0.18_a
Average	0.24	0.10	-0.01

From Esses and Zanna (1993).
Note. $N = 45$. The [#] indicated target groups for which post hoc comparisons revealed significant mood effects. For each of these target groups, means not sharing a common subscript differ from each other at the $p < .05$ level using Tukey's HSD test.

There are some anomalies in the findings, such as the fact that Chinese subjects did not describe their own group favorably, irrespective of mood. Perhaps this can be attributed to cultural norms of modesty. In addition, the effect of mood on perceptions of the English Canadian target group did not fit predictions for either the Chinese or Other identity subjects. For Chinese subjects, there was an effect of negative mood despite the use of quite favorable stereotypes in the positive and neutral mood conditions. For Other identity subjects, there was not

TABLE 4.3
Mean Expression of Ethnic Stereotypes as a Function of Mood Condition and
Target Ethnic Group: Chinese Subjects, Study 2

Target Ethnic Group	Mood Condition		
	Positive	Neutral	Negative
Jewish	0.34	0.26	0.30
Pakistani[#]	0.17_b	0.10_{ab}	-0.24_a
Chinese	0.14	0.16	-0.03
English Canadian[#]	0.46_b	0.35_{ab}	-0.05_a
Native Indian[#]	0.11_b	-0.14_{ab}	-0.40_a
Arabic[#]	0.14_{ab}	0.21_b	-0.21_a
Average	0.23	0.16	-0.09

From Esses and Zanna (1993).
Note. $N = 33$. The [#] indicates target groups for which post hoc comparisons revealed significant mood effects. For each of these target groups, means not sharing a common subscript differ from each other at the $p < .05$ level using Tukey's HSD test.

TABLE 4.4
Mean Expression of Ethnic Stereotypes as a Function of Mood Condition and
Target Ethnic Group: Other Identity Subjects, Study 2

	Mood Condition		
Target Ethnic Group	Positive	Neutral	Negative
Jewish	0.44	0.41	0.45
Pakistani[#]	0.24$_b$	0.15$_b$	-0.28$_a$
Chinese	0.47	0.54	0.34
English Canadian	0.16	0.08	0.11
Native Indian[#]	-0.08$_b$	-0.09$_b$	-0.52$_a$
Arabic[#]	0.21$_b$	0.21$_b$	-0.21$_a$
Average	0.24	0.22	-0.02

From Esses and Zanna (1993).
Note. N = 45. The [#] indicates target groups for which post hoc comparisons revealed significant mood effects. For each of these target groups, means not sharing a common subscript differ from each other at the $p < .05$ level using Tukey's HSD test.

an effect of negative mood, although the stereotypes provided in the positive and neutral mood conditions were not very favorable. Perhaps these findings are related to the status of English Canadians as the majority group in Canada.

As in the initial study, we also examined the separate components of the stereotype scores in order to determine what was being affected by mood. Once again, we found that subjects' mood state influenced only the valence of characteristics attributed to the groups. Irrespective of ethnic identity, mood predominantly had an effect on the proportion of very unfavorable characteristics utilized (characteristics assigned a double negative valence). In particular, subjects who were in a negative mood used a higher proportion of very unfavorable characteristics in describing Pakistani, Native Indian, and Arabic people, and, for Chinese subjects, English Canadian people.

The results of this second study demonstrate that the effect of negative mood on the accentuation of negative stereotypes is not limited to self-referent methods of mood induction or to English Canadian subjects. This increases the generalizability of our findings. In addition, this study provides some evidence to discredit a pure downward comparison explanation of the effects obtained. First, the negative musical mood induction procedure was unlikely to have been perceived as a threat to self-esteem as required by downward comparison theory. Second, the effect of negative mood was evident for Other identity subjects, despite the fact that they were not making an explicit comparison to their own group. Finally, English Canadian and Chinese subjects in the negative mood condition showed no evidence of own group enhancement, which would maximize the psychological distance between the self and less fortunate others. The fact that this own group enhancement occurred in the initial study suggests that downward comparison may play a role when the determinant of negative mood state is of a self-referent nature.

Our proposal that the findings are mediated predominantly by the effect of mood on information processing is supported by an additional study (Schiff, Esses, & Lamon, 1992) that utilized a more unusual method of mood induction—the unilateral contraction of facial muscles (Schiff & Lamon, 1989). In this procedure, subjects are asked to contract the muscles of one side of their face by pulling back and raising that corner of their mouth four times for a duration of 45 seconds each time. The study in which we used this procedure was similar to those described previously, except that a positive or negative mood state was induced through right or left facial contractions. In contrast to most, if not all, other methods of mood induction, these facial contractions give rise to mood states without cognitive mediation. In fact, the contractions produce effects that mimic those of other mood induction procedures without requiring subjects' conscious awareness that they are experiencing the mood state intended (Schiff & Lamon, 1993). It has been suggested that the contractions operate through the direct activation of contralateral cerebral hemispheres. As a result, contractions of the right side of the face produce effects similar to those of a positive mood state and contractions of the left side of the face produce effects similar to those of a negative mood state.

How did these contractions influence the expression of ethnic stereotypes? Although subjects were not aware of being in a negative or positive mood state, those who performed the left-sided contractions (negative mood inducer) expressed more negative stereotypes than did those who performed the right-sided contractions (positive mood inducer). Once again, the effect was specific to three target groups: Pakistani, Native Indian, and Arabic people. This replication without subjects' conscious awareness of mood state argues against mediation through controlled, motivated processes, such as downward comparison for purposes of self-enhancement. Instead, it is likely that the effects obtained are mediated by mood's influence on cognitive processes.

Mood and Change in Meaning

The advantage of our individual stereotypes measure is that it elicits spontaneous attributions about groups, that is, the characteristics that come to mind when individuals are asked to describe members of groups. However, because subjects in the studies described so far provided their own lists of characteristics and then immediately assigned valences and percentages to these characteristics, it was unclear exactly what was being influenced by mood. We knew that in terms of the stereotype scores, it was the valences that were affected and not the percentages. However, we did not know whether subjects who were in different mood states used different types of characteristics to describe the affected target groups or whether the meaning of the characteristics (as indicated by valence) changed as a function of mood. In other words, mood may have influenced the actual characteristics that were attributed to certain groups. Then, because subjects listed these characteristics, they assigned valences accordingly. Alternatively, mood may have influenced the meaning attached to similar characteristics. When subjects assigned valences to the characteristics, their interpretation of the characteristics may have differed depending on mood.

In order to get at this, we might try to have naive judges look at the characteristics listed in the previous studies and rate them for favorability. Then, we could examine average favorability ratings of characteristics listed in the different mood conditions. However, this would be defeating the purpose of our individual stereotypes measure, which takes into account the meaning individuals invest in characteristics when using them to describe members of particular groups. Rather, it seemed to us that the best judges we could use to interpret the characteristics would be the subjects themselves. In two further studies we did just that (Esses & Zanna, 1993). We used subjects as their own raters by separating in time their listing of characteristics of groups and their interpretation of these characteristics.

The first study included two separate conditions: (a) a standard condition, and (b) a delayed condition. The procedure followed in the standard condition was the same as that of the previous studies using a musical mood induction procedure. Subjects underwent a positive or negative musical mood induction procedure and then completed the usual individual stereotypes measure—they listed characteristics of each group and assigned valences and percentages to the characteristics immediately. The procedure followed in the delayed condition was similar to that of the standard condition with one important difference. Subjects in this condition came back to the laboratory 2 days later to assign valences and percentages to the characteristics. In other words, in the first session, they underwent a positive or negative musical mood induction procedure and listed characteristics of each group. In the second session 2 days later, they were presented with the list of characteristics that they had personally attributed to each group earlier and were asked to assign valences and percentages to the characteristics as used to describe members of that group.

As is evident in Table 4.5, it makes a difference whether subjects assign valences and percentages to the characteristics while still in different mood states. In the standard condition, once again we found that mood influenced perceptions of Pakistani, Native Indian, and Arabic people, plus one additional group, Chinese people. In contrast, in the delayed condition, there were no significant effects of mood. That is, the characteristics listed immediately following the positive and negative mood inductions were later not rated as differing in valence.

On the basis of these results, we were tempted to conclude that mood must be influencing the meaning attached to characteristics, rather than influencing the

TABLE 4.5
Mean Expression of Ethnic Stereotypes as a Function of When Valences and Percentages Are Assigned to Characteristics

| | STANDARD | | DELAYED | |
| | Mood Condition | | Mood Condition | |
Target Ethnic Group	Positive	Negative	Positive	Negative
Jewish	0.52	0.13	0.23	0.11
Pakistani	* 0.16	-0.30	-0.07	-0.35
Chinese	* 0.83	0.12	0.23	0.13
English Canadian	0.22	-0.09	-0.01	0.00
Native Indian	* 0.19	-0.53	0.01	-0.38
Arabic	* 0.29	-0.37	-0.07	0.18
Average	0.37	-0.17	0.05	-0.05

Note. From Esses and Zanna (1993). $N = 52$. The * indicates where post hoc comparisons revealed significant mood effects at the $p < .05$ level using Tukey's HSD test.

sort of characteristics used to describe target groups. In the delayed condition, subjects were acting as their own "objective" raters of characteristics generated previously while in an induced positive or negative mood state. The stereotype scores computed on the basis of the valences and percentages they later assigned to these characteristics provided no clear evidence that there were actual differences between the type of characteristics being attributed to the groups in different mood states. In the absence of such evidence, it would seem to be the immediate interpretation of the characteristics that varied depending on mood.

Further examination of cell means prevented us from being completely confident of this interpretation of the findings. When one looks at the cell means in the delayed condition, it is apparent that, although not significant, a similar pattern to that of the standard condition is obtained for the Pakistani and Native Indian target groups. In fact, statistical comparisons between the standard and delayed conditions revealed significant differences for only the Chinese target group in the positive mood condition and the Arabic target group in the negative mood condition. Thus, at least for the Pakistani and Native Indian target groups, it was conceivable that mood influenced both the meaning attached to characteristics and the actual type of characteristics utilized. It was possible that only when these two effects could occur concurrently, that is, in the standard condition, would significant effects be obtained.

In order to address this issue, we performed one more study. We knew now that mood's effect on the type of characteristics utilized was not strong enough by itself to account for our earlier findings. Therefore, in this final study, we determined whether mood's effect on the meaning attached to characteristics would be powerful enough to produce significant results. In other words, would our initial findings replicate when mood could only influence the meaning attached to characteristics and not the type of characteristics utilized? The procedure followed in this study was similar to that of the delayed condition in the previous study, with one important difference. The mood induction occurred at the beginning of the second session immediately before subjects assigned valences and percentages to the characteristics, rather than in the first session before they listed characteristics of the groups. In other words, in the first session, all subjects were treated alike; they were all asked to list characteristics of each group. In the second session 2 days later, subjects first underwent a positive, neutral, or negative musical mood induction procedure. Then, they were presented with the list of characteristics that they had personally attributed to each group earlier and were asked to assign valences and percentages to the characteristics as used to describe members of that group.

Unexpectedly, and for the first time, we encountered a slight problem in this study with our musical mood induction procedure. Our mood manipulation check indicated that, although in the appropriate direction, subjects in the positive and neutral mood conditions did not differ significantly in their self-reports of mood following the induction procedure. Fortunately, we were primarily interested in possible differences between these two conditions and the negative mood condition. Therefore, we collapsed across the positive and neutral mood conditions for our analysis of stereotype scores.

As shown in Table 4.6, once again there are differences between mood conditions in perceptions of Pakistani, Native Indian, and Arabic people. In particular, subjects who were in a negative mood were more negative in their perceptions of these groups. Because subjects were randomly assigned to mood induction con-

TABLE 4.6
Mean Expression of Ethnic Stereotypes When Mood Induction Procedure Occurs Immediately
Prior to Assignment of Valances and Percentages to Characteristics

	Mood Condition	
Target Ethnic Group	Positive/Neutral	Negative
Jewish	0.12	0.36
Pakistani[#]	-0.04	-0.36
Chinese	0.41	0.43
English Canadian	0.07	0.12
Native Indian[#]	0.11	-0.25
Arabic[#]	0.21	-0.24
Average	0.15	0.01

From Esses and Zanna (1993).
Note. $N = 45$. The [#] indicates target groups for which post hoc comparisons revealed significant mood effects at the $p < .05$ level using Tukey's HSD test.

ditions after they had listed characteristics of the groups and immediately prior to assigning valences and percentages to these characteristics, these results demonstrate that mood does influence the meaning attached to characteristics used to describe the affected target groups.

Another way of looking at these data is to examine the valences assigned to characteristics listed in common by subjects in different mood conditions. Although we have not observed a lot of consensus among our subjects in the characteristics they attribute to the groups, our colleagues have been urging us to attempt this type of analysis. In the previous studies, we hesitated to do so because mood might be having a quite subtle effect on the exact wording of characteristics that we would mistakenly categorize together. In this final study, because the mood induction procedure occurred after the listing of characteristics of the groups, the characteristics themselves could not be influenced by mood state. Therefore, in this study, we examined the average valence assigned to characteristics listed in common by at least three subjects in each of the two conditions for the three affected target groups. As shown in Table 4.7, although there are indeed not a lot of consensus among subjects, the valences they assigned to the characteristics listed most frequently showed a consistent effect of mood. That is, with only one exception (Arabic: dark skinned), being in a negative mood caused subjects to interpret characteristics they attributed to Pakistani, Native Indian, and Arabic people in an especially unfavorable light. Thus, on the basis of the full analysis of stereotype scores and this more descrip-

TABLE 4.7
Average Valence Assigned to Most Frequently Occurring Characteristics as a Function of Mood Condition and Target Ethnic Group

Target Ethnic Group and Characteristic	Mood Condition	
	Positive/Neutral	Negative
Pakistani		
Dark skinned	0.00 (8)	-0.50 (4)
Hard working	2.00 (4)	0.75 (4)
Poor	-0.83 (6)	-2.00 (3)
Religious	0.29 (7)	0.00 (6)
Native Indian		
Alcoholic	-1.50 (6)	-1.80 (5)
Dark skinned	0.00 (5)	-0.25 (4)
Lazy	-1.33 (3)	-1.75 (4)
Proud	1.50 (4)	1.00 (4)
Arabic		
Aggressive	-1.17 (6)	-2.00 (4)
Dark skinned	0.00 (7)	0.00 (5)
Religious	0.88 (14)	-0.50 (4)

From Esses and Zanna (1993).
Note. Numbers in parentheses indicate the number of subjects who listed that characteristic.

tive examination of specific characteristics, we can conclude that mood influences the interpretation of characteristics typically attributed to certain groups.

These findings fit in well with some previous research showing that the meaning of characteristics attributed to groups is indeed open to interpretation. First, groups providing reciprocal stereotypes may agree on the characteristics of their own and the other group but differ in their evaluation of these characteristics (Campbell, 1967; Peabody, 1968). As a result, they may use different terms to refer to the same general class of behavior (e.g., we are *thrifty* vs. they are *stingy;* we are *generous* vs. they are *extravagant*). But it is not necessary to use different words to indicate one's interpretation of a characteristic. Rather, the same word can be infused with different meanings. For example, in the early 1950s, Saenger and Flowerman (1954) found that there was almost complete overlap in the stereotypes that university students ascribed to Americans (own group) and Jews. However, these stereotypes assumed a different meaning, or tone, depending on the context. The students evaluated traits such as *aggressive, materialistic,* and *mercenary* more unfavorably in the context of describing Jews than in the context of describing themselves. Similarly, Smedley and Bayton (1978) found that characteristics such as *rebellious, aggressive,* and *demanding* are evaluated more or less favorably depending on one's own group and the group to which the characteristic is attributed. Our current findings suggest that this change in meaning can also be mediated by changes in one's mood state.

CONCLUSIONS

Our program of research demonstrates that negative mood does accentuate the expression of negative stereotypes. That is, in five separate studies we found that when individuals are in a negative mood, they are especially likely to describe certain ethnic groups using characteristics that they perceive to be very unfavorable. This applies irrespective of the method of mood induction and, within the bounds examined, irrespective of the population of subjects. That is, it was demonstrated for both males and females, for English Canadian and Chinese subjects, and for a mixed group of subjects who were not asked to make an explicit comparison to their own group. In terms of why this effect occurs, our use of mood induction procedures that are not self-referent and of an induction procedure that operates without subjects' conscious awareness of mood state suggests that controlled, motivated processes are not operating. Instead, we suggest that the findings are mediated by the effect of mood on cognitive processes.

How do our findings fit into the mood and information-processing model we presented earlier? Our fourth study suggests that mood does not have a large impact, if any, on the accessibility of specific characteristics. In contrast, our final study demonstrates that mood definitely affects the meaning attached to these characteristics, as indicated by the valences used to interpret them. That is, when people are in a negative mood, they are likely to interpret their stereotypes of certain groups in a particularly unfavorable light. Two complementary processes may be operating in order to produce this effect. First, when individuals are in a negative mood, stereotypes may take on a different meaning because of the abundance of negative supporting information that comes to mind. Second, the increased accessibility of negative interpretive categories ensures that this supporting information is interpreted in a particularly negative way. In addition, irrespective of any supporting information that comes to mind, the increased accessibility of negative interpretive categories may directly influence the connotation of stereotypes utilized.

This interpretation of our findings fits well with the fact that only certain target groups are affected—those that are perceived least favorably when individuals are not in a negative mood. These are the groups for which negative information is most available should interpretation or elaboration of stereotypes of these groups be required. For example, when someone who is in a negative mood says that members of one of these groups are *aggressive,* the person might conjure up images of fist fights and being accosted on the street, rather than images of the group standing up for its rights. In addition, the preponderance of initially neutral and negative stereotypes of these groups is most susceptible to increased negativity of interpretation. That is, it would be credible to interpret these stereotypes in a particularly unfavorable way. Thus, it would be more plausible to interpret the rather ambiguous characteristic *aggressive* as very unfavorable than it would be to interpret a more obviously favorable characteristic, such as *intelligent,* in this light.

We now return to our initial description of the negative perceptions of refugees reported in the local newspaper of a small Ontario community. As the reader will recall, our interest in the possible relation between mood and the expression of stereotypes was stimulated by our observation that the expression of these negative perceptions was accompanied by descriptions of unpleasant, yet unrelated, events. In light of the research that we have conducted since that time, we suggest that being in a bad mood primarily influenced what people meant when they used terms such as *radical* to describe refugees, rather than having much effect on whether they used these terms at all. In turn, the meaning they attached to these stereotypes may have determined these people's response to the question of whether refugees should be allowed into Canada. Indeed, we recently obtained preliminary evidence to suggest that individuals who are in a negative mood not only express more negative stereotypes but also express more unfavorable overall evaluations of the groups in question (Haddock, Zanna, & Esses, 1992). Thus, being in a bad mood may not only have a negative impact on people's perceptions of certain groups, but may, in turn, influence their general attitudes toward and policies regarding these groups. We suspect that we will find that mood also influences other significant components of intergroup attitudes, such as symbolic beliefs (beliefs that social groups promote or hinder cherished values and norms) and feelings (specific emotional responses to social groups) (Esses et al., 1993). These are issues for future research to address. For the present, we do know that people who are in a negative mood are especially likely to place a negative interpretation onto the characteristics they typically attribute to various groups.

ACKNOWLEDGMENTS

Preparation of this chapter was facilitated by a Canada Research Fellowship from the Social Sciences and Humanities Research Council of Canada to Victoria M. Esses. The research on which this chapter is based was supported, in part, by a research grant from the Social Sciences and Humanities Research Council of Canada to Victoria M. Esses and Mark P. Zanna.

We would like to thank Robert Gardner and James Olson for their helpful comments on an earlier draft of this chapter. We would also like to thank Michael Ross for suggesting the design of the final study reported.

REFERENCES

Anderson, N. H. (1981). *Foundations of information integration theory.* New York: Academic Press.

Ashmore, R. D., & Del Boca, F. K. (1981). Conceptual approaches to stereotypes and stereotyping. In D. L. Hamilton (Ed.), *Cognitive processes in stereotyping and intergroup behavior* (pp. 1–35). Hillsdale, NJ: Lawrence Erlbaum Associates.

Berkowitz, L. (1989). Frustration–aggression hypothesis: Examination and reformulation. *Psychological Bulletin, 106,* 59–73.

Berkowitz, L. (1990). On the formation and regulation of anger and aggression: A cognitive neo-associationistic analysis. *American Psychologist, 45,* 494–503.

Berkowitz, L., & Troccoli, B. T. (1986). An examination of the assumptions in the demand characteristics thesis: With special reference to the Velten mood induction procedure. *Motivation and Emotion, 10,* 337–349.

Berkowitz, L., & Troccoli B. T. (1990). Feelings, direction of attention, and expressed evaluations of others. *Cognition and Emotion, 4,* 305–325.

Blaney, P. H. (1986). Affect and memory: A review. *Psychological Bulletin, 99,* 229–246.

Boucher, D. (1987, March 18). Street wise. *The Milton Observer,* p. 3.

Bower, G. H. (1981). Mood and memory. *American Psychologist, 36,* 129–148.

Bower, G. H., & Mayer, J. D. (1985). Failure to replicate mood-dependent retrieval. *Bulletin of the Psychonomic Society, 23,* 39–42.

Bower, G. H., & Mayer, J. D. (1989). In search of mood-dependent retrieval. *Journal of Social Behavior and Personality, 4,* 121–156.

Brewer, M. B., & Kramer, R. M. (1985). The psychology of intergroup attitudes and behavior. *Annual Review of Psychology, 36,* 219–243.

Brigham J. C. (1971a). Ethnic stereotypes. *Psychological Bulletin, 76,* 15–38.

Brigham, J. C. (1971b). Racial stereotypes, attitudes, and evaluations of and behavioral intentions toward Negroes and Whites. *Sociometry, 34,* 360–380.

Campbell, D. T. (1967). Stereotypes and the perception of group differences. *American Psychologist, 22,* 817–829.

Clark, D. M. (1983). On the induction of depressed mood in the laboratory: Evaluation and comparison of the Velten and musical procedures. *Advances in Behaviour Research and Therapy, 5,* 27–49.

Clark, M. S., & Isen, A. M. (1982). Toward understanding the relationship between feeling states and social behavior. In A. Hastorf & A. M. Isen (Eds.), *Cognitive social psychology* (pp. 73–108). New York: Elsevier.

Crocker, J., Thompson, L. L., McGraw, K. M., & Ingerman, C. (1987). Downward comparison, prejudice, and evaluations of others: Effects of self-esteem and threat. *Journal of Personality and Social Psychology, 52,* 907–916.

Dollard, J., Doob, L., Miller, N., Mowrer, O., & Sears, R. (1939). *Frustration and aggression.* New Haven: Yale University Press.

Dovidio, J. F., & Gaertner, S. L. (1986). Prejudice, discrimination, and racism: Historical trends and contemporary approaches. In J. F. Dovidio & S. L. Gaertner (Eds.), *Prejudice, discrimination, and racism* (pp. 1–34). Orlando, FL: Academic Press.

Eagly, A. H., & Mladinic, A. (1989). Gender stereotypes and attitudes toward women and men. *Personality and Social Psychology Bulletin, 15,* 543–558.

Ellis, H. C., & Ashbrook, P. W. (1988). Resource allocation model of the effects of depressed mood states on memory. In K. Fiedler & J. Forgas (Eds.), *Affect, cognition and social behavior* (pp. 25–43). Toronto: Hogrefe.

Esses, V. M. (1989). Mood as a moderator of acceptance of interpersonal feedback. *Journal of Personality and Social Psychology, 57,* 769–781.

Esses, V. M., Haddock, G., & Zanna, M. P. (1993). Values, stereotypes, and emotions as determinants of intergroup attitudes. In D. M. Mackie & D. L. Hamilton (Eds.), *Affect, cognition, and stereotyping: Interactive processes in group perception.* (pp. 137–166). New York: Academic Press.

Esses, V. M., & Zanna, M. P. (1989, August). *Mood and the expression of ethnic stereotypes.* Paper presented at the annual meeting of the American Psychological Association, New Orleans, LA.

Esses V. M., & Zanna, M. P. (1993). *Mood and the expression of ethnic stereotypes.* Manuscript submitted for publication.

Evans, M. G. (1991). The problem of analyzing multiplicative composites: Interactions revisited. *American Psychologist, 46,* 6–15.

Forgas, J. P., & Bower, G. H. (1987). Mood effects on person-perception judgments. *Journal of Personality and Social Psychology, 53,* 53–60.

Forgas, J. P., & Bower, G. H. (1988). Affect in social and personal judgments. In K. Fiedler & J. Forgas (Eds.), *Affect, cognition and social behavior* (pp. 183–208). Toronto: Hogrefe.

Gardner, R. C. (1993). Stereotypes as consensual beliefs. In M. P. Zanna & J. M. Olson (Eds.), *The psychology of prejudice: The Ontario symposium* (Vol. 7, pp. 1–31). Hillsdale, NJ: Lawrence Erlbaum Associates.

Haddock, G., Zanna, M. P., & Esses, V. M. (1992, August). *Affect intensity, intergroup attitudes, and the "feelings-as-information" hypothesis.* Paper to be presented at the annual meeting of the American Psychological Association, Washington, DC.

Isen, A. M. (1984). Toward understanding the role of affect in cognition. In R. S. Wyer & T. K. Srull (Eds.), *Handbook of social cognition* (Vol. 3, pp. 179–236). Hillsdale, NJ: Lawrence Erlbaum Associates.

Izard, C. E. (1972). *Patterns of emotions: A new analysis of anxiety and depression.* New York: Academic Press.

Karlins, M., Coffman, T. L., & Walters, G. (1969). On the fading of social stereotypes: Studies in three generations of college students. *Journal of Personality and Social Psychology, 13,* 1–16.

Katz, D., & Braly, K. (1933). Racial stereotypes of one hundred college students. *Journal of Abnormal and Social Psychology, 28,* 280–290.

Kenealy, P. M. (1986). The Velten mood induction procedure: A review. *Motivation and Emotion, 10,* 315–325.

Mayer, J. D. (1986). How mood influences cognition. In N. E. Sharkey (Ed.), *Advances in cognitive sciences I.* (pp. 290–314). Chichester: Ellis Horwood.

Peabody, D. (1968). Group judgments in the Philippines: Evaluative and descriptive aspects. *Journal of Personality and Social Psychology, 10,* 290–300.

Pignatiello, M. F., Camp, C. J., & Rasar, L. (1986). Musical mood induction: An alternative to the Velten technique. *Journal of Abnormal Psychology, 95,* 295–297.

Riskind, J. H. (1989). The mediating mechanisms in mood and memory: A cognitive-priming formulation. In D. Kuiken (Ed.), Mood and memory: Theory, research, and applications [Special issue]. *Journal of Social Behavior and Personality, 4*(2), 173–184.

Saenger, G., & Flowerman, S. (1954). Stereotypes and prejudicial attitudes. *Human Relations, 7,* 217–238.

Schiff, B. B., Esses, V. M., & Lamon, M. (1992). Unilateral facial contractions produce mood effects on social cognitive judgements. *Cognition and Emotion, 6,* 357–368.

Schiff, B. B., & Lamon, M. (1989). Inducing emotion by unilateral contraction of facial muscles: A new look at hemispheric specialization and the experience of emotion. *Neuropsychologia, 27,* 923–935.

Schiff, B. B., & Lamon, M. (1993). *Inducing emotions without cognitive mediation.* Manuscript submitted for publication.

Schwarz, N. (1990). Feelings as information: Informational and motivational functions of affective states. In E. T. Higgins & R. M. Sorrentino (Eds.), *Handbook of motivation and cognition: Foundations of social behavior* (Vol. 2, pp. 527–561). New York: Guilford.

Schwarz, N., & Clore, G. L. (1983). Mood, misattribution, and judgments of well-being: Informative and directive functions of affective states. *Journal of Personality and Social Psychology, 45,* 513–523.

Schwarz, N., & Clore, G. L. (1988). How do I feel about it? The informative function of affective states. In K. Fiedler & J. Forgas (Eds.), *Affect, cognition and social behavior* (pp. 44–62). Toronto: Hogrefe.

Singer, J. A., & Salovey, P. (1988). Mood and memory: Evaluating the network theory of affect. *Clinical Psychology Review, 8,* 211–251.

Smedley, J. W., & Bayton, J. A. (1978). Evaluative race–class stereotypes by race and perceived class of subjects. *Journal of Personality and Social Psychology, 36,* 530–535.

Smith, W. E. (1989, February 27). Hunted by an angry faith. *Time,* pp. 14–20.

Stroebe, W., & Insko, C. A. (1989). Stereotype, prejudice, and discrimination: Changing conceptions in theory and research. In D. Bar-Tal, C. F. Graumann, A. W. Kruglanski, & W. Stroebe (Eds.), *Stereotyping and prejudice: Changing conceptions* (pp. 3–34). New York: Springer-Verlag.

Teasdale, J. D. (1983). Affect and accessibility. *Philosophical Transactions of the Royal Society of London 302,* 403–412.

Velten, E. (1968). A laboratory task for induction of mood states. *Behaviour Research and Therapy, 6,* 473–482.

Wallace, C. (1988, September 2). Iraq using gas on Kurds, rebels say. *Toronto Star,* p. A20.

Wills, T. A. (1981). Downward comparison principles in social psychology. *Psychological Bulletin, 90,* 245–271.

Zawadzki, B. (1948). Limitations on the scapegoat theory of prejudice. *Journal of Abnormal and Social Psychology, 43,* 127–141.

Expectancy-Confirmation Processes in Stereotype-Tinged Social Encounters: The Moderating Role of Social Goals

5

Steven L. Neuberg
Arizona State University

Theorists and laypersons alike have argued that one can eliminate inaccurate stereotypes by having the holders of such beliefs meet and interact with individual members of the stereotyped group. If people merely experience firsthand what members of such groups are truly like, the reasoning goes, inaccurate stereotypes will prove themselves to be of little use and will gradually disappear. This notion—the *contact hypothesis*—has been with social scientists for a while now and admittedly possesses much intuitive appeal (Allport, 1954; Cook, 1978).

Unfortunately, empirical evidence does not strongly support the contact notion, at least not in its simple form. Indeed, real-world interventions often reveal that contact can paradoxically serve to maintain, and even intensify, stereotypes and prejudices (for a review, see Miller & Brewer, 1984).

Why is this? Why is contact so often ineffective at reducing stereotypes and prejudices? To answer this question, one must focus on two fundamental aspects of the stereotype-change process. First, to change a stereotype or a prejudice, a person must obtain information about the group that is accepted as being incongruous with the stereotype or prejudice. Second, the person must use this information to modify his or her beliefs and feelings toward the group in general. Stated in terms most relevant to the situation of interpersonal contact between a potential stereotyper and the potential stereotypee, we can thus pose two broad questions: (a) What are the processes inherent to stereotype-tinged social encounters that determine whether or not individual members of a stereotyped group are viewed as being confirming or disconfirming of their group stereotypes? And (b) What are the processes that determine whether or not the impressions formed of these individuals subsequently influence the perceiver's group-level stereotypes and prejudices?

This chapter focuses on the former question—the nature of stereotype-tinged social interactions—for two reasons. First, as stated previously, to alter people's stereotypes and prejudices, disconfirming information must be available to those people. Although people may passively acquire disconfirming evidence from many sources (e.g., media, peer groups, family), acquiring such evidence via direct experience—that is, via contact with individual members of stereotyped groups—may be particularly influential (Fazio & Zanna, 1981). Thus, like many others before me, I believe that an understanding of the dynamics of interpersonal contact situations, specifically with respect to the conditions encouraging the formation of stereotype-inconsistent impressions, is critical if one desires to reduce the existence of inaccurate stereotypes.[1]

Second, beyond an interest in stereotype- and prejudice-change, such contact situations are clearly interesting and significant in their own right. Each day, the outcomes of social encounters determine friendship choices, educational opportunities, job hirings, housing decisions, the ability of people to get along peacefully with each other, and so forth. When stereotypes and prejudices color such encounters, leading people to form mistaken impressions of others, the personal consequences of these encounters can be momentous for all parties involved.

An understanding of the behavioral and cognitive dynamics of stereotype-tinged interactions is thus important for both theoretical and practical reasons. In this chapter, I describe a framework I developed to help understand the nature of such interactions. My approach takes as its foundation previous theoretical and empirical investigations of expectancy-confirmation processes, investigations that make salient the cognitive and behavioral biases that can result from possessing inaccurate stereotypes and unjustified prejudices. The present framework builds upon this earlier work, articulating the conditions under which stereotypes and prejudices may, or may not, have such influences. Specifically, I propose that a careful analysis of social motives is necessary for a thorough understanding of the stereotype-confirmation process.

The present perspective is thus similar to several recent conceptualizations that address, to varying degrees, the importance of understanding the motivational context in which expectancy-tinged interactions occur (Deaux & Major, 1987; Fiske & Neuberg, 1990; Hilton & Darley, 1991; Jones, 1986; Miller & Turnbull, 1986; Snyder, 1992; Swann, 1984). The present approach differs from each of these others, however, in at least several of the following respects:

1. The present conceptualization focuses on both behavioral and cognitive mechanisms underlying expectancy confirmation.

---

[1]Note that I am not arguing that encounters with individuals who disconfirm the stereotypes and prejudices held of their groups are sufficient for stereotype and prejudice change. This is clearly not the case (see Rothbart & John, 1985). Rather, I am merely suggesting that such encounters may be a necessary starting point; without stereotype-disconfirming interactions, stereotype and prejudice reduction may be extremely difficult, if not impossible.

2. The framework makes predictions about the potential moderating roles of a relatively large variety of social motives, relating to both impression-formation and self-presentational concerns.

3. It focuses on the roles played both by the holders of interpersonal expectancies and by the targets of these expectancies.

4. It posits the importance of resource availability as a crucial limit on the ability of social goals to successfully moderate the expectancy-confirmation process.

5. The present analysis occurs at the level of the specific behaviors and thought processes demonstrated to mediate the expectancy-confirmation process.

I begin by arguing for the legitimacy of conceptualizing stereotypes and prejudices as expectancies. I then present a brief overview of what is known of the expectancy-confirmation process, focusing on the behavioral and cognitive mechanisms that enable the formation of expectancy-consistent impressions. Based on this mediational analysis, I propose that the social goals of the interactants should play an important role in determining whether or not expectancy confirmation actually occurs. In support of this analysis, I review research addressing the key aspects of the emerging framework. Finally, I discuss conceptual and practical implications of the proposed model, focusing on its ramifications for intergroup contact.[2]

THE EXPECTANCY-CONFIRMATION APPROACH

Stereotypes and Prejudices as Interpersonal Expectancies

What are stereotypes and prejudices? For my purposes here, simple definitions suffice: Stereotypes are beliefs about the characteristics of members of a group, and prejudice is the feeling one has toward members of a group. Although stereotypes and prejudices potentially serve many functions (see Snyder & Miene, chapter 2, this volume), they importantly serve the function of being *interpersonal expectancies*. An interpersonal expectancy, loosely defined, is a belief that an individual will be in a particular state, possess a certain trait or ability, or act in certain manner at some point in the future. Thus, stereotypes are expectancies in that they suggest what an individual member of a group might be like, with respect to that individual's traits, physical characteristics, abilities, behaviors, and so forth. Prejudices are expectancies as well, in that they suggest what one is

---

[2]A more comprehensive presentation of this framework can be seen in Neuberg (1992); here, given space concerns, I broadly sketch the model's basic premises and the data relevant to them.

likely to feel toward such an individual. In this sense, stereotypes and prejudices are functionally similar to other kinds of expectancies, such as those suggested by third parties ("Be careful of Joe . . . he's a back stabber!") or by previous direct experience with that particular individual ("The last time I worked with Frank he was really unmotivated.").

Note that from the expectancy perspective, one need not conceptualize stereotypes or prejudices as being negative, consensual, or, in terms of group-level prediction, even inaccurate. Although many stereotypes and prejudices are indeed negative, people clearly possess positive stereotypes about many groups and hold many groups in high esteem; because positive and negative expectancies both have the potential to influence one's interactions with others and the way one forms impressions of them, the framework presented here does not distinguish between them. Likewise, although many stereotypes and prejudices are shared by significant portions of any population, it is important to recognize that expectancies have the potential to constrain social interaction and impression formation both when they are consensually agreed upon and when they merely reflect an individual perceiver's idiosyncrasies; thus, the consensuality of stereotypes and prejudices is largely irrelevant to the processes I discuss here. Finally, given that any set of group-based expectancies is likely to be somewhat inaccurate when applied to any individual group member (as one rarely encounters the group prototype), and given that this chapter focuses on the processes underlying individual-to-individual social interactions, issues of whether or not a particular set of stereotypes represent a group well in the aggregate are also largely immaterial.

Expectancy Influences on the Outcomes
of Social Interaction

People's impressions of others can be strongly influenced by their preinteraction expectancies, such that they may often form expectancy-consistent impressions even when their initial expectancies are inaccurate (for reviews, see Darley & Fazio, 1980; Fiske & Taylor, 1991; Hamilton, Sherman, & Ruvulo, 1990; Higgins & Bargh, 1987; Jussim, 1986; Miller & Turnbull, 1986; Snyder, 1984). When they expect to dislike others, they find that they often do. When they hold strong stereotypes of certain groups, they often cannot help but take note of the many individuals who are indeed as they expected them to be. What is it about the nature of social interactions that enables the confirmation of one's expectancies?

One potential source of expectancy influence originates in the ways that people cognitively process information about others. For example, when people are merely presented with information about others and play no role in the gathering of such information, they often form impressions that are consistent with their expectancies, especially when the target information is somewhat ambiguous (for reviews, see Fiske & Neuberg, 1990; Fiske & Taylor, 1991; Hamilton et al., 1990; Higgins & Bargh, 1987; Nisbett & Ross, 1980). Numerous studies indicate that identical behavior is often perceived differently, depending on the target's group membership; these biases in impressions are often in the direction of confirming the perceiver's stereotype-based expectancies (Darley & Gross, 1983; Langer & Abelson, 1974; Taylor, Fiske, Etcoff, & Ruderman, 1978; for reviews, see Brigham, 1971; Farina, 1982; Ruble & Ruble, 1982; Tavris & Offir, 1977).[3] For example, behaviors performed by White children may be viewed as appropriately assertive, whereas the identical behaviors performed by Black children may be viewed as overly aggressive (Duncan, 1976; Sagar & Schofield, 1980). Several studies go so far as to indicate that under some circumstances, targets are viewed in an expectancy-consistent manner even when their behavior is objectively inconsistent with the perceivers' expectancies (Farina & Ring, 1965; Ickes, Patterson, Rajecki, & Tanford, 1982; Major, Cozzarelli, Testa, & McFarlin, 1988; Swann & Snyder, 1980). It is clear, then, that expectancy-consistent impressions may result from biases in the ways that perceivers cognitively assess target behavior.

A second source of expectancy bias derives from the behavioral dynamics of the interaction itself. Under some circumstances, perceivers act in ways that lead targets to behave in an objectively expectancy-consistent manner, even if such behavior is typically uncharacteristic of them. For example, in one classic study (Snyder, Tanke, & Berscheid, 1977), men believing (erroneously) that their female conversation partners were physically attractive—thus invoking stereotypes that such partners were also interpersonally skilled, friendly, and so on—created interactions in which their partners actually behaved in a more sociable manner, thus confirming the male perceivers' stereotypes. Such examples of the *self-fulfilling prophecy* (Merton, 1948), sometimes termed *behavioral confirmation* (Snyder & Swann, 1978a), have been demonstrated with many different stereotypes and in many different domains (for reviews, see Brophy, 1983; Darley & Fazio, 1980; Jussim, 1986; Miller & Turnbull, 1986; Rosenthal, 1974; Snyder, 1984).

Perceivers may thus form expectancy-consistent impressions for several reasons. They may cognitively assess targets' behavior as being expectancy-consistent when it is indeed not, and/or they may create self-fulfilling prophecies, in which they behaviorally constrain targets to act in an expectancy-consistent manner.

The existence of preinteraction expectancies, however, does not imply the formation of expectancy-consistent impressions. Indeed, much data indicate that

---

[3]Researchers studying expectancy confirmation typically refer to the holders of expectancies as *perceivers* and to the targets of these expectancies as, not surprisingly, *targets*. I adopt this convention as well, acknowledging, however, that each participant is typically both a perceiver and a target in most dyadic social interactions.

perceivers do not always cognitively process information in an expectancy-biased way, nor do they always elicit self-fulfilling prophecies (Andersen & Bem, 1981; Babad, Inbar, & Rosenthal, 1982; Darley, Fleming, Hilton, & Swann, 1988; Hilton & Darley, 1985; Neuberg, 1989; Neuberg & Fiske, 1987; Swann & Ely, 1984; for reviews, see Brophy, 1983; Fiske & Neuberg, 1990; Higgins & Bargh, 1987; Hilton & Darley, 1991; Jussim, 1986, 1991; Miller & Turnbull, 1986; Neuberg, 1992; Snyder, 1992). In fact, some reviewers suggest that expectancy biases are rare and are typically of only small magnitude (Brophy, 1983; Brophy & Good, 1974; Cooper, 1979; Jussim, 1991; West & Anderson, 1976; but see Rosenthal & Rubin, 1978). It is thus important to ask the following: Under what circumstances do people form expectancy-consistent impressions of others? To answer this question, I must first explicate in greater detail the mechanisms underlying expectancy confirmation when it does indeed occur. I do this now.

Mechanisms Mediating the Formation of Expectancy-Consistent Impressions

How does expectancy confirmation come about? That is, what behavioral and cognitive processes mediate the formation of expectancy-consistent impressions?

First, recent findings indicate that expectancy-based cognitive biases are often mediated by biased perceiver attentional and interpretational processes (Erber & Fiske, 1984; Fiske, Neuberg, Beattie, & Milberg, 1987; Kruglanski & Freund, 1983; Neuberg & Fiske, 1987; Omoto & Borgida, 1988). More specifically, when perceivers attend in only a limited fashion to targets' own individuating features and interpret these features, when ambiguous, as being expectancy-congruent, they form expectancy-consistent impressions. In contrast, when perceivers increase their attention to targets' individuating features and interpret these features in a manner unbiased by their expectancies, they form less biased impressions (see Fiske & Neuberg, 1990). Thus, expectancy-based impression biases may be mediated by biases in perceiver attentional and interpretational processes.

Moreover, with respect to the creation of self-fulfilling prophecies, it is clear that expectancy-biased perceiver information-gathering behaviors can play an important role. For example, several studies demonstrate that people with expectancies may ask questions of targets that either are leading—in that they encourage the targets to provide expectancy-consistent information—or that make it difficult for targets to provide expectancy-disconfirming information (see Snyder, Campbell, & Preston, 1982; Snyder & Gangestad, 1981; Snyder & Swann, 1978b; Swann & Ely, 1984). Other studies indicate that perceivers ask less favorable questions of targets about whom they possess negative expectancies (Neuberg, 1989), as well as ask such targets fewer questions (Harris & Rosenthal, 1985) and conduct shorter interactions with them (Word, Zanna, & Cooper, 1974). In turn, such perceiver behaviors can lead targets to present themselves in an expectancy-consistent, albeit personally unrepresentative, manner. Thus, expectancy-biased, perceiver information-gathering behaviors serve as potential mediators of the self-fulfilling prophecy process.

Perceiver expectancy-revealing expressive behaviors also mediate the self-fulfilling prophecy process. For example, the holders of unfavorable expectancies may "leak" their negative feelings or discomfort for the target, via a lack of warmth and general sociability (Babad et al., 1982; Harris & Rosenthal, 1985; Snyder et al., 1977), fewer expressions of positive affect (Ickes et al., 1982), greater interpersonal distance (Ickes et al., 1982; Word et al., 1974), an increase in speech errors (Word et al., 1974), and so forth. To the extent that such behaviors inform people as to others' feelings toward them and because the rules of interaction often encourage people to reciprocate the behaviors of others (Goffman, 1959), such perceiver behaviors may lead targets to respond with "cold" behaviors of their own, in this manner fulfilling unfavorable perceiver expectancies. The existence of such a mediational process is further supported by the finding that targets particularly skilled at decoding nonverbal communications are especially likely to confirm perceiver expectancies (Cooper & Hazelrigg, 1988). Thus, expectancy-revealing expressive behaviors can also play a major role in the mediation of self-fulfilling prophecies.

Finally, self-fulfilling prophecies are more likely when targets accept the interactional script created by perceivers' expressive and information-gathering behaviors (see Jones, 1986). In some sense, one can conceptualize behavioral confirmation as being a deference behavior, with the target deferring to the constraints and assumptions of the perceiver. In such instances, the target chooses to accommodate, rather than to challenge, the perceiver. So the target's decision to defer, be it either thoughtful or automatically activated by the situation, can also play a critical role mediating self-fulfilling prophecies.

The expectancy-confirmation process can thus be characterized in the following way: A perceiver, possessing expectancies, exhibits expectancy-revealing expressive behaviors and/or expectancy-biased, information-gathering behaviors. The target decides to defer to the behavioral script implied by these perceiver behaviors, thus behaviorally confirming the perceiver's expectancies. Moreover, even under circumstances in which a target's behavior is ambiguous with respect to the perceiver's expectancies, the perceiver may utilize biased attentional and interpretational processes in the cognitive assessment of this behavior, resulting in an expectancy-consistent impression of the target.

Thus, strong expectancy biases in attentional and interpretational processes are sufficient to create expectancy confirmation. In the absence of such cognitive biases, the presence of either expectancy-biased perceiver expressive or information-gathering behaviors can produce target behavioral confirmation, given that the target decides to accommodate the perceiver's interactional script.[4]

SOCIAL GOALS AS MODERATORS
OF EXPECTANCY CONFIRMATION

Of course, expectancy-tinged social interactions do not always result in expectancy-consistent impressions. People sometimes like those they expected to hate, they often decide that an individual is unrepresentative of his or her group, and so on. This should not be surprising, as the four mediating processes outlined previously are unlikely to occur in every expectancy-tinged interaction: Perceivers do not always engage in biased attentional and interpretational processes, they do not always gather information in biased ways, their expressive behaviors do not always reveal their expectancies, and targets do not always accommodate the whims of their perceivers. When these mediators fail to unfold, expectancy confirmation is less likely. It follows that those factors that regulate the likelihood of these processes determine whether or not expectancy confirmation occurs. Hence, factors that encourage expectancy-based perceiver biases in attention, interpretation, information gathering, or expression or that encourage target deference make expectancy confirmation more likely. In contrast, those factors that reduce expectancy-based perceiver biases in attention, interpretation, information gathering, or expression or that discourage target deference make expectancy confirmation less likely.

Based on this mediational analysis, I propose that several classes of participant motivations—perceiver impression-formation and self-presentational goals, and target self-presentational goals—play a critical role in moderating expectancy confirmation. Below, I theoretically justify my proposal, and present the results of empirical studies relevant to this conceptualization.

Perceiver Impression-Formation Goals

Impression-formation goals are those motives aimed at producing specified outcomes of the impression-formation process. For instance, when one depends on others for something of value, one often has the goal of forming accurate impres-

---

[4]This chapter focuses on the interpersonal and intrapersonal processes occurring within expectancy-tinged social encounters. I would be remiss, however, if I failed to note one of the more common mechanisms through which people enable the survival of their inaccurate expectancies: the avoidance, either deliberate or not, of the targets of their expectancies. That is, to the extent that people avoid confronting the targets of their expectancies (which, of course, is especially likely to occur when their expectancies are based on negative stereotypes and prejudices), they are unlikely to obtain the disconfirming evidence needed to alter their expectancies.

sions of them; when one's expectancies or stereotypes are of personal importance, perhaps because of their links to one's self-concept, one may be actively motivated to confirm them; when under time pressures, one may desire to form impressions rapidly. How do perceivers implement such goals? What cognitive and behavioral strategies do perceivers use to construct their desired impressions. How do these strategies influence the likelihood of expectancy confirmation?

If one desires to form a particular impression, one needs information compatible with that desired impression. That is, if one wants to confirm an existing expectancy, one needs to generate target information consistent with that expectancy. If one wants to form an accurate impression, one needs to generate a great deal of unbiased target information, sampling from a wide range of relevant target domains. One can generate goal-compatible information in several ways. One can search for information compatible with one's goal—either behaviorally or via attentional processes—or one can *interpret* existing information in a way that renders it acceptable to one's goal.

Of course, as discussed previously, such information collection and interpretational processes are also critical to the expectancy-confirmation process. It follows that impression formation goals moderate the expectancy-confirmation process by regulating the ways that perceivers behaviorally gather and cognitively assess target information. To the extent that a perceiver's impression-formation goal encourages the active gathering of expectancy-biased target information, the focusing of attentional resources on expectancy-consistent target information, and the interpretation of ambiguous target behaviors as being expectancy-consistent, the perceiver is increasingly likely to confirm his or her expectancies. In contrast, to the extent that a perceiver's impression-formation goal discourages such behaviors and cognitions, the perceiver becomes less likely to confirm his or her expectancies.

To illustrate, consider a perceiver who is actively motivated to confirm a particular expectancy (e.g., that a Hispanic job applicant is unqualified for a job). The perceiver may ask the target biased questions ("So Mr. Gomez, tell me about a recent job of yours in which you didn't quite perform as well as you would have liked."), pay particular attention to expectancy-consistent target behaviors (e.g., by taking special note of the fact that Mr. Gomez got lost trying to find the personnel office), and interpret ambiguous and expectancy-inconsistent behaviors as expectancy-consistent (e.g., by interpreting Mr. Gomez's layoff from his previous job as a firing). These behavioral and cognitive processes are, of course, those presented previously as facilitating expectancy confirmation. Straightforwardly, when people desire to confirm their expectancies, they are indeed likely to do so.

In contrast, consider a perceiver motivated to form an accurate impression. This perceiver may ask many questions, attempting to be as unbiased as possible (e.g., by also asking Mr. Gomez about his past successes). He or she may also be more likely to accept the target behaviors for what they seem, avoiding where possible expectancy biases in attention and interpretation. Such accuracy-driven behaviors and thought processes, however, run counter to those facilitative of expectancy confirmation. For this reason, a perceiver motivated to form accurate impressions should be less likely to form expectancy-consistent impressions.

Finally, consider a perceiver motivated to form a rapid impression. He or she is likely to limit the amount of target information gathered. Moreover, given that expectancy-consistent information is easier to process cognitively than is expectancy-inconsistent information (see Fiske & Neuberg, 1990), the perceiver may seek expectancy-consistent information, focus limited attentional resources on expectancy-consistent target behaviors, and bias his or her interpretational processes toward expectancy consistency. Because these goal-driven processes happen to be those encouraging of expectancy confirmation, this perceiver is likely to form an expectancy-consistent impression of the target.

Because perceiver impression-formation goals regulate information gathering and cognitive processes—processes critical to expectancy confirmation—one would expect these goals to influence the likelihood of expectancy confirmation. Reviewing first the literature on cognitive impression-formation processes (see Fiske & Neuberg, 1990, for a more comprehensive discussion), there is a reasonable amount of evidence supporting this premise. For example, a series of studies by Fiske and her colleagues suggests that when a perceiver's own personal fate rests somewhat in the hands of the target—ostensibly eliciting accuracy concerns within the perceiver—expectancy confirmation is less likely. This occurs within both cooperative (Neuberg & Fiske, 1987) and competitive (Ruscher & Fiske, 1990) outcome-dependency situations. Moreover, when perceivers are made aware that their impressions have important implications for the targets (Freund, Kruglanski, & Shpitzajzen, 1985) or that objective standards of accuracy exist (Tetlock & Kim, 1987), their impressions are also less biased by expectancy information. Finally, direct experimental manipulations of accuracy motivation also reduce expectancy influences. In one study, subjects motivated to form accurate impressions of a supposed schizophrenic reduced their reliance on their stereotypes of schizophrenics and increased their reliance on the targets' individuating behaviors (Neuberg & Fiske, 1987).

Furthermore, such accuracy-driven attenuations in expectancy influence are mediated by an increase in unbiased attentional processes, as proposed. For example, perceivers become more attentive to targets' individuating characteristics when outcome-dependent on them (Berscheid, Graziano, Monson, & Dermer, 1976; Neuberg & Fiske, 1987; Ruscher & Fiske, 1990). This increase in attention is particularly focused on individuating characteristics that are expectancy-inconsistent (Erber & Fiske, 1984). Moreover, the Neuberg and Fiske (1987) studies indeed demonstrate the ability of such attentional processes to mediate the influence of initial expectancies on ultimate impressions. Thus, within the domain of cognitive impression formation, it is clear that a perceiver's impression-formation goal can moderate expectancy confirmation, apparently through its ability to regulate attentional and interpretational processes.

Evidence within the domain of behavioral interaction is also compatible with the notion that perceiver impression-formation goals moderate the influence of preinteraction expectancies on impressions. Several studies, for instance, demonstrate that perceivers who are explicitly motivated to form accurate impressions show a decrease in expectancy bias following their interactions with the targets (Fein, von Hipple, & Hilton, 1989; Neuberg, 1989). Moreover, in situations where one might presume that perceivers are likely to be motivated to form accurate impressions, expectancy bias in impressions also is attenuated. For example, when perceivers are highly uncertain of their expectancies, expectancy confirmation is less likely (Swann & Ely, 1984).

In contrast, several studies reveal that self-fulfilling prophecies are more likely when perceivers are those who dispositionally tend to make stereotypical interpretations (Babad et al., 1982; Harris & Rosenthal, 1986) or are strongly sex typed (Andersen & Bem, 1981). It is quite possible that such perceivers are likely motivated to confirm their expectancies—the "biased" or dogmatic perceivers may dispositionally desire to retain their prior beliefs, whereas the sex-typed perceivers may especially wish to confirm their sex-relevant expectancies for others. Consequently, the existence of self-fulfilling prophecies under these circumstances might well be anticipated.

Thus, perceiver impression-formation goals indeed moderate the behavioral-confirmation process. Importantly, several studies suggest the proposed mechanism (i.e., the regulation of perceiver information-gathering behaviors) through which impression formation goals have their influence. For example, in one study, perceivers interviewing targets as potential partners for future interactions—and consequently, driven by the goal of impression accuracy—were more likely to ask expectancy-relevant as opposed to expectancy-irrelevant questions, in this manner providing their interaction partners with an opportunity to dispel the perceivers' inaccurate expectancies (Darley et al., 1988). Several other studies in which perceivers were apparently motivated by accuracy concerns—because of either a short-term control deprivation (Swann, Stephenson, & Pittman, 1981) or a more chronic depressive state (Hildebrand-Saints & Weary, 1989)—reveal that such perceivers were especially likely to seek diagnostic information from their targets.

Finally, a recent study of mine (Neuberg, 1989) directly tests the hypothesis that perceiver impression-formation goals moderate the behavioral-confirmation process by regulating the ways that perceivers gather information about targets. Subjects were recruited to participate in a study on interview styles and were randomly assigned to be either an interviewer or an applicant for a hypothetical job as student manager for a campus travel agency. Interviewer subjects conducted two interviews; they were given negative expectancies for one of the applicants (bogus personality inventories revealed that the applicant was relatively deficient on the dimensions of interpersonal skills, goal directedness, and general problem-solving abilities) and no expectancies for the other (because of a computer glitch, these particular scores were unavailable). Moreover, interviewers were either presented with no explicit motivation or prompted to be as accurate in their impressions as possible. Applicant targets were motivated to present themselves well in the interview, and prizes of $50 served as rewards for outstanding performances. Interviewers generated their own questions and were encouraged to structure the over-the-phone interviews however they liked. When the interviews were complete, interviewers and applicants provided their impressions of each other. Moreover, hidden microphones recorded the interviews, thus providing behavioral data as well.

Results are highly compatible with the present conceptualization. First, as anticipated, the no-goal interviewers formed less favorable impressions of the negative-expectancy applicants than of the no-expectancy applicants; this is the basic expectancy-confirmation effect. In contrast, the accuracy-goal interviewers displayed no such bias. Thus, the goal of impression accuracy successfully served to attenuate the expectancy-confirmation effect.

How? Judges, naive to the expectancy and motivational manipulations, listened to the audiotaped interactions and evaluated the favorability of the applicants' performance. Whereas negative-expectancy applicants tended to perform less favorably than their no-expectancy counterparts when interviewed by no-goal perceivers, reflecting the presence of a self-fulfilling prophecy, the negative-expectancy applicants interviewed by the accuracy-goal perceivers actually performed better than their no-expectancy counterparts. Thus, interviewers motivated to be accurate did not elicit self-fulfilling prophecies but instead enabled their negative-expectancy applicants to excel.

An analysis of interviewer behavior suggests how this occurred. First, accuracy-goal interviewers asked their applicants, especially the negative-expectancy applicants, questions that provided them with a greater opportunity to present themselves favorably (i.e., the questions tended to be positively valenced, open-ended, and novel, as opposed to negatively valenced, closed-ended, and redundant). Second, these interviewers spent a smaller proportion of their time talking during the interviews, thus enabling the applicants to provide more information about themselves. And third, these interviewers provided more "encouragements," or prompts for additional information. As a result of these information-gathering behaviors, the negative expectancy applicants had a greater opportunity to overcome the unfavorable initial impressions held of them.

Finally, a structural modeling analysis reveals the predicted mediational path. The accuracy goal attenuated the unfavorable impact that negative perceiver expectancies had on perceiver information gathering. These changes in information gathering translated into improved target performance that in turn, led to reduced bias in perceiver impressions.[5]

Thus, along with the other findings reviewed previously, these data not only suggest an important moderating role for perceiver impression-formation goals but also speak to the mechanisms through which such influences occur: Impression-formation goals moderate the influences of expectancies by regulating the ways in which perceivers gather, attend to, and interpret target information.

Perceiver Self-Presentational Goals

People frequently desire others to view them in certain ways. Sometimes they want others to like them; at other times, they want to be seen as competent; sometimes they want to be intimidating; and so on (cf. Jones & Pittman, 1982). I argue here that perceiver self-presentational goals also play an important role in moderating the expectancy-confirmation process.

Recall that expectancy confirmation is facilitated when perceivers reveal their expectancies to targets via their expressive behaviors, when they gather expectancy-biased information from targets, and when they utilize biased attentional and interpretational processes. How might a perceiver's self-presentational goals influence these behaviors and thought processes and the likelihood of expectancy confirmation?

First, it is clear that perceivers often choose to regulate strategically their expressive behaviors in order to create in the targets the desired image. For example, if I want to be liked, I may smile a lot, provide others with positive feedback ("That's a very interesting idea, Ms. Brown."), exhibit "warm" body language, maintain eye contact, and so on. If I want to be intimidating, I may glower at others and act condescendingly. Indeed, for many desired images, there exists in the mind of an actor a strategic set of potentially facilitative expressive behaviors.

---

[5]It is interesting to note that here and in the Neuberg et al. (1993) Liking-Goal study to be presented later the negative-expectancy applicants were treated better than the no-expectancy applicants when interviewed by perceivers explicitly motivated to form an accurate impression of them (or in the Neuberg et al. study, when motivated to get the applicants to like them). Such "bending over backwards" patterns are reported elsewhere as well (Ickes et al., 1982). It is likely that such overcompensation stems from the extra difficulties anticipated in implementing one's goals when interacting with a target of one's unfavorable expectancies. That is, the goal of forming an accurate impression may be perceived as being particularly difficult upon realizing that one must overcome a set of negative biases in order to effectively do so. As a consequence, a perceiver may be especially likely to focus on careful information-gathering behaviors, providing these targets with uncommon opportunities for favorable self-presentation. In a similar vein, the task of getting targets to like oneself is also seen as especially difficult when the targets are initially expected to be somewhat dislikable. In this case, greater focus on the positivity of one's expressive behaviors results, again providing these targets with notable opportunities to present themselves well.

Of course, expressive behaviors play an important role in expectancy confirmation, with expectancy-revealing expressions facilitating the occurrence of self-fulfilling prophecies. To the extent that self-presentational tactics serve to mask such expressions—for example, expressive behaviors designed to obtain an individual's positive regard may conceal one's stereotype-based dislike for that individual—they should reduce the likelihood of self-fulfilling prophecies, thus making less likely the formation of expectancy-consistent impressions. To the extent, however, that self-presentational concerns evoke expectancy-consistent expressions—as in the case of the perceivers who desire to intimidate the targets of their negative prejudices—self-fulfilling prophecies and expectancy-consistent perceiver impressions should become more likely. Thus, perceiver self-presentational goals moderate the expectancy-confirmation process by determining the nature of perceiver expressive behaviors.

Second, to implement certain self-presentational aims, perceivers also strategically regulate their information-gathering behaviors. For example, in an interview setting, if one wants to be liked, one may ask others questions that focus on their positive features and that avoid their weaknesses (e.g., "So Ms. Brown, you seem to have been very successful in all your previous jobs; to what do you attribute such outstanding performance?"). If one desires to be seen as competent and fair, one might conduct a long, comprehensive interview, asking many questions that cover a wide range of domains. If one desires to communicate superiority, one may contemptuously question the applicant's flaws. In these first two cases, the self-presentational goals elicit behaviors incompatible with expectancy-driven information-gathering practices, making self-fulfilling prophecies less likely. In the latter case, the self-presentational goal evokes information-gathering behaviors of the sort that make self-fulfilling prophecies more likely.

Finally, a perceiver's self-presentational concerns may indirectly influence that perceiver's attentional and interpretational processes by eliciting a particular impression-formation goal. For example, consider the case of a racist personnel officer who wants to be viewed as highly perceptive by his or her discerning boss. To create this image, the interviewer may adopt an accuracy set while evaluating Black job applicants. As a result, the interviewer successfully reduces stereotype-based attentional and interpretational biases when assessing these applicants, enabling him or her to form a more accurate impression of each applicant's individual abilities and characteristics. From the interviewer's perspective, such impressions contribute to the interviewer's desired image—that of a perceptive, astute judge of job applicants. To the extent, then, that a perceiver's self-presentational concerns have implications for attentional and interpretational processes, they have an impact on the expectancy-confirmation process more generally.

Although not much research directly assesses the previous notions, some relevant data are available. For example, although not addressing issues of expectancy confirmation per se, a study by Baumeister, Hutton, and Tice (1989) illustrates the ability of perceivers' self-presentational goals to elicit in targets reciprocal behaviors; perceivers who were motivated to self-promote led their targets to act in a self-promoting manner, whereas perceivers motivated to be modest elicited greater modesty in their targets.

Moreover, other studies suggest an ability of perceiver self-presentational goals to regulate expectancy confirmation via a cognitive route. For example, when perceivers anticipate having to explain their impressions to others, these impressions become less stereotypical (Kruglanski & Freund, 1983). Similarly, Snyder et al. (1982) demonstrated that perceivers are more likely to attend to targets' individuating features when they fear being viewed by others as being prejudiced.

A recent study from my own lab (Neuberg, Judice, Virdin, & Carrillo, 1993) more directly suggests an important moderating role of perceiver self-presentational goals. Similar to the accuracy-goal study discussed previously (Neuberg, 1989), subjects in this study were randomly assigned to the roles of interviewer or applicant for a hypothetical job opening. Interviewers were led to believe that one of their two applicants was likely unqualified for the job, while receiving no job-relevant information about the other applicant. This time, however, half of the interviewers were motivated to get the applicants to like them, whereas the remaining interviewers were given no explicit motivation. We again encouraged applicants to present themselves favorably. The phone interviews were conducted, behavioral measures were obtained via unobtrusive audiorecording, and postinteraction impressions were collected.

As predicted, interviewers in the no-goal conditions formed expectancy-consistent impressions of their applicants; negative-expectancy applicants were evaluated less favorably than were no-expectancy applicants. In contrast, for the liking-goal interviewers, this expectancy-based impression bias was not only eliminated but actually reversed, with negative-expectancy applicants receiving more favorable evaluations than the no-expectancy applicants. Thus, the influence of preinteraction expectancies on impressions was moderated by the perceivers' self-presentational concerns.

Moreover, the liking goal had its moderating influence on the nature of the behavioral interaction itself. Again, as anticipated, the no-goal interviewers created interactions in which the negative-expectancy applicants tended to objectively perform less favorably than their no-expectancy counterparts, as assessed by naive judges listening to interview audiotapes; this reflects a self-fulfilling prophecy. In contrast, the liking-goal interviewers created interactions in which the negative-expectancy applicants performed better than the no-expectancy applicants (again, see footnote 5).

What did the liking-goal interviewers do to counteract the influence of their expectancies on applicant behavior? As anticipated, these interviewers were warmer than their no-goal counterparts, beginning their interviews with friendlier openings and using the applicants' names more frequently throughout their sessions. Moreover, whereas no-goal interviewers spent less time listening to the negative-expectancy applicants (relative to the no-expectancy applicants), the liking-goal interviewers exhibited no such bias. Finally, and perhaps most important, the liking-goal interviewers went out of their way to avoid asking their negative-expectancy applicants about unfavorable experiences and were also less likely to probe these applicants deeply, perhaps trying to avoid the possibility of embarrassing them or of causing them to "lose face." Indeed, path analyses reveal that these interviewer behaviors mediated the influence of interviewer goal on applicant behavior.

This study thus suggests the potential importance of perceiver self-presentational goals as moderators of expectancy confirmation. As a perceiver's self-presentational goals change, so too change the perceiver's expressive and information-gathering behaviors, thus altering the nature of expectancy-tinged interactions.

Target Self-Presentational Goals

Up to this point, I have focused on the motivations of the perceivers. One should be careful, however, not to neglect the role of the targets. After all, in most cases, the targets are in ultimate control of their own behaviors and determine the extent to which they behaviorally confirm the perceivers' expectancies.

Hence, I look here at target self-presentational goals. Like perceivers, targets desire to project particular images. Moreover, like perceivers, targets possess a repertoire of behaviors believed to create the desired image when implemented in the proper fashion. To the extent that such strategic behaviors are compatible with the perceivers' expectancies, there is evidence of self-fulfilling prophecies and subsequently, of postinteraction expectancy confirmation. To the extent, however, that such strategic self-presentations are incompatible with perceiver expectancies, evidence of self-fulfilling prophecy is lacking, making postinteraction expectancy confirmation less likely.[6]

If the earlier conceptualization is correct—namely, that the target's "decision" to defer to the perceiver's behavioral script mediates the self-fulfilling prophecy— then target self-presentational goals should have their moderating influences by regulating this deference decision. Although no empirical evidence directly addresses the target decision process per se, some evidence is consistent with such a regulatory role.

---

[6]I should note that a target's behavioral disconfirmation of a perceiver's expectancies certainly does not guarantee that the perceiver will form an expectancy-inconsistent impression. Indeed, a perceiver may still cognitively interpret these behaviors as being expectancy consistent or focus attention only on those target behaviors that are either expectancy consistent or ambiguous, thus enabling an expectancy-consistent impression.

First, consider the case in which a target may see it to be in his or her best self-presentational interest to accommodate the perceiver's script. This may occur because the target has no proactive self-presentational goals of his or her own, and merely desires to avoid participating in an awkward interaction; such a state of affairs may indeed characterize many social encounters. As Jones (1986) has argued, to directly challenge the assumptions of another violates a face-saving contract implicit to social interaction (Goffman, 1959) and conversation (Grice, 1975). As a consequence, in unimportant interactions, one may decide not to rock the boat, acquiescing to the perceiver's assumptions and thus facilitating a comfortable, albeit expectancy-confirming, interaction.

Of course, even in significant interactions, targets may decide to defer to the perceivers' scripts, thus creating self-fulfilling prophecies. For example, if one's goal is to be viewed as likable, accommodation is often a useful strategy. Likewise, a desired image of being weak, supplicant, or vulnerable also elicits a deferential strategy. Several studies by Zanna and his colleagues support such a notion. For example, female targets acted more sex role traditionally (Zanna & Pack, 1975) and dressed more "femininely" (von Baeyer, Sherk, & Zanna, 1981) when interacting with an attractive male known to be chauvinistic, suggesting that accommodation is a self-presentational strategy of choice under some circumstances.

Moreover, challenging the assumptions of others potentially carries with it serious costs; such costs may be especially salient when the perceiver is of higher status than the target. Thus, one would expect the decision to defer, and thus behavioral confirmation, to be more likely in circumstances in which the target perceives himself or herself to be of relatively low status. Indeed, a recent experiment by Copeland (1991) indicates that behavioral confirmation is especially likely to occur when the perceiver is placed in a position of relative power over the target and both parties are aware of this power distinction.

Moreover, a study from our lab suggests that the mere (inaccurate) perception by a target that a perceiver is of higher relative status may be sufficient to promote expectancy confirmation (Virdin & Neuberg, 1990). Perceivers interacted with two targets, their purpose being to assess the targets' degrees of optimism so that we could ostensibly evaluate the validity of a newly designed personality scale of optimism/pessimism. They were led to believe that one of these targets was dispositionally optimistic whereas the other was dispositionally pessimistic. Targets, on the other hand, were told that they were interacting with people who were a part of a special interpersonal skills training program and that their role was to help assess the effectiveness of that training. Targets were further led to believe that the perceiver was either a high school student (perceiver low-status condition), another college student (perceiver equal-status condition), or a doctoral student (perceiver high-status condition); perceivers (all college students) were unaware of the status manipulation. Following the telephone conversations, perceivers evaluated the targets' levels of optimism.

Perceiver impressions indicated that target perceptions of status served to moderate the expectancy-confirmation process. Perceivers believed by the targets to be of high status were especially likely to attribute more optimism to the optimism-expectancy target than to the pessimism-expectancy target; perceivers believed by the targets to be of low status were least likely to demonstrate this expectancy-confirmation effect.

Thus, in a situation in which the role of deference decisions is perhaps most salient—the situation of perceived differential status—expectancy confirmation is most likely when targets view themselves as being of low relative status.

Other data are also consistent with the conceptualization of behavioral confirmation as deference: Men are more likely to elicit behavioral confirmation whereas women are more likely to succumb to it (Christensen & Rosenthal, 1982), and individuals who are dispositionally "influenceable" are also more likely to behaviorally confirm others' expectancies (Cooper & Hazelrigg, 1988; Harris & Rosenthal, 1986). If one assumes that women and influenceable individuals are dispositionally more accommodating, these data fit well with the present perspective. Thus, the data reviewed to this point suggest not only that targets play a large role in determining whether or not expectancy confirmation occurs but also that the deference decision is a potential mediator of this process.

Of course, targets often possess self-presentational goals incompatible with such deference decisions; under such circumstances, expectancy confirmation is less likely. For example, in one study, targets were informed that perceivers held unflattering expectations for them (Hilton & Darley, 1985). Given that these particular targets were efficacious Princeton students, the existence of such negative expectancies likely elicited an explicit goal of positive self-presentation; it is thus not surprising that expectancy confirmation was attenuated in these interactions (in contrast to the noninformed sessions). Moreover, targets who are high in self-certainty are also less likely to behaviorally confirm the expectations of others (Swann & Ely, 1984). Again, this fits with the present view if one assumes that highly self-certain individuals are less likely to decide to accept the perceivers' script when it apparently conflicts with their own self-presentational agenda.

Although only a limited amount of empirical data exist testing these notions, it seems clear that a target's own self-presentational concerns serve to moderate the expectancy-confirmation process. When a target's self-presentational concerns elicit deference as an appropriate strategy, self-fulfilling prophecies occur; when such accommodation is incompatible with a target's self-presentational goal, self-fulfilling prophecies become less likely.

The Role of Limited Resources

In the previous pages, I proposed that perceiver and target motivations play a crucial role in moderating the expectancy-confirmation process via their ability to regulate the mechanisms mediating expectancy confirmation. Positing a role for motivations, however, requires one to consider the issue of availability of cognitive and behavioral resources. I briefly do so here.

Simply put, it typically takes resources to implement any goal. If I desire to form an accurate impression, I must allocate behavioral resources to the unbiased gathering of target information and cognitive resources to the unbiased attention to, and interpretation of, such gathered information. If I wish to get another to like me, I must allocate cognitive resources to the monitoring of both my own and others' behaviors and behavioral resources to the strategic actions deemed necessary. If resources are lacking, my ability to realize my goals are greatly reduced.

This recognition of the importance of available resources has implications for our conceptualization of the expectancy-confirmation process. In particular, it suggests the necessity of positing a set of "default" behavioral strategies— strategies that occur "automatically" when resources are scarce. Briefly, I argue that the following defaults will typically hold.

First, when resources are scarce, the gathering of information is in general reduced, with the focus on the gathering of expectancy-consistent target information; cognitively processing expectancy-inconsistent information is relatively difficult and is likely to be avoided under such circumstances. Second, because expectancy-inconsistent information is more difficult to process, perceiver attentional and interpretational processes should also favor expectancy consistency. Third, perceiver expressive behaviors should reflect underlying expectancies when resources are tight; to monitor one's own expressive behaviors and to control the leakage of sentiments is not always a simple task and requires resources that may not be available. Finally, under circumstances of limited resources, one would expect targets to choose to defer to the behavioral script initiated by the perceivers, as it is typically easier to accommodate the script of another than it is to coax another into a script of one's own.

If the defaults are indeed as proposed, expectancy confirmation should be increasingly likely when resources are scarce. Indeed, stereotype-based judgments are more likely when perceivers are under time pressures (Bechtold, Naccarato, & Zanna, 1986; Kruglanski & Freund, 1983) and when perceivers are highly aroused (Kim & Baron, 1988; Wilder & Shapiro, 1989). To the extent that time pressures and arousal reduce the availability of cognitive resources, such findings are consistent with the present view. Moreover, a recent study by Bodenhausen (1990) indicated that *morning people* (i.e., those who reach their peak of cognitive functioning early in the day) are more likely to rely on their stereotypes at night, whereas *night people* (i.e., those who reach their peak of cognitive functioning late in the day) are more likely to rely on their stereotypes in the morning. Again, these data are consistent with the present notion if one considers these circadian variations to have implications for resource availability.

Finally, the issue of resource availability has important implications for expectancy influences under circumstances of multiple goals. More specifically, to the extent that an interactant focuses resources on one goal, he or she necessarily is less able to implement effectively other goals. In such cases, one would predict the posited default processes to occur in the goal domains relatively neglected by the interactant, leading to expectancy biases in these domains (for similar discussions within other contexts, see Baumeister et al., 1989; Gilbert, Krull, & Pelham, 1988; Lord & Saenz, 1985; Saenz & Lord, 1989).

No existing data directly address this issue, although some findings from the Neuberg (1989) study are suggestive. Most important, although the accuracy-driven interviewers demonstrated a lack of expectancy bias in their information-gathering behaviors, they nonetheless revealed an expectancy bias in their cognitive processing of the applicants' behaviors. One interpretation of this finding is that the interviewers' focus on information gathering left them with few remaining resources for the cognitive impression-formation task; as a consequence, these perceivers were compelled to adopt expectancy-biased default processes in this latter domain. Thus, although a particular goal may serve to eliminate expectancy-based biases in one behavioral or cognitive domain, its implementation may ironically increase the likelihood of expectancy-based biases in another.

Summary

Up to this point, I elaborated on previous theoretical and empirical work, providing a motivational framework for understanding the behavioral and cognitive dynamics of expectancy-tinged dyadic social interactions (see Fig. 5.1.). The present conceptualization is highly interactional, focusing not only on the abilities of both participants to influence each other throughout the encounter but also on the dynamic interplay of expectancies, motives, resources, and cognitive processing occurring within each participant.

Four fundamental premises shape the proposed framework, emphasizing the critical role that social motives play in moderating expectancy-confirmation processes. These premises, when employed as an integrated set of guiding principles, are proposed to enable reasonably precise predictions regarding the outcomes of expectancy-tinged encounters:

1. Perceiver impression-formation goals moderate the influence of perceiver expectancies on perceiver impressions by moderating the impact that these expectancies have on perceiver information-gathering behaviors and attentional and interpretational processes.

2. Perceiver self-presentational goals moderate the influence of perceiver expectancies on perceiver impressions by moderating the impact that these expectancies have on perceiver expressive behaviors, information-gathering behaviors, and attentional and interpretational processes.

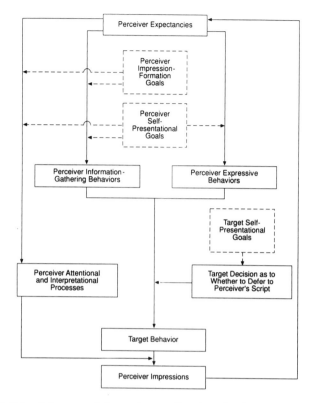

FIG. 5.1.   A framework for understanding the role of social motives in expectancy-tinged social interactions. The moderating influences of perceiver and target goals are represented by dotted arrows. Moderating influences of resource availability are not represented here.

3. Target self-presentational goals moderate the influence of perceiver expectancies on perceiver impressions by determining the extent to which the target decides to accommodate the behavioral script implicated by the perceiver's information-gathering and expressive behaviors.

4. The ability of perceiver and target goals to moderate the influence of perceiver expectancies on perceiver impressions is constrained by the availability of behavioral and cognitive resources; low-effort, default processes, increasing the likelihood of expectancy confirmation, occur in those goal domains receiving insufficient resources.

Having presented my framework, I move to apply these notions more explicitly to the stereotype-tinged contact situation presented at the beginning of this chapter.

STEREOTYPE-DISCONFIRMING CONTACT SITUATIONS

According to the present framework, what kinds of circumstances must exist in order for individuals to form impressions of others that are unbiased by their inaccurate stereotypes and prejudices?

First, stereotype confirmation is clearly less likely when perceivers are motivated to form accurate impressions of their targets. The motivation to be accurate not only has potentially important influences on the ways that perceivers cognitively process targets' behaviors—reducing stereotype-based biases in attentional and interpretational processes—but also plays a large role in determining the behavioral dynamics of the interaction itself, making it less likely that targets will behaviorally confirm perceivers' inaccurate stereotypes. When perceivers are instead motivated to confirm their stereotypes or to form rapid impressions, the resulting perceiver impressions are much more likely to be stereotype consistent.

Second, the confirmation of negative stereotypes and prejudices is also less likely when the perceivers are motivated to ingratiate their targets. The behavioral process of getting others to like us can have powerful influences on both information-gathering and expressive behaviors, reducing the creation of self-fulfilling prophecies. In contrast, perceiver self-presentational styles driven by motives to appear superior, intimidating, and the like create unfavorable target presentations, supporting negative preconceptions held by the perceivers. Thus, the self-presentational goal of ingratiation also contributes to a reduced impact of negative stereotypes and prejudices on postinteraction impressions.

Third, targets of perceiver stereotypes and prejudices are less likely to fall into behavioral confirmation to the extent that they are motivated to impose upon perceivers self-presentational agendas of their own. Deciding to accommodate a biased perceiver's interactional script is the self-presentational death knell of any target wishing to be viewed as an individual distinct from his or her stereotyped label. To defer to a biased perceiver's behavioral agenda is often to confirm that perceiver's inaccurate stereotypes and prejudices. Targets need to possess proactive self-presentational agendas of their own and need to adjust the behavioral dynamics of the social encounter appropriately. To the extent that a perceiver is motivated to be accurate or to ingratiate, this self-presentational task becomes easier for the target, as such perceiver motivations often create the needed opportunity.

Fourth, and perhaps most critical, both perceivers and targets need to have at their disposal the cognitive and behavioral resources required to implement their goals. It takes a good deal of resources to eliminate biases in information-gathering and cognitive processing; it takes resources to monitor one's own expressive behaviors to make sure that negative sentiments do not leak; and it

124

takes a significant amount of resources to shift carefully an interactional script from one compatible with stereotype confirmation to one compatible with stereotype disconfirmation. Without such resources, stereotype confirmation is much more likely.

Thus, to create stereotype disconfirmation, one should (a) motivate the holders of stereotypes and prejudices to form accurate impressions of others, (b) motivate these perceivers to be likable and ingratiating, (c) create in the stereotyped targets the motivation to challenge the interactional assumptions of perceivers and provide these targets with low-cost opportunities to indeed do so, and (d) provide an environment in which the absence of resource-draining stressors and distractions enable interactants to implement these aims.

Given this analysis, it is not surprising that research on stereotype-tinged contact reveals that stereotype-consistent impressions are less likely as individuals interact under circumstances of (a) cooperative interdependence, (b) equal status, and (c) egalitarian norms (for reviews, see Miller & Brewer, 1984).

Cooperative interdependence—when interactants must cooperate with each other in order to achieve some commonly desired aim—likely attenuates the impact of stereotypes and prejudices because it activates particular participant impression-formation and self-presentational goals. Specifically, it is important under such circumstances for the participants to understand each other, to form accurate impressions of each other. If I need to work together with another person to achieve my own ambitions, I want to understand that other person so that I may predict his or her behavior and, thus, control my own outcomes. Moreover, if coordinated cooperation is needed, it also behooves me to get that other person to like me; to effectively ingratiate another is to create a smooth, and thus potentially productive, interaction environment. And as I have discussed, such motivational states make stereotype-biased cognitive and behavioral processes less likely.

Equal status, from the perspective of the present framework, may have its positive influences for several reasons. First, when biased perceivers see themselves in a position of relatively high status or local superiority, their motivations to form accurate impressions of low status others is minimal; after all, under such circumstances, the costs of making a mistake are low. Similarly, high status perceivers have little reason to ingratiate themselves to low status targets, as not much is gained by the affections of such targets. Additionally, when such status differentials exist, it is both more difficult for targets to challenge the interactional scripts of high status perceivers—as the potential costs increase—and less likely that high status perceivers will indeed provide such targets with reasonable opportunities to do so.

Finally, the presence of egalitarian norms may be advantageous to such contact situations for similar reasons. Because egalitarian norms increase the likelihood of perceiver accuracy and ingratiation goals and because they legitimize for stereotyped targets their desires for a self-determined self-presentation, they make it more likely that such targets will successfully challenge perceivers' stereotypic assumptions.

Thus, although the present framework was conceptualized independently of the intergroup contact literature, it nonetheless makes some of the same predictions. Importantly, given its more explicit focus on underlying psychological states and mechanisms central to the stereotype-tinged interaction process, the present framework helps to explain why contact factors such as cooperative interdependence, equal status, and egalitarian norms have the effects that they do, as well as to suggest somewhat finer-grained intervention strategies.

Of course, the creation of such contact circumstances is no easy task, as students of desegregation already know. Moreover, even when such circumstances are indeed created and perceivers indeed form unbiased impressions of their interaction partners, generalization of these nonstereotypic impressions from the target individual to the target's more general group affiliation is far from guaranteed (see Brewer & Miller, 1984; Cook, 1984; Rothbart & John, 1985; Weber & Crocker, 1983). Nonetheless, learning via social interaction that individual targets of our stereotypes and our prejudices are not as we expect them to be and that they do not always conform to our preconceived notions is a critical, perhaps even necessary, first step toward changing stereotypes and prejudices.

In sum, the purpose of the present chapter is to begin explicating the interpersonal and intrapersonal dynamics of stereotype-tinged social interactions. The framework presented here emphasizes the importance of the motivational context in which these interactions occur. It is hoped that the present framework furthers theoretical understanding of these important social encounters. Given the everyday significance of such interactions, I also cannot help but hope that this framework may someday provide even a small contribution toward the creation of more effective contact interventions.

ACKNOWLEDGMENTS

I would like to thank Mark Zanna, Jim Olson, Jenny Crocker, and the participants and attendees of the Ontario Symposium for their many helpful questions and comments. Preparation of this chapter was supported by National Institute of Mental Health Grant No. MH45719.

REFERENCES

Allport, G. W. (1954). *The nature of prejudice.* Reading, MA: Addison-Wesley.
Andersen, S. M., & Bem, S. L. (1981). Sex typing and androgeny in dyadic interaction: Individual differences in responsiveness to physical attractiveness. *Journal of Personality and Social Psychology, 41,* 74–86.

Babad, E. Y., Inbar, J., & Rosenthal, R. (1982). Pygmalian, Galatea, and Golem: Investigations of biased and unbiased teachers. *Journal of Educational Psychology, 74,* 459–474.

Baumeister, R. F., Hutton, D. G., & Tice, D. M. (1989). Cognitive processes during deliberate self-presentation: How self-presenters alter and misinterpret the behavior of their interaction partners. *Journal of Experimental Social Psychology, 25,* 59–78.

Bechtold, A., Naccarato, M. E., & Zanna, M. P. (1986, June). *Need for structure and the prejudice–discrimination link.* Paper presented at the annual meeting of the Canadian Psychological Association, Toronto.

Berscheid, E., Graziano, W., Monson, T., & Dermer, M. (1976). Outcome dependency: Attention, attribution, and attraction. *Journal of Personality and Social Psychology, 34,* 978–989.

Bodenhausen, G. V. (1990). Stereotypes as judgmental heuristics: Evidence of circadian variations in discrimination. *Psychological Science, 1,* 319–322.

Brewer, M. B., & Miller, N. (1984). Beyond the contact hypothesis: Theoretical perspectives on desegregation. In N. Miller & M. B. Brewer (Eds.), *Groups in contact: The psychology of desegregation* (pp. 281–302). San Diego, CA: Academic Press.

Brigham, J. C. (1971). Ethnic stereotypes. *Psychological Bulletin, 76,* 15–38.

Brophy, J. E. (1983). Research on the self-fulfilling prophecy and teacher expectations. *Journal of Educational Psychology, 75,* 631–661.

Brophy, J. E., & Good, T. (1974). *Teacher–student relationships: Causes and consequences.* New York: Holt, Rinehart, & Winston.

Christensen, D., & Rosenthal, R. (1982). Gender and nonverbal decoding skill as determinants of interpersonal expectancy effects. *Journal of Personality and Social Psychology, 42,* 75–87.

Cook, S. W. (1978). Interpersonal and attitudinal outcomes in cooperating interracial groups. *Journal of Research and Development in Education, 12,* 97–113.

Cook, S. W. (1984). Cooperative interaction in multiethnic contexts. In N. Miller & M. B. Brewer (Eds.), *Groups in contact: The psychology of desegregation* (pp. 155–185). San Diego, CA: Academic Press.

Cooper, H. (1979). Pygmalian grows up: A model for teacher expectation communication and performance influence. *Review of Educational Research, 49,* 389–410.

Cooper, H., & Hazelrigg, P. (1988). Personality moderators of interpersonal expectancy effects: An integrative research review. *Journal of Personality and Social Psychology, 55,* 937–949.

Copeland, J. T. (1991). *Motivational implications of social power for behavioral confirmation.* Unpublished doctoral dissertation, University of Minnesota.

Darley, J. M., & Fazio, R. H. (1980). Expectancy confirmation processes arising in the social interaction sequence. *American Psychologist, 35,* 867–881.

Darley, J. M., Fleming, J. H., Hilton, J. L., & Swann, W. B., Jr. (1988). Dispelling negative expectancies: The impact of interaction goals and target characteristics on the expectancy confirmation process. *Journal of Experimental Social Psychology, 24,* 19–36.

Darley, J. M., & Gross, P. H. (1983). A hypothesis-confirming bias in labeling effects. *Journal of Personality and Social Psychology, 44,* 20–33.

Deaux, K., & Major, B. (1987). Putting gender into context: An interactive model of gender-related behavior. *Psychological Review, 94,* 369–389.

Duncan, S. L. (1976). Differential social perception and attribution of intergroup violence: Testing the lower limits of stereotyping of blacks. *Journal of Personality and Social Psychology, 34,* 590–598.

Erber, R., & Fiske, S. T. (1984). Outcome dependency and attention to inconsistent information. *Journal of Personality and Social Psychology, 47,* 709–726.

Farina, A. (1982). The stigma of mental disorders. In A. G. Miller (Ed.), *In the eye of the beholder; Contemporary issues in stereotyping* (pp. 305–363). New York: Praeger.

Farina, A., & Ring, K. (1965). The influence of perceived mental illness on interpersonal relations. *Journal of Applied Social Psychology, 70,* 47–51.

Fazio, R. H., & Zanna, M. P. (1981). Direct experience and attitude–behavior consistency. In L. Berkowitz (Ed.), *Advances in experimental social psychology* (Vol. 14, pp. 162–203). New York: Academic Press.

Fein, S., von Hipple, W., & Hilton, J. L. (1989, August). *The impact of interaction goals on expectancy confirmation.* Paper presented at the annual meeting of the American Psychological Association, New Orleans.

Fiske, S. T., & Neuberg, S. L. (1990). A continuum of impression formation, from category-based to individuating processes: Influences of information and motivation on attention and interpretation. In M. P. Zanna (Ed.), *Advances in experimental social psychology* (Vol. 23, pp. 1–74). New York: Academic Press.

Fiske, S. T., Neuberg, S. L., Beattie, A. E., & Milberg, S. J. (1987). Category-based and attribute-based reactions to others: Some informational conditions of stereotyping and individuating processes. *Journal of Experimental Social Psychology, 23,* 399–427.

Fiske, S. T., & Taylor, S. E. (1991). *Social cognition* (2nd ed.). New York: McGraw Hill.

Freund, T., Kruglanski, A. W., & Shpitzajzen, A. (1985). The freezing and unfreezing of impression primacy: Effects of the need for structure and the fear of invalidity. *Personality and Social Psychology Bulletin, 11,* 479–487.

Gilbert, D. T., Krull, D. S., & Pelham, B. W. (1988). Of thoughts unspoken: Social inference and the self-regulation of behavior. *Journal of Personality and Social Psychology, 55,* 685–694.

Goffman, E. (1959). *The presentation of self in everyday life.* Garden City, NY: Doubleday.

Grice, H. P. (1975). Logic in conversation. In P. Cole & J. L. Morgan (Eds.), *Syntax and semantics* (Vol. 3, pp. 41–58). New York: Academic Press.

Hamilton, D. L., Sherman, S. J., & Ruvulo, C. M. (1990). Stereotype-based expectancies: Effects on information processing and social behavior. *Journal of Social Issues, 46,* 35–60.

Harris, M. J., & Rosenthal, R. (1985). Mediation of interpersonal expectancy effects: 31 meta-analyses. *Psychological Bulletin, 97,* 363–386.

Harris, M. J., & Rosenthal, R. (1986). Counselor and client personality as determinants of counselor expectancy effects. *Journal of Personality and Social Psychology, 50,* 362–369.

Higgins, E. T., & Bargh, J. A. (1987). Social cognition and social perception. *Annual Review of Psychology, 38,* 369–425.

Hildebrand-Saints, L., & Weary, G. (1989). Depression and social information gathering. *Personality and Social Psychology Bulletin, 15,* 150–160.

Hilton, J. L., & Darley, J. M. (1985). Constructing other persons: A limit on the effect. *Journal of Experimental Social Psychology, 21,* 1–18.

Hilton, J. L., & Darley, J. M. (1991). The effects of interaction goals on person perception. In M. P. Zanna (Ed.), *Advances in experimental social psychology* (Vol. 24, pp. 235–267). San Diego, CA: Academic Press.

Ickes, W., Patterson, M. L., Rajecki, D. W., & Tanford, S. (1982). Behavioral and cognitive consequences of reciprocal versus compensatory responses to pre-interaction expectancies. *Social Cognition, 1,* 160–190.

Jones, E. E. (1986). Interpreting interpersonal behavior: The effects of expectancies. *Science, 234,* 41–46.

Jones, E. E., & Pittman, T. S. (1982). Toward a general theory of strategic self-presentation. In J. Suls (Ed.), *Psychological perspectives on the self* (pp. 231–262). Hillsdale, NJ: Lawrence Erlbaum Associates.

Jussim, L. (1986). Self-fulfilling prophecies: A theoretical and integrative review. *Psychological Review, 93,* 429–445.

Jussim, L. (1991). Social perception and social reality: A reflection–construction model. *Psychological Review, 98,* 54–73.

Kim, H-S, & Baron, R. S. (1988). Exercise and the illusory correlation: Does arousal heighten stereotypic processing? *Journal of Experimental Psychology, 24,* 366–380.

Kruglanski, A. W., & Freund, T. (1983). The freezing and unfreezing of lay-inferences: Effects of impressional primacy, ethnic stereotyping, and numerical anchoring. *Journal of Experimental Social Psychology, 19,* 448–468.

Langer, E. J., & Abelson, R. P. (1974). A patient by any other name . . . : Clinician group difference in labeling bias. *Journal of Consulting and Clinical Psychology, 42,* 4–9.

Lord, C. G., & Saenz, D. S. (1985). Memory deficits and memory surfeits: Differential cognitive consequences of tokenism for tokens and observers. *Journal of Personality and Social Psychology, 49,* 918–926.

Major, B., Cozzarelli, C., Testa, M., & McFarlin, D. B. (1988). Self-verification versus expectancy confirmation in social interaction: The impact of self-focus. *Personality and Social Psychology Bulletin, 14,* 346–359.

Merton, R. K. (1948). The self-fulfilling prophecy. *Antioch Review, 8,* 193–210.

Miller, D. T., & Turnbull, W. (1986). Expectancies and interpersonal processes. *Annual Review of Psychology, 37,* 233–256.

Miller, N., & Brewer, M. B. (1984). *Groups in contact: The psychology of desegregation.* San Diego, CA: Academic Press.

Neuberg, S. L. (1989). The goal of forming accurate impressions during social interactions: Attenuating the impact of negative expectancies. *Journal of Personality and Social Psychology, 56,* 374–386.

Neuberg, S. L. (1992). *Expectancy influences in social interaction: The moderating role of social goals.* Unpublished manuscript, Arizona State University.

Neuberg, S. L., & Fiske, S. T. (1987). Motivational influences on impression formation: Outcome dependency, accuracy-driven attention, and individuating processes. *Journal of Personality and Social Psychology, 53,* 431–444.

Neuberg, S. L., Judice, T. N., Virdin, L. M., & Carrillo, M. (1993). Perceiver self-presentational goals as moderators of expectancy influences: Ingratiation and the disconfirmation of negative expectancies. *Journal of Personality and Social Psychology, 64,* 409–420.

Nisbett, R. E., & Ross, L. (1980). *Human inference: Strategies and shortcomings of social judgment.* Englewood Cliffs, NJ: Prentice-Hall.

Omoto, A. M., & Borgida, E. (1988). Guess who might be coming to dinner?: Personal involvement and racial stereotypes. *Journal of Experimental Social Psychology, 24,* 571–593.

Rosenthal, R. (1974). *On the social psychology of the self-fulfilling prophecy: Further evidence for Pygmalion effects and their mediating mechanisms.* New York: MSS Modular Publications (Module 53).

Rosenthal, R., & Rubin, D. B. (1978). Interpersonal expectancy effects: The first 345 studies. *Behavioral and Brain Sciences, 3,* 377–386.

Rothbart, M., & John, O. P. (1985). Social categorization and behavioral episodes: A cognitive analysis of the effects of intergroup contact. *Journal of Social Issues, 41,* 81–104.

Ruble, D. N., & Ruble, T. L. (1982). Sex stereotypes. In A. G. Miller (Ed.), *In the eye of the beholder: Contemporary issues in stereotyping* (pp. 188–252). New York: Praeger.

Ruscher, J. B., & Fiske, S. T. (1990). Interpersonal competition can cause individuating impression formation. *Journal of Personality and Social Psychology, 58,* 832–842.

Saenz, D. S., & Lord, C. G. (1989). Reversing roles: A cognitive strategy for undoing memory deficits associated with token status. *Journal of Personality and Social Psychology, 56,* 698–708.

Sagar, H. A., & Schofield, J. W. (1980). Racial and behavioral cues in black and white children's perceptions of ambiguously aggressive acts. *Journal of Personality and Social Psychology, 39,* 590–598.

Snyder, M. (1984). When belief creates reality. In L. Berkowitz (Ed.), *Advances in experimental social psychology* (Vol. 18, pp. 248–306). New York: Academic Press.

Snyder, M. (1992). Motivational foundations of behavioral confirmation. In M. P. Zanna (Ed.), *Advances in Experimental Social Psychology* (Vol. 25, pp. 67–114). San Diego, CA: Academic Press.

Snyder, M., Campbell, B. H., & Preston, E. (1982). Testing hypotheses about human nature: Assessing the accuracy of social stereotypes. *Social Cognition, 1,* 256–272.

Snyder, M., & Gangestad, S. (1981). Hypothesis-testing processes. In J. H. Harvey, W. Ickes, & R. F. Kidd (Eds.), *New directions in attribution research* (Vol. 3, pp. 171–198). Hillsdale, NJ: Lawrence Erlbaum Associates.

Snyder, M., & Swann, W. B., Jr. (1978a). Behavioral confirmation in social interaction: From social perception to social reality. *Journal of Experimental Social Psychology, 14,* 148–162.

Snyder, M., & Swann, W. B., Jr. (1978b). Hypothesis-testing processes in social interaction. *Journal of Personality and Social Psychology, 36,* 1202–1212.

Snyder, M., Tanke, E. D., & Berscheid, E. (1977). Social perception and interpersonal behavior: On the self-fulfilling nature of social stereotypes. *Journal of Personality and Social Psychology, 35,* 656–666.

Swann, W. B., Jr. (1984). Quest for accuracy in person perception: A matter of pragmatics. *Psychological Review, 91,* 457–477.

Swann, W. B., Jr., & Ely, R. J. (1984). A battle of wills: Self-verification versus behavioral confirmation. *Journal of Personality and Social Psychology, 46,* 1287–1302.

Swann, W. B., Jr., & Snyder, M. (1980). On translating beliefs into action: Theories of ability and their applications in an instructional setting. *Journal of Personality and Social Psychology, 38,* 879–888.

Swann, W. B., Jr., Stephenson, B., & Pittman, T. S. (1981). Curiosity and control: On the determinants of the search for social knowledge. *Journal of Personality and Social Psychology, 40,* 635–642.

Tavris, C., & Offir, C. (1977). *The longest war: Sex differences in perspective.* New York: Harcourt Brace Jovanovich.

Taylor, S. E., Fiske, S. T., Etcoff, N. L., & Ruderman, A. J. (1978). Categorical bases of person memory and stereotyping. *Journal of Personality and Social Psychology, 36,* 778–793.

Tetlock, P. E., & Kim, J. I. (1987). Accountability and judgment processes in a personality prediction task. *Journal of Personality and Social Psychology, 52,* 700–709.

Virdin, L. M., & Neuberg, S. L. (1990, August). *Is perceived status a moderator of expectancy confirmation?* Paper presented at the annual meeting of the American Psychological Association, Boston.

von Baeyer, C. L., Sherk, D. L., & Zanna, M. P. (1981). Impression management in the job interview: When the female applicant meets the male (chauvinist) interviewer. *Personality and Social Psychology Bulletin, 7,* 45–51.

Weber, R., & Crocker, J. (1983). Cognitive processes in the revision of stereotypic beliefs. *Journal of Personality and Social Psychology, 45,* 961–977.

West, C., & Anderson, T. (1976). The question of preponderant causation in teacher expectancy research. *Review of Educational Research, 46,* 613–630.

Wilder, D. A., & Shapiro, P. (1989). The role of competition-induced anxiety in limiting the beneficial impact of positive behavior by an outgroup member. *Journal of Personality and Social Psychology, 56,* 60–69.

Word, C. O., Zanna, M. P., & Cooper, J. (1974). The nonverbal mediation of self-fulfilling prophecies in inter-racial interaction. *Journal of Experimental Social Psychology, 10,* 109–120.

Zanna, M. P., & Pack, S. J. (1975). On the self-fulfilling nature of apparent sex differences in behavior. *Journal of Experimental Social Psychology, 11,* 583–591.

6 Reducing Prejudice in Right-Wing Authoritarians

Bob Altemeyer
University of Manitoba

Since its earliest days, the study of the authoritarian personality has been inti-mately involved with our struggle to understand prejudice (Adorno, Frenkel-Brunswik, Levinson, & Sanford, 1950). The famous team of researchers who collected around Nevitt Sanford at Berkeley during World War II set out, in the first instance, to understand the anti-Semitism then rushing to its catastrophic climax in Europe. The "Berkeley researchers" found that anti-Semites were profoundly ethnocentric as well, disliking a wide range of outgroups while overglorifying their own ingroups. Interviews of persons who scored highly on an Ethnocentrism scale revealed, the Berkeley team thought, an underlying personality structure that they labeled *prefascist*. Whereupon they developed another attitude scale to ensnare the potentially fascist personality. Remarkably, scores on that test, the Fascism scale, and ethnocentrism correlated about .75 over a wide range of samples.

It turned out, however, that those dazzling findings were largely produced by methodological shortcomings (Christie & Jahoda, 1954). In particular, the high E and F scale correlations were due to shared response sets. Some people answer-ing a psychological test tend to say "Yes" or "Agree" when they do not under-stand the question, have no real opinion, or (horrors!) do not particularly care about the researcher's quest. Others, perhaps positively unhappy about having been maneuvered into serving in the studies, *dis*agree right and left. Because all the items on the E and F scales were worded in the protrait, ethnocentric/fascist direction, the president of the American Civil Liberties Union would score higher than Adolf Hitler on these tests if, to get rid of the researcher, he or she merely said "agree" to each item. This yea-saying would bond the two scales together, whatever they measured.

An even larger, conceptual problem handicapped the Berkeley research program at the gate. The construct of the prefascist personality was rather vague and muddled. It was defined as the covariation of nine traits, such as "cynicism and destructiveness" and "sex." But *cynicism* is not the same thing as *destructiveness*, or even necessarily correlated with it. Furthermore, none of the "nine" traits was defined at any length. For example "sex" was defined as simply "an exaggerated concern with sexual 'goings-on'" (Adorno et al., 1950, p. 228). This would seem to apply equally to a bowdlerizing prude, the Marquis de Sade, and the man whose theory of personality inspired the Berkeley model, Sigmund Freud.

Even though these and other major problems were pointed out just a few years after *The Authoritarian Personality* appeared (Adorno et al., 1950), a publishing frenzy of F Scale studies broke out in the 1950s, and lasted well into the 1960s. For the most part it went nowhere, for the predictable reason that no one knew what the F Scale actually measured, and because so many of the findings contradicted one another (Altemeyer, 1981).

By the mid-1960s the literature on authoritarianism was so confused and frustrating that, one by one, investigators quietly gave up. Ironically, this was the time of Selma, Saigon, Kent State, and again, Berkeley. The world was embroiled with authoritarian issues, as it still is, and psychology was mired in confusion.

A CASE STUDY IN OVERCOMPENSATION

I on the other hand was too inexcusably ignorant to be confused. I first became acquainted with the study of authoritarianism in 1965, when Daryl Bem thoughtfully asked me a PhD candidacy exam question about the F Scale and response sets. (The question was inspired by the chapter on authoritarianism in Roger Brown's wonderful 1965 social psychology text. Ultimately, this is ALL BROWN'S FAULT.) I failed the question with distinction, and had to write a redemptive paper. You don't have to be much of an Adlerian to figure out the rest.

When I scrunched up my face and looked very critically at the F Scale literature I discovered that, from the original Berkeley data onward, the only appreciable level of covariation among the items on the test appeared among statements tapping the first three of the "nine" traits: (a) "conventionalism," (b) "authoritarian submission," and (c) "authoritarian aggression." This was still true in data I collected in Manitoba in the early 1970s. And though in subsequent studies I dealt in various other measures of "authoritarianism," such as Rokeach's (1960) Dogmatism Scale, nothing really hung together except these three kinds of attitudes. They still clustered together when I began mixing *contrait* versions of these sentiments into the stew.

Right-Wing Authoritarianism

As I experimented with different ways of tapping these attitudes, I began to sense what the underlying sentiments were. By 1973 I believed *right-wing authoritarianism* could be usefully defined as the covariation of three attitudinal clusters:

authoritarian submission—a high degree of submission to the authorities who are perceived to be established and legitimate in the society in which one lives;

authoritarian aggression—a general aggressiveness, directed against various persons, that is perceived to be sanctioned by established authorities.

conventionalism—a high degree of adherence to the social conventions that are perceived to be endorsed by society and its established authorities.

The same studies that led to this conceptualization (which is defined at length in Altemeyer, 1981) also eventually led to a balanced 30-item attitude scale to measure it, which I creatively named the RWA scale. Gratifyingly, this test proved more internally consistent, more unidimensional, and more empirically valid than five other measures of authoritarianism (including the original F scale) in a series of pitting studies conducted in Canada and the United States in 1973–1974.

Ten years after publishing these results, the cumulative evidence indicates that the RWA scale does actually measure right-wing authoritarianism. North Americans who score highly on the test tend to support many unlawful and unjust acts by their governments, such as illegal searches, denial of the right to peaceful protest, and systematic police harassment. Similarly, American High Right-Wing Authoritarians (RWAs) tended to support Richard Nixon to the very end of Watergate and afterwards felt he had done little wrong. They did not want Nixon put on trial. Nor are high RWAs punitive toward other authorities who beat prisoners in jail or who order the killing of civilians in war (Altemeyer, 1981).

On the other hand, Highs (i.e., the top quartile of a RWA scale distribution) tend to be quite punitive toward "common criminals" when they are asked to recommend sentences. They believe, more than most people do, that harsh punishment works and that criminals deserve it. But they also admit that they get some personal pleasure out of being able to punish criminals. Similarly, when subjects were given a chance to administer electric shocks (supposedly) to a peer during a fake learning experiment, high RWAs delivered significantly stronger shocks than did others (Altemeyer, 1981).

As for conventionalism, RWA scale scores are linked in many ways to various aspects of traditional religious behavior and outlook (Altemeyer, 1988). Highs tend to be the most orthodox members of all the denominations tested to date, believing most strongly whatever that particular religion traditionally teaches. They also tend to lead the league in feeling morally superior to persons who act differently from them. For example, they highly disapprove of homosexuality and do not think "gay bashing" is as serious a crime as most people do.

Politically, persons who score highly on the RWA scale tend to favor the "conservative" political parties in their countries: the Progressive Conservatives in Canada and the Republicans in the United States. Whereas the correlations summarized in the three preceeding paragraphs roam around in the .40s to .60s, the connections with political party preference in normal samples are much smaller. If, however, one takes into account how interested people are in politics, one finds more substantial connections. Indeed, the strongest RWA scale relationships discovered thus far appeared between "left-" and "right-wing" lawmakers in four Canadian provincial legislators (Altemeyer, 1988).

This is interesting, because a fair amount of evidence indicates High RWAs have very little commitment to democracy. Among university students and their parents, Highs usually claim to be the biggest patriots of all. But they are vulnerable to arguments that their country has "too much" freedom, so the Charter of Rights and Freedoms (in Canada) or the Bill of Rights (in the United States) should be repealed. If such a group of subjects is asked if they would be willing to locate and arrest Communists (or radicals, or homosexuals, or members of religious cults) and then have them tortured and even executed, most people say, "absolutely not." But High RWAs say, "Possibly" (Altemeyer, 1988).

So general is Highs' availability for "posse duty" that they are even relatively willing to help persecute "persons who are highly submissive to authorities, aggressive against anyone the authorities pick, and highly conventional." That is, themselves. This is funny only if one ignores the threat such people implicitly pose to a democratic society.

Consider these four protrait items from the current version of the RWA scale:

1. "Our country will be destroyed someday if we do not smash the perversions eating away at our moral fiber and traditional beliefs."
2. "The situation in our country is getting so serious, the strongest methods would be justified if they eliminated the troublemakers and got us back to our true path."
3. "Once our government leaders condemn the dangerous elements in our society, it will be the duty of every patriotic citizen to help stomp out the rot that is poisoning our country from within."
4. "What our country really needs is a strong, determined leader who will crush evil and take us back to our true path."

Most of the High RWAs in my university student/parent samples agree with these items that could easily appear in some Nazi cheerbook. That probably translates into tens of millions of North Americans.

RWA Scale Scores and Prejudice

Given all this, you will probably not be surprised to learn that RWA scale scores correlate significantly with various measures of prejudice. The *r*s with balanced ethnocentrism scales have been in the .30 to .50 range among North American students and their parents (Altemeyer, 1988). (Highs tend to show more prejudice when they answer anonymously, which may remind you of Batson's findings in chapter 7, this volume, concerning overt versus covert measures of prejudice.) RWA scale scores also correlate .50 to .65 with hostility toward homosexuals, which authoritarians are more willing to reveal than hostility toward Blacks, Jews, aboriginals, etc. Duckitt (1990) found RWA connections from .53 to .69 with a variety of measures of anti-Black prejudice among White South African students. McFarland, Ageyev, and Abalakina (1990) discovered RWA scale scores in the Soviet Union correlated .55 with anti-Semitism and .63 with dislike for ethnic nationalities in the country.

[As predicted, High RWAs in the Soviet Union support the Communist Party and oppose democratization. They also tend to support the "hard-line" Communist leaders, such as Prime Minister Pavlov, who staged the coup in August 1991 (McFarland, Ageyev, & Abalakina, 1991). In general, American and Russian Highs have mirror images of who caused the Cold War and who the "good guys" are (Altemeyer & Kamenshikov, 1992). Russian Highs dislike capitalism as much as American Highs dislike Communism. If they had grown up in the other country, they would probably feel just the opposite.]

Causes of Prejudice

Although the RWA-prejudice relationships discovered to date are relatively substantial, they do not support the Berkeley finding that the prefascist personality is a major source of prejudice. The highest RWA-ethnocentrism connection I have found is a .71 correlation among 204 American state legislators in 1991. Therefore, although authoritarians tend to be ethnocentric, so are some *non*authoritarians.

We can find other explanations in particular cases. For example, Hunsberger and I (Altemeyer & Hunsberger, 1992) recently discovered that persons who scored highly on a Religious Fundamentalism scale—or who scored low on an expanded version of Batson and Ventis' (1982) Quest scale—tended to be hostile toward homosexuals, even after hefty mutual correlations with RWA scale scores were partialled out. So prejudice against gays may arise independently from a certain kind of religious training.

But a more general answer to the question of what causes prejudice may lay in Tajfel's (1981) theory of social identity. People appear to divide the world rather automatically into favored ingroups and less favored outgroups (Tajfel, Billig, Bundy & Flament, 1971; Tajfel & Turner, 1979). This probably lays a foundation for ethnocentrism in nearly all of us.

We have additionally been exposed to societal stereotypes loaded with heavy emotional baggage, usually when we are young and learning such concepts as "Jew" and "Black." These give particular shape to the tendency to disparage outgroups. And some of us encounter persons who confirm these stereotypes (e.g. there *are* absent-minded whatchamacallits). And some people, living frustrated and unsuccessful lives, may seek others to blame for their failures. And we may personally prosper if others have less of a chance in life. And so on. You do not have to be authoritarian to be prejudiced.

But authoritarians do tend to be bigots. Indeed, RWA scale scores among White North Americans have correlated with prejudice against so many different minorities (Blacks, Hispanics, Jews, aboriginal peoples, Sikhs, Japanese, Chinese, Pakistanis, Filipinos, Africans, Arabs, feminists, homosexuals, and— where I come from—Francophones) that one could say right-wing authoritarians are "equal opportunity bigots" (Altemeyer, 1981, 1988). What is the cause of such wide-ranging hostility?

Causes of Authoritarian Prejudice

For starters, the mainspring of ethnocentrism that Tajfel discovered in his minimal group effect experiments appears to be wound a little tighter in right-wing authoritarians. In September 1990, I gave my two introductory psychology classes a logical reasoning test. Then I asked them if they thought one of the classes would score higher on the test. Most students sensibly said there would be no predictable difference. The students who did think one group would be superior almost always picked their own class (for which there was no known justification; actually, the students had only been together for one previous meeting). High RWAs were twice as likely to show this ingroup preference as were Low RWAs ($p < .02$). (This finding was replicated in September 1991.)

In the same vein, I gave the RWA scale and the initial version of Duckitt's Group Cohesiveness scale to 422 other introductory psychology students at the same time. The latter contains items such as "Our society cannot afford disunity in these difficult times" and (a contrait) "Diversity in culture and lifestyle must be encouraged in any healthy society." The two tests correlated .49, indicating again that High RWAs place greater value upon their group memberships than most people do.

Which other roots might authoritarian prejudice have, besides a heightened concern for social identity? The psychoanalytically inclined Berkeley researchers believed their prefascists were redirecting repressed hatred of their cold, harsh parents. However, Bandura's (1973) instigate–disinhibit social-learning model of aggressive behavior provides a better explanation (Altemeyer, 1988). High RWAs fear a dangerous world more than most people do and they are also self-righteous. Fear thus seems to tighten the finger on the trigger, whereas self-righteousness releases the safety on the gun. Studies in Canada (Altemeyer, 1988) and the United States have found that measures of these two variables can explain, between them, most of the connection between RWA scale scores and many examples of authoritarians' aggression, including their many prejudices.

All this fits rather well into our understanding of the origins of personal authoritarianism, which again follows a social learning model (Altemeyer, 1988). Most young children are authoritarian—in attitude anyway. But some become markedly less so during adolescence. Teenagers who experience—directly or vicariously—a lot of unfair treatment by authorities, who meet minorities, who have rewarding experiences with unconventional/forbidden behavior, and so on tend to be Low RWAs by the time they enter the university.

The incoming Highs, on the other hand, usually have not had these experiences, mainly because they travel in such small, tight circles that they seldom get to know gays, radicals, persons who use marijuana, and so on. The tight circles are to be expected from persons who emphasize group cohesiveness, just as that strong ingroup/outgroup dichotomization fits hand in glove with an underlying fear and self-righteousness.

The tight circles have further implications. When I have administered anonymous ethnocentrism scales and then asked respondents to estimate how prejudiced they will be compared with others serving in the study, High RWAs usually think they will be average. Their lack of insight may be due partly to common social comparison processes. Compared to the people Highs know, their prejudices probably are normal. They do not necessarily appreciate how prejudiced their circle of acquaintances is, relative to the rest of the population. (On the other hand most Low RWAs, having broader experiences, realize they are comparatively unprejudiced.)

The Defensiveness of Authoritarians

But this is only part of the reason authoritarians tend to be blind to themselves. Experiments have also indicated many Highs stiff arm ego-threatening material. In March 1989, I gave students bogus feedback about how they had scored on a self-esteem scale. Half were randomly told they had very high self-esteem, and the others were told the opposite. Then I offered the students information supporting the validity of the scale. Of the Low RWAs, 67% of those who had received high self-esteem scores, and 63% of those who had received low self-esteem scores wanted that information. And 73% of the High RWAs who had gotten good news about their self-esteem also asked for evidence that the measure was valid. But only 47% of the authoritarians who had gotten bad news about themselves asked for the information ($p < .001$).

(I dehoaxed the students immediately, and suggested that if they took their scores seriously, they probably gave too much credence to individual results on psychological tests.)

Direct evidence of some authoritarians' *I Don't Want To Know* attitude came in 1992 when I administered a booklet of surveys under "secret number" conditions. Students again answered anonymously, except they wrote down a personally relevant number that they would recognize when I (supposedly) brought individual feedback sheets to their class. After answering an ethnocentrism scale, the students were asked "If it turns out you are highly prejudiced compared with the others, do you want to be told?" Seventy-six percent of the Low RWAs said "yes," compared with 55% of the High RWAs ($p < .001$).

Changing Right-Wing Authoritarians' Prejudices

These results indicate it will be hard to change authoritarians' prejudices through self-insight. But a number of societal approaches can still be recommended. One obvious tack is to reduce Highs' fear and self-righteousness. The media might curb their tendencies to overemphasize violent crime (I am a dreamer, I know). Social reformers should devote themselves to nonviolent protest. Religions can strive to lower self-righteousness.

Another obvious tack is to help authoritarians move out of their tight circles. Accordingly, university education appears to lower Highs' authoritarianism (Altemeyer, 1988), perhaps because of their sterling professors and enlightening studies. But my own sermonizing against authoritarianism in class has always failed to show an effect when I made the mistake of including a control group. More likely, I think, university increases the radius of authoritarians' circle of acquaintances. Many of them probably meet more "different" people at college than they have met in all their previous years.

Rokeach's Value Confrontation Procedure

The value confrontation technique invented by Milton Rokeach (1973), although it is a "self-insight" approach, also catches one's eye. It has subjects rank a number of values, including *freedom* and *equality*. *Freedom* is usually ranked pretty high, *equality* rather low. Later, subjects are given back their own ratings, and told the average rankings obtained from the group studied. Attention is drawn to the discrepancy between the *freedom* and *equality* means, and it is pointed out that most people seem more interested in their own freedom than in that of others.

Rokeach believed this feedback produced feelings of self-dissatisfaction within those subjects who had a big spread between those rankings. He then nailed down his point about selfishness by presenting evidence that those who ranked *equality* close to *freedom* had positive attitudes toward civil rights demonstrations, whereas those who did not, did not.

Rokeach and his associates found this procedure not only raised ratings of *equality*, and produced verbal support for civil rights demonstrations up to 15 months later (Penner, 1971; Rokeach, 1973; Rokeach & Cochrane, 1972; Rokeach & McClellan, 1972; Sherrid & Beech, 1976), it also had long-term behavioral pay-offs. Michigan State students who underwent personal value confrontation in 1968 were three times as likely as control subjects to join a civil rights support group four months later (Rokeach, 1973). Furthermore, persons in eastern Washington who viewed without interruption all of a 30-minute television program on value inconsistency (which did *not* include personal confrontation) gave four to six times as much money as nonviewers to relevant causes several months later (Ball-Rokeach, Rokeach, & Grube, 1984).

As Cook and Flay (1978) observed, however, value confrontation has not always worked. Penner (1971) found no effect on the nonverbal behavior of White students interacting with a Black confederate 3 months after the manipulation. Rokeach and McClellan (1972) got very little support for a Committee To End Racism proposed to students 4 months after personal-value confrontation. And Sherrid and Beech (1976) found such confrontation had no effect 2 months later on New York City policemen's (limited) willingness to attend a seminar on human relations on their day off.

The record is by no means convincing, therefore. But the procedure was put to very demanding tests in some of these experiments. And we *are* a little short of effective antiprejudice techniques. So I recently set out to see if personal-value confrontation could reduce prejudice among right-wing authoritarians.

THE MAY 1990 STUDY

Method

In September 1989, I administered a booklet of surveys to 372 students attending two sections of the introductory psychology course at the University of Manitoba. As always, the first task in this booklet was the RWA scale. Task 2 asked the students to rank 10 values in terms of their personal importance:

A sense of accomplishment (5.29) [.03]
A world at peace (4.66) [−.06]
Equality (3.99) [−.19]
Family security (5.25) [.32]
Freedom (6.16) [−.07]
Happiness (7.72) [−.07]

Mature love (5.32) [−.01]
Self-respect (6.78) [−.05]
True friendship (5.46) [−.02]
Wisdom (4.41) [.06]

Task 3 (printed on the same page as the value rankings) reminded the students of the demonstrations that the Aboriginal community in Manitoba (its largest and most disadvantaged minority) had conducted "to protest their treatment by the police, and by bureaucrats and politicians in the government." After inviting the subjects to write down their reactions to these demonstrations, Task 3 asked them (again following Rokeach, 1973), "How, in general, do you react to Indian demands for a better place in society?" Three alternatives were presented:

1. Not much reaction, one way or the other.
2. I sympathize with them and support them.
3. I don't sympathize with them.

Preliminary Results.   The mean ranking of each value is printed in parentheses in the previous listing. (Subjects actually called their highest value "No. 1," but the scale has been reversed so that a high ranking results in a high number.) As seen, *happiness* has the highest average ranking, *freedom* places third, and (sadly) *equality* comes in dead last of these 10. The correlations between students' RWA scale scores and their rankings for each value are given in brackets. Only two attained significance: Highs tended to value *equality* less than Lows did, and family security more.

Most Lows (80%) and most Highs (85%) ranked *freedom* ahead of *equality*, but (as one would infer from the negative correlation with *equality* just reported) the gap between the two was significantly smaller for Lows (mean = 2.01) than it was for Highs (2.74) ($t = 1.72$; $p < .05$ by a one-tailed test).

On Task 3, 25% of the students said they were neutral toward the Aboriginal protest movement, 38% said they sympathize with it, and 37% said they did not. But Lows were significantly more sympathetic than were Highs. Twenty-three of the 92 Lows were neutral, 42 were sympathetic, and 27 were unsympathetic. The same values for the 91 Highs were 20, 28, and 43 (chi-squared = 6.64; $p < .05$).

The Value-Confrontation Manipulation.   In late March 1990, when the university's regular term was nearly over, I reappeared in the larger of these two classes to give feedback about the purpose of my September survey. After securing the students' promise to keep all I said secret, I spoke briefly about right-wing authoritarianism and then gave each student the Task2/Task3 sheet he or she had filled out 6 months earlier. One hundred and sixty-four were claimed; 93 absent students, for whom I had September answers, provided a control group (once I had eliminated the students who had dropped the course). There were only trivial overall differences in the September answers of the experimental and control groups.

I followed Rokeach's procedures as carefully as I could from his published descriptions. I wrote the 10 average value rankings on the blackboard and also chalked up a table of numbers which showed that sympathizers had a relatively small gap between their *freedom* and *equality* rankings, whereas neutrals had a larger gap, and nonsympathizers had the largest gap of all. The key statement in my talk, taken from Rokeach (1973), was:

> This raises the question as to whether those who don't sympathize with the native peoples are really saying they care a great deal about their own freedom, but are indifferent to other people's freedom. For such people, *equality* ranked very low. Those who sympathize with the native movement are perhaps really saying they not only want freedom for themselves, but for other people too. You can look at your own rankings, to see how much value you placed on *equality*, especially compared with that for *freedom*.

I asked for questions and was asked a lovely one about whether one would find the same relationship in South Africa among anti-Black Whites? (I replied, "probably.") I thanked the class and its instructor and left.

A Behavioral Measure of Change.   Seven weeks later, after the school year had ended, each of the Low and High RWA students who was still enrolled in the course in March was mailed a letter, printed on the university's Department of Native Studies letterhead, from the head of that department. The letter stated that the head was thinking of asking the university to set aside some of its general scholarship funds just for Native students. Specifically, the head was thinking of proposing that $1,000 scholarships be awarded each year to four Aboriginals. However, before proceeding he wanted to see how the student body in general reacted to this idea. The recipient was supposedly 1 of 100 students selected at random by the university's computer to answer a simple, anonymous poll on this matter.

A ballot was printed on the bottom of the letter, on which the student could indicate if she or he did or did not favor the proposal. These ballots were discretely coded to indicate if the student was a Low or High, experimental or control subject. A stamped envelope, addressed to the head of the Native Studies Department, accompanied the letter.

I should explain, before getting to the results, that I was purposely putting Rokeach's procedure to a stiff test here. The biggest complaint Caucasian students at my university have about Aboriginal people is that "they get everything free, and still are demanding more handouts and special treatment." (Some persons of Aboriginal descent in Canada are entitled by treaty to have their university expenses paid by the federal government. However, the funds are quite limited, and very few natives attempt a university education.) So from the perspective of many White students, seeking summer jobs in May so they could return to school in the fall, the affirmative action proposal to set aside scholarships just for natives would crash headlong into their foremost gripe about Indians. Many of them made this clear in comments they attached to their ballots.

I should also explain that $1,000 is not an insignificant sum in this context. Tuition for a year of study at my university this particular year was about $1600.

Results

Seventeen of the 65 September Lows (i.e., persons who scored less than 127 on the RWA scale; the bottom quartile) were not in class the day I performed the value confrontation, but were still in the course. Another 5 had dropped the course. Thirteen of these Low Controls returned their ballots, of whom 10 (77%) said they favored the proposal.

Of the 43 Lows who heard my presentation, 24 replied to the head's letter. Fifteen of these Low experimentals (62% approval—not significantly different from the Low Controls: $z = 0.89$; $p > .30$) favored establishing the Native scholarships.

Fifteen of the 64 September Highs (who scored over 162 on the RWA Scale; the upper quartile) formed the High control group. (Eight other Highs had dropped the course.) Eight returned their ballots, voting 6–2 against the proposal (25% approval).

Of the 41 Highs who experienced the value confrontation, 26 replied. They voted 15–11 in favor of the affirmative action program (58% approval). This High experimental value is significantly greater than the High control result ($z = 1.78$, $p < .04$ by a one-tailed test). It is also virtually the same as that found among the Low experimentals.

The December 1990 Follow-Up Study

About 7 months later I hired an experienced telephone pollster to phone as many of the Highs as could be located in the current student telephone directory. She reached 17 of the 41 experimental Highs and 5 of the 15 control Highs. (I have no way of knowing how many of these students had replied to the mail solicitation.)

My interviewer, blind to the purpose of the study, said she was working for Cross Canada Polls which was "doing a nationwide poll of university students' opinions about the big issues in the news during 1990. Your name was selected at random from the University of Manitoba Student Directory, and I'd like to ask you a few questions. It will only take a minute or so, OK?" (All agreed, showing these students had not been stung enough by magazine sellers, etc. over the phone yet.)

Questions were then asked about the Meech Lake Constitutional Accord and the proposed federal sales tax, basically to give the student some experience with the 5-point Likert response scale being used. Then the relevant question was posed:

"Do you personally oppose, or support, Canadian Indians' demands for self-government, quicker settlement of their land claims, and voting rights at constitutional conferences?" This too was a high ball proposition. It would give Canadian aboriginals virtually everything they had been demanding for years.

Three of the five control Highs *strongly opposed* this proposition, another was *somewhat opposed,* and the fifth *somewhat supported* it. On a 1–5 basis, the control mean was 1.8.

Two of the 17 experimental Highs were also strongly opposed, and 4 were somewhat opposed. But 3 were neutral, 7 somewhat supported the proposal, and 1 strongly supported it. The experimental mean of 3.06 was significantly higher ($t = 1.95$; $p < .05$ by a one-tailed test) than the controls. Seemingly then, the effect of the value confrontation lasted many months and was not just a one shot conscience salver.

THE MAY 1991 STUDY

Statistical significance notwithstanding, I simply do not believe one can wipe out the difference in prejudice between Lows and Highs in 20 minutes. So I laid my plans for replication and extension of the experiment during the following year.

Method

First, in the fall of 1990 I administered booklets of surveys containing the value ranking and reaction-to-aboriginal-demonstrations tasks to two sections of introductory psychology. I also gave out another booklet that included religious questionnaires to two other sections, and I sent similar booklets home to these latter students' parents.

Then, between March 19 and April 2, 1991, I appeared in each of these classes to give feedback about the purpose and results of my earlier surveys.

In the first such session, done with students who had ranked values in September, I swore them to secrecy and then gave them exactly the same blackboard feedback I had used the previous year. Only I did not hand back their personal answers from the fall, but instead just gave them unused rating forms so they could follow along with my chalk talk. Thus, these nonpersonal value confrontation subjects received the disconcerting group scores and the punch line about "This raises the question. . ." , but nothing that undeniably implicated them personally.

In my second and fourth feedback sessions, done with the two classes given religious surveys, I swore them to secrecy and then gave them veridical feedback about authoritarianism, religiosity, and prejudice. I reported that, for both students and their parents, High RWAs tend to score highly on the Religious Fundamentalism scale I mentioned earlier. And I reported that persons who agree with items such as:

> "God has given mankind a complete, unfailing guide to happiness and salvation, which must be totally followed," and "God's true followers must remember that he requires them to *constantly* fight Satan and Satan's allies on this earth,"

also tend to agree with such statements as:

> "Indians are spoiled; they should realize what a good deal they get in our country," and "Our native Indians should try to fit into the White man's society and stop acting like children and savages."

I made the point that "fundamentalists" appeared in all the religions covered in the sample, not just those sometimes named so. But again, all of this was general, not personal. These nonpersonal religious confrontation subjects did not get their original survey answers back.

Finally in the remaining class, visited on March 25th, I swore them to secrecy, too, and then repeated the personal value confrontation procedures used the previous year. That is, these subjects got exactly the same chalk talk and the value rankings and the reactions-to-aboriginal-demonstrations they had personally given 6 months earlier.

I passed an attendance sheet around in all four classes, supposedly for a study I was doing on class attendance at the end of the school year. The professors involved were kept blind as to my purpose and may only have suspected I was doing more than just giving feedback to their students when I later asked for a copy of their final class lists (needed to eliminate students who had dropped the course). Finally, I chose the class for the personal value confrontation, of the two available, by the flip of a coin.

In mid-May 1991, all of the experimental and control subjects were mailed the Aboriginal bursary letter used the previous year (updated) and a stamped, self-addressed envelope.

Results

Nonpersonal value confrontation had no effect on support for the Aboriginal bursaries. Of the 26 Lows who heard my presentation, 16 returned their ballots for this program. Eight of these (50%) supported the proposal. The figures for the 13 Control Lows, who were still enrolled in the course but not in class that day, were: 10 returned the ballot, of whom 6 (60%) favored the bursaries.

As for the 24 Highs who got only group results for the value confrontation, 16 responded to the mail-in poll, and 4 of these (25%) supported the scholarships. Seven Highs who were absent from class on the day of my presentation formed a High control group; of these, 6 gave replies, of whom 2 (33%) endorsed the bursaries.

You can see that Lows were, overall, significantly more in favor of the proposal than Highs were ($z = 1.74; p < .05$ by a one-tailed test). But that is old hat. Otherwise, things are pretty flat between controls and experimentals.

Neither did the nonpersonal religious confrontation do anything. The figures for the two classes combined (which were largely the same) were: Lows—33 heard that the more intensely "religious" they were, the more likely they were to be prejudiced against Indians. Of these, 24 answered the poll, of whom 14 (58%) voted for the special bursaries. Among the 16 controls, 8 responded, 4 (50%) in the affirmative.

Again, the Highs in these classes are less supportive than the Lows ($z = 2.54; p < .01$); but my "antireligion sermonette" had no effect upon them either: 29 heard it, 23 gave their opinions on the scholarships, of whom 7 (30%) supported them. The figures for the 18 control Highs were 2 (20%) of the 10 respondents in favor.

The Lows in the personal value confrontation condition resembled the Lows in the other classes. Of the 29 nonauthoritarians in class that day, 19 sent in their opinions, and 9 (47%) of them voted for special scholarships for aboriginals. Of the 33 control Lows, 22 responded, of whom 13 (59%) liked the idea. The difference between the two is nonsignificant ($z = 0.75; p > .30$).

Now to the crux. Of the 31 experimental Highs, 10 of the 18 respondents (56%) voted for the bursaries. This is again amazing. Except that among the 36 control Highs, 26 sent in their votes, of whom 13 (50%) answered positively. This difference between experimental and control Highs is NOT significant, nor is the overall difference between all Lows and all Highs ($z = 0.13; p > .70$).

The results of the first and second experiments are depicted in Fig. 6.1.

Discussion

Let us do the easy parts first. Nonpersonal value confrontation apparently does not make High RWAs more sympathetic to minorities, nor does nonpersonal religious confrontation. It is apparently easy to slough off group findings as personally irrelevant.

Secondly, authoritarians are ordinarily more prejudiced than nonauthoritarians, as evidenced in many samples, on many issues, for many minority targets. It is unusual for a group of Highs to be as unprejudiced as Lows drawn from the same source, as they were in the last condition. Something probably happened.

Did *personal* value confrontation change Highs? If we did not have the control group from this class, we would say, "Yes, unbelievably!" But within that class, those Highs who were confronted with their relatively low ranking of *equality*

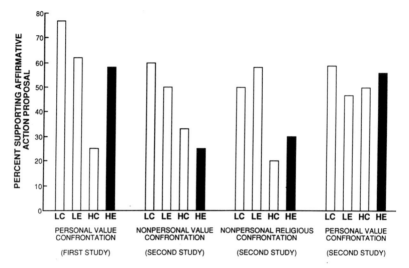

FIG. 6.1.   Creating support for an Affirmative Action Program among Right-Wing authoritarians. *Note:* LC = Low RWA Controls; LE = Low RWA Experimentals; HC = High RWA Controls; HE = High RWA Experimentals.

and their accompanying nonsupport of Aboriginals, did not support the affirmative action proposal any more than those Highs who missed this confrontation. (And I know the latter never saw their earlier responses, because I took them from the classroom with me.)

I questioned Dr. Hartsough, this section's instructor, at some length about his course and this particular class. Interestingly, he did not discuss prejudice at all in this course, or even social psychology. (Does that make students less prejudiced? Should we all shut up?) He also takes a rather idiographic approach, developing the theme that individuals are responsible for their own actions, and should not allow themselves to become group-formed group statistics. He did not think this class was different (e.g., in number of minorities) from classes he had had before. He does allow students who did well on earlier exams to skip the last one, which means brighter (Lows and Highs) were probably more likely to be in the control group in this class than in the others.

Pick your interpretation. For myself, I am still skeptical that Rokeach's technique works. (There is also a hint, in both studies, that it may backfire a bit among Lows.) But I am also sufficiently impressed by the big differences it produced—compared with other experimental approaches—to tell other researchers about these results now. Clearly we need more studies, with different populations and issues.

In closing, let me say I think Rokeach's procedure could conceivably change Highs. All of the feedback talks I gave probably made High RWAs defensive—

which we have seen is easily done—and hence likely to avoid thinking about the personal implications of the data. But the Highs in the personal value confrontation could see their own answers, so it was very difficult for them to kid themselves that the conclusion about equality and selfishness applied to someone else, but not to them.

I suspect personal value confrontation (and perhaps personal religious confrontation) would be particularly troubling to Highs, because they conceive of themselves as "the good people." When they could (or, had to) see a way in which they were falling short of their self-image, many may have resolved to change. They seemingly responded beautifully, nondefensively, constructively when an inconsistency in their thinking was pointed out. *Freedom* and *equality* are probably highly compartmentalized concepts in authoritarians' thinking, both endorsed with little thought, as cultural values. But when the connection was made between equality and other people's freedom, a more comprehensive, better integrated understanding of equality in society may have emerged.

Most Highs do not realize they are unusually submissive, conventional, and aggressive (Altemeyer, 1988). When they learn they are, they usually express some willingness to change. The right-wing authoritarians I study are not irredeemable Nazi-types as a rule, but fearful people whose circumstances have kept them in those tight circles. They would never suspect they are enemies of *freedom* or *equality*. But if one can get past the defenses they have thrown up to protect their vulnerabilities, as Rokeach's procedure might, Highs may be remarkably capable of change. This gives hope, if it is true.[1]

ACKNOWLEDGMENT

I would like to thank Professor Paul Chartrand and Frieda Ahenakew, Heads of the Department of Native Studies at my university, and Donald Salmon, Marvin Brodsky, Ross Hartsough, and Jim Shapiro, my colleagues teaching introductory psychology, for their valued cooperation in these studies.

REFERENCES

Adorno, T. W., Frenkel-Brunswik, E., Levinson, D. J., & Sanford, R. N. (1950). *The authoritarian personality*. New York: Harper & Row.
Altemeyer, B. (1981). *Right-wing authoritarianism*. Winnipeg: University of Manitoba Press.

---

[1]A replication of the personal value confrontation procedure in March 1992 produced the following results by the following summer: High controls ($N = 14$) = 21% support; High experimentals ($N = 14$) = 50% support; $z = 1.58$, $p < .15$ by a two-tailed test. Low controls ($N = 13$) = 54% support; Low experimentals ($N = 16$) = 56% support; $z = 0.13$, $p > .50$. A fourth experiment is being conducted in 1992–1993.

Altemeyer, B. (1988). *Enemies of freedom: Understanding right-wing authoritarianism.* San Francisco: Jossey-Bass.

Altemeyer, B., & Hunsberger, B. (1992). Authoritarianism, religious fundamentalism, quest and prejudice. *International Journal for the Psychology of Religion, 2,* 113–133.

Altemeyer, B., & Kamenshikov, A. (1991). Impressions of American and Soviet behaviour: RWA images in a mirror. *South African Journal of Psychology, 21,* 255–260.

Ball-Rokeach, S. J., Rokeach, M., & Grube, J. W. (1984). The great American values test. *Psychology Today, 18,* 34–41.

Bandura, A. (1973). *Aggression: A social learning analysis.* Englewood Cliffs, NJ: Prentice-Hall.

Batson, D., & Ventis, W. L. (1982). *The religious experience: A social psychological perspective.* New York: Oxford University Press.

Brown, R. (1965). *Social psychology.* New York: The Free Press.

Christie, R., & Jahoda, M. (Eds.). (1954). *Studies in the scope and method of "The authoritarian personality."* New York: The Free Press.

Cook, T. D., & Flay, B. R. (1978). The persistence of experimentally induced attitude change. In L. Berkowitz (Ed.), *Advances in experimental social psychology* (Vol. 11, pp. 2–57). New York: Academic Press.

Duckitt, J. H. (1990). *A social psychological investigation of racial prejudice among White South Africans.* Unpublished doctoral dissertation, University of Witwatersrand, Johannesburg.

McFarland, S., Ageyev, V. S., & Abalakina, M. A. (1990). *The authoritarian personality in the U.S.A. and the U.S.S.R.: Comparative studies.* Paper presented at the 13th meeting of the International Society of Political Psychology, Washington, DC.

McFarland, S., Ageyev, V. S., & Abalakina, M. A. (1991). *Russian authoritarianism and reactions to political leaders and events, and to conventional norms of distributive justice.* Paper presented at the 14th meeting of the International Society of Political Psychology, Helsinki.

Penner, L. A. (1971). Interpersonal attraction toward a Black person as a function of value importance. *Personality, 2,* 175–187.

Rokeach, M. (1960). *The open and closed mind.* New York: Basic Books.

Rokeach, M. (1973). *The nature of human values.* New York: The Free Press.

Rokeach, M., & Cochrane, R. (1972). Self-confrontation and confrontation with another as determinants of long-term value change. *Journal of Applied Social Psychology, 2,* 283–292.

Rokeach, M., & McClellan, D. D. (1972). Feedback of information about the values and attitudes of self and others as determinants of long-term cognitive and behavioral change. *Journal of Applied Social Psychology, 2,* 236–251.

Sherrid, S. D., & Beech, R. P. (1976). Self-dissatisfaction as a determinant of change in police values. *Journal of Applied Psychology, 61,* 273–278.

Tajfel, H. (1981). *Human groups and social categories.* Cambridge, England: Cambridge University Press.

Tajfel, H., Billig, M. G., Bundy, R. P., & Flament, C. (1971). Social categorization and intergroup behavior. *European Journal of Social Psychology, 1,* 149–178.

Tajfel, H., & Turner, J. C. (1979). An integrative theory of social conflict. In W. Austin & S. Worchel (Eds.), *The Social Psychology of Intergroup Relations* (pp. 33–47). Monterey, CA: Brooks/Cole.

7 Personal Religion: Depressant or Stimulant of Prejudice and Discrimination?

C. Daniel Batson
Christopher T. Burris
University of Kansas

Karl Marx described religion as the opiate of the masses. Adopting Marx's metaphor of religion as a drug, we wish to know whether religion is a depressant or stimulant of prejudice and discrimination. This question, although rarely cast in these terms, has been heavily researched by psychologists of religion.

The reason for interest in the effect of religion on prejudice is easy to understand. All major religions in our society preach love and acceptance of others. The acceptance is to be unconditional, not qualified by race, creed, sex, or color. Christianity in particular prides itself on its message of universal love: "There is neither Jew nor Greek, slave nor free, male nor female"—one might add, Black nor White—"for you are all one . . ." (Galatians 3:28). If a religion can indeed lead its followers to adopt and live such a belief, then it is a powerful antidote for prejudice—one overlooked by most social psychologists.

Yet, this preaching notwithstanding, history is littered with examples in which religion—Christianity included—has provided the justification if not the instigation for atrocious inhumanity to outgroups. Think of the Crusades, the Inquisition, witch hunts, slavery, missionaries' obliteration of native cultures, Northern Ireland, the Middle East; the list is endless. All too often, it seems, religion functions not as a prophetic voice calling the faithful to shed their intolerance and bigotry, but as a mighty fortress of ingroup superiority, one that justifies elitism, ethnocentrism, oppression, and even destruction of those who are different.

Robert Brannon (1970) observed, "Some critics of religion have gone so far as to charge that racial and ethnic intolerance is a natural extension of religious precepts" (p. 42). When one thinks back over the role of religion in Western civilization, this charge does not seem nearly as extreme as Brannon implies. Examples in which religious institutions and doctrines have encouraged racial

149

and ethnic intolerance come to mind at least as easily as examples in which religion has encouraged acceptance and tolerance. Before peddling the religious opiate as an antidote for prejudice and discrimination, then, one had best be sure of this drug's effects.

Psychologists of religion have attempted to move beyond the rhetoric of celebrating or castigating religion based on extreme examples, seeking empirical evidence to answer the question of whether personal religion is associated with decreased or increased prejudice and discrimination. We want to present an overview of what they have found. Before doing so, however, let us mention three characteristics of this research:

1. Different measures of intolerance, prejudice, and bigotry have been used. These measures include racism, ethnocentrism, anti-Semitism, and what we have called "other prejudice" (i.e., prejudice against other ethnic or national outgroups, such as Hispanics and Orientals).

2. The research focuses on the relation between personal religion and prejudice among White, middle-class Christians in the United States. This is both because of the accessibility of such individuals (most of the researchers have worked in the United States) and because prejudice within this group has been a major social problem over the past 5 decades.

3. The research is correlational. It does not actually assess the influence of religion on prejudice, only the relation between the two. Any relation found could result from the influence of prejudice on religion instead of the influence of religion on prejudice or from the influence of some third variable on each.

With these characteristics of the research in mind, let us take a look at what has been found.

PREJUDICE AND AMOUNT OF RELIGIOUS INVOLVEMENT

When persons are more religious, are they less prejudiced, more prejudiced, or is there no difference? Based on existing research, the answer is very clear: In spite of what religions preach about universal brotherhood, the more religious an individual is, the more prejudiced he or she is likely to be. In early studies, for example, Allport and Kramer (1946) found that Protestant and Catholic students were more likely than those with no religious affiliation to be prejudiced against Blacks. They also found that strong religious influence in the home correlated positively with racial prejudice. Rosenblith (1949) found a similar trend. Adorno, Frenkel-Brunswik, Levinson, and Sanford (1950) reported that both authoritarianism and ethnocentrism were higher among church attenders than among nonattenders. Kirkpatrick (1949) found that religious people had more punitive attitudes than nonreligious people toward criminals, delinquents, prostitutes, drug addicts, and those in need of psychiatric treatment. Stouffer (1955) demonstrated that among a representative sample of American church members, those who had attended church within the past month were more intolerant of nonconformists, socialists, and communists than were those who had not attended.

Rather than continue this litany, let us reproduce a line-score summary provided by Batson and Ventis (1982) of 44 findings concerning the relationship between one of the four types of intolerance and prejudice (racial prejudice, ethnocentrism, anti-Semitism, and other prejudice) and one of the three indexes of amount of religious involvement (church membership or attendance, positive attitudes toward religion, and orthodoxy or conservatism of religious beliefs). These findings were obtained across 36 different studies conducted between 1940 and 1975. (For a summary description of each study, including information concerning the population sampled, geographic location, religion measure used, prejudice measure used, and relationship reported, see Batson & Ventis, 1982, pp. 258–263.)

Although the uneven quality of research methods employed in these studies precludes a modern meta-analysis, one is not really necessary to determine the direction of the relationship. All it takes is a brief look at Table 7.1 to see that the score is very lopsided. Overall, 34 of the 44 findings reveal a positive relation between amount of prejudice and amount of interest in, involvement in, or

TABLE 7.1
Association Between Prejudice and Amount of Religious Involvement
(44 Findings from 36 Different Studies--1940-1975)

	Measure of Religious Involvement										
	Membership or Attendance			Strength of Religious Attitude			Strength of Orthodoxy or Conservatism			Total		
Measure of Prejudice	+	?	-	+	?	-	+	?	-	+	?	-
Racial prejudice	6	2	0	3	0	0	4	2	0	13	4	0
Ethnocentrism	3	0	0	3	0	1	2	0	0	8	0	1
Anti-Semitism	4	1	0	0	1	0	4	1	0	8	3	0
Prejudice against other minorities	2	0	0	1	0	0	2	1	1	5	1	1
Total	15	3	0	7	1	1	12	4	1	34	8	2

Note. Column entries in the table indicate: (a) the number of reports of a positive relationship between prejudice and amount of religious involvement, (b) the number of reports of no relationship, and (c) the number of reports of a negative relationship. Adapted by permission from *The Religious Experience* by C. D. Batson and W. L. Ventis. Copyright (1982) by Oxford University Press.

adherence to religion. Eight findings show no clear relationship; most of these were conducted in the northern United States. Only two findings indicate a negative relationship, and each is based on adolescent or preadolescent samples (Nias, 1972; Strommen, 1967). The different columns and rows in Table 7.1 show that the pattern of results is highly consistent regardless of how religion or prejudice is measured. The pattern is also highly consistent over time. The evidence summarized in Table 7.1 suggests a clear conclusion: Among White, middle-class Christians in the United States, religion is not associated with increased love and acceptance but with increased intolerance, prejudice, and bigotry.

PREJUDICE AND DIFFERENT WAYS OF BEING RELIGIOUS: THE EXTRINSIC–INTRINSIC DISTINCTION

One can well imagine the consternation among religious leaders as the evidence for a positive correlation between religion and prejudice began to pile up. Actually, the consternation was short lived, for several social psychogists—most notably Adorno et al. (1950) and Allport (1950, 1966)—pointed out a basic flaw in these studies: It is inappropriate to lump together all White, middle-class people who identify themselves as Christians. Allport (1966) argued most persuasively that one must distinguish between two ways of being religious: an *extrinsic* orientation, in which religion is a means to other ends, such as achieving social status or security, and an *intrinsic* orientation, in which religion is an end in itself, the "master motive" in life. He claimed that "both prejudice and religion are subjective formulations within the personal life. One of these formulations (the extrinsic) is entirely compatible with prejudice; the other (the intrinsic) rules out enmity, contempt, and bigotry" (Allport, 1966, p. 456). Allport's distinction implies that among individuals who are religious, the correlation between measures of the extrinsic orientation and prejudice may be positive, but the correlation between measures of the intrinsic orientation and prejudice should be negative.

To assess Allport's claim, some way of measuring extrinsic and intrinsic religion was needed. The most popular measurement strategy has been to type individuals as extrinsic or intrinsic based on relative scores on the Extrinsic and Intrinsic scales introduced by Allport and Ross (1967), or on similar instruments. The 11 items on the Extrinsic scale include, for example:

"Although I believe in my religion, I feel there are many more important things in my life."
"The church is most important as a place to formulate good social relationships."

"What religion offers me most is comfort when sorrows and misfortunes strike."

The 9 items on the Intrinsic scale include, for example:

"I try hard to carry my religion over into all my other dealings in life."
"If I were to join a church group, I would prefer to join a Bible study group rather than a social fellowship."
"My religious beliefs are what really lie behind my whole approach to life."

A second strategy has also been used. Gorsuch and McFarland (1972) noted that a fairly reliable measure of the distinction between extrinsic and intrinsic religion could be obtained by simply asking people about the frequency of their involvement in religious activities. The extrinsically religious should limit their involvement to a moderate level, because for them religion is subsumed under more important values and goals. The intrinsically religious, on the other hand, should be highly involved, because for them religion is the master motive in life. Employing this logic, a number of researchers have used three levels of involvement in religious activities to assess differences in religious orientation: (a) no or low involvement (e.g., less than four times a year), (b) moderate involvement (e.g., less than weekly), and (c) high involvement (e.g., at least weekly). The three levels are assumed to identify the nonreligious, extrinsically religious, and intrinsically religious, respectively. Consistent with this assumption, among religious individuals more involvement is highly positively correlated with scores on the Intrinsic scale but not with scores on the Extrinsic scale (Donahue, 1985; Gorsuch & McFarland, 1972). (Because attention has shifted from whether one is religious to how, and because it only makes sense to ask how one is religious if one is, nonreligious individuals are typically not included in research assessing different ways of being religious.)

Equipped with these two ways of operationalizing the extrinsic versus intrinsic distinction, we turn to empirical research on the relationship between each of these orientations and prejudice. Table 7.2 reproduces a line-score summary provided by Batson and Ventis (1982) of 40 findings obtained across 31 different studies conducted between 1949 and 1977. The first three columns of the table report 14 findings from 12 studies that used some form of questionnaire or interview data to make the distinction between extrinsic and intrinsic religion. The next three columns report 26 findings from 22 studies in which religious orientation was assessed by amount of religious activity broken into moderate (M) and high (H). The final three columns provide totals across both measurement strategies. (For a summary description of each study, including information concerning the population sampled, geographic location, religion measure used,

TABLE 7.2
Association Between Prejudice and Extrinsic Versus Intrinsic Religion
(40 Findings From 31 Different Studies--1949-1977)

	Measure of Religious Orientation								
	Extrinsic versus Intrinsic			Moderate versus High Attendance			Total		
Measure of Prejudice	E < I	E = I	E > I	M < H	M = H	M > H			
Racial prejudice	0	0	6	0	2	10	0	2	16
Ethnocentrism	0	0	1	0	0	2	0	0	3
Anti-Semitism	0	0	3	0	0	6	0	0	9
Prejudice against other minorities	0	0	4	0	0	6	0	0	10
Total	0	0	14	0	2	24	0	2	38

Note. Column entries in the table indicate: (a) the number of reports that E < I (extrinsic less prejudiced than intrinsic) or M < H (moderate attenders less prejudiced than high attenders), (b) the number of reports of no difference, and (c) the number of reports that E > I or M > H. Adapted by permission from *The Religious Experience* by C. D. Batson and W. L. Ventis. Copyright (1982) by Oxford University Press.

prejudice measure used, and relationship reported, see Batson & Ventis, 1982, pp. 266–270.)

Once again, the pattern of results across the studies is extremely clear, even clearer than it is for the relationship between amount of religious involvement and prejudice. As predicted by Allport, the way one is religious makes a great difference; the more intrinsically religious are consistently found to be less prejudiced than the extrinsically religious. In all 14 findings in the first three columns of Table 7.2, those who were classified as intrinsic scored lower on prejudice, however measured, than those classified as extrinsic. In 24 of the 26 findings in the next three columns, those who were highly involved in religious activities scored lower on prejudice, however measured, than those who were only moderately involved. Moreover, one of the two studies that found no difference assessed attitudes toward political issues concerning minority rights, not prejudice (Rokeach, 1969). The other assessed racial attitudes of White Catholics in the Florida panhandle who had recently migrated from the North and were members of an integrated church (Liu, 1961). Self-selection as a member of an integrated church in the Deep South could easily account for the lack of difference in this study.

Clearly, the earlier conclusion that there is a positive relationship between religious involvement and prejudice needs to be revised. Apparently, in studies measuring the amount of religious involvement, the relatively low prejudice of the intrinsically religious minority was masked by the high prejudice of the extrinsically religious majority. When these different ways of being religious are taken into account, a more appropriate conclusion seems to be: The extrinsically religious may be high in intolerance and prejudice, but the intrinsically religious are relatively low. This revised conclusion has been widely accepted among psychologists interested in religion (e.g., Gorsuch, 1988; Gorsuch & Aleshire, 1974).

The question of the relation between religion and prejudice seems to be neatly answered. Although being more religious correlates with being more intolerant and prejudiced, this is true only among those who have emasculated the more profound claims of their religion and are using it as an extrinsic means to self-serving ends. In studies that include individuals who report low as well as moderate and high interest and involvement in religion, extrinsically religious individuals appear more prejudiced than individuals with little interest and involvement; correlations of the Extrinsic scale with measures of prejudice are typically positive (Donahue, 1985).

But those who take their religion seriously, dealing with it as an intrinsic end in itself, are not more prejudiced. Even though the intrinsically religious are rarely found to be less prejudiced than individuals with little interest and involvement in religion, they are not more so. In studies that include individuals who report low as well as moderate and high interest and involvement, correlations of the Intrinsic scale with measures of prejudice are typically near zero (Donahue, 1985). Intrinsic religion may not have the active ingredients that depress prejudice and bigotry that Allport (1966) claimed, but at least it does not seem to contain the stimulant that extrinsic religion does.

DOUBTS

Perhaps because this revised conclusion regarding the religion–prejudice relationship was far more satisfying to researchers interested in religion than was the original conclusion, it has seldom been questioned. We believe, however, that it should be. We have doubts about the adequacy of both the assessment of prejudice in the summarized research and the assessment of personal religion.

Self-Presentation on Overt, Questionnaire Measures of Prejudice

Concerning the assessment of prejudice, we worry about self-presentation (Jones & Pittman, 1982). In all but one of the studies summarized in Table 7.2, prejudice was measured by questionnaire, and prejudice questionnaires are usually quite transparent. Although none directly ask, "Are you a racist bigot?" many come close.

For example, on the prejudice measure used by Allport and Ross (1967) and called by them "subtly worded," respondents were asked their attitudes about a landlord in an all-White neighborhood refusing to rent to a young Black woman and about an informal business luncheon club refusing membership to a Jewish executive. We suspect that respondents, well aware of issues of prejudice and discrimination that have been so prominent over the past several decades, could easily detect the purpose of such questions and, if they were concerned to present themselves as free from prejudice, would mark the low-prejudice responses (see Crosby, Bromley, & Saxe, 1980; Gaertner & Dovidio, 1986; Karlins, Coffman, & Walters, 1969; Sigall & Page, 1971; Silverman, 1974, for more detailed discussion of self-presentation problems with questionnaire measures of prejudice).

Moreover, there is reason to believe that individuals scoring relatively high on intrinsic religion are likely to be more concerned with a "colorblind" self-presentation than individuals scoring relatively high on extrinsic religion. First, strong agreement with items assessing intrinsic religion (e.g., "I try hard to carry my religion over into all my other dealings in life") is likely to be more socially desirable than strong agreement with items assessing extrinsic religion (e.g., "Although I believe in my religion, I feel there are many more important things in my life"). Thus, high scores on the Intrinsic scale may reflect desire for positive self-presentation, at least in the religious domain, whereas high scores on the Extrinsic scale may not.

Consistent with this suggestion, Batson, Naifeh, and Pate (1978) found a moderate positive correlation between scores on the Intrinsic scale and the Marlowe–Crowne (1964) Social Desirability scale (SDS) (r (48) = +.36; $p <$ .01). Subsequent research (e.g., Watson, Morris, Foster, & Hood, 1986) also typically found a positive correlation between these two scales, although of a lower magnitude; a more accurate estimate of the correlation between these scales seems to be around +.20.[1] In contrast, correlations of the Extrinsic scale with the SDS are typically either close to zero or low negative.

---

[1]Interpretation of this relationship between the Intrinsic and Social Desirability scales has been the subject of some controversy. Watson et al. (1986) suggested that the Marlowe–Crowne SDS is not an appropriate measure of social desirability to use with intrinsically religious individuals because "over half of the SDS items have content relevant to religion and religious belief" (p. 228) and that "could put the intrinsic . . . subject at a selective disadvantage" (p. 227).

Leak and Fish (1989) challenged the Watson et al. (1986) argument on both logical and empirical grounds. Empirically, Leak and Fish found statistically significant ($p < .05$) low positive correlations between the Intrinsic scale and both subscales of the Paulhus (1984) Balanced Inventory of Desirable Responding (BIDR), an instrument proposed as an improvement on the Marlowe–Crowne and incorporating separate subscales to assess concern for public and private self-presentation. Correlations were +.23 for the public Impression Management subscale, +.27 for the private Self-Deception subscale, and +.30 for the total BIDR. Additionally, Leak and Fish found near-zero correlations between the Intrinsic scale and subject-rated religious relevance of the items of both BIDR subscales, using a rating procedure modeled after that of Watson et al. (1986). Overall, the research to date is generally consistent with the suggestion that individuals scoring higher on measures of intrinsic religion are more concerned with presenting themselves in a positive light, especially but not exclusively on issues related to their religious beliefs.

Second, as already noted, all major religions condemn prejudice and bigotry. Assuming that the religious community provides an especially important reference group and source of social and personal norms for the intrinsically religious, individuals so classified should be especially motivated to present themselves as free from prejudice and bigotry. One way to do so is by circling the easily discernible "right" responses on a prejudice questionnaire. If individuals classified as intrinsically religious present themselves as free from prejudice to a greater extent than individuals classified as extrinsic, then the result would be precisely the pattern found in Table 7.2: The former would appear less prejudiced than the latter. Yet the personal transformation that Allport (1966) claimed is associated with intrinsic religion may have reached only to the hand that marks the questionnaire, not to the heart.

A Three-Dimensional Model of Personal Religion

Concerning the assessment of personal religion, we recommend use of the three-dimensional model proposed by Batson (1976) and Batson and Ventis (1982) instead of Allport's bipolar extrinsic-intrinsic model. The bipolar model ran into problems early on, when Allport and Ross (1967) found that the Extrinsic and Intrinsic scales were not measuring opposite ends of the same continuum, as had been assumed, but defined two independent dimensions of personal religion. The extrinsic versus intrinsic classification employed in the research reported in the left side of Table 7.2 is based on the bipolar model; as a result, it involves an inappropriate confounding of these two dimensions.

The three-dimensional model proposed by Batson (1976) and Batson and Ventis (1982) includes two orthogonal dimensions that correspond conceptually to Allport's (1966) extrinsic and intrinsic orientations (and are measured principally by the Extrinsic and Intrinsic scales). These dimensions are called *religion as means* and *religion as end*, respectively.

The model also includes a third dimension, orthogonal to the other two, called *religion as quest* (measured principally by Batson's, 1976, Interactional—or Quest—scale, which includes items such as: "It might be said that I value my religious doubts and uncertainties." "God wasn't very important to me until I began to ask questions about the meaning of my own life." "Questions are far more central to my religious experience than are answers."). This third dimension of personal religion concerns the degree to which the individual seeks to face religious issues such as personal mortality or meaning in life in all their complexity, yet resists clear-cut, pat answers. An individual who approaches religion in this way recognizes that he or she does not know, and probably never will know, the final truth about such matters. Still, the questions are deemed important and, however tentative and subject to change, answers are sought.

A number of writers, both theologians (e.g., Bonhoeffer, 1953; Niebuhr, 1963) and psychologists (e.g., Barron, 1968; Fromm, 1950), emphasize the importance of the quest dimension of religion. Moreover, some researchers (e.g., Batson et al., 1978; McFarland, 1989) emphasize the importance of including the quest dimension when assessing the religion–prejudice relationship. They suggest that even if the intrinsic, end dimension is associated only with an increased desire to appear less prejudiced rather than a genuine reduction in prejudice, the quest dimension may be associated with a genuine reduction. (Support for the existence and independence of the means, end, and quest dimensions of personal religion is provided through principal–components analysis with orthogonal rotation—see Batson & Ventis, 1982, chapter 5.)

NEW RESEARCH STRATEGIES

These two doubts about the revised conclusion concerning the religion–prejudice relationship surfaced in the late 1970s. Since then, researchers have used two strategies to take a new look at the relationship between prejudice and different ways of being religious. One strategy still involves assessing prejudice using questionnaires but assessing prejudices that the respondents' religious community does not clearly proscribe, such as prejudice against non-Whites by Afrikaners in South Africa or prejudice against homosexuals or communists by members of mainline churches in the United States. The second strategy involves assessing religiously proscribed prejudices, such as racial prejudice by members of mainline churches in the United States, but doing so using covert, behavioral measures of prejudice, not questionnaires. Although relatively few studies of each type have been conducted, the results are, once again, remarkably consistent.

Questionnaire Measurement of Prejudices
Not Clearly Proscribed

Batson, Schoenrade, and Ventis (1993) recently summarized 24 findings from six different studies of the association between measures of one or more of the three dimensions of personal religion and some nonproscribed prejudice. The nonproscribed prejudices assessed include: (a) prejudice against Rastafarians by Seventh-Day Adventists in the Virgin Islands (Griffin, Gorsuch, & Davis, 1987), (b) prejudice against homosexuals by university students in the United States (Herek, 1987), (c) prejudice against homosexuals and communists by undergraduate and adult members of mainline churches in the United States (McFarland, 1989, 1990), (d) social distance from various ethnic minorities among university students in Venezuela (Ponton & Gorsuch, 1988), and (e) social distance from non-Whites among Afrikaners (Snook & Gorsuch, 1985). Eight findings assess the relation to nonproscribed prejudice for the extrinsic, means dimension; nine the relation for the intrinsic, end dimension; seven the relation for

TABLE 7.3
Association Between Dimensions of Personal Religion and Measures of Prejudices Not
Clearly Proscribed by Respondents' Religious Community
(24 Findings From 6 Different Studies—1985-1990)

Dimension of Personal Religion	Nature of Association		
	+	?	-
Extrinsic, means	1	7	0
Intrinsic, end	8	0	1
Quest	0	2	5

Note. Column entries in the table indicate: (a) the number of reports of a positive correlation between measures of each dimension of personal religion and some nonproscribed prejudice, (b) the number of reports of no reliable correlation, and (c) the number of reports of a negative correlation. Adapted by permission from *Religion and the Individual* by C. D. Batson, P. Schoenrade, and W. L. Ventis. Copyright (1993) by Oxford University Press.

the quest dimension.[2] Table 7.3 presents a line-score summary of the correlations for each of the three dimensions.

The patterns in Table 7.3 for the extrinsic, means and the intrinsic, end dimensions exactly reverse the patterns of correlations for these dimensions reported in Table 7.2 for proscribed prejudices (e.g., racial prejudice). For nonproscribed prejudices, the extrinsic, means dimension shows no clear relation to prejudice in seven of eight findings; the intrinsic, end dimension shows a positive relation to prejudice in eight of nine findings. Only the quest dimension shows evidence of a negative relation to prejudices that are not clearly proscribed by the religious community (five of seven findings).

Several comments should be made about the studies summarized in Table 7.3:

1. Two of the studies reviewed assess prejudice against women by members of mainline churches in the United States (McFarland, 1989, 1990). Given that these studies were both conducted in the late 1980s, we have considered this a proscribed prejudice. The validity of this assumption is supported by the tendency in these studies for correlations with prejudice against women to pattern much like correlations for prejudice against Blacks. If, however, one wishes to consider prejudice against women nonproscribed, then one can add two no-relation findings to the extrinsic, means row in Table 7.3, two no-relation findings to the intrinsic, end row, and two negative-correlation findings to the quest row. These additions do not substantially change the overall pattern.

---

[2]Typically, because these studies concern different dimensions of being religious, individuals with low interest or involvement in religion are not included. Researchers vary, however, in the criteria for exclusion of the nonreligious.

2. The one outlier in the extrinsic row, the one outlier in the intrinsic row, and one of the two no-relation findings in the quest row all come from a single study by Ponton and Gorsuch (1988). This study assessed the preferred social distance from various ethnic minorities by Spanish-speaking university students in Caracas, Venezuela. The ethnic minorities were Spaniards, Portuguese, Italians, Americans, Canadians, Colombians, Peruvians, and Chileans. Given that social contact with at least some of these groups might have been positively desired rather than merely tolerated, we doubt that the social distance measure in this study was a valid measure of prejudice. If this study is excluded from Table 7.3, as it probably should be, then the pattern of correlations becomes even clearer.

3. It is worth noting that four of the six studies summarized in Table 7.3 also included questionnaire measures of proscribed (racial) prejudice (Herek, 1987; McFarland, 1989, 1990; Snook & Gorsuch, 1985). Correlations of the measures of racial prejudice with the extrinsic, means and the intrinsic, end dimensions are much the same as in the earlier studies summarized in Table 7.2. The extrinsic, means dimension correlates positively with proscribed prejudice against Blacks in two of three findings (no-relation in the third); the intrinsic, end dimension is not reliably correlated with proscribed prejudice against Blacks in four of four findings.

4. Measures of the quest dimension are not included in any of the studies summarized in Table 7.2. Therefore, it is of particular interest to note that in the studies summarized in Table 7.3, the Quest scale is negatively correlated with proscribed prejudice against Blacks in three of three findings. As in all of the questionnaire-based research on the religion–prejudice relation, these three correlations are not especially large (rs ranging from $-.10$ to $-.30$), but they are all reliably different from zero.

Overall, the results summarized in Tables 7.2 and 7.3 strongly suggest that the association between the intrinsic, end dimension of personal religion and relatively low prejudice is not a general one but is limited to prejudices that are clearly proscribed by the religious community. Apparently, the intrinsic believer is not generally free from enmity, contempt, and bigotry, as Allport (1966) claimed, but is instead conforming to the "right" tolerances and the "right" prejudices as defined by the formal and informal teachings of his or her religious community.

This conclusion is further supported by three of the studies summarized in Table 7.3: Herek (1987); McFarland (1989); and McFarland (1990). In each, the positive relation of (a) the intrinsic, end dimension to (b) nonproscribed prejudice may be accounted for by the positive association of both a and b to devout, orthodox beliefs (also see Altemeyer & Hunsberger, 1991). To the degree that people value their religion intrinsically, believing what is taught, they are more likely to report being tolerant of those their religious community tells them they should tolerate and being intolerant of those the community tells them they should not tolerate. At best, the personal transformation produced by their religion seems circumscribed.

We must, however, question even this circumscribed transformation. The evidence suggests that the extrinsic, means dimension correlates positively with questionnaire measures of a clearly proscribed prejudice—racial prejudice; neither the intrinsic, end nor the quest dimensions do. The intrinsic, end dimension shows either no relation or a weak negative relation to questionnaire measures of racial prejudice; the quest dimension shows a weak-to-moderate negative relation. But does the tolerance reported on these racial prejudice questionnaires reflect an internalization of the values of the religious community or only presentation of oneself as exemplifying these values (Jones & Pittman, 1982)? To answer this question, it is necessary to move beyond overt, questionnaire assessment of racial prejudice to examine the relation of the various dimensions of personal religion to more covert, behavioral measures. This is the second strategy used to take a new look at the religion–prejudice relationship.

Covert, Behavioral Measurement of Racial Prejudice

Assessing prejudice through the use of behavioral measures is almost always more difficult and time consuming than administering a prejudice questionnaire. But behavioral measures have two important advantages:

1. The response required can be made more costly to the respondent.
2. The relevance of the response to prejudice can often be masked, making the measurement unobtrusive or covert.

If, for example, someone states on a questionnaire that race would make no difference in the choice of a roommate, this person need not fear that the statement will affect his or her room assignment. The statement carries no behavioral consequences, and so no cost. But what if the person makes the same statement on an application form from the housing office? Now it carries behavioral consequences and cost.

Not surprisingly, responses differ dramatically in these two situations, as Silverman (1974) cleverly demonstrated. He found that White incoming freshmen reported little concern about the race of their future roommate on an attitude questionnaire; they seemed quite colorblind. But other incoming freshmen from the same group, responding to the same question on a housing office application, reported a definite preference for a White rather than a Black roommate. As this experiment clearly shows, it is important to move beyond exclusive reliance on cost-free questionnaire measures of proscribed prejudice.

In Silverman's (1974) study, the application form not only involved potential cost but also provided an unobtrusive measure; respondents thought their housing assignment—not prejudice—was at issue. Costs may at times override the motivation to present oneself in a socially desirable light even on obtrusive behavioral measures, but it is preferable to make the measures unobtrusive or covert (Crosby et al., 1980). With a little imagination, this can usually be done.

Development of covert, behavioral measures is one of the major contributions of social psychology to the study of prejudice (see Gaertner & Doviodio, 1986, for a range of examples). Unfortunately, this strategy has rarely been employed in studies of the religion–prejudice relationship. We know of only three studies that have examined the relation between one or more of the dimensions of personal religion and prejudice using covert, behavioral measures. All three studies focus on racial prejudice.

Brannon (1970)

Brannon (1970) administered the Extrinsic and Intrinsic scales to 81 White members of a small Protestant church in a Southern city in the United States. The church had recently decided to racially integrate and, as an index of prejudice, Brannon noted whether each individual remained a member of the now-integrated church, showing racial tolerance, or left to join a newly formed splinter church that vowed to remain segregated. Brannon reported that those who remained with the old church scored significantly higher on the Intrinsic scale and significantly lower on the Extrinsic scale than did those who left, suggesting that the intrinsic, end dimension is negatively and the extrinsic, means dimension positively associated with racial prejudice, assessed behaviorally.

Unfortunately, there is an important confound in this study that clouds interpretation of the results. As previously noted, scores on the Intrinsic scale tend to be associated with greater overall religious activity, including church involvement. It is possible that the more intrinsic members stayed with the old church because of this attachment, not because they were more racially tolerant. To disentangle this confound, one needs to compare Brannon's results with results in a situation in which the old church remains segregated and the new splinter church integrates. As far as we know, this comparison has never been made.

Batson, Naifeh, and Pate (1978)

Adapting Silverman's (1974) strategy for covert, behavioral assessment of prejudice, Batson et al. (1978) placed 51 White undergraduates with at least a moderate interest in religion in a situation where their expressed readiness to interact with a Black individual would have behavioral consequences. This was done by telling the undergraduates that later in the study they would be interviewed in depth about their religious views. The undergraduates were given the opportunity to indicate which of the available interviewers they would like to have interview them. As a basis for their judgment, they were provided information sheets describing each interviewer. Although differing in particulars, each sheet described a well-rounded college graduate, interested in religion, who had grown up in a middle-class Protestant church. Clipped to each information sheet was a photograph. The photographs revealed that one interviewer was White, the other Black. Interviewers were always the same sex as the undergraduate, were nicely dressed and groomed, and had a friendly smile. In order to equalize information about interviewers other than race, information sheets and photographs were counterbalanced.

After reading the information sheets, the undergraduates were asked to rate how much they would like each interviewer to interview them. A difference score was created by subtracting the rating of the Black interviewer from the rating of the White. Relative preference for the White over the Black interviewer on this difference score reflected a preference to interact with one person rather than another solely on the basis of race, providing an index of racial prejudice.

To permit direct comparison of results using this behavioral measure with results using a questionnaire measure of prejudice, Batson et al. (1978) also administered the racial-prejudice questionnaire used by Allport and Ross (1967). Finally, the three dimensions of personal religion were assessed using six religious-orientation questionnaires.

Results of this study are summarized in Table 7.4. As can be seen, correlations between the religious dimensions and the questionnaire measure of prejudice are much as in previous research. The correlation for the extrinsic, means dimension is low positive ($r = .18$; ns); the correlations for the intrinsic, end and quest dimensions are negative ($rs = -.35$ and $-.34$; $ps < .05$).

For both the extrinsic, means dimension and the quest dimension, the correlations with prejudice using the behavioral measure do not differ from those using the questionnaire measure. But for the intrinsic, end dimension, there is a clear difference. Using the behavioral measure, the correlation with racial prejudice becomes significantly more positive ($r = .26$; $z = 3.21$; $p < .005$).

TABLE 7.4
Association Between Dimensions of Personal Religion and Overt Versus Covert Measures
of Racial Prejudice

	Measure of Racial Prejudice	
Dimension of Personal Religion	Overt (Questionnaire)	Covert (Interview Preference)
Extrinsic, means	.18	.17
Intrinsic, end	-.35*	.26
Quest	-.34*	-.16

From Batson, Naifeh, and Pate (1978).
Note. *$p < .05$, two-tailed.

These results are consistent with the suggestion that the intrinsic, end dimension of personal religion is associated more with an increased desire to avoid appearing racially prejudiced than with a genuine reduction of prejudice. Using the overt, questionnaire measure, this dimension has a significant negative correlation with racial prejudice; using the covert, behavioral measure, however, the correlation is nonsignificantly positive. Only the quest dimension appears to be associated with a genuine reduction of prejudice; it correlates negatively with both the overt and covert measures of prejudice, although the latter association is weak.

Batson, Flink, Schoenrade, Fultz, and Pych (1986)

Snyder, Kleck, Strenta, and Mentzer (1979) introduced a new technique for detecting prejudicial attitudes that people wish to conceal, a technique called *attributional ambiguity*. They demonstrated the usefulness of this technique in two studies assessing prejudice against the physically handicapped. In each study, subjects chose where they would sit to watch a movie: with either a handicapped person or a nonhandicapped person. In the low-attributional-ambiguity condition, the same movie was being shown in both locations; in the high-attributional-ambiguity condition, the movies were different. Snyder et al. found, as they had predicted, that people avoided a handicapped person more often if the decision to do so was also a decision between two different movies, allowing the avoidance to masquerade as a movie preference.

Batson et al. (1986) used this attributional-ambiguity technique to assess the religion–prejudice relationship. They had 44 White undergraduates with at least a moderate interest in religion first complete a battery of questionnaires, including the Extrinsic, Intrinsic, and Quest scales. At a later experimental session, these undergraduates participated individually in what was ostensibly a study of factors that affect liking for movies. They were given a choice of whether to watch a movie being shown in Theater A or Theater B. There was already a person (a confederate the same sex as the subject) sitting in each theater; one person was Black, the other White. Attributional ambiguity for the seating choice was manipulated by varying whether the movies being shown in the two theaters were the same (overt racial-prejudice condition) or different (covert racial-prejudice condition). Choosing to sit in the theater with the White person rather than the Black person was the measure of racial prejudice. Pairing of confederate with movie, of confederate with theater, of movie with theater, and of theater with side of room were all counterbalanced.

Results of this study are summarized in Table 7.5. As can be seen, they are quite consistent with those of the Batson et al. (1978) study. For the extrinsic, means dimension, there is no reliable correlation with preference for sitting with the White in either condition. For the intrinsic, end dimension, the correlation with choosing to sit with the White person is significantly negative in the overt

TABLE 7.5
Association Between Dimensions of Personal Religion and Overt Versus Covert Measures
of Racial Prejudice

	Measure of Racial Prejudice	
Dimension of Personal Religion	Overt (Same Movie)	Covert (Different Movie)
Extrinsic, means	-.21	-.01
Intrinsic, end	-.52*	-.08
Quest	-.10	-.45*

From Batson, Flink, Schoenrade, Fultz, and Pych (1986).
Note. *p < .05, two-tailed.

condition ($r = -.52; p < .05$) but near zero in the covert condition ($r = -.08$). For the quest dimension, the correlation is near zero in the overt condition ($r = -.10$) but significantly negative in the covert condition ($r = -.45; p < .05$).[3]

As in the Batson et al. (1978) study, then, the intrinsic, end dimension correlates negatively with an overt measure of racial prejudice. But this significant negative correlation disappears when choosing to sit with the White person could masquerade as a movie preference. The pattern of behavior associated with devout, intrinsic religion in these two studies is strikingly reminiscent of what Gaertner and Dovidio (1986) called *aversive racism*. The pattern suggests a concern on the part of the intrinsically religious not to be seen by others, or by themselves, as prejudiced; still, "the underlying negative portions of their attitudes are expressed, but in subtle, rationalizable ways" (Gaertner & Dovidio, 1986, p. 62). Only the quest dimension has a significant negative correlation with the covert measure of prejudice.

SUMMARY AND SOME IMPLICATIONS

We have traveled a long and winding path in this review of the religion–prejudice relationship, but we believe that we have gotten somewhere. First, we found much research suggesting a positive correlation between being religious and being prejudiced. Then we found much research suggesting that this was only

---

[3]To check the pattern of choices underlying the negative correlation for the quest dimension, we performed median splits on the (Quest) Interactional scale in each attributional-ambiguity condition. Among subjects scoring above the median, the proportions of subjects choosing to sit with the White person were .44 and .46 in the overt and covert prejudice conditions, respectively; among subjects scoring below the median, the proportions were .75 and .71. Thus, high scorers on the quest dimension showed no preference for Black or White persons in either condition, whereas low scorers showed a preference for sitting with the White person ($z = 2.13; p < .04$; observed proportions tested for difference from .50 across experimental conditions).

true for those persons who use their religion as an extrinsic means to self-serving ends. Among religious individuals, those who orient to their religion as an intrinsic end in itself almost invariably score lower on questionnaire measures of proscribed prejudice and discrimination (e.g., racism) than do the extrinsically religious (although the intrinsically religious rarely score lower on these measures than nonreligious individuals). For neither of these two dimensions of personal religion is there evidence that it is a depressant of intolerance and bigotry, but at least the devout, sincere belief reflected in the intrinsic, end dimension does not appear to be a stimulant of prejudice.

Although these results suggest a more comforting revised conclusion concerning the relationship between personal religion and prejudice, we have doubts. In virtually every study of the relationship between personal religion and proscribed prejudice, prejudice was measured by self-report questionnaire. Measuring prejudice in this way opens the door wide for individuals who wish to present themselves as unprejudiced to do so. There is reason to suspect that individuals scoring high on measures of intrinsic, end religion might wish to do so.

The few studies to date that have attempted to avoid the self-presentation problem, by either assessing forms of prejudice that are not proscribed by respondents' religious community or using covert, behavioral measures of prejudice, suggest a *revised* revised conclusion:

> The extrinsic, means dimension of personal religion is related to increased prejudice, but only when prejudice is proscribed. The quest dimension is related to decreased prejudice, both proscribed and not. The intrinsic, end dimension is related to the appearance of relatively low proscribed prejudice, but only the appearance. It is related to increased prejudice when the prejudice is not proscribed by the religious community.

This is a far more complex conclusion than we were seeking when we first asked whether religion is a depressant or stimulant of intolerance and bigotry; it is, however, the conclusion to which we believe the existing evidence points. Of course, future research may cause us to rethink matters yet again.[4]

In the interim, we must take issue with earlier reviews (e.g., Gorsuch, 1988; Gorsuch & Aleshire, 1974) and caution against peddling intrinsic religion as an

---

[4]The suggestion that the extrinsic, means dimension is related only to proscribed prejudice may need some explanation. Empirically, it seems true: Scores on the Extrinsic scale correlate positively with questionnaire measures of a wide range of proscribed prejudices (cf. Table 7.2) and generally correlate close to zero with questionnaire measures of nonproscribed prejudice (cf. Table 7.3). But why? One possibility is that whereas higher scores on the intrinsic, end dimension are associated with both knowledge of and cognitive—if not behavioral—acceptance of the teachings of one's religious institution about right and wrong prejudices, higher scores on the extrinsic, means dimension are associated with knowledge but not acceptance (and possibly rejection) of these teachings.

antidote for prejudice. The devout, sincere belief of the intrinsically religious seems to change the manifestations of prejudice, making it more covert. Yet prejudice remains, manifesting itself in subtle ways reminiscent of the aversive racism described by Gaertner and Dovidio (1986).

Our interpretation may, however, be too pessimistic. Devine's (1989) dissociation model suggests a more optimistic interpretation of the evidence we have reviewed concerning the relationship of devout, intrinsic religion to racial prejudice. Perhaps, stimulated by their religious beliefs and role models, the intrinsically religious are in the process of being resocialized away from prejudice, but the resocialization process is not complete. Like trying to break a bad habit, they slip back into their old ways when their new, unprejudicial thoughts and behaviors are not consciously activated by salient cues (cues such as being asked to complete a prejudice questionnaire or act in a way that might appear overtly prejudicial). If this interpretation is correct, then increasing the salience of the antiprejudice norm of the religious community (i.e., consciousness raising) may lead to reduced prejudice by the more intrinsically religious even in covert behavior, not just on questionnaires.

Once again, we have doubts. This dissociation, or resocialization, analysis rests on the assumption that the norm of the religious community is to eschew prejudice and discrimination, that the religious community teaches, to paraphrase McConahay (1986), the truly religious can't be racists and racists can't be truly religious. We wonder whether this is the norm. True, every major religion teaches tolerance, and every major denomination is on record opposing racial prejudice and discrimination. Yet we are given pause when we see a headline that reads, "Sunday morning at 11 remains most segregated hour of week" (*Atlanta Constitution*, August 9, 1987, p. 11-A). We suspect that in many cases the intrinsic believer, attending to the practice of the religious community as well as the preaching, is being resocialized to a very different, more pharisaical norm: The truly religious can't look racist. If so, then perhaps the resocialization process is complete, or if it is not, increased salience of the norm will not reduce the subtle, covert prejudice.

The potential for the open-ended, quest dimension of religion to serve as an antidote for prejudice seems more promising. This dimension generally correlates negatively with measures of both proscribed and nonproscribed prejudices, especially when prejudice is measured covertly. It remains unclear, however, whether the quest orientation to religion should get causal credit for its association with reduced prejudice or vice versa, or whether both the quest orientation to religion and reduced prejudice are expressions of a general personal disposition toward openness and tolerance (cf. Peters & Zanna, 1991). Panel studies may be necessary to address this key question of causation. Until it is answered, we recommend restraint on peddling even the quest derivative of the religion poppy.

REFERENCES

Adorno, T. W., Frenkel-Brunswik, E., Levinson, D. J., & Sanford, R. N. (1950). *The authoritarian personality.* New York: Norton.

Allport, G. W. (1950). *The individual and his religion.* New York: Macmillan.

Allport, G. W. (1966). Religious context of prejudice. *Journal for the Scientific Study of Religion, 5,* 447–457.

Allport, G. W., & Kramer, B. (1946). Some roots of prejudice. *Journal of Psychology, 22,* 9–30.

Allport, G. W., & Ross, J. M. (1967). Personal religious orientation and prejudice. *Journal of Personality and Social Psychology, 5,* 432–443.

Altemeyer, B., & Hunsberger, B. (1991). Authoritarianism, religious fundamentalism, quest, and prejudice. Unpublished manuscript, University of Manitoba, Winnipeg.

Atlanta Constitution (1987, August 9). Sunday morning at 11 remains most segregated hour of week (p. 11-A).

Barron, F. (1968). *Creativity and personal freedom.* Princeton: Van Nostrand.

Batson, C. D. (1976). Religion as prosocial: Agent or double agent? *Journal for the Scientific Study of Religion, 15,* 29–45.

Batson, C. D., Flink, C. H., Schoenrade, P. A., Fultz, J., & Pych, V. (1986). Religious orientation and overt versus covert racial prejudice. *Journal of Personality and Social Psychology, 50,* 175–181.

Batson, C. D., Naifeh, S. J., & Pate, S. (1978). Social desirability, religious orientation, and racial prejudice. *Journal for the Scientific Study of Religion, 17,* 31–41.

Batson, C. D., Schoenrade, P. A., & Ventis, W. L. (1993). *Religion and the individual: A social-psychological perspective.* New York: Oxford.

Batson, C. D., & Ventis, W. L. (1982). *The religious experience: A social-psychological perspective.* New York: Oxford.

Bonhoeffer, D. (1953). *Letters and papers from prison.* New York: Macmillan.

Brannon, R. C. L. (1970). Gimme that old time racism. *Psychology Today, 3,* 42–44.

Crosby, F., Bromley, S., & Saxe, L. (1980). Recent unobtrusive studies of Black and White discrimination and prejudice: A literature review. *Psychological Bulletin, 87,* 546–563.

Crowne, D. P., & Marlowe, D. (1964). *The approval motive: Studies in evaluative dependence.* New York: Wiley.

Devine, P. G. (1989). Automatic and controlled processes in prejudice: The role of stereotypes and personal beliefs. In A. R. Pratkanis, S. J. Breckler, & A. G. Greenwald (Eds.), *Attitude structure and function* (pp. 181–212). Hillsdale, NJ: Lawrence Erlbaum Associates.

Donahue, M. J. (1985). Intrinsic and extrinsic religiousness: Review and meta-analysis. *Journal of Personality and Social Psychology, 48,* 400–419.

Fromm, E. (1950). *Psychoanalysis and religion.* New Haven: Yale University Press.

Gaertner, S. L., & Dovidio, J. F. (1986). The aversive form of racism. In J. F. Dovidio & S. L. Gaertner (Eds.), *Prejudice, discrimination, and racism* (pp. 61–89). New York: Academic.

Gorsuch, R. L. (1988). Psychology of religion. *Annual Review of Psychology, 39,* 201–221.

Gorsuch, R. L., & Aleshire, D. (1974). Christian faith and ethnic prejudice: A review and interpretation of research. *Journal for the Scientific Study of Religion, 13,* 281–307.

Gorsuch, R. L., & McFarland, S. (1972). Single- versus multiple-item scales for measuring religious values. *Journal for the Scientific Study of Religion, 11,* 53–65.

Griffin, G. A. E., Gorsuch, R. L., & Davis, A. (1987). A cross-cultural investigation of religious orientation, social norms, and prejudice. *Journal for the Scientific Study of Religion, 26,* 358–365.

Herek, G. M. (1987). Religious orientation and prejudice: A comparison of racial and sexual attitudes. *Personality and Social Psychology Bulletin, 13,* 34–44.

Jones, E. E., & Pittman, T. S. (1982). Toward a general theory of strategic self-presentation. In J.

Suls (Ed.), *Psychological perspectives on the self* (pp. 231–262). Hillsdale, NJ: Lawrence Erlbaum Associates.

Karlins, M., Coffman, T. L., & Walters, G. (1969). On the fading of social stereotypes: Studies in three generations of college students. *Journal of Personality and Social Psychology, 13,* 1–16.

Kirkpatrick, C. (1949). Religion and humanitarianism: A study of institutional implications. *Psychological Monographs, 63* (No. 304).

Leak, G. K., & Fish, S. (1989). Religious orientation, impression management, and self-deception: Toward a clarification of the link between religiosity and social desirability. *Journal for the Scientific Study of Religion, 28,* 355–359.

Liu, W. T. (1961). The community reference system, religiosity, and race attitudes. *Social Forces, 39,* 324–328.

McConahay, J. B. (1986). Modern racism, ambivalence, and the Modern Racism scale. In J. F. Dovidio & S. L. Gaertner (Eds.), *Prejudice, discrimination, and racism* (pp. 91–125). New York: Academic.

McFarland, S. G. (1989). Religious orientations and the targets of discrimination. *Journal for the Scientific Study of Religion, 28,* 324–336.

McFarland, S. G. (1990, April). *Religiously oriented prejudice in communism and Christianity: The role of quest.* Paper presented at the Annual Convention of the Southeastern Psychological Association, Atlanta.

Nias, D. K. B. (1972). The structuring of social attitudes in children. *Child Development, 43,* 211–219.

Niebuhr, H. R. (1963). *The responsible self.* New York: Harper.

Paulhus, D. L. (1984). Two-component models of socially desirable responding. *Journal of Personality and Social Psychology, 46,* 598–609.

Peters, L. J., & Zanna, M. P. (1991, June). *Faith, doubt, and authority: The relation of intrinsic and quest religiosity with right-wing authoritarianism.* Paper presented at the annual meeting of the Canadian Psychological Association, Calgary.

Ponton, M. O., & Gorsuch, R. L. (1988). Prejudice and religion revisited: A cross-cultural investigation with a Venezuelan sample. *Journal for the Scientific Study of Religion, 27,* 260–271.

Rokeach, M. (1969). Religious values and social compassion. *Review of Religious Research, 11,* 24–38.

Rosenblith, J. (1949). A replication of "some roots of prejudice." *Journal of Abnormal and Social Psychology, 44,* 470–489.

Sigall, H., & Page, R. (1971). Current stereotypes: A little fading, a little faking. *Journal of Personality and Social Psychology, 18,* 247–255.

Silverman, B. I. (1974). Consequences, racial discrimination, and the principle of belief congruence. *Journal of Personality and Social Psychology, 29,* 497–508.

Snook, S. C., & Gorsuch, R. L. (1985, August). *Religion and racial prejudice in South Africa.* Paper presented at the 92nd Annual Convention of the American Psychological Association, Los Angeles, CA.

Snyder, M. L., Kleck, R. E., Strenta, A., & Mentzer, S. J. (1979). Avoidance of the handicapped: An attributional ambiguity analysis. *Journal of Personality and Social Psychology, 37,* 2297–2306.

Strommen, M. P. (1967). Religious education and the problem of prejudice. *Religious Education, 62,* 52–59.

Stouffer, S. A. (1955). *Communism, conformity, and civil liberties.* New York: Doubleday.

Watson, P. J., Morris, R. J., Foster, J. E., & Hood, R. W., Jr. (1986). Religiosity and social desirability. *Journal for the Scientific Study of Religion, 25,* 215–232.

Power, Gender, and Intergroup Discrimination: Some Minimal Group Experiments

8

Richard Y. Bourhis
Université du Québec à Montréal

> *Our definition of racism will go beyond belief or attitudes to include actions. The significant factor of ingroup preference, whether racially or ethnically based, is the POWER that the ingroup has over an outgroup.*
> —Jones, 1972, p. 117

Much of the early work on the social psychology of intergroup relations stresses intraindividual and interpersonal psychological processes contributing to prejudiced attitudes and discriminatory behavior (Adorno, Frenkel-Brunswik, Levinson, & Sanford, 1950; Billig, 1976). In contrast, Sherif's (1966) functional approach provides a true intergroup framework to the study of prejudice and discrimination by documenting how realistic conflict of interest over scarce resources leads to antagonistic intergroup relations. Though Sherif's realistic conflict theory (RCT) received much empirical support in the literature (Brown, 1988; Sherif, 1966), results from Tajfel's minimal group paradigm studies (MGP) show that conflicting group interests are not a necessary condition for intergroup discrimination (Tajfel, 1978).

Results of over three decades of research using the minimal group paradigm demonstrate that the mere categorization of people into two groups is sufficient to foster intergroup discrimination (Brewer, 1979; Diehl, 1990; Tajfel, 1981). Typically, the minimal group paradigm involves members of two arbitrary groups allocating pecuniary points to members of the ingroup and members of the outgroup. There is no social interaction either within or between anonymous group members; there is no previous history of relations between the groups and there are no instrumental links between subjects' responses and their self-interest. Although these procedures are designed to eliminate grounds for discriminatory behavior, results show that subjects, nevertheless, discriminate by choosing not only to give more points to ingroup members than to outgroup ones but also to maximize the difference between awards made to the ingroup and the outgroup, even at the cost of sacrificing maximum ingroup profit. The minimal group discrimination effect displays considerable robustness in being replicable across subjects of different ages, nationalities, and social classes and with different dependent measures including intergroup perceptions, evaluative ratings, and the distribution of valued resources such as points and money, using numerous types of allocation scales including the Tajfel matrices (Bourhis & Sachdev, 1986; Brewer, 1979; Brewer & Kramer, 1985; Diehl, 1990; Messick & Mackie, 1989; Tajfel, 1981; Turner, 1983a, 1983b).

Social identity theory (SIT) (Tajfel & Turner, 1986) proposes that this intergroup discrimination effect reflects a competition for a positive social identity. Within the experimental situation, the arbitrarily imposed categorizations provide subjects with social identities that contribute to their self-concepts. Subjects' desires for positive social identities are translated into seeking favorable social comparisons between the ingroup and the outgroup on the only available dimensions of comparison, namely, choices on resource distribution scales such as the Tajfel matrices. Thus, by creating favorable intergroup differences (i.e., discriminating), subjects in the minimal group studies are able to achieve a positive social identity. In support of this, Oakes and Turner (1980) and Lemyre and Smith (1985) reported that subjects who discriminated in their studies had higher self-esteem than those who did not (cf. Hogg & Abrams, 1990).

However, it must be noted that theoretical approaches of both Sherif (RCT) and Tajfel (SIT) were developed on the basis of research conducted with groups that were structurally equal in terms of power, status, and group numbers. Most real life intergroup relations involve minority and majority groups who differ in terms of their relative power and status within the intergroup structure. Sociologists have noted that although dominant groups often enjoy status positions commensurate with their ascribed or achieved power position, instances exist in which power and status positions in the social structure are discrepant (Lenski, 1984). For instance, although trade unions have rarely been ascribed much status in British society, unions have at times been quite powerful within the British economy. In contrast, the English aristocracy has enjoyed a high status position long after it ceased occupying a dominant position within English society. Furthermore, scholars of ethnic relations concur in considering differential power between ethnic groups as one of the more important determinants of discrimination and ethnic stratification in multiethnic societies (Barth & Noel, 1972; Marger, 1991; Schermerhorn, 1970). Status differentials between groups are less predictive of discriminatory behaviors and ethnic stratification, because such differentials are more often seen as a consequence of power differentials between ethnic groups in stratified societies. Such patterns, as well as others in the ethnic relation literature, attest to the need for considering status, power, and group number as variables having independent and combined effects on the dynamics of minority and majority group relations.

In contrast to sociological approaches, social psychology focuses largely on cognitive and motivational aspects of discrimination and intergroup behavior (Abrams & Hogg, 1990; Brown, 1988; Dovidio & Gaertner, 1986; Hogg &

Abrams, 1988; Stroebe, Kruglanski, Bar-Tal, & Hewstone, 1988; Taylor & Moghaddam, 1987; Turner, 1987; Turner & Giles, 1981; Worchel & Austin, 1986). Within social psychology, statements concerning the impact of sociostructural variables on intergroup behavior either treat group numbers, power, and status variables interchangeably or do not address the issue (Deaux, 1985; Tajfel, 1982). The lack of attention paid to these sociostructural variables within social psychology is surprising, given their key role in shaping the dynamics of intergroup relations and group conflicts (Giles, Bourhis, & Taylor, 1977). It is clear that the impact of sociostructural variables on intergroup behavior remains to be integrated conceptually and empirically within the current intergroup relation literature. The main goal of this chapter is to contribute to this task, especially as regards the role played by group power in the actualization of intergroup discrimination.

At this point, it is necessary to provide more precise definitions of the terms *group power, social status,* and *group numbers.* Given the range of circumstances in which different forms of power can be exerted, Ng (1980) pointed out that no single, all inclusive definition of power is possible or desirable within social psychology. The sources of social power range from reward power to coercive, legitimate, expert, informational, and referent power (Deschamps, 1982; Kipnis, 1972; Raven & Kruglanski, 1970). However, given the present focus on power differentials between social groups, the intergroup definition of social power provided by Jones (1972) is most pertinent and refers to "the degree of control that one group has over its own fate and that of outgroups" (p. 117). Following Tajfel and Turner (1986), group status is defined as the relative position of groups on valued dimensions of comparison such as educational achievement, occupational status, speech styles, etc. Finally, Sachdev and Bourhis (1984) defined majorities and minorities strictly in terms of the relative numerical compositions of group members within their particular setting. This definition is more precise than that found in many sociological accounts (Farley, 1982), because the latter often assume that minorities are usually subordinate low-status groups whereas majorities are dominant high-status groups.

Recently, Richard Bourhis and colleagues conducted field and laboratory experiments designed to explore the independent and combined effects of status, power, and group numbers on intergroup behavior (Bourhis, Cole, & Gagnon, 1992; Bourhis & Hill, 1982; Cole & Bourhis, 1990, 1991; Sachdev & Bourhis, 1984, 1985, 1987, 1990, 1991). This research program seeks to build a long-needed rapprochement between some key sociological and social-psychological approaches to the study of discrimination and intergroup relations. Given space constraints, this chapter focuses primarily on a series of four laboratory experiments investigating the effects of power differentials on the discriminatory behavior of mixed-gender, same-gender, and opposite-gender groups. Results obtained in each of these intergroup studies are discussed as they relate to both social identity theory (Tajfel & Turner, 1986) and issues pertinent to female–

male relations (Ashmore & Del Boca, 1986). The chapter concludes with a brief analysis of group power as a key determinant of discrimination in both stable and unstable intergroup power structures.

STUDY 1: POWER DIFFERENTIALS BETWEEN MIXED-GENDER GROUPS

Over 3 decades have passed since Cartwright (1959) advocated the introduction of power in social psychologists' formulations about interpersonal and intergroup relations. Whereas social psychologists have been quite active in addressing power relations between individuals (Ellyson & Dovidio, 1985; Tedeschi, 1974), they have only begun to touch on the issue of power in analyses of relations between social groups (Apfelbaum, 1979; Ng, 1980). For instance, Deschamps (1982) suggested that members of dominated groups may not only be refused material rewards but may also be denied opportunities to determine their own sense of social identity. These are privileges that members of dominant groups enjoy as a function of their power advantage. As regards intergroup discrimination, Ng (1980) argued that whatever the psychological antecedent to discrimination may be, there must be at the same time a "usable power" so that prejudice can be translated into effective discrimination.

Although traditional minimal group studies never addressed the issue of power directly, categorized subjects in such studies are supposedly given the freedom to distribute resources without concerning themselves with the degree of control they have over their own and others' fate in the experiments. Rather than eliminating power considerations, the minimal group procedures essentially create a situation where ingroup and outgroup members have equal power in their decisions to distribute resources (Ng, 1982). Thus, the designs of minimal group experiments not only induce social categorization but also implicitly introduce a bilateral-and-equal-power relation between ingroup and outgroup members. It is this relation that makes it possible for group members to discriminate in minimal group experiments. However, in the real world, groups of equal power are rare. Instead, we find that dominant and subordinate groups are the rule rather than the exception in most intergroup situations (Marger, 1991).

To explore the impact of power differentials on intergroup discrimination, Sachdev and Bourhis (1985) conducted a minimal group study involving dominant and subordinate groups within a stable intergroup situation. Middle-class English Canadian undergraduates ($N = 200$) attending an Ontario university were recruited to participate in a decision-making study that involved deciding how to distribute an extra course credit for taking part in the experiment. Subjects were told that the study was aimed at uncovering how individuals reach decisions in situations where they have little information on which to base such decisions. Following a random categorization of undergraduates into Group Z and Group W using a toss of the coin, students were told that they would all receive one credit for taking part in the study but that they had the chance to give and receive a second course credit that would exempt them from writing an obligatory essay for their introductory psychology course. Thus, the psychology undergraduates were making decisions that involved the distribution of a valued resource, namely the extra course credit for taking part in the experiment.

Before subjects began the decision task, the power manipulation was achieved by telling subjects that decisions made by members of one group would have more weight in the experimenter's calculation of the course credits than decisions made by members of the other group. Perceptions of arbitrary power differentials were created by a random toss of a coin to determine which group's decisions had greater weight (i.e., control) in the distribution of the extra credit. Three intergroup power situations were investigated. Extremes in power differentials were explored by creating an intergroup situation in which one group had 100% control (absolute-power group); whereas its outgroup had 0% control (no-power group) in the distribution of the course credit. In the intermediary power-differential situation, one group had 70% control (high-power group); whereas its outgroup had 30% control (low-power group) over the distribution of resources. The third situation consisted of the usual minimal group condition in which each group had 50% control (equal-power groups) over the distribution of the extra course credit.

The main dependent measures were subjects' course credit allocations to ingroup and outgroup others using the Tajfel matrices. Using a standard instructional set, subjects were told how to use the Tajfel matrices for distributing points to ingroup and outgroup others. Subjects were told that their point distribution using the Tajfel matrices represented units of course credits that were used by the experimenter to calculate the final course credit allocated to each participants in the study.

For the sake of illustration, a stylized Tajfel matrix is presented in Table 1. Four basic strategies are assessed using the Tajfel matrices (Turner, Brown, & Tajfel, 1979). The four strategies are described from the point of view of a member of Group Z distributing resources to two anonymous individuals: One is a member of the ingroup, Group Z; the other is a member of the outgroup, Group W.

TABLE 8.1
Stylized Tajfel Matrix

Points to Member A of Group Z:	11	12	13	14	15	16	17	18	19	20	21	22	23
Points to Member B of Group W:	5	7	9	11	13	15	17	19	21	23	25	27	29
Points to Member A of Group Z: —													
Points to Member B of Group W:—													

Parity (P) represents a choice that awards an equal number of points to a recipient from the ingroup and a recipient from the outgroup. The parity response available in the Tajfel matrix presented in Table 8.1 is box 17/17. Maximum joint profit (MJP) represents a choice that maximizes the combined number of points to both ingroup and outgroup recipients. Maximum joint profit (MJP) is most clearly represented in box 23/29, which totals 52 points obtained from the experimenter (23 + 29 = 52). MJP is the most economically rational strategy because it maximizes the number of points obtained for all subjects in the experiment.

Maximum ingroup profit (MIP) represents a choice that awards the highest absolute number of points to the ingroup member regardless of awards made to the outgroup member. As seen from Tab. 8.1, box 23/29 represents the MIP strategy, because 23 points is the highest award that can be granted to the ingroup member. Note that in this stylized Tajfel matrix, maximum ingroup profit (MIP) also coincides with the maximum joint profit (MJP) strategy.

Maximum differentiation (MD) is a discrimination strategy par excellence and refers to a choice that maximizes the difference in points awarded to two recipients, the difference being in favor of the ingroup member but at the cost of sacrificing maximum ingroup profit. In the matrix example presented in Table 8.1, it is box 11/5 that most strongly represents a maximum differentiation (MD) strategy. Note that by choosing box 11/5, (MD), the Group Z respondent sacrifices 12 points that could otherwise have been gained for the ingroup had the 23/29 (MJP) box been selected (23 − 11 = 12). However, the 11/5 (MD) box offers an ingroup–outgroup differential of six points in favor of the ingroup (11 − 5 = +6). In contrast, the 23/29 (MJP) box represents an ingroup–outgroup differential of six points in favor of the outgroup (23 − 29 = −6). The maximum differentiation (MD) strategy is clearly not an economically rational strategy, although it does offer the greatest possible differentiation outcome between ingroup and outgroup fate, this differential being in favor of the ingroup.

Note that the other numerical options presented in box form within the Tajfel matrix represent intermediary choices between the four basic strategies discussed previously. Note as well that the Tajfel matrices are arranged so that subjects never allocate points to themselves personally. The previous four strategies are presented to the subjects in different combinations and permutations using different numerical presentations of the Tajfel matrices. These presentations yield matrix types that are used to measure the strengths or pulls of combinations of the previous strategies on subjects' choices. Most studies using the Tajfel matrices measure the strength of the following strategies: three types of discrimination strategies, one parity strategy, and one maximum joint profit strategy.

The first discrimination strategy is MD on MIP + MJP, which represents a preference for the maximum differentiation (MD) strategy when it is pitted against a combination of maximum ingroup profit (MIP) and maximum joint profit (MJP) strategies. In this case a strong pull of MD indicates that an individual prefers to maximize the difference between ingroup and outgroup points (MD) even when offered the alternative of combining maximum ingroup profit with maximum joint profit (MIP + MJP). Ingroup favoritism (FAV) is also a discrimination strategy, because it represents a choice that combines both maximum differentiation (MD) and maximum ingroup profit (MIP). There are two types of ingroup favoritism strategies (FAV). FAV on P represents a choice for ingroup favoritism (FAV) when it is pitted against parity (P). Respondents choosing FAV on P deliberately prefer to discriminate (FAV), even when this strategy is pitted against parity (P). FAV on MJP is also a preference for ingroup favoritism (FAV) but this time when it is pitted against the option of choosing maximum joint profit (MJP). Monitoring two types of ingroup favoritism (FAV) strategies is akin to measuring the degree of preference for apples in two ways: (a) when the choice is between an apple and an orange, and (b) when the choice is between an apple and a banana. Thus, one may be more or less tempted by the ingroup favoritism (FAV) strategy depending on whether it is pitted against parity (P) or against maximum joint profit (MJP). In most studies using the Tajfel matrices, there is a slightly stronger preference for FAV when it is pitted against maximum joint profit (FAV on MJP) than when it is pitted against parity (FAV on P). Taken together, the independent measurement of three different types of discriminatory strategies allow for more detailed and subtle analyses of discriminatory responses in various types of intergroup relation situations.

The P on FAV strategy represents the choice of parity (P) when it is pitted against the option of choosing ingroup favoritism (FAV = MIP + MJP). In most studies using the Tajfel matrices, the strength or pull of the parity strategy is stronger than the strength of any of the three discriminatory strategies. However, the advantage of using the Tajfel matrices lies in the fact that one can measure the strength of the three types of discrimination strategies independently of the strength of the parity strategy.

The MJP on FAV strategy represents a preference for maximum joint profit when it is pitted against ingroup favoritism (FAV = MIP + MD). As mentioned earlier, maximum joint profit (MJP) is the most economically rational strategy to adopt for respondents. However, many intergroup studies using the Tajfel matrices show that MJP is not a very popular strategy among group members. This is the case in the studies discussed in this chapter and no further mention of this strategy is made herein.

The order of presentation of each matrix is randomized for each subject. Each pull has a theoretical range from -12 to $+12$. As seen in the figures presented in this chapter, positive strategy pulls on MD, FAV on P, and FAV on MJP indicates discriminatory behaviors. Negative strategy pulls indicate pursuit of their psychological opposites. For instance, negative FAV on P or negative FAV on MJP indicates outgroup favoritism: awarding more points to an outgroup than ingroup recipient.

Although there has been some controversy about the use and scoring of the

Tajfel matrices, evidence from a great deal of previous research suggests that the matrices do monitor subjects' social orientations in a valid, reliable, and sensitive manner (see Bornstein, Crum, Wittenbraker, Harring, Insko, & Thibaut, 1983a, 1983b; Bourhis & Sachdev, 1986; Brown, Tajfel, & Turner, 1980; Diehl, 1990; Messick & Mackie, 1989; Rabbie, Schot, & Visser, 1989; Turner, 1980, 1983a, 1983b). Note that a detailed account of how to construct and score the Tajfel matrices is available in a publication by Bourhis & Sachdev (1986). A summary of the method used to administer and score the Tajfel matrices discussed herein is presented in chapter 9 (Bourhis, Sachdev, & Gagnon, chapter 9, this volume).

The present power-differential study also included an extensive postsession questionnaire designed to monitor how subjects felt as group members within the experiment. After completing the Tajfel matrices, subjects completed questionnaire items dealing with their own group identification, their feelings towards ingroup and outgroup members, their perceptions of the intergroup power structure, and their self-reports of the strategies they used while completing the Tajfel matrices. All of these postsession questionnaire items were measured using 7-point Likert scales. After their debriefing, subjects were told that they would all receive two course credits for having taken part in the experiment.

According to SIT, subjects in minimal group experiments realize their motivations for a positive social identity through intergroup discrimination. Sachdev and Bourhis (1985) argued that the hypothesized need for a positive social identity coupled with the perception of having usable power enables subjects to effectively maximize their relative superiority over the outgroup through discrimination. Therefore, greater group power should lead to concomitant increases in discrimination against the outgroup. Dominant group members should show greater discrimination than subordinate group members. Conversely, lack of usable power should rob low-power group members of the capacity to discriminate effectively. Thus, subordinate group members were expected to show lower discrimination than dominant group members.

Which strategies did dominant and subordinate group members use in their distribution of credit resources to ingroup and outgroup members? Wilcoxon Matched Pairs Tests were performed on the pull scores of each strategy to determine which Tajfel strategy was used significantly by subjects within each cell of the design (Turner, 1983a). As is usually the case in minimal group studies, results show that group members were more parity oriented than discriminatory in their responses. Also, group members did not differ much in their use of the parity strategy depending on their power ascription. However, group members did differ significantly in their use of the discrimination strategies depending on their position in the power structure. Figure 8.1 illustrates this pattern by representing the mean pull scores of each discrimination strategy within each of the five power conditions. Note that this style of presentation is used to describe the main results of the other studies discussed in this chapter.

As seen in Fig. 8.1, the within condition Wilcoxon Matched Pairs Tests

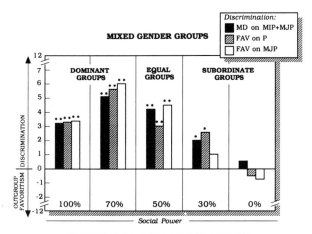

FIG. 8.1. Discrimination between dominant and subordinate groups of mixed-gender composition. Tajfel matrices results (Sachdev & Bourhis, 1985).

clearly show that discrimination strategies were used to a significant degree by absolute- (100%), high- (70%), equal- (50%) and low- (30%) power group members. It is important to note that equal-power group members (50%) discriminated against outgroups on the three measures of discrimination, thus replicating the usual minimal group studies (Brewer, 1979; Messick & Mackie, 1989; Tajfel, 1982). In contrast, Fig. 8.1 clearly shows that discrimination strategies were not used by subjects in the no- (0%) power group position. For group members without any power, social categorization could not lead to effective discrimination. Thus, the classic minimal group effect was eliminated in the no-power group condition, indicating that usable power is a necessary condition for discrimination in the minimal group paradigm.

A MANOVA analysis conducted on the matrix pull scores as dependent variables reveals a main effect for the power variable. Univariate analyses indicate that the power-main effect was reliable ($p < .001$) for the three discrimination strategies. Group members did differ in their use of the discrimination strategies (MD, FAV on P, and FAV on MJP) depending on their position in the power structure. Although more female than male subjects took part in each experimental condition, no gender effects emerged in the use of the distribution strategies in the five power conditions.

As hypothesized, dominant and equal-power group members were more discriminatory than subordinate group members. Duncan's Multiple Range Tests showed that equal- (50%), high- (70%), and total- (100%) power group members were significantly more discriminatory (FAV on MJP) than low-power group members (30%). These results show that the greater the power of the ingroup, the more capable its members are of effective discrimination.

Duncan's Multiple Range Tests also showed that high-power (70%) group members were significantly more discriminatory on the FAV on P strategy than all other groups in the study including absolute- (100%) power group members. Apfelbaum (1979) noted that intense discrimination by high-power group members may be characteristic of groups who seek to maintain their power advantage in settings where outgroup members nevertheless command some power in the intergroup structure (i.e., 30% power group). Why were absolute-power group members (100%) less discriminatory than the high-power (70%) group members? It seems that absolute-power group members could afford to exhibit a certain degree of benevolent paternalism or noblesse oblige vis-à-vis their totally powerless (0%) outgroups (Sachdev & Bourhis, 1985). However, it remains that absolute-power group members were more discriminatory than no- and low-power group members and at least as discriminatory as equal-power group members.

Were subjects accurate in reporting the parity and discrimination strategies they used in the study? Correlations computed between self-reports of distribution strategies and actual matrix pull scores show that variations in matrix strategies are significantly and positively related to subjects' self-reports (P on FAV, MD, FAV on MJP). Subjects' estimates of how other ingroup and outgroup members used the strategies relative to themselves show that subjects felt they used more parity than other ingroup and outgroup members. Subjects also estimated that outgroup members and other ingroup members were more discriminatory than themselves. These patterns show that parity rather than discrimination is the socially desirable behavior for group members in such studies. Similar patterns of self-reports were obtained in the other studies discussed in this chapter, thus confirming that parity is the more socially desirable response in such intergroup studies (Turner, 1983a, 1983b).

Other postsession questionnaire results were analysed using MANOVA procedures. Importantly, results show that categorization per se led to more ingroup than outgroup liking for group members. Intergroup perception measures show that all group members, regardless of their power ascription, liked members of their own group more than members of the outgroup. Thus, whereas minimal categorization was sufficient to trigger more ingroup than outgroup liking, power differentials were more predictive of discriminatory behavior.

SIT postulates that discrimination serves to establish a positive social identity within minimal group studies. Group members who discriminate should have more positive feelings about their group membership than those who do not discriminate (Tajfel, 1981). These expectations are supported by results that show that the absolute-, high-, and equal-power group members reported feeling more comfortable, satisfied, and happy about their group membership than did low- and no-power group members. Although all group members identified with their ascribed own group, high-power (70%) group members, who were the most discriminatory group in the study, also reported the highest level of identification with their own group.

The results of the present study perhaps identify the minimal effects of power differentials on intergroup discrimination. Individuals in dominant group position used their power to discriminate against subordinate outgroup members. Individuals in the equal-power (50%) position also discriminated, thus replicating the classic minimal group effect. Even group members who were subordinate but had some power (30%) did use the little power they had to discriminate against outgroup members. However, the minimal group effect was eliminated in the no-power group situation. Group members without power did not discriminate at all against outgroup members. Taken together, these results suggest that usable power is a necessary condition for effective discrimination (Sachdev & Bourhis, 1985; Ng, 1982). To further test the validity of these conclusions, the next series of studies was conducted with real life category group members, namely same-gender and opposite-gender groups.

STUDY 2: POWER DIFFERENTIALS BETWEEN SAME-GENDER GROUPS

In a recent review of the male–female relation literature, Ashmore and Del Boca (1986) pointed to the growing need to consider males and females not just as individuals but also as group members whose conduct could be examined using an intergroup relation approach (see also Hacker, 1951; Lips, 1981). Although recognizing that relations between the genders have a number of unique features (marriage, procreation), numerous authors have noted that power differentials between males and females as group members do exist and are represented differently in terms of their perceived legitimacy and stability in the intergroup structure (Archer & Lloyd, 1985; Deaux, 1985; Del Boca & Ashmore, 1986; Ellyson & Dovidio, 1985). However, despite calls for studying male–female relations from an intergroup perspective, little empirical research using such an approach has emerged in the literature (however, see Dion, 1986; Gurin & Markus, 1989; Lorenzi-Cioldi, 1988).

The next three studies address both the conceptual and empirical lacunas in the area of male–female intergroup relations. The first two laboratory studies explore the effect of power differentials on the discriminatory and parity strategies of same-gender and opposite-gender groups using our previous power study as a comparison baseline (Sachdev & Bourhis, 1985). The last laboratory study focuses on social change strategies adopted by opposite-gender groups in a situation where the power differential between the groups is unstable. Theoretically, these laboratory studies are significant, because they use real-life social groups to test and modify key aspects of social identity theory (Skevington &

Baker, 1989). In turn, the adoption of SIT as a framework for analyzing male–female relations as group members provides a much needed complimentary approach to the existing body of research dealing with men and women as individuals (Deaux & Major, 1987; Eagly, 1987; Ellyson & Dovidio, 1985).

Williams and Giles (1978) proposed the first analysis of male–female intergroup relations from the perspective of social identity theory. However, SIT research conducted in the laboratory has been criticized by Williams (1984) who noted that most studies have either used only males as subjects or have used mixed-gender ingroup–outgroup categorizations without adequate checks for possible gender effects in minimal group results. Furthermore, SIT theorists have also been criticized for failing to consider possible differences in the social identities of males and females as gender groups (Skevington & Baker, 1989).

Williams (1984) claimed that men and women derive their self-esteem from group membership in fundamentally different ways. As in SIT, males, through socialization, strive for favorable social comparisons and group distinctiveness, given their primary concerns with achievement, competition, and success. Williams (1984) labeled this an *agentic* social identity. However, Williams argued that positive social identity may also be attained through interpersonal attachments and through within and between group cooperation for which SIT fails to account. Social identity derived from such relational concerns is referred to as *communal* and could be seen as the main concern of female group members. This communal orientation may lead females to be more concerned with parity strategies as a way of achieving a positive group distinctiveness rather than through discrimination as is usually the case in minimal group research.

The agentic versus communal explanation of gender differences in group behavior represents a "dispositional" approach in which male and female behavior depends on internalized factors that act to produce a distinctive male behavior versus a distinctive female behavior. According to this approach, these pervasive behaviors represent basic and fundamental differences between the genders. Indeed, Katz (1986) proposed that men and women develop distinctive "gender identities" related to the experiences and feelings that individuals derive as a result of membership in their gender group. Core gender identities are developed as early as 3 years of age and serve as "the foundation on which other aspects of identity rest" (Katz, 1986, p. 33). Once formed, gender identity is thought to be relatively stable and pervasive, causing members to actively compare and evaluate themselves and others in accordance with gender group membership. Thus, gender groups are well suited for intergroup analysis because many of the central features of gender identity can be understood from a SIT perspective (Skevington & Baker, 1989; Williams & Giles, 1978).

Although the agentic–communal distinction has received some empirical support in pay allocation paradigms among male and female individuals (e.g., Watts, Messe, & Vallacher, 1982), as yet no empirical research has systematically addressed this distinction in the context of male–female intergroup relations. Although a dispositional approach to male–female intergroup behavior could be partially explained as a social creativity strategy, SIT must still account for the possibility that males and females derive their positive social identity from different types of group distinctiveness dimensions (Skevington, 1989). Thus, if a dispositional explanation were supported in the present research, SIT would have to be modified by including the possibility of a communal-derived social identity, in addition to the competitive group distinctiveness notion that is more characteristic of an agentic orientation.

Theorists such as Breakwell (1979) questioned the dispositional approach and argued that gender differences in intergroup behavior are not rooted in the sexes themselves as gender-typical behavior but are determined situationally by virtue of the status and power position occupied by male and female group members in the social structure. For instance, Bartol and Martin (1986) suggested that apparent gender differences in group behavior can be explained by initial differences in status between males and females as they entered their experimental task groups. Thus, in certain settings, gender is seen mainly as a status characteristic reflecting sex typed roles in which, for instance, males act as high-status group members whereas females act as low-status group members (Eagly & Wood, 1982; Eagly, 1987). This is essentially the line of argument proposed by expectation states theory within the sociological literature on interpersonal relations (Berger, Fisek, & Norman, 1989; Berger, Rosenholtz, & Zelditch, 1980).

A similar line of argument has been used to help account for interpersonal visual displays of dominance between men and women in mixed-gender interactions. Using expectation states theory as a conceptual framework, Dovidio, Ellyson, Keating, Hettman, & Brown (1988) showed that both men and women high in expert or reward power displayed high visual dominance vis-à-vis opposite-gender interlocutors with low expert or reward power. In contrast, men and women low in expert or reward power displayed low visual dominance vis-à-vis high-power, opposite-gender interlocutors. However, in conditions where both male and female individuals did not possess differential expertise or reward power, visual displays of power were related to the gender of the interactants. In this case, males engaged in visual displays of dominance toward females, whereas females engaged in low displays of visual dominance toward males, thus reflecting consensual stereotypes about the relative power position of males and females in the social structure (Ellyson & Dovidio, 1985).

In another study of interpersonal relations between male and female individuals, Molm (1985) investigated the effects of gender on the evaluation of others in powerful and less powerful positions. The study varied the gender of the powerful and powerless person in same-gender and opposite-gender dyads. An analysis of the social interaction of the dyads along with subjects' perceptions of each other in the situation indicates that power rather than gender had the greatest effect on the perceived power and evaluative ratings of the powerful and less powerful interactants. Likewise, results show that the power position per se rather than the gender of the interactants best accounts for the use of power in both the same-gender and opposite-gender dyads. Molm (1985) concluded that it is the power position of individuals rather than their gender per se that best accounts for their perceptions and behaviors in the study.

Taken together, these studies of interpersonal relations between dominant and subordinate individuals suggest that a sociostructural account may be most pertinent in accounting for the intergroup behavior of same-gender and opposite-gender groups. It is the position of gender groups in the social structure rather than their dispositional agentic or communal orientation which may best predicts the intergroup behavior of males and females as group members. We note that no empirical research focuses on how males and females use power as group members to distribute valued resources between ingroup and outgroup members. It is to explore this important issue of intergroup power and gender that the following series of laboratory experiments were conducted.

The use of male and female undergraduates to study relations between males and females as group members in laboratory experiments raises the important issue of the beliefs and ideologies such students have concerning the nature of female–male group relations as they enter the experimental situation (Eagly & Mladinic, 1989; Lips, 1981; Williams & Giles, 1978). Beliefs about the stability and legitimacy of status and power differentials existing between males and females as groups in society and in the university setting were surveyed by Cole and Bourhis (1988) with 310 English Canadian undergraduates attending the same Ontario university as the subjects who took part in the laboratory experiments. Survey results show that male and female undergraduates identified strongly with their gender group and felt highly positive, secure, and happy about their gender-group membership. Although both males and females had quite liberal sex-role ideologies as measured on the Attitude Towards Women scale (AWS), female undergraduates had significantly more liberal sex-role ideologies than did the male undergraduates (Spence, Helmreich, & Stapp, 1973). The students perceived power and status to be important for both males and females as gender groups. However, both male and female undergraduates perceived that men have more power and status than women in society in general, in the workforce, and on the university campus. Although both males and females felt this power imbalance was illegitimate, female undergraduates felt this even more strongly than males. Male and female undergraduates perceived women, as a group, to be gaining in power and status, whereas they perceived men to be losing power and status in the long run. Taken together, these survey results show that power and status differentials between gender groups are important for female and male undergraduates and that students perceive relations between the gender groups as being somewhat unfair but in the process of changing towards greater equality.

The design, procedures, and subjects used in this group-power experiment are virtually identical to those used in the Sachdev and Bourhis (1985) study conducted with mixed-gender groups. However, in this study, power differentials were established within same-gender groups (Cole & Bourhis, 1990). That is, distribution of resources was always made between ingroup and outgroup members whose gender was the same as the subject. The subjects who took part in this study were 178 female and 169 male English Canadian undergraduates attending the same Ontario university as those who took part in the mixed-gender study. Using the same procedures as in the Sachdev and Bourhis (1985) study, three intergroup-power situations were created: (a) absolute- (100%) versus no-power groups (0%), (b) high- (70%) versus low-power groups (30%), and (c) equal-power groups (50%). The study yields a 2 × 5 factorial design with two levels of gender (male–female) and five levels of power (100%, 70%, 50%, 30%, and 0% power). Subjects were involved in the same decision task as the Sachdev and Bourhis (1985) study and distributed the extra course credit to ingroup and outgroup others using not only the Tajfel matrices but also a 100-point, zero-sum distribution. Intergroup perception items used in the mixed-gender study were supplemented with items pertinent to the gender composition of the groups.

If the sociostructural analysis were to prevail, then power differentials between groups rather than their gender composition would emerge as the main determinant of intergroup behavior between same-gender groups. Under such circumstances, a replication of the Sachdev and Bourhis (1985) results could be expected. Regardless of the gender composition of the groups, equal-power group members would be expected to discriminate against outgroups, thus replicating previous minimal group studies. Further, one could expect dominant group members to be more discriminatory than subordinate groups. Finally, no-power groups regardless of gender would not be expected to discriminate against dominant outgroups, thus confirming that power is a necessary condition for effective discrimination.

Alternatively, differences in the agentic versus communal orientation of male and females may be the main determinant of intergroup behavior in the study. Regardless of their power ascription, female group members may be more concerned with parity than with discrimination when distributing the resources, thus reflecting a fundamentally communal orientation upon which female social identity may be based. In contrast, male group members may be quite discriminatory, reflecting a basically competitive agentic male social identity. Patterns of results showing that males are more discriminatory than females across power conditions would more strongly support the dispositional than the sociostructural explanation of male–female behavior in group relations.

Results presented in Fig. 8.2 and Fig. 8.3 show the mean scores for the three discrimination strategies obtained in the five power conditions with female and male group members. Within condition Wilcoxon Matched Pairs Tests show that male and female group members with power discriminate against same-gender outgroup members on both the Tajfel matrices and the 100-point, zero-sum distribution. As in the usual minimal group studies, both male and female group

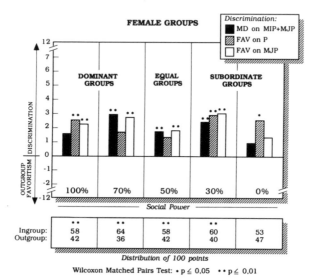

FIG. 8.2. Discrimination between dominant and subordinate female groups. Tajfel matrices and zero-sum distribution of 100 points (Cole & Bourhis, 1990).

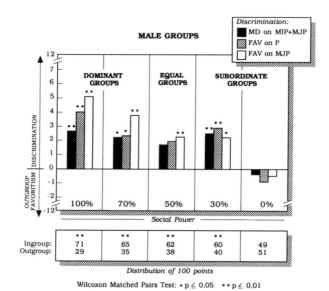

FIG. 8.3. Discrimination between dominant and subordinate male groups. Tajfel matrices and zero-sum distribution of 100 points (Cole & Bourhis, 1990).

members with 50% power discriminate against the outgroup. Both male and female group members who were dominant (100% and 70% power) discriminated against subordinate outgroup members. Subordinate groups with 30% power also discriminated against the outgroup. As in the mixed-gender study, group members with no power did not discriminate against dominant out-group members (one single exception being powerless females who discriminated somewhat on the FAV on P strategy). Methodologically, it is important to note that these Tajfel matrices results are corroborated by results obtained on the 100-point, zero-sum distributions.

To test for between-condition effects, a 5 × 2 MANOVA was conducted on the parity and discrimination strategies. The analysis shows no gender-main effect and no gender by power interaction on the distribution strategies. However, a power-main effect shows that group members differed in their use of the discrimination strategies depending on their position in the power structure. Univariate analyses clearly showed that both male and female group members with power (100%, 70%, 50%, and 30%) were more discriminatory than no (0%) power group members. Univariate analysis conducted on the parity strategy shows that group members were equally parity oriented regardless of their position in the power structure. As is usually the case in minimal group studies, both male and female group members across the design were more parity oriented than discriminatory in orientation.

The results of the postsession questionnaire items provide additional insights on how male and female group members felt in the study. Overall, MANOVA analyses (2 × 5) show power main effects but few gender or power × gender interactions. Both male and female group members identified with their own power group regardless of their power ascription. However, dominant and equal power group members had a more positive social identity than subordinate group members. Dominant (100%, 70%) and equal- (50%) power group members felt more comfortable, satisfied, and happy with their group membership than did subordinate group members (30% and 0% groups). Dominant and equal power group members also liked being members of their own group more than did subordinate group members. Importantly, the usual categorization effect was obtained: Regardless of their power position, group members liked members of their own group more than they liked members of the outgroup.

How did male and female subjects feel as members of their own gender group in the experiment? First of all, both female and male subjects identified strongly with their own gender group and felt highly positive, secure, and happy about their gender-group membership regardless of their power ascription in the experiment. Though both gender groups had very liberal sex-role ideologies as measured by the AWS scale (Spence et al., 1973), females emerged with significantly more liberal sex-role ideologies than did male undergraduates. Female undergraduates also defined themselves more as somewhat "feminist" in ideological orientation than did male undergraduates. Virtually identical patterns of gender identification and sex-role ideologies were obtained with male and female undergraduates who took part in the other laboratory studies discussed in this chapter. Taken together, these patterns of results confirm that the students who took part in our three laboratory studies were equivalent with regard to their respective gender identities and beliefs.

Overall, results of this study support the sociostructural analysis rather than the dispositional one. No differences emerged in the parity and discriminatory behavior of male and female group members. Female group members were no less discriminatory than male group members. Instead, it is the position of group members in the power structure that best accounts for male and female discriminatory behavior. Both male and female group members with power discriminated against the outgroup, whereas group members without power did not discriminate. These results corroborate the Sachdev and Bourhis (1985) study with mixed-gender groups, showing that usable power is a necessary condition for effective discrimination. However, rejection of the dispositional explanation of male–female intergroup behavior is premature until the effects of power differentials on discrimination are tested not only in same-gender group settings but also in opposite-gender group situations. This is the focus of the third laboratory experiment presented in this chapter.

STUDY 3: POWER DIFFERENTIALS BETWEEN OPPOSITE-GENDER GROUPS

Cole and Bourhis (1990) established power differentials between opposite-gender groups using an experimental design and procedures that are virtually identical to those used in the same and mixed-gender studies (Sachdev & Bourhis, 1985). Subjects were 165 male and 176 female undergraduates whose background was English Canadian and who attended the same Ontario university as the subjects in the previous studies. Using identical procedures as the same-gender study, three intergroup power situations were created: (a) absolute- (100%) versus no-power groups (0%), (b) high- (70%) versus low-power groups (30%), and (c) equal-power groups (50%). The study yields a 2 × 5 factorial design with two levels of gender and five levels of power. Subjects were involved in the same decision task as the Sachdev and Bourhis (1985) study and distributed the extra course credit to ingroup and outgroup others, using not only the Tajfel matrices but also a 100 point, zero-sum distribution. However, in this study the distribution of resources was always made between an ingroup member of one's own gender and an outgroup member of the opposite gender. Intergroup perception items used in the mixed-gender study were again supplemented with items pertinent to the gender composition of the groups.

If power remains the main determinant of intergroup behavior, one would expect the opposite-gender study to replicate the results of the mixed- and same-gender studies by showing that group members with power discriminate whereas group members without power do not. Alternatively, differences in the agentic versus communal orientation of males and females may be the main determinant of intergroup behavior in the study. Regardless of their power ascription, female group members may be more concerned with parity than with discrimination, reflecting a communal orientation, whereas male group members may be more discriminatory, reflecting a basically competitive agentic orientation.

However, unlike the same-gender study, the opposite-gender situation provides an experimental categorization that coincides with a real-life gender categorization of male and female groups. This double categorization accentuates the ingroup–outgroup dichotomy thus making the intergroup situation more salient and vivid (Deschamps & Doise, 1978; Vanbeselaere, 1987). Under such circumstances one would expect both male and female group members to discriminate more against outgroups than in the same-gender study.

Furthermore, it must be noted that the opposite-gender study is not strictly minimal in MGP terms, because exceptionally in this setting, ingroup and outgroup members are not entirely anonymous, given that group categorization is based on the sex of the subjects present in the same experimental room. Attraction between members of the opposite sex could influence patterns of intergroup discrimination over and above the power ascriptions imposed by the experimenter (Huston & Ashmore, 1986). Thus, compared to subjects in the same-gender study, males and females in the present study may emerge as less discriminatory against outgroup individuals who happen to be attractive members of the opposite sex.

Results presented in Fig. 8.4 and Fig. 8.5 show the mean scores for the three discrimination strategies obtained in the five power conditions with female and male group members. As seen in Fig. 8.4, within-condition Wilcoxon Matched Pairs Tests clearly show that female group members with power discriminated against outgroup males on both the Tajfel matrices and the 100-point, zero-sum distribution. Female group members with 50% power discriminated against outgroup males, thus replicating the usual minimal group effect. Dominant group females (100% and 70% groups) discriminated against subordinate males, whereas low-power females discriminated somewhat (MD) against dominant outgroup males. Female group members with no power whatsoever did not discriminate at all against dominant outgroup males. As seen in Fig. 8.4, these Tajfel matrices results are corroborated by the 100-point, zero-sum distributions.

Results presented in Fig. 8.5 show that male group members with 100% and 30% power discriminated against outgroup females. However, contrary to expectation, male group members with 50% and 70% power did not discriminate significantly against female outgroup members. In line with responses obtained with other powerless groups, male group members with no power (0%) did not discriminate at all against outgroup females.

To test for between condition effects, a 5 × 2 MANOVA was conducted on the

190   BOURHIS

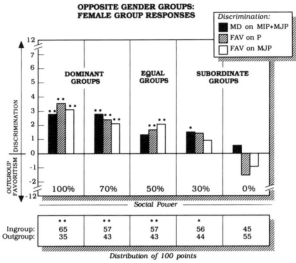

FIG. 8.4. Female group discrimination toward male outgroups, depending on group power. Tajfel matrices and zero-sum distribution of 100 points (Cole & Bourhis, 1990).

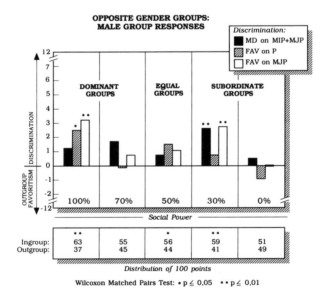

FIG. 8.5. Male group discrimination toward female outgroups, depending on group power. Tajfel matrices and zero-sum distribution of 100 points (Cole & Bourhis, 1990).

mean scores of the Tajfel distribution strategies. The analysis shows no gender-main effect and no gender-by-power interaction on the distribution strategies. However, a power-main effect shows that group members differed in their use of the discrimination strategies, depending on their position in the power structure. Univariate analyses show that, combined, male and female group members with power (100%, 70%, 50%, and 30%) were more discriminatory than no-power group members. The fact that powerless groups did not discriminate at all in this study corroborates results of the mixed-gender and same-gender studies and confirms the notion that power is a necessary condition for effective discrimination.

Univariate analysis conducted on the parity strategy shows that group members were equally parity oriented regardless of their position in the power structure. As is usually the case in minimal group studies, both male and female group members across the design were more parity oriented than discriminatory in orientation.

Results from the postsession questionnaire provide insights that help account for the intergroup behavior of the male and female group members in this study. As in the same-gender study, both male and female subjects identified with their own gender group, regardless of their power ascription. Dominant (70% and 100%) and equal-power group members felt more comfortable, satisfied, and happy with their power group membership than did subordinate group members (0% and 30%). Importantly, dominant and equal-power group members also liked being members of their own group more than did subordinate group members.

Across the design, female group members reported liking members of their own gender group more than members of the male outgroup. This result is in line with previous studies that show that social categorization per se is sufficient to foster more ingroup than outgroup liking (Brewer & Kramer, 1985). However, unlike any other social categorization study, male group members, regardless of their power ascription, reported liking female outgroup members just as much as they liked male ingroup members. This pattern of intergroup liking helps explain why male group members with 50% and 70% power did not discriminate against female outgroup members. Nevertheless, despite liking female outgroup members, male group members with 30% and 100% power used their power to discriminate against outgroup females. Overall, these results suggest that opposite-sex attraction cannot be excluded from accounts of intergroup behavior between males and females as group members (Huston & Ashmore, 1986). That opposite-sex liking emerged for male group members but not for female group members reflects the enduring position of females as the objectified targets of male attention in society at large (Wolf, 1990). Clearly, both power differentials between group members and the special nature of male–female relations are needed to properly account for the intergroup behavior of opposite-gender groups (Lips, 1981; Skevington & Baker, 1989).

Taken together, results from the mixed-gender, same-gender, and opposite-gender studies show that group power is a necessary condition for intergroup discrimination. Regardless of the gender composition of the groups, dominant group members discriminated against subordinate outgroup members. In contrast, group members without power did not discriminate against the dominant outgroup. Without power, social categorization is not sufficient to trigger discriminatory behavior against outgroups.

STUDY 4: UNSTABLE POWER DIFFERENTIALS BETWEEN OPPOSITE-GENDER GROUPS

The results obtained in the power differential studies between the mixed-gender, same-gender, and opposite-gender experiments were obtained in intergroup settings that were meant to be and were perceived to be both stable and legitimate. Within these experimental situations, no alternative was explicitly present that allowed group members to challenge the imposed power structure between the groups. However, existing power and status differentials between real-life groups are often perceived as illegitimate and unstable and are thus seen as susceptible to efforts aimed at changing the structure of the intergroup situation (Tajfel, 1978). For instance, efforts by women acting as group members to change their power and status position within the social structure have been linked to perceptions that existing relations between the genders are illegitimate, unstable, and likely to change (Williams & Giles, 1978). Such social change beliefs were precisely those held by male and, especially, female undergraduates in the survey of male–female group relations conducted by Cole and Bourhis (1988) in the Ontario university in which the present series of studies took place.

Although intergroup situations that are perceived to be illegitimate are often considered unstable, many instances arise in which illegitimacy and instability can be treated as orthogonal variables (Turner & Brown, 1978). For instance, low-power group members may perceive their position to be illegitimate but highly stable, because their position is difficult to change precisely because they suffer from unfair disadvantages. Conversely, democratic systems can foster very unstable power relationships between contrasting political groups through the vagaries of voting outcomes that are nevertheless perceived to be quite legitimate.

In its analysis of social change, social identity theory emphasizes the relation between insecure social identity, discrimination, and social change phenomena. Within SIT, Tajfel (1978) proposed that perceived illegitimacy and/or instability of the intergroup situation contributes to insecure group identity and can be related to group members' attempts to change the structure of the intergroup situation (Turner & Brown, 1978). In such circumstances, SIT proposes that group members who have an insecure social identity discriminate in order to make their social identity more secure and satisfying.

Whereas SIT suggests that the desire for a positive social identity is at the root of social-change phenomena, theorists such as Russell (1938) and Ng (1982) argued that the desire for power per se is the key factor bringing about competition between groups in stratified societies. To the degree that power is seen as a desirable scarce resource unrelated to the social identity of groups, the desire for power per se may reflect processes related to realistic conflict theory (RCT) as proposed by Sherif (1966).

Questionnaire responses obtained in the Cole and Bourhis (1990) same- and opposite-gender power studies provide some support for the previous analysis. All subjects in the same-gender ($N = 347$) and opposite-gender ($N = 341$) studies were asked about how they felt concerning their power ascription in the experiments. If the study were to be run again, dominant and subordinate group members, regardless of their gender, declared they would prefer to be members of the dominant rather than the subordinate group. Furthermore, when asked to ascribe power differentials as a percentage between the ingroup and the outgroup for a subsequent study, male and female subjects in each study reported they would prefer their own group to have twice as much power (65%) as the outgroup (35%). These results show that a strong power advantage over subordinate outgroups rather than parity is seen as the more desirable position to hold within the power structure. However, it is notable that total hegemony (95%–100% power) over the outgroup is not the power differential option preferred by group members in these studies. Group members may feel that total hegemony over subordinate outgroups is more difficult to legitimize, especially if such an extreme power advantage is seen as unstable.

Only rarely has the critical issue of legitimacy and stability been addressed in empirical studies exploring how power and status differentials affect the intergroup behavior of group members (Caddick, 1982; Turner & Brown, 1978; Ellemers, Knippenberg, & Wilke, 1990). Given the paucity of empirical research on this fundamental aspect of SIT, Bourhis (1985, 1987a, 1987b) investigated the impact of insecure social identity on the intergroup behavior of both power and status differential groups within minimal group laboratory studies.

The focus here is on one study conducted with opposite-gender groups whose power differentials were perceived as unstable but fundamentally legitimate. In this study with opposite-gender groups, Bourhis (1990) created a legitimate but fundamentally unstable intergroup situation among 100% versus 0% power groups, 70% versus 30% power groups, and equal-power groups (50%). The study yields a 2×5 factorial design with two levels of gender and five levels of power. As in previous studies (Cole & Bourhis, 1990), power differentials between male and female groups were made legitimate by using a toss of a coin to determine which gender group was dominant and which was subordinate. However, unlike the previous studies, group members were asked to make two rather than just one set of decisions regarding the distribution of resources within the experiment. In the first decision task, the initial power structure was made unstable by giving group members a say in deciding how the power would be distributed between the groups within the experiment. Subjects made decisions about the distribution of power using a first set of Tajfel matrices made up of power points for ingroup and outgroup members. Subjects were told that both the experimenter's initial power ascription and those made by ingroup and outgroup members using the first set of power matrices would be combined to determine the definitive power distribution between the two groups. Without being told of the final outcome of the power distribution between the groups, subjects proceeded with the second decision task consisting of distributing the extra course credit to ingroup and outgroup members using credit matrices. Thus, unlike any previous minimal group studies, the decision-making task consisted of the completion of two rather than one Tajfel matrix booklet. As usual, Tajfel matrices responses were complemented with 100-point, zero-sum distributions. There were 221 English Canadian undergraduates who took part in this study (95 males and 126 females) conducted in the same Ontario university as the other studies presented in this chapter.

According to SIT, unstable intergroup situations contribute to insecure social identity and can trigger group members' attempts to change their position within the social structure (Tajfel, 1978). Consequently, it was hypothesized that, regardless of their power ascription, male and female group members in such unstable conditions would discriminate against outgroups in both their power and resource distribution decisions. Alternatively, differences in the agentic versus communal orientation of males and females may determine intergroup behavior in the study. Female group members may be more concerned with parity than discrimination, reflecting a communal orientation, whereas male group members may be more discriminatory, reflecting a basically competitive agentic orientation. Finally, given that this MGP study is not strictly anonymous, attraction between members of opposite-sex groups could lessen intergroup discrimination in the study.

The distribution strategies on the two sets of Tajfel matrices were analysed using a $2 \times 5 \times 2$ MANOVA analysis consisting of two levels of gender, five levels of power, and repeated measure on power-share versus course-credit distribution. The MANOVA analysis revealed no gender-main effect, no power-main effects, and no gender-by-power interactions. However, the MANOVA analysis did reveal a consistent and significant repeated-measure effect on both the parity and discrimination matrices. Overall, subjects, regardless of their gender or power ascription, discriminated more and were less parity oriented when distributing the share of power within the experiment than when they allocated the course credits between ingroup and outgroup members. This pattern of results also held for the 100-point distribution of the power and course-credit resources.

Taken together, these results provide some support for an important proposition put forward by power theorists (Russell, 1938; Marger, 1991). In the long run, achieving a greater share of power in the intergroup structure seems more important for own-group advancement than simply seeking the accumulation of pecuniary resources available in the intergroup setting. Achieving a greater share of power in the intergroup structure insures that empowered groups can consistently exert more choices about how they wish to discriminate—or not discriminate—in their distribution of resources to ingroup and outgroup members.

Within each condition, Wilcoxon Matched Pair Tests were conducted on the matrices and the 100-point distributions. Analyses conducted on the discrimination strategies revealed differential patterns of results between gender and power groups which are presented in Fig. 8.6 and Fig. 8.7 for female group members and in Fig. 8.8 and Fig. 8.9 for male group members.

As seen in Fig. 8.6 and Fig. 8.8 the importance of the present results is most manifest when they are contrasted with results obtained in the stable opposite-gender power study conducted by Cole and Bourhis (1990; see Fig. 8.4 and Fig. 8.5). Unlike the nondiscriminatory behavior of no-power group members in the stable opposite-gender study, powerless male and female group members in the unstable intergroup context discriminated a great deal when distributing the share

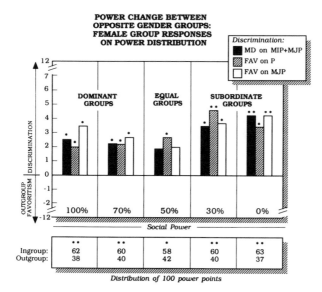

FIG. 8.6. Female group discrimination toward male outgroups, depending on group power that has been destabilized. Power distribution on Tajfel matrices and using zero-sum distribution of 100 power points (Bourhis, 1990).

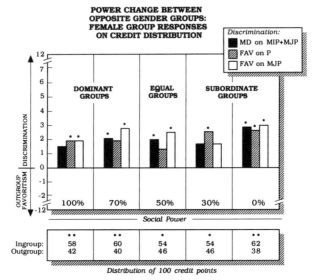

FIG. 8.7.   Female group discrimination toward male outgroups, depending on group power that has been destabilized. Credit distribution on Tajfel matrices and using zero-sum distribution of 100 credit points (Bourhis, 1990).

of power within the intergroup structure. Thus, powerless males and females in the unstable intergroup structure did not hesitate to discriminate against dominant opposite-gender groups if this meant they could improve their power position within the intergroup structure.

With regard to discrimination on the credit resource allocations, results presented in Fig. 8.7 show that no-power (0%) female groups discriminated strongly against outgroup males. However, as seen in Fig. 8.9, it is noteworthy that ascribed no-power (0%) males did not discriminate at all against dominant outgroup females in the distribution of the course credits. So, although no-power males discriminated against dominant females to gain usable power on the power distribution matrices (Fig. 8.8), they did not use their power gain to discriminate against females in the second distribution task dealing with the credit resource allocations.

Fig. 8.6 and Fig. 8.8 also show that low-power (30%) male and female group members discriminated strongly in their power distribution relative to the credit distribution strategies of low-power groups in the more stable power structure created in the Cole and Bourhis (1990) study (cf. Fig. 8.4 and Fig. 8.5). However, although low-power (30%) males and females discriminated strongly against dominant outgroups to gain usable power on the power matrices, they did not

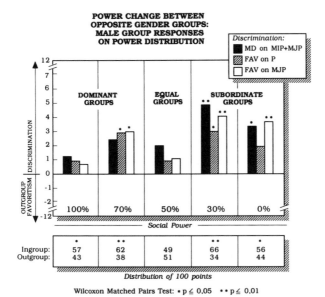

FIG. 8.8.   Male group discrimination toward female outgroups, depending on group power that has been destabilized. Power distribution on Tajfel matrices and using zero-sum distribution of 100 power points (Bourhis, 1990).

discriminate as much when it came time to allocate credit resources to ingroup and outgroup members.

Taken together, these results clearly support a basic premise of the present study: Subordinate and powerless groups discriminate against dominant outgroups in unstable intergroup situations, especially in cases where such discrimination improves the position of subordinate groups in the power structure.

Dominant (100% and 70%) and equal- (50%) power female group members in the unstable power study were consistent in their discriminatory behavior against outgroup males (Fig. 8.6 and Fig. 8.7). These results are consistent with those obtained with females in the stable opposite-gender study (cf. Fig. 8.4). However, male group members with power were not systematic in their discriminatory behavior against outgroup females, results that are also consistent with male responses in the opposite-gender study (cf. Fig. 8.5). As seen in Fig. 8.8 and Fig. 8.9, male group members with 100% and 50% power did not discriminate against outgroup females on either the power or credit matrices nor on any of the 100-point distribution items. Overall, we had expected much stronger and consistent discriminatory tendencies among dominant group members (100% and 70% power groups) whose ascendency was threatened by the unstable power structure created in the study.

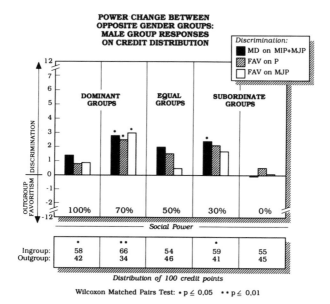

FIG. 8.9. Male group discrimination toward female outgroups, depending on group power that has been destabilized. Credit distribution on Tajfel matrices and using zero-sum distribution of 100 credit points (Bourhis, 1990).

Results from the postsession questionnaire provide insights that help account for the intergroup behavior of the female and especially the male group members in this study. As in the stable opposite-gender study, both male and female subjects identified with their own power group, regardless of their gender and power ascription. Again, the quality of group members' social identity was affected by their position in the power structure. Subordinate group members (0% and 30%) felt less comfortable, satisfied, and happy with their power group membership than did dominant group members (70% and 100%). Importantly, subordinate group members did not like being members of their own group as much as the dominant and equal-power group members.

However, the opportunity to improve one's own group position in the power structure did have a positive effect on how much subordinate group members liked being members of their own group. Results clearly show that subordinate group members liked being members of their own group more after they had a chance to improve their power share in the experiment than immediately following their initial ascription as subordinate groups. Improving one's own group share of power within the intergroup structure may be the strategy par excellence for achieving a more satisfactory social identity in the intergroup setting.

Despite the instability of the intergroup structure, dominant individuals liked being members of their own group more than did subordinate group members. However, dominant groups were somewhat affected by the instability of the intergroup structure, because they liked being members of their own group less following the power-change phase of the study than after the initial power ascription. It is clear that dominant groups have more to lose from a destabilized intergroup structure than do subordinate groups. It is no coincidence that in real life, dominant groups are more likely to support the perpetuation of stable intergroup power structures than is the case for subordinate groups (Marger, 1991).

Did group members expect their power-distribution strategies on the matrices to actually change their respective position in the power structure? Results from the questionnaire items dealing with this issue clearly show that they did. Subordinate group members (0% and 30%) rated their power position as significantly improved following the power-distribution task. In contrast, dominant group members (70% and 100%) believed their power positions dropped significantly after completion of the power-distribution task. Equal-power group members did not report any change in their power position during the experiment.

Despite a perceived substantial reduction in power differentials between the groups, subjects nevertheless expected the power structure to remain intact in favor of the ascribed dominant group. Results show that dominant group members still rated their own group power to be more substantial than what subordinate group members rated their own group power to be. It is also the case that dominant group members expected that they were more likely to obtain the extra course credit at the end of the experiment than did subordinate group members. Thus, the strong feelings of power advantage felt by dominant group members at the beginning of the study may have compensated somewhat for the insecurity created by the unstable intergroup situation. Through noblesse oblige, dominant group members may not have felt as compelled to discriminate against subordinate outgroups. This post hoc account seems most pertinent in the case of the absolute power, male group members, who did not discriminate at all against outgroup females in the study.

Results show that group members, regardless of their gender or power ascription, liked members of their own group more than members of the outgroup. These intergroup-liking results help explain the consistently discriminatory behavior of female group members against outgroup males. However, the male ingroup-liking results fail to account for their unsystematic discriminatory behavior towards outgroup females. These ambivalent male responses toward outgroup females again indicate that opposite-sex attraction cannot be excluded from accounts of intergroup behavior between male and female group members (Huston & Ashmore, 1986).

Finally, if the study were run again, dominant and subordinate group members, regardless of their gender, declared they would prefer to join the dominant rather than the subordinate group. Furthermore, when asked to ascribe power differentials between the ingroup and the outgroup for a subsequent study, subjects from both gender groups reported they would prefer their own group to have twice as much power (64%) as the outgroup (36%), thus corroborating the patterns obtained with same-gender and opposite-gender group members in our previous studies. Clearly, gaining a substantial power advantage is an important consideration for subordinate, equal, and dominant groups within both stable and unstable intergroup structures. Results showing such consistent desires for gaining dominance over outgroup members suggest that social psychologists can no longer afford to ignore group power as a key factor in the conduct of intergroup relations.

In line with social identity formulations (Tajfel, 1978), this study shows that subordinate groups in unstable intergroup structures do discriminate, especially in circumstances where such behaviors empower disadvantaged groups by improving their power position in the intergroup structure. This pattern of discrimination was obtained with both male and female subordinate and powerless group members, thus providing support for the sociostructural rather than the dispositional explanation of gender group behavior in unstable power structures. Furthermore, results show that group members were more discriminatory and less parity oriented in their power distributions than when they were involved in distributing the credit resources. Achieving a better share of power in the intergroup structure is more vital for effective group functioning, because it allows empowered groups to have more choices about how they wish to discriminate in their distribution of resources to ingroup and outgroup members.

CONCLUDING NOTES

The premise of the present research program is that the sociostructural position of laboratory and real-life groups plays an important role in determining the intergroup behavior of group members (Bourhis et al. 1992; Sachdev & Bourhis, 1990, 1991). The laboratory results discussed in this chapter highlight the central role that power plays in determining the discriminatory behaviors of dominant and subordinate gender groups within both stable and unstable intergroup power structures.

Taken together, the results of these laboratory studies show that dominant groups discriminate more than subordinate groups, whereas powerless groups do not discriminate at all against dominant outgroups. This was shown to be the case in stable power differential studies involving mixed-gender groups, same-gender groups, and opposite-gender groups. These results confirm a boundary condition to the now classic minimal-group effect. Without power, social categorization is not sufficient to trigger discriminatory behavior (Ng, 1982; Sachdev & Bourhis, 1985). Power is a necessary condition for effective intergroup discrimination. This conclusion is in line with Jones' (1972) classic writings on the relationship between power, prejudice, and racism. Jones wrote, "Racism results from the transformation of race prejudice and/or ethnocentrism through the exercise of power against a racial group. . ." (p. 117).

Clearly, more research is needed to better understand how group power plays its role in actualizing prejudicial attitudes into discriminatory behavior. Group power is too central a concept to be left out of current theorizing concerning the relationship between prejudice, stereotyping, and discrimination.

Overall, our laboratory results were obtained regardless of the gender composition of the groups, suggesting that it is the position of individuals in the power structure rather than their dispositional orientations that best accounts for discriminatory behavior in such intergroup settings. Since the late 1970s, many of the observed gender differences attributed to dispositional factors have been questioned in the light of more parsimonious sociostructural explanations of such differences. For instance, gender differences are more readily explained by power and/or status differentials between the sexes than by dispositional gender characteristics in studies dealing with (a) task orientation within face to face groups (Lockheed & Hall, 1976; Wood & Karten, 1986), (b) social influence (Eagly & Wood, 1982; Pugh & Warhman, 1983), (c) nonverbal power displays (Dovidio et al., 1988), (d) reward-allocation preferences (Reis & Jackson, 1981), and (e) interpersonal sensitivity (Snodgrass, 1985). The sociostructural accounts of the discrimination results obtained in this chapter are in line with these interpretations. However, our interpretations are formulated in intergroup terms as they apply to males and females acting as group members within stable and unstable power structures. Much conceptual and empirical work remains to be done to better integrate interindividual with intergroup analyses of male and female behaviors in these different domains of social behavior.

That both male and female group members across the three laboratory studies ($N = 909$) preferred their own experimental group to have twice as much power (65%) than the outgroup (35%) also attests to the desirability of achieving a favorable power position in the intergroup structure. Dominant group members across the studies also felt more comfortable, satisfied, and happy with their group membership than subordinate group members. Dominant group members also liked being members of their own group more than did subordinate group members, again suggesting that the former have a more satisfactory social identity than subordinate group members. Taken together, these patterns of intergroup perceptions, feelings, and behaviors attest to the key role of power in shaping the social identity of dominant and subordinate group members.

These laboratory studies also show that in unstable power situations, subordinate and powerless groups discriminated in order to improve their power position within the intergroup structure. These discriminatory responses were obtained with both male and female subordinate groups, thus providing additional support for the sociostructural rather than the dispositional explanation of group behavior in such power structures. That group members were more discriminatory and less parity oriented in their power distributions than when they were distributing credit resources attests to the importance of power in attaining a more favorable position in the intergroup structure. Gaining a stronger power position increases the effectiveness of discriminatory behaviors meant to increase the accumulation of valued resources for the ingroup. With the appropriation of valued resources that comes with greater social power, favorable comparisons with outgroups on valued dimensions such as wealth and status become more easily attainable and contribute to a more positive social identity.

Conceptually, the effects of power on intergroup behavior may be discussed in terms of Tajfel and Turner's (1986) social identity theory. According to SIT, group number and power are seen as any other valued dimension of comparison contributing to status differentials between groups (Tajfel & Turner, 1986). Thus, social power is seen as any other scarce resource (e.g., wealth) that contributes favorably or unfavorably to social status, depending on the outcome of social comparisons with outgroups. Although social status is considered central to SIT, group power is seen as just one of many comparison dimensions likely to contribute to the establishment of status differentials between groups. As such, SIT considers status differentials rather than power differentials as contributing most directly to social identity and intergroup discrimination. This conceptualization differs from the ethnic relations approach, which, as seen earlier, considers power differentials between groups as the crucial factor in accounting for discriminatory behaviors and the establishment of status differentials between groups (Jones, 1972; Marger, 1991). This conceptualization is also at odds with the results obtained in the power-differential studies presented in this chapter. Given the effect of power on social identity and its role in the actualization of discriminatory behavior, it seems that group power must be more centrally integrated within SIT (Tajfel & Turner, 1986). Empirically, a first step toward such a goal is to investigate the relative effect of group power, social status, and group numbers on both social identity and intergroup discrimination.

In a recent laboratory study, Sachdev and Bourhis (1991) obtained results showing that power, status, and group numbers—independently and in combination—have a strong impact on the parity and discriminatory behavior of minority and majority groups. Using the minimal group paradigm, group members who varied in power, status, and group numbers completed a decision-making task involving the distribution of valued resources to members of the ingroup and outgroup. Results clearly show that dominant group members were much more discriminatory and less parity oriented toward outgroup members than were subordinate group members. Members of high-status groups were more discriminatory and less parity oriented than members of low-status groups. More importantly for our current interest are the results that show that low-status groups who were dominant (i.e., powerful) were more discriminatory than low-status groups who were subordinate (i.e., powerless). Thus, despite their inferior status on a salient dimension of comparison, low-status dominant groups used their power advantage to discriminate against high-status outgroups who were subordinate.

Results also show that high-status group members felt more comfortable, satisfied, and happy with their group membership than did low-status group members. Status ascription contributed directly and significantly to the quality of group members' social identity, an effect that SIT predicts. In contrast, group power had virtually no such effect in this study. However, power position was much more predictive of actual discriminatory behavior than social status, a result that corroborates the results presented in this chapter and supports scholars of ethnic relations who consider power differentials between groups as the crucial factor in accounting for discriminatory behaviors (Jones, 1972; Marger, 1991). Clearly, group power is playing a much more central role within social identity theory than was originally anticipated (Tajfel & Turner, 1986).

Finally, original SIT formulations anticipated the role of stability and legitimacy in bringing about social change between groups (Tajfel, 1978; Turner & Brown, 1978). Ongoing laboratory and field research should help uncover the full implications of dominant and subordinate group relations, not only in stable and unstable intergroup relation situations but also in group relations where power and status differentials are perceived to be illegitimate and likely to change (Bourhis, 1985, 1987b; Ellemers et al., 1990).

The social psychology of intergroup relations has a rich tradition of focusing on the cognitive and motivational processes that account for prejudice, stereotyping and discrimination. The laboratory studies presented in this chapter highlight the equally important role of sociostructural factors such as group power, social status, and group numbers in accounting for the dynamics of intergroup perceptions and behaviors. The research agenda of the 1990s must be broadened to a more pluralistic theoretical and empirical approach that integrates cognitive, motivational, and sociostructural factors to better account for manifestations of both prejudice, stereotyping, and discrimination. This plea for a more pluralistic approach to the study of intergroup relations is not new. Was it not embodied in the classic contribution by Allport (1954) in *The Nature of Prejudice?*

ACKNOWLEDGMENTS

The research presented in this chapter was made possible thanks to grants from the Social Sciences and Humanities Research Council of Canada awarded to Richard Y. Bourhis. A version of this chapter was presented at the 7th Ontario Symposium on Personality and Social Psychology: The Psychology of Prejudice, held at the University of Waterloo, Kitchener-Waterloo, Ontario, Canada, June 1991.

The author wishes to thank the following individuals for their very useful comments on earlier versions of this chapter: Richard Ashmore, Marilynn Brewer, Rochelle Cole, Alice Eagly, André Gagnon, Léna Céline Moïse, Donald E. Taylor, and Mark Zanna. Comments and suggestions concerning this chapter would be much appreciated and should be addressed to: RICHARD Y. BOUR-HIS, Département de Psychologie, Université du Québec à Montréal, C.P. 8888, Succ. A, Montréal, Québec, Canada, H3C 3P8.

REFERENCES

Abrams, D., & Hogg, M. A. (Eds.). (1990). *Social identity theory: Constructive and critical advances.* New York: Harvester/Wheatsheaf.

Adorno, T. W., Frenkel-Brunswik, E., Levinson, D. J., Sanford, R. N. (1950). *The authoritarian personality.* New York: Harper.

Allport, G. (1954). *The nature of prejudice.* Reading, MA: Addison-Wesley.

Apfelbaum, E. (1979). Relations of domination and movements for liberation: An analysis of power between groups. In W. G. Austin & S. Worchel (Eds.), *The social psychology of intergroup relations* (pp. 188–204). Monterey, CA: Brooks/Cole.

Archer, J., & Lloyd, B. (1985). *Sex and gender.* New York: Cambridge University Press.

Ashmore, R. D., & Del Boca, F. (1986). Toward a social psychology of female–male relations. In R. D. Ashmore & F. Del Boca (Eds.), *The social psychology of female–male relations* (pp. 1–17.) New York: Academic Press.

Barth, E., & Noel, D. (1972). Conceptual frameworks for the analysis of race relations. *Social Forces, 50,* 333–348.

Bartol, K., & Martin, D. (1986). Women and men in task groups. In R. D. Ashmore & F. Del Boca (Eds.), *The social psychology of female–male relations* (pp. 259–310). New York: Academic Press.

Berger, J., Fisek, M., & Norman, R. (1989). The evolution of status expectations: A theoretical extension. In J. Berger, M. Zelditch, Jr., M. and B. Anderson (Eds.), *Social theories in progress* (pp. 73–99). London: Sage.

Berger, J., Rosenholtz, S., & Zelditch, Jr. M. (1980). Status organizing processes. *Annual Review of Sociology, 6,* 479–508.

Billig, M. (1976). *Social psychology and intergroup relations.* London: Academic Press.

Bornstein, G., Crum, L., Wittenbraker, J., Harring, K., Insko, C. A., & Thibaut, J. (1983a). On the measurement of social orientations in the minimal group paradigm. *European Journal of Social Psychology, 13,* 321–350.

Bornstein, G., Crum, L., Wittenbraker, J., Harring, K., Insko, C. A., & Thibaut, J. (1983b). Reply to Turner's comments. *European Journal of Social Psychology, 13,* 369–381.

Bourhis, R. Y. (1985). *Social change and power differentials in groups.* Grant from the Social Sciences and Humanities Research Council of Canada, Ottawa.

Bourhis, R. Y. (1987a). *Status and power differentials in male and female group relations.* Research grant from the Social Sciences and Humanities Research Council of Canada, Ottawa.

Bourhis, R. Y. (1987b). *Instability and power change in group relations.* Paper presented at the Social Identity Conference, Exeter, England.

Bourhis, R. Y. (1990). *Stable and unstable power differentials between same sex and opposite sex groups.* Paper presented at the 10th annual Nags Head Conference, Kill Devill Hills, NC.

Bourhis, R. Y., Cole, R., & Gagnon, A. (1992). Sexe, pouvoir et discrimination: Une analyse intergroupes des rapports Femmes-Hommes. [Sex, power and discrimination: An intergroup analysis of female-male relations]. *Revue Québécoise de Psychologie, 13,* 103–127.

Bourhis, R. Y., & Hill, P. (1982). Intergroup perceptions in British higher education: A field study. In H. Tajfel (Ed.), *Social identity and intergroup relations* (pp. 423–468). Cambridge & Paris: Cambridge University Press & Editions de la Maison des Sciences de l'Homme.

Bourhis, R. Y., & Sachdev, I. (1986). *The Tajfel matrices as an instrument for conducting intergroup research.* Hamilton, Ontario: McMaster University Mimeo.

Breakwell, G. M. (1979). Woman: Group and identity. *Women's Studies International Quarterly, 2,* 9–17.

Brewer, M. B. (1979). Ingroup bias in the minimal group situation: A cognitive–motivational analysis. *Psychological Bulletin, 86,* 307–324.

Brewer, M. B., & Kramer, R. M. (1985). The psychology of intergroup attitudes and behavior. *Annual Review of Psychology, 36,* 219–243.

Brown, R. J. (1988). *Group Processes: Dynamics within and between groups.* New York: Blackwell.

Brown, R. J., Tajfel, H., & Turner, J. (1980). Minimal group situations and intergroup discrimination: Comments on the paper by Aschenbrenner and Schaefer. *European Journal of Social Psychology, 10,* 399–414.

Caddick, B. (1982). Perceived illegitimacy and intergroup relations. In H. Tajfel (Ed.), *Social identity and intergroup relations* (pp. 137–154). Cambridge: Cambridge University Press.

Cartwright, D. (1959). Power: A neglected variable in social psychology. In D. Cartwright (Ed.), *Studies in social power* (pp. 1–14). Ann Arbor, MI: Institute of Social Research.

Cole, R., & Bourhis, R. Y. (1988). *Perceptions of power and status differentials between the sexes: Two survey studies.* Poster presented at the 49th Annual Conference of the Canadian Psychological Association, Montreal.

Cole, R., & Bourhis, R. Y. (1990). *Power differentials between the sexes: Two intergroup studies.* Paper presented at the 51st Annual Conference of the Canadian Psychological Association, Ottawa.

Cole, R., & Bourhis, R. Y. (1991). *Social identity, power and "passing": A field study of members of two sex segregated labour federations in Ontario.* Paper presented at the 52nd Annual Conference of the Canadian Psychological Association, Calgary.

Deaux, K. (1985). Sex and gender. *Annual Review of Psychology, 36,* 49–81.

Deaux, K., & Major, B. (1987). Putting gender into context: An interactive model of gender-related behavior. *Psychological Review, 94,* 369–389.

Del Boca, F., & Ashmore, R. (1986). Male–female relations: A summing up and notes toward a social-psychological theory. In R. D. Ashmore & F. Del Boca (Eds.), *The social psychology of female–male relations* (pp. 311–332). New York: Academic Press.

Deschamps, J. C. (1982). Social identity and relations of power between groups. In H. Tajfel (Ed.), *Social identity and intergroup relations* (pp. 85–98). Cambridge: Cambridge University Press.

Deschamps, J. C., & Doise, W. (1978). Crossed category memberships in intergroup relations. In H. Tajfel (Ed.), *Differentiation between social groups* (pp. 141–158). London: Academic Press.

Diehl, M. (1990). The minimal group paradigm: Theoretical explanations and empirical findings. In W. Stroebe & M. Hewstone (Eds.), *European Review of Social Psychology,* (Vol. 1, pp. 263–292). Chichester, England: Wiley.

Dion, K. (1985). Sex, gender, and groups: Selected issues. In V. O'Leary, R. K. Unger, & B. Strudler Wallston (Eds.), *Women, gender, and social psychology* (pp. 293–347). Hillsdale, NJ: Lawrence Erlbaum Associates.

Dovidio, J., Ellyson, S., Keating, C., Heltman, K., & Brown, C. (1988). The relationship of social power to visual displays of dominance between men and women. *Journal of Personality and Social Psychology, 54,* 233–242.

Dovidio, J., & Gaertner, S. (1986). *Prejudice, discrimination, and racism.* Orlando, FL: Academic Press.

Eagly, A. H. (1987). *Sex differences in social behavior: A social-role interpretation.* Hillsdale, NJ: Lawrence Erlbaum Associates.

Eagly, A. H., & Wood, W. (1982). Inferred sex differences in status as a determinant of gender stereotypes about social influence. *Journal of Personality and Social Psychology, 43,* 915–928.

Eagly, A. H., & Mladinic, A. (1989). Gender Stereotypes and Attitudes towards Women and Men. *Personality and Social Psychology Bulletin, 15,* 543–558.

Ellemers, N., Knippenberg, A., & Wilke, H. (1990). The influence of permeability of group status on strategies of individual mobility and social change. *British Journal of Social Psychology, 29,* 233–246.

Ellyson, S., & Dovidio, J. (1985). Power, dominance, and nonverbal behavior: Basic concepts and issues. In S. Ellyson & J. Dovidio (Eds.), *Power, dominance, and nonverbal behavior* (pp. 1–27). New York: Springer-Verlag.

Farley, J. (1982). *Majority–minority relations.* Englewood, NJ: Prentice-Hall.

Giles, H., Bourhis, R. Y., & Taylor, D. E. (1977). Towards a theory of language in ethnic group relations. In H. Giles (Ed.), *Language, ethnicity, and intergroup relations* (pp. 307–348). New York: Academic Press.

Gurin, P., & Markus, H. (1989). Cognitive consequences of gender identity. In S. Skevington & D. Baker (Eds.), *The social identity of women* (pp. 152–172). London: Sage.

Hacker, H. (1951) Women as a minority group. *Social Forces, 30,* 60–69.

Hogg, M. A., & Abrams, D. (1988). *Social identifications: A social psychology of intergroup relations and group processes.* London: Routledge.

Hogg, M. A., & Abrams, D. (1990). Social motivation, self-esteem and social identity. In D. Abrams & M. A. Hogg (Eds.), *Social identity theory: Constructive and critical advances* (pp. 28–47). New York: Harvester/Wheatsheaf.

Huston, T., & Ashmore, R. D. (1986). Women and men in personal relationships. In R. D. Ashmore and F. Del Boca (Eds.), *The social psychology of female–male relations* (pp. 167–210). New York: Academic Press.

Jones, J. M. (1972). *Prejudice and racism.* Reading, MA: Addison-Wesley.

Katz, P. A. (1986). Gender identity: Development and consequences. In R. D. Ashmore & F. Del Boca (Eds.), *The social psychology of female–male relations* (pp. 21–67). New York: Academic Press.

Kipnis, D. (1972). Does power corrupt? *Journal of Personality and Social Psychology, 24,* 33–41.

Lemyre, L., & Smith, P. (1985). Intergroup discrimination and self-esteem in the minimal group paradigm. *Journal of Personality and Social Psychology, 49,* 660–670.

Lenski, G. (1984). *Power and privilege: A theory of social stratification.* Chapel Hill, NC: The University of North Carolina Press.

Lips, H. (1981). *Women, men, and the psychology of power.* Englewood Cliffs, NJ: Prentice-Hall.

Lockheed, M., & Hall, K. (1976). Conceptualizing sex as a status characteristic: Applications to leadership training strategies. *Journal of Social Issues, 32,* 111–124.

Lorenzi-Cioldi, F. (1988). Individus dominants et groupes dominés. Images masculines et féminines [Dominant individuals and subordinated groups. Masculine and feminine images]. Grenoble: Presses Universitaires de Grenoble.

Marger, M. N. (1991). *Race and ethnic relations: American and global perspectives* (2nd ed.). Belmont, CA: Wadsworth.

Messick, D. M., & Mackie, D. M. (1989). Intergroup relations. *Annual Review of Psychology, 40,* 45–81.

Molm, L. (1985). Gender and power use: An experimental analysis of behavior and perceptions. *Social Psychology Quarterly, 48,* 285–300.

Ng, S. H. (1980). *The social psychology of power.* New York: Academic Press.

Ng, S. H. (1982). Power and intergroup discrimination. In H. Tajfel (Ed.), *Social identity and intergroup relations* (pp. 179–206). Cambridge & Paris: Cambridge University Press & Edition de la Maison des Sciences de l'Homme.

Oakes, P., & Turner, J. C. (1980). Social categorization and intergroup behaviour: Does minimal intergroup discrimination make social identity more positive? *European Journal of Social Psychology, 10,* 295–301.

Pugh, M., & Warhman, R. (1983). Neutralizing sexism in mixed-sex groups: Women have to be better than men? *American Journal of Sociology, 88,* 746–762.

Rabbie, J. M., Schot, J. C., & Visser, L. (1989). Social identity theory: Conceptual and empirical critique from the perspective of a behavioural interaction model. *European Journal of Social Psychology, 19,* 171–202.

Raven, B. H., & Kruglanski, A. W. (1970). Conflict and power. In P. G. Swingle (Ed.), *The structure of conflict* (pp. 69–110). New York: Academic.

Reis, H., & Jackson, L. (1981). Sex differences in reward allocation: Subjects, partners, and tasks. *Journal of Personality and Social Psychology, 40,* 465–478.

Russell, B. (1938). *Power: A new social analysis.* London: Allen & Unwin.

Sachdev, I., & Bourhis, R. Y. (1984). Minimal majorities and minorities. *European Journal of Social Psychology, 14,* 35–52.

Sachdev, I., & Bourhis, R. Y. (1985). Social categorization and power differentials in group relations. *European Journal of Social Psychology, 15,* 415–434.

Sachdev, I., & Bourhis, R. Y. (1987). Status differentials and intergroup behavior. *European Journal of Social Psychology, 17,* 277–293.

Sachdev, I., & Bourhis, R. Y. (1990). Language and social identification. In D. Abrams & M. Hogg (Eds.), *Social identity theory: Constructive and critical advances* (pp. 211–229). New York: Harvester-Wheatsheaf.

Sachdev, I., & Bourhis, R. Y. (1991). Power and status differentials in minority and majority group relations. *European Journal of Social Psychology, 21,* 1–24.

Schermerhorn, R. A. (1970). *Comparative ethnic relations: A framework for theory and research.* New York: Random House.

Sherif, M. (1966). *Group conflict and co-operation.* London: Routledge & Kegan Paul.

Skevington, S. (1989). A place for emotion in social identity theory. In S. Skevington & D. Baker (Eds.), *The social identity of women* (pp. 40–57). London: Sage.

Skevington, S., & Baker, D. (1989). Introduction. In S. Skevington & D. Baker (Eds.), *The social identity of women* (pp. 1–14). London: Sage.

Snodgrass, S. E. (1985). Women's intuition: The effect of subordinate role on interpersonal sensitivity. *Journal of Personality and Social Psychology, 49,* 146–155.

Spence, J., Helmreich, R., & Stapp, J. (1973). A short version of the Attitudes Toward Women Scale (AWS). *Bulletin of the Psychonomic Society, 2,* 219–220.

Stroebe, W., Kruglanski, A., Bar-Tal, D., & Hewstone, M. (Eds.). (1988). *The social psychology of intergroup conflict.* Berlin: Springer-Verlag.

Tajfel, H. (Ed.). (1978). *Differentiation between social groups.* London: Academic Press.

Tajfel, H. (1981). The social psychology of minorities. In H. Tajfel (Eds.), *Human groups and social categories* (pp. 309–343). Cambridge: Cambridge University Press.

Tajfel, H. (1982). Social psychology of intergroup relations. *Annual Review of Psychology, 33,* 1–39.

Tajfel, H., & Turner, J. C. (1986). The social identity theory of intergroup behavior. In S. Worchel & W. G. Austin (Eds.), *Psychology of intergroup relations* (2nd ed., pp. 7–24). Chicago: Nelson-Hall.

Taylor, D. M., & Moghaddam, F. M. (1987). *Theories of intergroup relations: International social psychological perspectives.* New York: Praeger.

Tedeschi, J. T. (1974). *Perspectives on social power.* Chicago: Aldine.

Turner, J. C. (1980). Fairness of discrimination in intergroup behavior? A reply to Branthwaite, Boyle, and Lightbown. *European Journal of Social Psychology, 10,* 131–147.

Turner, J. C. (1983a). Some comments on "the measurement of social orientations in the minimal group paradigm." *European Journal of Social Psychology, 13,* 351–367.

Turner, J. C. (1983b). A second reply to Bornstein, Crum, Wittenbraker, Harring, Insko and Thibaut on the measurement of social orientations. *European Journal of Social Psychology, 13,* 383–387.

Turner, J. C. (Ed.). (1987). *Rediscovering the social group: A self-categorization theory.* Oxford: Blackwell.

Turner, J. C., & Brown, R. J. (1978). Social status, cognitive alternatives, and intergroup relations. In H. Tajfel (Ed.), *Differentiation between social groups* (pp. 201–234). London: Academic Press.

Turner, J. C., Brown, R. J., & Tajfel, H. (1979). Social comparison and group interest in ingroup favoritism. *European Journal of Social Psychology, 9,* 187–204.

Turner, J. C., & Giles, H. (1981). *Intergroup behavior.* Oxford: Blackwell.

Vanbeselaere, N. (1987). The effects of dichotomous and crossed social categorizations upon intergroup discrimination. *European Journal of Social Psychology, 17,* 143–156.

Watts, B. L., Messe, L. A., & Vallacher, R. (1982). Toward understanding sex differences in pay allocation: Agency, communion, and reward distribution behavior. *Sex Roles, 8,* 1175–1187.

Williams, J. A. (1984). Gender and intergroup behaviour: Towards an integration. *British Journal of Social Psychology, 23,* 311–316.

Williams, J. A., & Giles, H. (1978). The changing status of women in society: An intergroup perspective. In H. Tajfel (Ed.), *Differentiation between social groups* (pp. 431–469). London: Academic Press.

Wolf, N. (1990). *The beauty myth.* Toronto: Vintage Books, Random House.

Wood, W., & Karten, S. J. (1986). Sex differences in interaction style as a product of perceived sex differences in competence. *Journal of Personality and Social Psychology, 50,* 341–347.

Worchel, S., & Austin, W. G. (Eds.). (1986). *Psychology of intergroup relations* (2nd. ed.). Chicago: Nelson-Hall.

9 Intergroup Research With the Tajfel Matrices: Methodological Notes

Richard Y. Bourhis
Université du Québec à Montréal

Itesh Sachdev
University of London, England

André Gagnon
Université du Québec à Montréal

The Tajfel matrices are dependent measures often associated with what is known in the intergroup literature as the *minimal group paradigm*. In the now classic minimal group studies, Tajfel and colleagues sought to uncover the necessary and sufficient conditions that foster intergroup discrimination (Tajfel, Flament, Billig, & Bunay, 1971). In the minimal group procedure, subjects are randomly categorized as members of one of two arbitrary groups specifically created for the purpose of the experiment. Factors known to contribute to discriminatory behavior, such as objective conflict of interest, intergroup contact, history of intergroup rivalry, intragroup loyalties, and self-interest, are systematically eliminated from the experimental intergroup situation. Despite these minimal intergroup circumstances, it was found that the mere categorization of subjects into ingroup and outgroup is sufficient to trigger intergroup discrimination (Tajfel et al., 1971). During the last 3 decades, a large number of studies have corroborated the effect of social categorization on intergroup discrimination (Billig, 1976; Brewer, 1979; Brewer & Kramer, 1985; Diehl, 1990; Messick & Mackie, 1989; Tajfel, 1978, 1981; Turner, 1978, 1981; Wilder, 1981).

Within minimal group studies, group members completed decision tasks that involved the distribution of valued resources to anonymous ingroup and outgroup individuals. The distribution was made using the series of point allocation scales known as the Tajfel matrices. Even though the Tajfel matrices are the dependent measures first used within minimal group studies, these matrices are quite useful for monitoring the discriminatory and parity behavior of individuals within other types of laboratory and field studies (Bourhis & Sachdev, 1986). Thus, the Tajfel matrices constitute a sensitive dependent measure that need not be limited to intergroup studies related to the minimal group paradigm.

The major goal of this chapter is to provide the methodological information needed to use and score the Tajfel matrices as an instrument for conducting intergroup research. The Tajfel matrices have been at the center of a lively methodological and conceptual debate in the intergroup literature. However, research evidence suggests that the Tajfel matrices do monitor subjects' social orientations in a valid, reliable, and sensitive manner (Aschenbrenner & Schaefer, 1980; Branthwaite, Doyle, & Lightbown, 1979; Bornstein, Crum, Wittenbraker, Harring, Insko, & Thibaut, 1983a, 1983b; Bourhis & Sachdev, 1986; Brewer, 1979; Brown, Tajfel, & Turner, 1980; Messick & Mackie, 1989; Turner, 1980, 1983a, 1983b). It is not the aim of this chapter to reiterate issues related to the previously mentioned debate. However, notwithstanding the efforts by Turner, Brown and Tajfel (1979), it is our opinion that some questions raised by the use of the Tajfel matrices have emerged because many researchers were not given a first hand opportunity to learn how to construct such scales and correctly calculate pull scores from the matrices. As an attempt to remedy this situation, this chapter deals with three practical concerns:

1. A brief description of the Tajfel matrices.
2. A step-by-step guide for calculating the pull scores from the Tajfel matrices.
3. Social orientations and the Tajfel matrices.

We hope that a detailed explanation of the use and scoring of these matrices will foster a broader use of the Tajfel matrices as a research tool for the study of intergroup behavior in both laboratory and field settings.

DESCRIPTION OF THE TAJFEL MATRICES

The Tajfel matrices were designed to measure the relative strength or pull of a variety of allocation strategies used by subjects in group experiments. The Tajfel matrices monitor five basic allocation strategies:

1. Fairness, or more precisely parity (P), consists of a choice that awards an equal number of points to ingroup and outgroup members. Note that the term *parity* is more precise than the term *fairness,* because parity clearly refers to the numerically equal distribution of points to ingroup and outgroup members. The term fairness is less adequate, because group members may distribute points unequally between ingroup and outgroup members, rationalizing that this distribution is only "fair" given the "superiority" of one group over the other.
2. Maximum joint profit (MJP) represents a choice that maximizes the

total combined number of points to both ingroup and outgroup recipients. MJP is an economically rational strategy, because it maximizes the the number of points obtained for all subjects in the experiment.

3. Maximum ingroup profit (MIP) is a strategy that awards the highest absolute number of points to ingroup members, regardless of awards made to outgroup members.

4. Maximum differentiation (MD) is a discrimination strategy that refers to a choice that maximizes the difference in points awarded to two recipients, the difference being in favor of the ingroup member but at the cost of sacrificing maximum ingroup profit. The maximum differentiation strategy is not economically rational, although it offers the greatest possible differentiation outcome between ingroup and outgroup fate, this differential being in favor of the ingroup.

The term *ingroup favoritism* (FAV) is used to denote a choice that combines both the maximum ingroup profit and maximum differentiation strategies. Thus, ingroup favoritism is used as a convenient way of representing a basically discriminatory orientation consisting of a combination of the MIP + MD strategies.

5. The Tajfel matrices also allow the measurement of what is known as outgroup favoritism (OF) which consists of allocating more points to outgroup members than to ingroup members. Negative scores on the ingroup favoritism (−FAV) strategy combination represent an orientation in favor of outgroup members. Outgroup favoritism is also reflected in a negative score on the maximum differentiation strategy (−MD) which denotes a concern for maximizing differentials between ingroup and outgroup allocations, but this time in favor of the outgroup. The outgroup favoritism strategies are least economically rational from the point of view of ingroup members, but such responses are nevertheless obtained in studies in which low-status groups acknowledge their inferiority vis-à-vis high-status outgroups (Sachdev & Bourhis, 1987, 1991).

Descriptions of the matrices and the strategies they assess are presented in Turner (1978) and Turner, Brown, & Tajfel (1979). The full range of methodological, statistical, and scaling issues related to the use of the Tajfel matrices are discussed in Bourhis and Sachdev (1986), Brown et al. (1980), and Turner (1983a). Table 9.1 provides examples of the most commonly used versions of the Tajfel matrices as reported in Turner et al. (1979). Typically, three classic matrix types are used:

1. *Matrix Type A* compares ingroup favoritism (FAV or MIP + MD) with maximum joint profit (MJP).

TABLE 9.1
Tajfel Allocation Matrices

Matrix Type A: FAV (MIP + MD) vs. MJP, strategies opposed (O) from the point of view of a member of Group Z:

Points to Member S of Group Z:	19	18	17	16	15	14	13	12	11	10	9	8	7
Points to Member P of Group W:	1	3	5	7	9	11	13	15	17	19	21	23	25

Matrix Type A: FAV (MIP + MD) vs. MJP, strategies together (T) from the point of view of a member of Group Z:

Points to Member E of Group Z:	25	23	21	19	17	15	13	11	9	7	5	3	1
Points to Member J of Group W:	7	8	9	10	11	12	13	14	15	16	17	18	19

Matrix Type B: MD vs. MIP + MJP, strategies opposed (O) from the point of view of a member of Group Z:

Points to Member H of Group Z:	19	18	17	16	15	14	13	12	11	10	9	8	7
Points to Member N of Group W:	25	23	21	19	17	15	13	11	9	7	5	3	1

Matrix Type B: MD vs. MIP + MJP, strategies together (T) from the point of view of a member of Group Z:

Points to Member M of Group Z:	1	3	5	7	9	11	13	15	17	19	21	23	25
Points to Member R of Group W:	7	8	9	10	11	12	13	14	15	16	17	18	19

Matrix Type C : P vs. FAV (MIP + MD), strategies opposed (O) from the point of view of a member of Group Z:

Points to Member V of Group Z:	16	17	18	19	20	21	22	23	24	25	26	27	28
Points to Member T of Group W:	16	15	14	13	12	11	10	9	8	7	6	5	4

Matrix Type C : P vs. FAV (MIP + MD), strategies together (T) from the point of view of a member of Group Z:

Points to Member O of Group Z:	4	5	6	7	8	9	10	11	12	13	14	15	16
Points to Member D of Group W:	28	27	26	25	24	23	22	21	20	19	18	17	16

2. *Matrix Type B* compares maximum difference in favor of ingroup (MD) with a combination of absolute ingroup profit (MIP) and maximum joint profit (MJP).

3. *Matrix Type C* compares parity (P) with ingroup favoritism (FAV).

Consider the two forms of Matrix Type A presented in Table 9.1. Subjects are required to choose only *one column/box* per matrix. Each column is made up of a top and bottom row. For the sake of illustration, assume that you are Member A of Group Z, and your task is to distribute monetary reward to individual members of your own group (Group Z) and the outgroup (Group W). Notice that as Member A of Group Z you are never allocating points to yourself. In this case, numbers in the top rows represent allocations that are made to an ingroup member (Group Z), whereas numbers in the bottom rows represent allocations to an outgroup member (Group W). If you choose to give 10 points to a member of your own group (Group Z), you must consider that you are also giving 19 points to a member of the outgroup (Group W). Subjects are specifically instructed to pay attention to awards made to both ingroup and outgroup members as is evident from the fact that only one column/box may be chosen from each matrix. A standard version of the instructional set used with subjects for completing the Tajfel matrices is provided in Appendix A of this chapter.

Generally, each point in the matrix has some value associated with it, such as money, points, scores, course credits, and so on. By comparing each subject's response in the series of different matrices presented in Table 9.1, pull scores that represent the relative strengths of different resource allocation strategies can be derived. In Table 9.1, consider Matrix Type A (strategies opposed), which measures the degree to which subjects are tempted to maximize ingroup favoritism when this strategy is pitted against the temptation to use maximum joint profit. In Matrix Type A, where allocations to the ingroup member are in the top row, a predominance of responses by Group Z members toward the left extreme suggests that subjects are discriminating in favor of their own group by employing FAV. Choices towards the right extreme of the same matrix are indicative of the influence of maximum joint profit (MJP). Note that option 7/25 represents the best maximum joint gain on this matrix because 32 points (7 + 25 = 32) can be gained by subjects in the experiment. In contrast, the FAV choice maximizes ingroup profit (19/1) but at the cost of sacrificing 12 points in maximum joint profit (19 + 1 = 20). However, in the strategies together (T) version of Matrix Type A, the optimum points of FAV and MJP coincide at the extreme left column of the matrix for members of Group Z. Thus, choices towards the left extreme of matrix A strategies together indicate the joint influence of ingroup favoritism (FAV) and maximum joint profit (MJP).

As seen in Table 9.1, Matrix Type B (strategies opposed) consists of MD vs. MIP + MJP and offers a Group Z member the choice between maximum differentiation (MD) and a combination of maximum ingroup profit (MIP) and maximum joint profit (MJP). In this case, the strongest option for maximum differentiation (MD) is the 7/1 choice in which a positive differential of 6 is achieved between the score awarded to an ingroup member of Group Z and an outgroup member of Group W. However, note that such an MD choice is achieved at the cost of the MIP + MJP option. In this case, the Group Z member is willing to sacrifice 12 points (19 − 7 = 12) in absolute ingroup gain for the sake of achieving a maximum differentiation of +6 between ingroup and outgroup fate.

Note as well that the MD choice is also achieved at the cost of maximum joint profit (MJP) because the 19/25 option represents a joint gain of 44 points (19 + 25 = 44), whereas the MD option represents a joint gain of only 8 points (7 + 1 = 8). It is clear that the MD strategy represents a differentiation strategy that in economic terms is not rational. Pitted as it is against a more rational combination of MIP and MJP, maximum differentiation (MD) is a discrimination strategy par excellence that offers a strong test of the need for intergroup differentiation postulated within social identity theory (Tajfel & Turner, 1986).

As seen in Table 9.1, the MD vs. MIP + MJP strategy is also offered in its strategies together (T) version. In this version of Matrix Type B, the optimum points of MD and MIP + MJP coincide at the extreme right column of the matrix (25/19) for members of Group Z. Thus, choices towards the right extreme of Matrix B (strategies together) indicate the joint influence of maximum differentiation (MD) and a combination of maximum ingroup profit (MIP) and maximum joint profit (MJP).

The parity (P) strategy represented in Matrix Type C (strategies opposed) represents an occasion to choose parity when it is pitted against the option of choosing ingroup favoritism (FAV = MIP + MJP). As seen in Table 9.1, the parity strategy (16/16) is clearly opposed to a strategy that combines MIP and MD (28/4). The parity (P) strategy is also presented in its strategies together (T) version where both parity and FAV coincide at the right extreme of Matrix C. Note that across the six types of matrices presented in Table 9.1, the option to choose a parity (P) response is always available. However, the advantage of using the Tajfel matrices lies in the fact that one can measure the strength of different types of discriminatory strategies independently of the more socially desirable use of the parity strategy.

Note that the same numbers are used in the two versions of each Matrix Type (A, B, and C) except that compared to the strategies opposed (O) version, the strategies together (T) version is arranged by reversing the matrix rows top to bottom and by reversing the columns left to right. The strategies together (T) version could also be achieved by simply reversing the Group Z and Group W labels so that outgroup allocations are on the top row, and ingroup allocations are on the bottom row of the matrix (outgroup/ingroup version of Matrix A compared to ingroup/outgroup version of Matrix A). Note that the ingroup/outgroup and outgroup/ingroup versions of Matrices A, B, and C are the usual ways of constructing the strategies opposed (O) and strategies together (T) version of each matrix type in previous studies and discussions (Bourhis & Sachdev, 1986; Turner et al., 1979; Turner, 1983a, 1983b).

Each of the six matrices described in Table 9.1 is provided on a separate page presented in booklet form to the subject. The order of matrix presentation is randomized within each booklet and varies from one booklet to another. For each booklet, the title page is followed by a second page on which subjects indicate to which of the two groups they have been assigned in the particular experiment.

CALCULATING THE PULL SCORES FROM THE TAJFEL MATRICES

Instead of using simple rank data from single matrices, Turner (1978) recommended the use of differences in simple ranks from the strategies opposed (O) and strategies together (T) versions of the same matrix type to assess subjects' distribution strategies. This procedure enables subjects to be used as their own controls against their idiosyncratic, extraneous response biases (for more details, see Bourhis & Sachdev, 1986; Brown et al., 1980; Turner, 1980, 1983a, 1983b). Difference scores obtained from this procedure are referred to as pull scores. Pull scores enable the assessment of the unconfounded influence of a variety of distribution strategies.

From each matrix type, two pulls are calculated. For instance, in matrix Type A, the pull of FAV on MJP and the pull of MJP on FAV are calculated using the strategies opposed (O) and the strategies together (T) versions of the matrix. Taken together, the two versions of Matrix Types A, B, and C allow for the measurement of six matrix distribution strategy pulls:

1. Pull of FAV (MIP + MD) on MJP.
   Matrix Type A
2. Pull of MJP on FAV (MIP + MD).
3. Pull of MD on MIP + MJP.
   Matrix Type B
4. Pull of MIP + MJP on MD.
5. Pull of P on FAV (MIP + MD).
   Matrix Type C
6. Pull of FAV (MIP + MD) on P.

With 13 columns per matrix, each pull has a theoretical range from -12 to $+12$. Negative pull scores are also considered to be psychologically meaningful strategies. Thus, negative FAV and negative MD implies outgroup favoritism, (OF), negative MJP indicates minimum joint profit, etc. (Turner, 1983a, 1983b).

The step-by-step method for scoring pull scores from Tajfel's matrices is summarized below as adapted from Brown and Bourhis (1978) and Bourhis and Sachdev (1986). Let us say that as Member A of Group Z you completed the six matrix pages as depicted in Table 9.2. (These matrices are the same as those presented in Table 9.1). For the sake of convenience, let us label each of the six matrices in Table 9.2 by a page number from 1 to 6. In an actual matrix booklet, pages should not be numbered because the matrix type on each page is presented in random order in each booklet.

Let us start with the matrix completed on page 1:

1. First identify the type of matrix you are dealing with, considering that you completed this matrix as Member A of Group Z. In this case, it is Matrix Type A in which FAV (MIP + MD) is pitted against MJP.

TABLE 9.2
Example of Tajfel Matrices presented in Random Order Completed by Either a Hypothetical
Member of Group Z or Group W.

Page 1
Points for Member Q of Group Z:

19	18	17	16	15✓	14	13	12	11	10	9	8	7

Points for Member R of Group W

1	3	5	7	9	11	13	15	17	19	21	23	25

Points awarded to member Q of Group Z: **15**
Points awarded to Member R of Group W: **9**

Page 2
Points for Member J of Group Z:

1	3	5	7	9	11	13	15	17	19	21✓	23	25

Points for Member F of Group W:

7	8	9	10	11	12	13	14	15	16	17	18	19

Points awarded to Member J of Group Z: **21**
Points awarded to Member F of Group W: **17**

Page 3
Points for Member L of Group Z:

16	17	18	19	20	21✓	22	23	24	25	26	27	28

Points for Member D of Group W:

16	15	14	13	12	11	10	9	8	7	6	5	4

Points awarded to Member L of Group Z. **21**
Points awarded to Member D of Group W: **11**

Page 4
Points for Member T of Group Z:

25	23	21	19	17✓	15	13	11	9	7	5	3	1

Points for Member H of Group W:

7	8	9	10	11	12	13	14	15	16	17	18	19

Points awarded to Member T of Group Z: **17**
Points awarded to Member H of Group W: **11**

Page 5
Points for Member C of Group Z:

19	18	17	16	15	14	13	12	11	10	9✓	8	7

Points for Member E of Group W:

25	23	21	19	17	15	13	11	9	7	5	3	1

Points awarded to Member C of Group Z: **8**
Points awarded to Member E of Group W: **3**

Page 6
Points for Member P of Group Z:

4	5	6	7	8	9	10	11	12	13	14	15✓	16

Points for Member I of Group W:

28	27	26	25	24	23	22	21	20	19	18	17	16

Points awarded to Member P of Group Z: **16**
Points awarded to Member I of Group W: **16**

See Tables 9.3 and 9.4 for scoring pull scores from the point of view of a member of Group Z (Table 9.3)
or from the point of view of a member of Group W (Table 9.4).

2. Determine whether the two sets of strategies are presented in the strategies opposed (O) or strategies together (T) form. In this case, Matrix Type A
is presented in the strategies opposed form:

Group Z :	19	. . .	7
Group W	1		25
	FAV	. . .	MJP

3. Locate the maximum value of the stationary variable (or pair of variables), that is, the one on which you are measuring the pull. In this case with Matrix Type A, it is MJP: 7/25. In this case, 7/25 serves as the zero point from which subjects move as they are tempted by FAV: 19/1.

4. Count the number of ranks (columns) from the MJP (7/25) zero point to the point the subject chose. In this case, as a Group Z member you chose:

$$\begin{array}{ll} \text{Group Z:} & 15 \\ \hline \text{Group W:} & 9 \end{array}$$

This choice represents a rank score of 8 for Matrix A when the strategies are opposed. If the temptation of FAV on MJP had been nonexistent for you, you would have chosen the 7/25 option, and the score would have been zero for this presentation of the matrix. However, in this example you have a rank score of 8 on the strategies opposed (O) form of Matrix Type A. This score should be entered in the scoring sheet presented in Table 9.3.

5. Because Matrix Type A (strategies opposed) is the first matrix type you came across in this booklet, you should search the strategies together (T) form of Matrix Type A in the matrix booklet. In this case, the strategies together (T) version of Matrix A is presented on page 4:

$$\begin{array}{llll} \text{Group Z:} & 25 & & 1 \\ \hline \text{Group W:} & 7 & \cdots & 19 \end{array}$$

Because FAV and MJP coincide at the 25/7 end of the matrix, use this as the zero point from which to calculate the rank score for the strategy together (T) version of Matrix Type A. Because you chose:

$$\begin{array}{ll} \text{Group Z:} & 17 \\ \hline \text{Group W:} & 11 \end{array}$$

the rank score for the strategy together (T) version of Matrix Type A is 4 and should be entered as such on the scoring sheet.

6. As seen on Table 9.3, the pull of FAV on MJP (Matrix Type A) is calculated by subtracting the rank score for strategies together (T) from the rank score obtained for the strategies opposed (O) versions of:

$$\text{pull of FAV on MJP} = O - T$$
$$8 - 4 = 4$$

TABLE 9.3
Scoring Sheet for Calculating Pull Scores From the Tajfel Matrices: Matrix Choices Completed by
a Member of Group Z

Condition:_____   Subject Number:_____

Matrix Type	Strategies Together (T)	Strategies Opposed (O)	Pull Scores
Type A:	Pull of FAV on MJP	Pull of FAV on MJP	Pull of FAV on MJP: 4
FAV(MIP + MD) vs. MJP	Group Z: 25 . . . 1 Group W: 7 19 * Zero point at 25/7 Matrix chosen: 17/11 Rank score (T) = 4	Group Z: 19 . . .7 Group W: 1 25 * Zero point at 7/25 Matrix chosen: 15/9 Rank score (O) = 8	O - T = 8 - 4 = 4 Pull of MJP on FAV: 0 (12 - O) - (T) = (12 - 8) - (4) = 0
Type B:	Pull of MD on MIP + MJP	Pull of MD on MIP + MJP	Pull of MD on MIP + MJP: 9
MD vs. MIP + MJP	Group Z: 1 . . . 25 Group W: 7 19 * Zero point at 25/19 Matrix chosen: 21/17 Rank score (T) = 2	Group Z: 19 . . .7 Group W: 25 1 * Zero point at 19/25 Matrix chosen: 8/3 Rank score (O) = 11	O - T = 11 - 2 = 9 Pull of MIP + MJP on MD: -1 (12 - O) - (T) = (12 - 11) - 2 = -1
Type C:	Pull of P on FAV	Pull of P on FAV	Pull of P on FAV: 7
P vs. FAV(MIP + MD)	Group Z: 4 . . . 16 Group W: 28 16 * Zero point at 16/16 Matrix chosen: 16/16 Rank score (T) = 0	Group Z: 16 . . .28 Group W: 16 4 * Zero point at 28/4 Matrix chosen: 21/11 Rank score (O) = 7	O - T = 7 - 0 = 7 Pull of FAV on P: 5 (12 - O) - (T) = (12 - 7) - 0 = 5

*The zero points identified for each of the strategies presented on this table are only relevant for the particular format presentation of the Tajfel matrices depicted in Table 9.2. Right-to-left and/or top-to-bottom reversals of rows and columns result in different zero points reflecting new configurations of strategies-together and strategies-opposed combinations.

7. As a short cut, one can calculate the pull of MJP on FAV (Matrix Type A) by using the following formula:

$$\text{pull of MJP on FAV} = (12 - O) - T$$
$$(12 - 8) - 4 = 0$$

8. As seen from Table 9.3 Matrix Type B, strategies opposed (O) (page 5) and strategies together (T) (page 2) are used to calculate:

The pull of MD on MIP + MJP and the
The pull of MIP + MJP on MD using the procedures described previously (Steps 1 to 8)

9. Likewise, calculations of:

The pull of P on FAV and
The pull of FAV on P

are obtained from the analysis of Matrix Type C, strategies opposed (O) (page 3) and strategies together (T) (page 6).

10. Pull scores of each strategy combination are quickly calculated using the scoring sheet presented in Table 9.3. Group means for the six strategy pulls are calculated from the pull scores obtained with each subject making up the respective groups in the study. Note that the score sheet presented in Table 9.3 allows an analysis of the strategies adopted by each subject individually. This allows the constitution of subgroups of individuals who may share common orientations as regards the completion of the Tajfel matrices across the design of the study (Platow, McClintock, & Liebrand, 1990).

To get a better feel of how the matrices work, practice calculating the pull score from the example given in Table 9.2 assuming that the responses were produced by Member B of Group W. The new pull scores generated from responses given by Member B of Group W are shown on the scoring sheet presented in Table 9.4. Note that Table 9.3 and Table 9.4 are worth printing as Tajfel matrices scoring sheets, because they can be used as a convenient method for calculating the pull scores of each individual member of Group Z (Table 9.3) and Group W (Table 9.4) who take part in a given study.

It must be pointed out that there are no mathematical reasons for two pulls calculated from the same matrix type to be negatively correlated a priori (Turner et al., 1979). For instance, in the case of Matrix Type C, the pull of P on FAV should be mathematically independent of the pull of FAV on P. However, it is customary to test for artifactual dependence between pull scores calculated from the same matrix type. The statistical procedure needed to test for artifactual dependence between pull scores is described in Turner et al. (1979). In most cases, correlation results show that obverse pulls obtained from the same matrix type are independent of each other (e.g., Sachdev & Bourhis, 1985, 1987, 1991). Thus, Tajfel's multichoice matrices provide a large number of distinctive alternative strategies whose precise relative strengths can be systematically measured.

How does one interpret the pull scores obtained in Table 9.3 and Table 9.4? Let us assume that the pull score obtained on Table 9.3 and Table 9.4 are mean scores obtained from two groups of subjects—members of Group Z and members of Group W, respectively. Let us assume, following appropriate statistical tests, that all pulls from Group Z members except MJP on FAV and MIP + MJP on MD are significant. Likewise, let us assume that all pull scores from Group W members are significant except the pulls of MJP on FAV and MIP + MJP on MD. Following appropriate between-subject group analyses, one can then com-

TABLE 9.4
Scoring Sheet for Calculating Pull Scores From the Tajfel Matrices: Matrix Choices Completed by
a Member of Group W

Condition:_____   Subject Number:_____

Matrix Type	Strategies Together (T)	Strategies Opposed (O)	Pull Scores
Type A:	Pull of FAV on MJP	Pull of FAV on MJP	Pull of FAV on MJP: -4
FAV(MIP + MD) vs. MJP	Group Z: 19 . . . 7 Group W: 1 25 * Zero point at 7/25 Matrix chosen: 15/9 Rank score (T) = 8	Group Z: 25 . . .1 Group W: 7 19 * Zero point at 25/7 Matrix chosen: 17/11 Rank score (O) = 4	O - T = 4 - 8 = -4 Pull of MJP on FAV: 0 (12 - O) - (T) = (12 - 4) - (8) = 0
Type B: MD vs. MIP + MJP	Pull of MD on MIP + MJP Group Z: 19 . . . 7 Group W: 25 1 * Zero point at 19/25 Matrix chosen: 8/3 Rank score (T) = 11	Pull of MD on MIP + MJP Group Z: 1 . . .25 Group W: 7 19 * Zero point at 25/19 Matrix chosen: 21/17 Rank score (O) = 2	Pull of MD on MIP + MJP: 9 O - T = 2 - 11 = -9 Pull of MIP + MJP on MD: -1 (12 - O) - (T) = (12 - 2) - 11 = -1
Type C: P vs. FAV(MIP + MD)	Pull of P on FAV Group Z: 16 . . . 28 Group W: 16 4 * Zero point at 16/16 Matrix chosen: 21/11 Rank score (T) = 5	Pull of P on FAV Group Z: 4 . . .16 Group W: 28 16 * Zero point at 4/28 Matrix chosen: 16/16 Rank score (O) = 12	Pull of P on FAV: 7 O - T = 12 - 5 = 7 Pull of FAV on P: -5 (12 - O) - (T) = (12 - 12) - 5 = -5

*The zero points identified for each of the strategies presented on this table are only relevant for the
particular format presentation of the Tajfel matrices depicted in Table 9.2. Right-to-left and/or top-to-
bottom reversals of rows and columns result in different zero points reflecting new configurations of
strategies-together and strategies-opposed combinations.

pare mean pull scores obtained from Group Z members with those obtained from
Group W members. Note that a summary of the usual statistical procedures used
to analyze pull scores from the Tajfel matrices is provided in Appendix B of this
chapter.

From such analyses, one can point out that parity is an influential strategy for
both Group Z and Group W members (pull of P on FAV = 7 for both groups).
However, results show that members of Group Z consistently discriminated
against members of the outgroup (Group W); they did so not only through use of
the two ingroup favoritism strategies (FAV on P = 5, FAV on MJP = 4) but also
by using the maximum differentiation strategy (MD on MIP + MJP = 9). In

contrast, Group W members were not only fair on the parity strategy (P on FAV = 7) but displayed a consistent pattern for outgroup favoritism as is evident from the negative pull scores on FAV on MJP = -4, and FAV on P = -5. In addition Group W members also sought maximum differentiation in favor of the outgroup as is evident from the negative pull of MD on MIP + MJP = -9.

From this hypothetical case, one can conclude that whereas members of Group Z discriminate a great deal against outgroup members, members of Group W consistently opted for strategies of outgroup favoritism and maximum difference in favor of the outgroup (e.g., Sachdev & Bourhis, 1987, 1991). The usefulness of presenting group members with the full range of Tajfel matrices is evident when one considers that although Group Z and Group W responses did not differ on the parity strategy, they differed a great deal on the ingroup favoritism and maximum differentiation strategies.

SOCIAL ORIENTATIONS AND THE TAJFEL MATRICES

As a further illustration of the use of the Tajfel matrices for conducting intergroup research, it is worthwhile to consider the pull scores presented in Table 9.5. The pull scores obtained for each of the six strategies (rows) presented in Table 9.5 were calculated on the basis of various resource allocation orientations (columns) that include: (a) maximum differentiation, (MD); (b) maximum ingroup profit, (MIP); (c) two types of maximum joint profit orientations (MJPa, MJPb); (d) parity, (P) and (e) outgroup favoritism (OF). It is important to note that the social orientations depicted in Table 9.5 are extreme ones, because actual subjects completing the matrices usually compromise between different social orientations rather than opt for a single orientation strategy. As seen in Table 9.5, other permutations of social orientation strategies are possible, including a combination of MIP + MJP and a strategy of seeking minimum outgroup profit (MOP) regardless of ingroup profit. However, these latter orientations serve as illustration and are not discussed further in this chapter. The important point to note is that each of these different strategy orientations can be clearly differentiated by analyzing the pattern of results obtained across *all* six pull scores calculated from the Tajfel matrices.

Let us assume that the pull scores presented in Table 9.5 were completed by six different members of Group Z who each completed the six matrices presented in Table 9.2. For the purpose of the present discussion, please ignore the ticked choices already marked in Table 9.2.

The pull scores presented in the first column of Table 9.5 represent the scores obtained by a member of Group Z who completed the Table 9.2 matrices with only one concern: that of maximizing the difference between points awarded to a member of his own group and a member of the outgroup, with the difference in favor of the ingroup member (MD). The raw scores reflecting this extreme MD

TABLE 9.5
Some of the Social Orientations Possible From the Tajfel Matrices

Tajfel Matrices: Pull Scores [1]	MD^2	MIP	MJPa	MJPb	P	OF	MIP + MJP	MOP
1. Pull of P on FAV (MIP + MD)	0	0	0	12	12	0	-12	0
2. Pull of FAV (MIP + MD) on MJP	12	12	0	0	0	-12	0	12
3. Pull of FAV (MIP + MD) on P	12	12	12	0	0	-12	0	12
4. Pull of MD on MIP + MJP	12	0	0	0	0	0	0	0
5. Pull of MIP + MJP on MD	0	12	12	12	0	12	12	0
6. Pull of MJP on FAV (MIP + MD)	0	0	12	12	0	0	12	0

Total and Percentage Points From Matrix Raw Scores

	MD^2	MIP	MJPa	MJPb	P	OF	MIP + MJP	MOP
1. (a) Total profit from E (in + outgroup)	168	204	216	216	168	204	216	132
(b) % of maximum profit from E	78%	94%	100%	100%	78%	94%	100%	61%
2. (a) Total of points to the ingroup	120	132	120	108	84	72	108	96
(b) % of maximum ingroup profit	91%	100%	91%	82%	64%	55%	82%	73%
3. (a) Total of points to the outgroup	48	72	96	108	84	132	108	36
(b) % of maximum outgroup profit	36%	55%	73%	82%	64%	100%	82%	27%
4. Difference between in/outgroup	72	60	24	0	0	-60	0	60

Note. The MJPa score is calculated from matrix scores in which the orientation in favor of MJP is expressed in conjunction with choices favoring the ingroup. The MJPb orientation is expressed in conjunction with choices favoring parity.

1. Matrices represent a 13-point scale with calculated pull scores that range in value from +12 through 0 to -12.
2. MD = maximum differentiation; MIP = maximum ingroup profit; MJPa = maximum joint profit favoring the ingroup; MJPb = maximum joint profit favoring parity; P = parity; OF = outgroup favoritism; MIP + MJP = maximum ingroup profit and maximum joint profit; MOP = minimum outgroup profit regardless of ingroup profit.

orientation involve the following matrix choices on each page of the matrix booklet presented in Table 9.2: (a) page 1: 19/1, (b) page 2: 25/19, (c) page 3: 28/4, (d) page 4: 25/7, (e) page 5: 7/1, (f) page 6: 16/16. These raw scores obtained on the Tajfel matrices are calculated as pull scores using the calculating scheme presented in Table 9.3. The six pull scores resulting from this pure MD strategy orientation are presented in the first column of Table 9.5. Note that a social orientation concerned with nothing else than maximum differentiation (MD in favor of the ingroup) yields maximum pulls of 12 on the three discrimination strategies (FAV on MJP, FAV on P, MD on MIP + MJP) but zero pulls on the other three strategies.

The pull scores presented in the second column of Table 9.5 represent scores obtained by another member of Group Z who in this case completed the Table 9.2 matrices with only one concern: that of maximizing the number of points awarded to a member of his own group regardless of the number of points allotted to members of the outgroup (MIP). The matrix choices reflecting this extreme MIP orientation involve the following matrix choices on each page of the matrix booklet presented in Table 9.2: (a) page 1: 19/1, (b) page 2: 25/19, (c) page 3: 28/4, (d) page 4: 25/7, (e) page 5: 19/25, (f) page 6: 16/16. The pull scores presented in the second row of Table 9.5 summarize this orientation using the calculation scheme presented in Table 9.3. Note that for this respondent concerned only with maximum ingroup profit, maximum pulls of 12 are obtained on the two FAV strategies and on the MIP + MJP on MD strategy. However, note that pulls of zero are obtained on the remaining strategies, including the MD on MIP + MJP matrix strategy.

The pull scores presented in the third column of Table 9.5 represent scores obtained from a Group Z member concerned with only one orientation: that of distributing the highest possible combined number of points to ingroup and outgroup others (MJP). The matrix choices reflecting this maximum joint profit orientation involve the following choices on each page of the matrix booklet presented in Table 9.2: (a) page 1: 7/25, (b) page 2: 25/19, (c) page 3: 28/4, (d) page 4: 25/7, (e) page 5: 19/25, (f) page 6: 16/16. However, note that in this case the MJP orientation also reflected a concern for favoring the ingroup on Matrix C (Table 9.2: page 3: 28/4, page 6: 16/16). As seen in Table 9.5, this first type of maximum joint profit (MJPa) orientation yields maximum pulls of 12 on the MJP on FAV strategy as well as on the FAV on P and MIP + MJP on MD strategies. The pull scores presented in the fourth column of Table 9.5 also represent a maximum joint profit orientation (MJPb) but this time with a concern for parity. This second MJPb orientation expressed in conjunction with choices favoring parity yields a pull of P on FAV of +12 and a pull of FAV on P of zero (Table 9.2 raw scores: page 3: 16/16, page 6: 16/16). Thus, two maximum joint profit orientations can be differentiated using the Tajfel matrices.

The pull scores presented in the fifth column of Table 9.5 represent scores obtained from a member of Group Z who completed the Table 9.2 matrices with only one concern: that of always distributing equal numbers of points to a member of his own group and to a member of the outgroup. The matrix choices reflecting this single-minded parity (P) orientation involve choosing either the 13/13 or 16/16 options of each page of the matrix booklet presented in Table 9.2. Note that the resulting calculations for such matrix choices yield zero pull scores for all strategies except the one of concern, namely a score of 12 on the P on FAV strategy.

Finally, the pull scores presented in the sixth column of Table 9.5 represent scores obtained from a member of Group Z who completed the Table 9.2 matrices with only one concern: that of always awarding more points to a member of the outgroup regardless of the number of points allocated to members of the ingroup. The matrix choices reflecting this extreme outgroup favoritism (OF) orientation involve the following matrix choices on Table 9.2: (a) page 1 = 7/25, (b) page 2 = 25/19, page 3 = 16/16, (d) page 4 = 1/19, (e) page 5 = 19/25, (f) page 6 = 4/28. As one would expect, the outgroup favoritism (OF) orientation yields a pull of −12 on the two FAV strategies, whereas a pull of +12 is obtained on the MIP + MJP on MD strategy.

The pattern of results presented in Table 9.5 shows how each unique social orientation betrays its presence by producing distinctive sets of pull scores (Turner 1983a, 1983b). It is by considering the pattern of results obtained across the six pull scores that one can more readily identify the distinctive orientations adopted by group members in their allocation of resources to ingroup and outgroup members. However, it is important to note that results obtained using the Tajfel matrices are rarely extreme, because matrix choices usually reflect compromises subjects make between these extremes in social orientation.

The second part of Table 9.5 illustrates the internal consistency of the Tajfel matrices. For each of the six social orientations discussed previously, one can calculate the total number of points allocated to ingroup and outgroup members across the six Tajfel matrices presented in Table 9.2. By combining points allocated to ingroup and outgroup members within each social orientation, one can also determine the total number of points gained by subjects from the experimenter (E). Note that it is the raw scores presented as options within each of the Tajfel matrices that serve as a basis for the calculations presented in Table 9.5. These calculations help clarify the economic underpinnings of each social orientation from the point of view of ingroup respondents, outgroup recipients, and the combination of ingroup/outgroup subjects vis-à-vis the experimenter (E).

As seen in Table 9.5, the two maximum joint profit (MJPa,b) orientations indeed yield the maximum number of points possible from the experimenter (E) to the two groups of subjects (216 points, 100%). Thus, maximum joint profit (MJP) is the most economically rational strategy to adopt when using the Tajfel matrices. However, as noted earlier, the MJPa orientation provides a small economic advantage to the ingroup (120 points) relative to the outgroup (96 points). In contrast, the MJPb orientation has a parity component that equalizes ingroup/outgroup gain at 108 points each thus providing both groups with 82% of the total ingroup gain possible within the matrix system.

In contrast to the MJP orientation, the parity strategy is not the most economically rational orientation. The parity orientation yields 168 points from the experimenter, constituting only 78% of the total possible gain that can be obtained from the matrices for ingroup and outgroup members. However, parity does guarantee equal gain for ingroup and outgroup members, even though this strategy yields only 64% of the total number of points that can be gained for members of the ingroup within the Tajfel matrices.

A maximum ingroup profit (MIP) orientation yields 204 points or 94% of the total joint gain that can be obtained from the experimenter using the Tajfel matrices. However, note that as expected, MIP yields the maximum number of points that can be gained for ingroup members using the Tajfel matrices (132 points = 100% of possible total). With only 72 points allocated to members of the outgroup, the maximum ingroup profit (MIP) orientation yields a differential between ingroup and outgroup gain of 60 points in favor of ingroup members.

As seen in Table 9.5, maximum differentiation (MD) is among the least economically rational orientation, yielding only 168 points or 78% of the total joint gain that can be obtained from the experimenter using the Tajfel matrices. Although contributing 120 points to ingroup members (91% of the possible total), the MD orientation yields the least number of points to outgroup members (48 points or 36% of the possible total). As expected, the maximum differentiation (MD) orientation yields the greatest differential between ingroup and outgroup gain, amounting to 72 points in favor of ingroup members.

Relative to the other social orientations presented in Table 9.5, outgroup favoritism (OF) is the orientation that yields the least number of points to members of the ingroup (72 points or 55% of the possible total). In contrast, it is the only orientation that offers the maximum possible number of points to outgroup members (132 points, 100% of the possible total). As expected, the outgroup favoritism orientation yields a differential between ingroup and outgroup gain that favors the outgroup rather than the ingroup (−60 points).

The previous calculations demonstrate the internal validity of the Tajfel matrices. Fundamental features of the social orientations presented in Table 9.5 are reflected in calculations based on raw scores obtained from the Tajfel matrices depicted in Table 9.2. Taken together, both the configurations of pull scores and the matrix calculations presented in Table 9.5 clearly differentiate key resource allocation strategies such as maximum joint profit, (MJP), parity, (P), maximum ingroup profit (MIP), maximum differentiation, (MD) and outgroup favoritism (OF). The previous calculations show that the Tajfel matrices can be used as a subtle tool for monitoring the resource distribution strategies of group members in different intergroup relation situations.

CLOSING NOTES

The effect of categorization on intergroup discrimination has been obtained in minimal group studies using dependent measures other than the Tajfel matrices. For instance, Brewer and Silver (1978), using numerical values, reported the overall percentage and proportions of subjects following strategies of parity, ingroup favoritism and outgroup favoritism on a resource allocation task. Results obtained on such measures replicated the usual minimal group effect. Numerous categorization studies employing a variety of dependent measures also replicated the minimal group discrimination effect. Dependent measures ranging from free-choice (Locksley, Oritz, & Hepburn, 1980; Ng, 1981) to binary (Bornstein et al., 1983b) and multiple allocation matrices (Brewer and Silver, 1978) have been employed. Minimal social categorization has led to intergroup discrimination on these measures (Brewer & Kramer, 1985; Diehl, 1990; Hogg & Abrams, 1988; Messick & Mackie, 1989).

However, it is difficult to gauge from these less sensitive measures the relative influence of strategies such as maximum differentiation (MD) and maximum joint profit (MJP). For example a strong score for the pull of MD on MIP + MJP is considered an important strategy that typifies discrimination against an out-group. This is the case because subjects are sacrificing maximum ingroup and joint profit for the sake of maximizing in their favor the difference in points between their own group and the outgroup. The MD strategy is also reflected in real-life situations when group members are ready to sacrifice a certain amount of ingroup profit for the sake of "putting down" outgroup members. Within social identity theory, the use of maximum differentiation (MD) is identified as a key discriminatory strategy reflecting group members' desire for achieving a positive social identity (Tajfel & Turner, 1986; Wilder, 1981). Therefore, the Tajfel matrices have an advantage over the less sensitive methods of free-choice and binary-choice allocations, because they allow for a fuller variety of psychologically meaningful strategies to be systematically assessed (Turner, 1980, 1983a, 1983b). Both theory and data suggest that pull scores provide a "convenient and representative description of the actual distribution strategies" employed by subjects (Brown et al., 1980, p. 409).

The Tajfel matrices have also been adapted successfully for use in various laboratory and field settings. The matrices have been modified to measure: (a) performance evaluations (Sachdev & Bourhis, 1987; Turner & Brown, 1978), (b) real-life salary differentials (Brown, 1978; Bourhis & Hill, 1982), (c) teachers' allocation of financial resources to rival labor federations using simplified Tajfel matrices (Cole & Bourhis, 1991), (d) the allocation of additional course credits for participation in psychology experiments (Bourhis, chapter 8, this volume; Sachdev & Bourhis, 1985, 1991), and (e) monetary allocations among 7–11-year-old children using three column matrices presented as dominoes (Moise,

Bourhis, & Gagnon, 1990; Vaughan, Tajfel, & Williams, 1981; Wetherhell, 1982). These considerations show that the Tajfel matrices can be adapted to suit the particularities of various groups of respondents in different types of intergroup settings. The results of the studies conducted so far show that the Tajfel matrices can provide psychologically meaningful and valid measures of intergroup behaviors. Although the Tajfel matrices are used mainly for intergroup research dealing with aspects of social identity theory (Abrams & Hogg, 1990; Hogg & Abrams, 1988; Tajfel, 1978, 1982), there is no reason why they should not be used as a research tool to explore issues related to other aspects of intergroup relations (Dovidio & Gaertner, 1986; Worchel & Austin, 1986). Thus, the Tajfel matrices can be adapted to examine key aspects of intergroup behavior related to: (a) equity and justice (Greenberg & Cohen 1982; Ng, 1984), (b) relative deprivation (Walker & Pettigrew, 1984), (c) intergroup contact (Hewstone & Brown, 1986), (d) bargaining and negotiation (Stephenson, 1984), and (e) realistic conflict of interest (Blake & Mouton, 1984; Sherif, 1966).

ACKNOWLEDGMENTS

The authors with to thank the following individuals for their comments on earlier versions of the manuscript: Rupert Brown, Léna Céline Moïse, and John Turner. Comments or suggestions concerning this manuscript would be much appreciated and should be addressed to: Richard Y. Bourhis, Département de psychologie, Université du Québec à Montréal C.P. 8888, Succ. A, Montréal, Québec, Canada, H3C 3P8.

REFERENCES

Abrams, D., & Hogg, M. A. (Eds). (1990). *Social identity theory: Constructive and critical advances.* New York: Harvester/Wheatsheaf.

Aschenbrenner, K. M., & Schaefer, R. E. (1980). Minimal group situations: Comments on a mathematical model and on the research paradigm. *European Journal of Social Psychology, 10,* 389–398.

Billig, M. (1976). *Social psychology and intergroup relations.* London & New York: Academic.

Blake, R. R., & Mouton, J. S. (1984). *Solving costly organizational conflicts.* San Francisco: Jossey Bass.

Bornstein, G., Crum, L., Wittenbraker, J., Harring, K., Insko, C. A., & Thibaut, J. (1983a). On the measurement of social orientations in the minimal group paradigm. *European Journal of Social Psychology, 13,* 321–350.

Bornstein, G., Crum, L., Wittenbraker, J., Harring, K., Insko, C. A., & Thibaut, J. (1983b). Reply to Turner's comments. *European Journal of Social Psychology, 13,* 369–381.

Bourhis, R. Y., & Hill, P. (1982). Intergroup perceptions in British higher education: A field study.

In H. Tajfel (Ed.), *Social identity and intergroup relations* (pp. 423–468). Cambridge & Paris: Cambridge University Press & Edition de la Maison des Sciences de l'Homme.

Bourhis, R. Y., & Sachdev, I. (1986). *The Tajfel matrices as an instrument for conducting intergroup research.* Hamilton, Ontario: McMaster University Mimeo.

Branthwaite, A., Doyle, S., & Lightbown, N. (1979). The balance between fairness and discrimination. *European Journal of Social Psychology, 9,* 149–163.

Brewer, M. B. (1979). Ingroup bias in the minimal group situation: A cognitive–motivational analysis. *Psychological Bulletin, 86,* 307–324.

Brewer, M. B., & Kramer, R. M. (1985). The psychology of intergroup attitudes and behavior. *Annual Review of Psychology, 10,* 399–414.

Brewer, M. B., & Silver, M. (1978). Ingroup bias as a function of task characteristics. *European Journal of Social Psychology, 8,* 393–400.

Brown, R. J. (1978). Divided we fall: An analysis of relations between sections of a factory workforce. In H. Tajfel (Ed.), *Differentiation between social groups,* (pp. 395–429). London & New York: Academic Press.

Brown, R., & Bourhis, R. Y. (1978). *Instructions for scoring intergroup matrices.* Bristol: University of Bristol Mimeo. 6 pages.

Brown, R. J., Tajfel, H., & Turner, J. C. (1980). Minimal group situations and intergroup discriminations: Comments on the paper by Aschenbrenner and Schaefer. *European Journal of Social Psychology, 10,* 399–414.

Cole, R., & Bourhis, R. Y. (1991). *A field study of power differentials between members of two sex segregated labour federations in Canada.* Paper presented at the Annual Conference of the Canadian Psychological Association, Calgary.

Diehl, M. (1990). The minimal group paradigm: Theoretical explanations and empirical findings. In W. Stroebe & M. Hewstone (Eds.), *European Review of Social Psychology* (Vol. 1, 263–292). Chichester: Wiley.

Dovidio, J., Gaertner, S. (1986). *Prejudice, discrimination, and racism.* Orlando, FL: Academic Press.

Greenberg, J., & Cohen, R. L. (Eds.). (1982). *Equity and justice in social behavior.* New York: Academic.

Hewstone, M., & Brown, R. (Eds.). (1986). *Contact and conflict in intergroup relations.* Oxford: Blackwell.

Hogg, M. A., & Abrams, D. (1988). *Social identifications: A social psychology of intergroup relations and group processes.* London: Routledge.

Locksley, A., Oritz, V., & Hepburn, C. (1980). Social categorization and intergroup behaviour: Extinguishing the minimal group discrimination effect. *Journal of Personality and Social Psychology, 39,* 773–783.

Messick, D. M., & Mackie, D. M. (1989). Intergroup relations. *Annual Review of Psychology, 40,* 45–81.

Moise, L. C., Bourhis, R. Y., & Gagnon, A. (1990). Passage intergroupe et discrimination chez les enfants. [Intergroup passing and discrimination amongst children.] Poster presented at the 13th Annual Conference of the Societe Quebecoise pour la Recherche en Psychologie, Montreal.

Ng, S. H. (1981). Equity theory and the allocations of rewards between groups. *European Journal of Social Psychology, 11,* 439–443.

Ng, S. H. (1984). Social psychology and political economy. In H. Tajfel (Ed.), *The social dimension* (Vol. 2, pp. 624–645). Cambridge & Paris: Cambridge University Press & Editions de la Maison des Sciences de l'Homme.

Platow, M. J., McClintock, C. G., & Liebrand, W. (1990). Predicting intergroup fairness and ingroup bias in the minimal group paradigm. *European Journal of Social Psychology, 20,* 221–239.

Sachdev, I., & Bourhis, R. Y. (1985). Social categorization and power differentials in group relations. *European Journal of Social Psychology, 15,* 415–434.

Sachdev, I., & Bourhis, R. Y. (1987). Status differentials and intergroup behaviours. *European Journal of Social Psychology, 17,* 277–293.

Sachdev, I., & Bourhis, R. Y. (1991). Power and status differentials in minority and majority group relations. *European Journal of Social Psychology, 21,* 1–24.

Sherif, M. (1966). *Group conflict and cooperation: Their social psychology.* London: Routledge & Kegan Paul.

Stephenson, G. (1984). Intergroup and interpersonal dimensions of bargaining and negotiation. In H. Tajfel (Ed.), *The Social Dimension* (Vol. 2, pp. 646–667). Cambridge & Paris: Cambridge University Press & Editions de la Maison des Sciences de l'Homme.

Tajfel, H. (1978). The psychological structure of intergroup relations. In H. Tajfel (Ed.), *Differentiation between social groups* (pp. 27–98). London: Academic.

Tajfel, H. (1981). *Human groups and social categories.* Cambridge: Cambridge University Press.

Tajfel, H. (Ed.). (1982). *Social identity and intergroup relations.* Cambridge & Paris: Cambridge University Press, & Editions de la Maison des Sciences de l'Homme.

Tajfel, H., Flament, C., Billig, M., & Bundy, R. (1971). Social categorization and intergroup behaviour. *European Journal of Social Psychology, 11,* 149–178.

Tajfel, H., & Turner, J. C. (1986). The social identity theory of intergroup behaviour. In S. Worchel & W. G. Austin (Eds.), *Psychology of intergroup relations* (2nd ed., pp. 7–24). Chicago: Nelson-Hall.

Turner, J. C. (1978). Social categorization and social discrimination in the minimal group paradigm. In H. Tajfel (Ed.), *Differentiation between social groups* (pp. 101–140). London: Academic Press.

Turner, J. C. (1980). Fairness or discrimination in intergroup behaviour? A reply to Branthwaite, Doyle and Lightbown. *European Journal of Social Psychology, 10,* 131–147.

Turner, J. C. (1981). The experimental social psychology of intergroup behaviour. In J. C. Turner & H. Giles (Eds.), *Intergroup behaviour* (pp. 66–101). Oxford: Blackwell.

Turner, J. C. (1983a). A second reply to Bornstein, Crum, Wittenbraker, Harring, Insko and Thibaut on the measurement of social orientations. *European Journal of Social Psychology, 13,* 383–387.

Turner, J. C. (1983b). Some comments on 'the measurement of social orientations in the minimal group paradigm'. *European Journal of Social Psychology, 13,* 351–367.

Turner, J. C., & Brown, J. R. (1978). Social status, cognitive alternatives, and intergroup relations. In H. Tajfel (Ed.), *Differentiation between social groups* (pp. 201–234). London: Academic.

Turner, J. C., Brown, R. J., & Tajfel, H. (1979). Social comparison and group interest in intergroup favouritism. *European Journal of Social Psychology, 9,* 187–204.

Vaughan, G. M., Tajfel, H., & Williams, J. (1981). Intergroup and interindividual discrimination in British children. *Social Psychology Quarterly, 44,* 37–42.

Walker, I., & Pettigrew, T. F. (1984). Relative deprivation theory: An overview and conceptual critiques. *British Journal of Social Psychology, 23,* 301–310.

Wetherhell, M. (1982). Cross-cultural studies of minimal groups: Implications for the social identity theory of intergroup relations. In H. Tajfel (Ed.), *Social identity and intergroup relations* (pp. 207–240). Cambridge & Paris: Cambridge University Press & Editions de la Maison des Sciences de l'Homme.

Wilder, D. A. (1981). Perceiving persons as a group: Categorization and intergroup relations. In D. L. Hamilton (Ed.), *Cognitive processes in stereotyping and intergroup behavior* (pp. 211–257). Hillsdale, NJ: Lawrence Erlbaum Associates.

Worchel, S., & Austin, W. G. (Eds.). (1986). *The psychology of intergroup relations* (Vol. 2). Chicago: Nelson-Hall.

APPENDIX A: INSTRUCTIONAL SET FOR COMPLETION OF THE TAJFEL MATRICES

Here is the way to complete your response booklet. Each page in the response booklet contains one matrix. A matrix consists of 13 boxes, each containing two numbers. On each matrix you are to award points (or money or credits) to two other people in this room. The top row of numbers within the boxes are the points to be awarded to Individual A from Group Z, and the bottom row are points to be given to Individual B from Group W. After looking at each box of the matrix, you must choose only one box that represents your choice of how you wish to award the points.

Let me give you an example of how to use the matrix. Let us say you are faced with the following matrix that we have on display for you on this chart. In addition to your group label (point on chart), each of you has received a personal identification letter (point).

Points to Member A of Group Z	11	12	13	14	15	16	17	18	19	20	21	22	23
Points to Member B of Group W	5	7	9	11	13	15	17	19	21	23	25	27	29

Points given to Member A of Group Z: _____
Points given to Member B of Group W: _____

Now suppose you are distributing points for Member A of Group Z and Member B of Group W. Think very carefully about all the numbers in the boxes. There are a variety of choices you can make. Let us say that you decide to choose a box toward the left-hand edge of this matrix, for example, Box 11,

                                              5

This means that you decide to give 11 points to Member A of Group Z and 5 points to Member B of Group W. Alternatively, you might choose Box 15

                                              13

This means you are giving 15 points to Member A of Group Z and 13 points to Member B of Group W. On the other hand, you might decide to choose Box 17

                                              17

which means that Member A of Group Z and Member B of Group W each get 17 points. Another option is choosing Box 20

                                              23

This means you are willing to give 20 points to Member A of Group Z, whereas Member B of Group W gets 23 points.
Further on in the matrix you can choose Box 23

                                              29

in which Member A of Group Z gets 23 points, whereas Member B of Group W gets 29 points.

Once again, you are not allowed to choose different numbers from different boxes on the same page. For instance, in our example here, you are not allowed to give 18 points to Member A of Group Z and 25 points (from another box) to Member B of Group W. If you decide to give 18 points to Member A of Group Z, then it means that you have also chosen 19 points for Member B of Group W. So please consider your choices carefully when you make them.

Now, each matrix page in the booklet contains different matrices, with different combinations of numbers in the boxes. So, as you go from one page to another, choose your boxes very carefully. Please note that you are never awarding points to yourself. We arranged the booklets so that your own individual identification letter never appears on the matrices in your booklet. Of course, we do not want you to give points to yourselves.

Regardless of your final choices, make sure that before each decision you carefully examine the two numbers contained in each box of the matrix. Once you make your decision, tick the box you chose and also write the numbers representing your choice in the spaces provided below each scale . . . (show this on chart). You may proceed now.

APPENDIX B: ANALYZING PULL SCORES FROM THE TAJFEL MATRICES

Two sets of statistical analyses are usually conducted to examine group pull scores on the Tajfel matrices: (a) matrix strategy analyses *within* each treatment condition and (b) matrix strategy analyses *between* treatment condition (Sachdev & Bourhis, 1991).

(A) The within treatment condition analysis of the pull scores is of more immediate concern because this analysis is the one required to determine if pull scores obtained from subjects within each treatment condition are significantly different from zero use on the $+12$ to -12 matrix pull scales. It is clear that one must first determine if subjects actually used any of the six strategy pulls (P on FAV, MD on MIP $+$ MJP, FAV on MJP, etc.) before determining whether differential use of the strategies were made by groups of subjects across treatment conditions within the study. The usual within treatment analysis is to apply a Wilcoxon Matched Pairs Test on the difference in scores between the opposed (O) and together (T) rank scores of each matrix type (Turner, 1983a). In the example depicted in Table 9.3, one would test for the significance of group pull score of FAV on MJP by conducting a Wilcoxon Matched Pairs Test on the difference in score between the opposed and together rank score of Matrix Type A (O $-$ T). In turn, the significance of group pull scores of the obverse pull, MJP on FAV, is determined by conducting a Wilcoxon Matched Pairs Test on the difference in scores between the $(12 - $ opposed) and together rank scores of Matrix Type A: $(12 - O) - T$. Similar Wilcoxon Matched Pairs Tests are conducted to test the significance of the pull scores obtained from the remaining four strategies (MD on MIP + MJP; MIP + MJP on MD; P on FAV, and FAV on P; Sachdev & Bourhis, 1991).

(B) The between treatment condition analyses of the six matrix pull scores usually involve parametric analyses (e.g., MANOVA) that are specific to the experimental design (Sachdev & Bourhis, 1987). It is assumed that pull scores are distributed normally in such analyses (see Turner, 1980).

10 Dimensions of Perceived Discrimination: The Personal/Group Discrimination Discrepancy

Donald M. Taylor
McGill University

Stephen C. Wright
University of California, Santa Cruz

Lana E. Porter
McGill University

Acts of discrimination necessarily involve two participants, the perpetrator and the victim. With a few important exceptions (e.g., Birt & Dion, 1987; Crocker & Major, 1989; Crosby, 1982, 1984a, 1984b; Crosby, Muehrer, & Loewenstein, 1986; Dibble, 1981; Dion, 1986; Dion & Earn, 1975; Lalonde & Cameron, in press; Major, Carrington, & Carnevale, 1984) the focus of most theory and research is on the persons or groups who hold prejudices and practice the discrimination. In this chapter, the emphasis is exclusively on persons who belong to groups that are potential targets for discrimination. Specifically, the question addressed here is to what extent such persons perceive or judge behavior directed at them personally or at their group to be discrimination, regardless of whether this perception reflects objective reality or not.

Our specific interest in this question arises because of a robust finding that has surfaced in a number of studies on discrimination. The phenomenon involves members of minority groups perceiving more discrimination directed at their group in general compared to themselves personally as a member of that group; a phenomenon that Taylor, Wright, Moghaddam, and Lalonde (1990) labeled the personal/group discrimination discrepancy. This pattern of perceptions is, on the surface, irrational. If all minority group members perceive relatively little discrimination directed at them personally, where are the group members who are discriminated against at such a high level that it would warrant the high ratings of group discrimination that emerge so consistently? Implied in this rhetorical question is the paradox contained in the personal/group discrimination discrepancy. Being a target of discrimination is a profound emotional experience that requires effective coping mechanisms. Insights into such a traumatic experience may well

233

be gained by understanding discrepancies between one's perceptions of discrimination at the personal and group levels.

The chapter addresses five issues needed for one to understand the personal/group discrimination discrepancy and appreciate its implications. These issues are: (a) The robustness of the phenomenon. (b) The psychological significance of perceived discrimination. (c) Potential motivational explanations for the perceived discrepancy in discrimination. (d) The extent to which perceptions of discrimination are reality based. (e) The relationship of self-identity to perceptions of discrimination.

THE PERSONAL/GROUP DISCRIMINATION DISCREPANCY: A ROBUST PHENOMENON

The tendency to perceive more discrimination at the group compared to the individual level was first documented by Crosby (1982, 1984a, 1984b) in her study of working women in the Boston area. Since then, the same perceptual discrepancy has arisen with a variety of minority groups, including Anglophone Quebecers (Taylor, Wong-Reiger, McKirnan & Bercusson, 1982), Francophone Quebecers (Guimond & Dubé-Simard, 1983), women in Quebec and France (Dubé-Simard & Abbondanza, 1985) and more recently, South Asian and Haitian immigrant women (Taylor et al., 1990).

An appreciation for the consistency of the finding is gained by examining Fig. 10.1, where perceptions of discrimination are illustrated for a variety of groups. The number and diversity of circumstances in which the discrepancy arises is striking:

1. The phenomenon holds across a variety of minority groups. In addition to women, published reports involve Anglophones and Francophones (two nonvisible ethnolinguistic minorities) and visible minority women. Moreover, unpublished results from our laboratory establish strong evidence for the personal/group discrimination discrepancy among minority groups as disparate as Jewish Montrealers, middle-class and inner-city African-Americans from Miami, and the Inuit of Arctic Quebec. Thus, the phenomenon is consistent across a wide variety of minority groups: this is underscored by the diversity of groups serving as exemplars in Fig. 10.1.

2. It is clear from Fig. 10.1 that the discrepancy remains as prominent for those minority group members who perceive relatively low levels of discrimination directed at their group or themselves personally as members of that group (e.g., women, Inuit) as those who perceive high levels of discrimination (e.g., Haitian women, Africans).

3. As illustrated in Fig. 10.1, the personal/group discrimination discrepancy arises when minority group members are asked about the overall level of

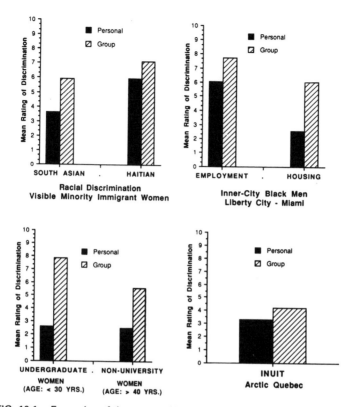

FIG. 10.1.   Examples of the personal/group discrimination discrepancy.

discrimination they perceive or their perception of discrimination in a particular context (e.g., housing, employment).

The personal/group discrimination discrepancy, then, is a phenomenon that is robust. It is so robust that the empirical challenge is not to replicate the finding but rather to find an exception; yet, to date, no such exception has been found. The consistency of the phenomenon poses a fundamental dilemma. On the one hand, its pervasiveness makes it a phenomenon that has profound psychological implications. For example, perceptions of personal and group discrimination may well be associated with consequent actions, ranging from passive acceptance by an individual to collective violence at the group level. On the other hand, the perceived discrepancy is so invariant that it may imply that the phenomenon is obvious, superficial, or both.

This dilemma is too important to ignore; it is necessary to address the question of the extent to which the personal/group discrimination discrepancy arises for obvious or superficial reasons or whether it constitutes a phenomenon of psychological importance.

THE PSYCHOLOGICAL SIGNIFICANCE OF PERCEIVED DISCRIMINATION

One obvious explanation for the personal/group discrimination discrepancy is that because of a systematic bias in the various samples, respondents' ratings of personal and group discrimination reflect objective reality. That is, if only the more privileged members of various stigmatized groups are sampled, then in reality such respondents might be personally the least discriminated against in their group.

The results presented in Fig. 10.1 make such a sampling bias unlikely: (a) The discrepancy in perceived discrimination is as prominent for working women as it is for university students. (b) More convincing perhaps is that the phenomenon arises in two domains for a sample of unemployed Black men living in housing projects in Miami. By any objective standards, they represent the least privileged among the community. Thus, it is unlikely that the discrepancy in perceived discrimination arises because of a systematic sampling bias.

The pervasiveness of the personal/group discrimination discrepancy raises another possible artifactual explanation. Perhaps some nonobvious aspect of the wording of the questions about discrimination prompts minority group members to respond as they do. The questions ask respondents to rate, usually on Likert-type scales, the extent to which "your minority group" (e.g., North American women as a group) and "you personally as a member of that group" (e.g., you personally as a woman) are discriminated against.

In order to explore the potential role of the wording of these questions on respondents, several samples of university student women were asked to rate their experiences with discrimination using a variety of wordings. In addition to the two standard questions, different samples were asked to rate the *frequency* with which they perceived discrimination at both the group and personal level and the *severity* of the discrimination they perceived at the two levels. A final sample had the standard group question (North American women as a group) replaced by the phrase "average North American woman."

The results were conclusive in the sense that despite variations in the wording, respondents consistently perceived more discrimination directed at women in general, compared to themselves personally as women. With minor fluctuations, group level ratings were consistently higher than the corresponding personal ratings for all four wordings of the question: (a) women, (b) average woman, (c) frequency, or (d) severity.

Further evidence that the personal/group discrimination discrepancy is not an artifact of the format and wording of items or the particular minority group being questioned, comes from the replies of African-Americans to a *Newsweek* poll

(Gelman, Springen, Brailsford, & Miller, 1988). The poll concerned race relations in the United States; fortuitously for us, there were two questions that asked African-Americans to compare their current situation with the way it was 5 years ago. Specifically, when asked about their personal situation, 44% responded that it is better now. However, when asked about African Americans as a group, only 33% perceived that life is better today compared to 5 years ago. Thus, even with different contexts and formats to the questions, respondents perceived their personal position in a more positive light than the position of the group as a whole.

Although any effect due to the wording of questions has theoretical import in its own right, the lack of any effect for wording rules out the possibility that the personal/group discrimination discrepancy phenomenon is due to some artifact of the wording of questions.

Beyond checking for the effect of wording, a second possible explanation for the perceived discrepancy must be ruled out. It may be that the label group connotes more than personal for the simple reason that a group, by definition, is comprised of more than one person. This straightforward association of *group with more* might explain the consistently higher ratings for group compared to personal discrimination.

Two sources of evidence converge on this question. The first arises out of the investigation for the effects of wording on the personal/group discrimination discrepancy. One of the options offered to a sample of women was the label *average woman* as a substitute for the standard wording *women as a group*. The average woman label was chosen in part because it refers to women as a group, but captured, as a composite, all women into one woman in the form of an average.

If the sheer numbers connoted by group lead to higher ratings for group-level discrimination, these higher ratings should be eliminated, or at least, greatly reduced when the label *average woman* is substituted. The findings belie this interpretation. The discrepancy in perceived discrimination in favour of the group is as pronounced for the *average woman* label as for the standard *women as a group* wording.

A second source of evidence bearing on the association of group with more explanation is found in the Taylor et al. (1990) study of South Asian and Haitian women. In that study, respondents were not only asked about discrimination at the group and personal levels but also about their privileged treatment at the same two levels. If a group-means-more process were operating, respondents should parallel their discrimination ratings by rating group-based privilege higher than personally directed privilege.

Respondents' pattern of ratings for privilege, however, does not parallel those for discrimination. Instead, both South Asian and Haitian women rated higher privilege at the personal level than they did for the group as a whole. Clearly these findings are inconsistent with the hypothesis that group ratings are higher because the label *group* connotes more than an individual label.

The two sources of evidence that rule out a simple group-means-more explanation, although consistent, are not conclusive. The average woman label, although explicitly singular, might still evoke an image of women in their plurality. The contrary ratings in the case of privileged treatment could arise because it is a somewhat bizarre question to ask of disadvantaged, visible minority groups who have been the targets for so much societal discrimination.

Nevertheless, the evidence suggests that there is more to the personal/group discrimination discrepancy than any artifact due to wording or simple process that compels people to always associate group with more. It is with some confidence then that our attention can be turned to the potential psychological processes that underlie the apparently nonobvious discrepancy in the perception of discrimination at the group and personal level.

MOTIVATIONAL EXPLANATIONS FOR PERCEIVED DISCRIMINATION

The most popular explanation for the personal/group discrimination discrepancy to date is the denial of personal discrimination (see Crosby, 1984a, 1984b; Taylor & Dubé, 1986; Zanna, Crosby, & Loewenstein, 1986). These explanations are based on the implicit assumption that the high levels of group discrimination reported so often reflect objective reality. The distortion is assumed to arise at the personal level, for a variety of reasons:

1. Personal denial might be the result of self-blame, where the individual assumes personal responsibility for receiving poor treatment.

2. Personal denial may be the result of the individual's desire to avoid pinpointing a particular villain as the source of discrimination against the self (Crosby, 1984a).

3. Perhaps individuals are evaluating their own personal situation through intragroup comparisons, whereas they are evaluating their group status through intergroup comparisons (Zanna et al., 1986).

4. Another possibility evokes cognitive dissonance; denying discrimination against the self may help the individual to justify not taking action against the perpetrator of discrimination (Taylor & Dubé, 1986).

5. It may be that individual disadvantaged group members feel relatively well off compared to the dramatic examples of discrimination that are highlighted by the mass-media (Taylor & Dubé, 1986).

There are three good reasons why, in the absence of any direct empirical evidence, the denial of personal discrimination has, until recently, emerged as the most obvious explanation:

1. In Crosby's (1984a, 1984b) research with working women, although ratings of group discrimination were pronounced, ratings for personal discrimination were literally zero or near zero which is highly suggestive of denial.

2. As our review suggests, there are a variety of compelling denial explanations that spring quickly to mind.

3. Denial explanations presuppose that ratings of group discrimination are a reflection of reality. To assume the converse, that is, to assume that personal ratings are reality based and that minority group members distort the amount of discrimination directed at their group, would be a highly unpopular theoretical stance.

The attractiveness of a denial explanation, then, is understandable. And yet, as Taylor et al. have (1990) argued, the exaggeration of group discrimination is as plausible an explanation for the perceived discrepancy in discrimination as any form of personal denial. Here, too, intuitively appealing explanations can be found. For example, the exaggeration of group discrimination is self-serving for minority group members. It serves as an external cause that offers a self-serving explanation for failure, one that enhances the self even further in cases of success (see Crocker & Major, 1989). This is captured eloquently in the women's movement slogan, "We have to be twice as good in order to achieve the same as men." Of course, the slogan highlights the theoretical challenge: Are women making a self-serving attribution of simply "telling it like it is?"

The results of our study involving South Asian and Haitian immigrant women shed some light on the complementary motivational explanations of denial of personal discrimination and exaggeration of group discrimination. Women in that study were asked to rate their experience with personal and group-level discrimination along four separate dimensions: (a) race, (b) culture, (c) newcomer status to Canada, and (d) gender.

The results, of course, confirm the personal/group discrimination discrepancy, and the specific ratings for one of the four dimensions, race, appears in the top-left quadrant of Fig. 10.1. These results alone shed some light on the motivational basis for the phenomenon. Clearly, neither the South Asian or Haitian women are denying personal discrimination. Ratings of 3.75 (South Asian) and 5.97 (Haitian) for personal discrimination do not constitute denial, especially compared to the women in Crosby's (1984a, 1984b) study who reported very little or no experience with personal discrimination. At best, then, the denial explanation must be relabeled the *minimization* of personal discrimination.

Beyond this, many of the denial explanations are less compelling when subjects report moderate to high levels of personal discrimination. For example, one of these explanations involves denial allowing the individual to escape from seeking out a specific villain. If respondents deny individual discrimination by shifting their ratings from 7.09 for group discrimination to 5.97 for personal discrimination (Haitians), the need to find a villain is reduced slightly, but is clearly not avoided.

Similarly, such ratings for personal discrimination are not likely to have much effect on the cognitive dissonance arising from the lack of direct action. Dissonance is only dramatically reduced if ratings for personal discrimination fall to a near zero level. At best, then, the Haitian and South Asia respondents were reducing their dissonance only slightly.

The present data also raises questions about the social comparison explanation (Zanna et al., 1986). In Crosby's (1984a, 1984b) research, the women were never explicitly asked if they were personally discriminated against on the basis of their gender. The conclusion that women were not reporting sexual discrimination at the personal level was inferred from women's responses on measures of job satisfaction, compared to answers to the same questions by a sample of working men. Also, sex discrimination was rarely mentioned by women in their answers to open-ended questions about working conditions. Thus, the high levels of personal job satisfaction may have arisen because the women limited their social comparisons to in-group members (other working women). By contrast, in the study involving South Asian and Haitian women, respondents were asked about discrimination directed at them personally as a woman. In this sense, respondents were led to make comparisons with those outside their own group, namely the potential perpetrators of discrimination, men. Nevertheless, it is still possible that when asked about personal discrimination, respondents compare their plight to others in their own group, and this possibility needs to be examined directly.

In summary, the relatively high ratings for personal discrimination reported by the Haitian and South Asian respondents (see Fig. 10.1) in and of themselves challenge certain of the denial explanations that have been offered to date. The media hypothesis, on the other hand, is entirely consistent with the present findings. That is, dramatic media presentations of discrimination may serve to reduce the comparative feeling of personal discrimination although they may not be enough to force the individual to completely ignore more personal experiences. In addition, dramatic media presentations may lead to an exaggerated estimate of group-based discrimination. Thus, the results for the South Asian and Haitian women do not rule out the possibility that some form of denial or minimization process is operating, but they certainly raise questions about its role.

Despite the clear and consistent pattern for perceptions of group discrimination to be higher than those for personal discrimination among the South Asian and Haitian women, individual differences in this tendency did arise. These differences were explored in a post hoc analysis designed to examine the extent to which respondents tended to deny personal discrimination, exaggerate group discrimination, or use some combination of both. For each respondent, a discrepancy score was computed by subtracting reported personal from group discrimination. For the questions involving racial discrimination, 32% of the Haitians and 24% of the South Asians had a discrepancy score of zero. For the questions concerning culture, 23% of the Haitians and 30% of the South Asians indicated that they were personally receiving treatment equal to that of their group. For newcomer, 30% of the Haitians and 24% of the South Asians have a discrepancy score of zero. For the questions concerning gender, 28% of the Haitians and 36% of the South Asians indicated no difference between personal and collective treatment.

By definition, these individuals are not manifesting the effects of denial of personal discrimination or of exaggeration of collective discrimination. Thus, this small no-discrepancy group makes an excellent comparison group for exploration of what is responsible for the personal/group discrepancy reported by the remaining respondents, who make up the majority.

From the remaining subjects, two additional subgroups were created: (a) those manifesting a moderate discrepancy between individual and group discrimination, and (b) those whose discrepancy was relatively large. No objective difference score criterion was established. Rather, an attempt was made to create, for each of the two ethnic groups on each of the four separate dimensions of discrimination, an equal number of subjects who, relatively speaking, could be classified as manifesting no discrepancy, a moderate discrepancy, or a large discrepancy in terms of perceived personal and group discrimination. The results for this arbitrary classification are presented in Fig. 10.2.

Only two of the eight patterns presented in Fig. 10.2 lend themselves to a strict denial-of-personal-discrimination explanation. The Haitian patterns for race and newcomer show that in comparing the no, moderate, and large discrepancy subsamples, the level of perceived personal discrimination systematically declines, as would be predicted from a denial-of-personal-discrimination explanation. However, these are precisely the two situations where group discrimination ratings are so high that a ceiling effect is likely. Even for the no-discrepancy groups, ratings for group discrimination are so high that there is little opportunity for these ratings to become even higher for the moderate- and large-discrepancy groups.

The arbitrary classification of the subgroups makes any formal analysis problematic. Nevertheless, a one-way analysis of variance was performed across the three subgroups (no, moderate, and large discrepancy), first for personal and separately for group discrimination. Such an analysis, suspect as it is, nevertheless bolsters the claim that in the cases of race and newcomer for the Haitian sample, denial of personal discrimination, not exaggeration of group discrimination, explains the individual differences in discrepancy. In both cases the group analysis was nonsignificant, and the "personal" analysis yielded a significant effect.

However, it is equally clear that, for the remaining six patterns (four South Asian and two Haitian), there is every indication that exaggeration of group discrimination is as prevalent as denial of personal discrimination. In all six

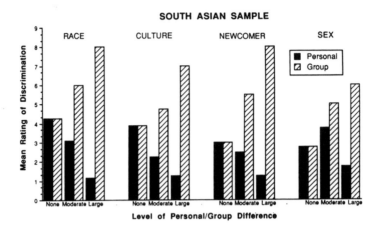

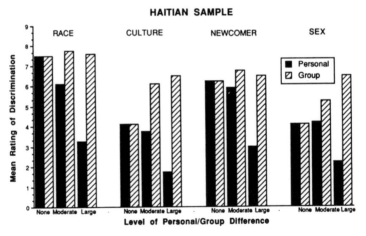

FIG. 10.2.   Histogram depicting ratings of discrimination for subsamples.

cases, one-way analyses of variance indicated that, as the discrepancy increases from the no- to the moderate- to the large-discrepancy subsamples, perceptions of personal discrimination decrease significantly, whereas perceptions of group discrimination increase significantly. Although not conclusive, this pattern of results offers as much support for the exaggeration of group as it does for the denial of personal discrimination perspectives.

Our exploration for a possible motivational basis to the personal/group discrimination discrepancy offers few solid conclusions. It is clear that the assumption of some basic denial process is not always consistent with the empirical evidence. Moreover, the evidence is at least as compelling for an exaggeration-of-group explanation as it is for any of the denial-of-personal-discrimination explanations that have been offered to date.

The explanatory door, then, is thrown wide open. Putting into question any simple form of denial and finding evidence that is consistent with exaggerations at the group level offers no direct evidence for or against these motivational explanations. The personal/group discrimination discrepancy, then, remains as intriguing a phenomenon as ever, and there is no one theoretical avenue to pursue that is necessarily more compelling than any other.

IS PERCEIVED DISCRIMINATION REALITY BASED?

Explanations for the personal/group discrimination discrepancy make implicit assumptions about the extent to which perceived discrimination is reality based. Denial-of-personal-discrimination explanations are based on the assumption that people's perceptions of group discrimination have a basis in reality. Conversely, explanations that focus on exaggerations at the group level assume that people are accurate in their perceptions at the personal level. Empirically testing the extent to which perceptions of discrimination are reality based is virtually impossible in a completely natural setting. Members of groups who are potential targets for discrimination base their perceptions on a lengthy and complex set of intergroup relations and on a complex personal history as a member of a potentially discriminated-against group. Moreover, even the simplest interaction involving a member of a stigmatized group is ambiguous with respect to the role of discrimination. Crocker and Major (1989) addressed this interactional ambiguity in their research into the attributions made by members of stigmatized groups when they are the recipients of positive or negative feedback. This same ambiguity makes it extremely difficult for human rights groups to obtain judgments in cases involving alleged discrimination. As much as the victim claims discrimination, the perpetrator argues that incompetence or provocation is the motivation for reprimanding or being belligerent with the victim. The point is that in naturally occurring interactions involving groups with a complex history of antagonism, it is extremely difficult to establish the extent to which perceived discrimination has a basis in reality.

What is needed is an experimental paradigm where control can be exercised over the extent to which a subject receives discriminatory treatment, so that perceptions of discrimination can be checked against an objective criterion. This experimental challenge is exacerbated by the need to independently manipulate group-directed and personally-directed discrimination.

Taylor, Wright, and Ruggiero (1991) made an initial attempt to develop a paradigm that independently manipulates personal and group discrimination in the laboratory. This was achieved by having women participate in an experiment ostensibly designed to assess problem solving. In the control condition, women were asked by the experimenter to solve two problems chosen randomly from an array of four. For the group discrimination/personal discrimination condition, the experimenter explained that he or she was working for a senior professor and that he or she was convinced that two of the four problems discriminate against women. The subject was told that she was one of the last to be run and unfortunately, according to the computer random-search list, she had been assigned the two problems that discriminate against women.

In order to introduce group discrimination with no personal discrimination, the subject was told about the two problems that discriminated against women as a group. However, the subject was told that fortunately she had been assigned the two tests that do not discriminate against women.

Finally, the biggest experimental challenge was to introduce personal discrimination without also including group discrimination. This was partially accomplished by again explaining that two of the tests discriminate against women. The subject was told that she was among the last to be run and that up until that point, the experimenter had been able to avoid ever giving the two discriminatory problems to any previous woman subject. It was explained, however, that in order to avoid suspicion from the supervising professor, it would be necessary for the present subject to be the first woman to attempt the two discriminatory problems.

The ratings of subjects in terms of perceived discrimination at the personal and group level for each of the four experimental conditions are presented in Fig. 10.3. These results clearly indicate that subjects' perceptions were entirely consistent with the treatment they received in the experiment. Subjects only conform

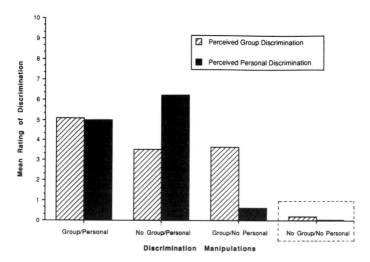

FIG. 10.3.   Mean ratings for effects of experimental conditions on perceived personal and group discrimination. (Dotted lines indicate cell is not included in the formal analysis.)

to the usual personal/group discrimination discrepancy when they are confronted with group discrimination in the absence of personal discrimination. Where both levels of discrimination are introduced, both are perceived equally; when no discrimination occurs, none is perceived. Finally, and most striking, in the appropriate condition they actually rate personal discrimination higher than group discrimination.

The results indicate, then, that at least in the simplified and immediate context of the laboratory, group members perceive both personal and group discrimination in a manner that is consistent with objective reality. Moreover, the objective reality created by the different experimental conditions involved the introduction of personally-directed and group-directed discrimination in a form that is consistent with what society generally regards as wholly unacceptable behaviour, in label as well as deed. Thus, in various forms, the experimenter used the label *discrimination,* and behaved in a manner that placed people at a disadvantage solely on the basis of their social category. That subjects perceived discrimination at the personal and group level in a manner consistent with the experimental conditions has implications for the personal/group discrimination discrepancy. Specifically, it indicates that when people respond to the usual generic questions about discrimination that are used in questionnaires, they are using the concept in the manner intended in the questions.

Interestingly, when the same subjects who took part in the experiment were asked later, in the context of a number of filler items, to rate their perceptions of discrimination against women in general and themselves as women, the usual personal/group discrimination discrepancy arose. From the results of the laboratory experiment, it is tempting, but perhaps premature, to conclude that ratings of minority group members' perceptions of personal and group-based discrimination, have at least some basis in reality. It is clear that the operational definition of discrimination used in the experiment was consistent with subjects' own understanding of what is meant by discrimination.

Finally, the responses of subjects to the experimentally induced personal and group discrimination do not provide any support for the motivational explanations of personal denial or group exaggeration. Denial explanations presuppose that perceptions at the group level are reality based, and exaggeration explanations are based on the assumption that personal perceptions have a basis in reality. In the present experiment, perceptions at both the personal and group levels reflect reality, and thus no clear support for either denial or exaggeration emerges.

LINKING THE PERSONAL SELF TO THE SOCIAL SELF

The roots of the discrimination discrepancy have to do with perceptions at two levels, the individual and the group. Aside from the momentary confines of the laboratory, ratings of discrimination at the group level are consistently and dramatically higher than ratings at the individual level. However, there is also a good deal of individual variation in terms of perceptions of discrimination within any particular minority group (see Fig. 10.2), including a minority of respondents who make identical ratings for personal and group discrimination.

The personal/group discrimination discrepancy as a phenomenon is not intuitively obvious because we assume that perceiving one's group and perceiving oneself as a member of that group are part of the same basic self-schema. The discrepancy raises questions about the structure of the two levels of perception and their relative contributions to the person's sense of self. Brewer (1991) and Turner, Hogg, Oakes, Reicher, and Wetherell (1987) come closest to addressing issues of identity that are relevant to the dilemma here. They argue that there are two important dimensions to self-definition: (a) personal identity, and (b) social (group) identity. Both theorists posit that for different individuals and indeed for the same individual at different times, different dimensions of the self are more or less salient.

One of the implications of a distinction between personal and social identity is that individuals differ in terms of the relative importance or salience of the two dimensions. At one extreme is a person whose personal and social identities overlap almost completely. To use women as an example, the woman who interprets even the most personal of interactions in terms of an intergroup issue involving men and women clearly derives much of her personal identity from her identity with the group, women. For such a woman, an attack on "me" is an attack on all women, and conversely, an attack on women is also an attack on "me" personally.

Contrast this pattern of identity with a woman who derives little of her identity from the group. For such a woman, an attack against women in general may not implicate "me" personally, and not all attacks against "me" are necessarily an affront to all women.

One would expect the two prototypic women described here to respond differently to questions about personal and group discrimination. The woman for whom personal and social identity are synonymous would not distinguish between person- and group-directed discrimination; in short, she would not evidence the usual personal/group discrimination discrepancy. The discrepancy would be expected for women who distinguish their personal from their social identity, such that perceptions at one level may or may not implicate perceptions at the other. Given the personal/group discrimination phenomenon, it would be expected that the discrepancy would involve higher ratings for group than for personal discrimination.

In order to test this basic hypothesis, it is first necessary to devise a test of individual differences in terms of the extent to which women associate their group identity with their personal identity. The often-used tests of modern versus traditional women or androgyny do not seem appropriate for the present context, because their focus is more on role definition and male–female trait attribution.

Examples are the Bem Sex Role Inventory (Bem, 1974) and the Personal Attributes Questionnaire (Spence & Helmreich, 1978). Such instruments assess how people define the social category *woman,* or query women about their personal preference in terms of competing definitions of the social category *women.* They do not, however, focus directly on the extent to which a woman derives her sense of self from the social category, women, or more personal characteristics that are unique to the self. Our aim is to develop a concrete and realistic context in which to ask women directly about the extent to which their personal or social identity is predominant. Where social identity predominates, there is a tendency for a woman to associate her personal identity with her social identity as a woman and vice versa. For women who dissociate their personal and social identities, their social identity as a woman is less salient.

Porter and Taylor (1992) assessed the salience of social identity by presenting women with pairs of scenarios. Each scenario describes an interaction between two coworkers. A male coworker initiates a behavior, and the woman in the scenario shares her thoughts in the form of her interpretation of the male coworker's behavior. The four actual scenarios presented to women are described here. The first pair of scenarios involves attacks at the personal level; the second pair of scenarios focuses on attacks at the group level:

Pair 1: Personally Directed Behavior

Scenario 1

Bob: "You know, Carol, you're really holding us up on the Solomon Report. Just because you're a woman doesn't mean you don't have to do your share of the work."

Carol: (thinking to herself): "I don't know how I got stuck working with Bob on this report. I really resent how he attacks me on the basis of being a woman. And, actually, I think that his comment against me personally as a woman is also meant to be some kind of attack against women in general."

Scenario 2

Bob: "You know, Carol, you're really holding us up on the Solomon Report. Just because you're a woman doesn't mean you don't have to do your share of the work."

Carol: (thinking to herself): "I don't know how I got stuck working with Bob on this report. I really resent how he attacks me on the basis of being a woman. But I don't think that his comment against me personally as a woman is meant to be some kind of attack against women in general."

Pair 2: Group-Directed Behavior

Scenario 1

Dan: (while throwing a stack of folders on Carol's desk and muttering loud enough for Sue to hear): "Women just never do their share of the work!"

Sue: (thinking to herself): "I don't know how I got stuck working with Dan on this report. I really resent how he attacks women in general like that. And, actually, I think his comment against women in general is meant to be some kind of attack against me personally as a woman."

Scenario 2

Dan: (while throwing a stack of folders on Carol's desk and muttering loud enough for Sue to hear): "Women just never do their share of the work!"

Sue: (thinking to herself): "I don't know how I got stuck working with Dan on this report. I really resent how he attacks women in general like that. But I don't think his comment against women in general is meant to be some kind of attack against me personally as a woman."

The scenarios were presented in pairs. Within each pair, the male coworker's comment was the same. So, for the first pair, the man's attack was directed at the woman personally. For the first scenario of the pair, the victim interpreted the male coworker's comment not only as an attack against her personally but also as an attack against women in general. Thus, the female coworker associated herself personally as a woman with women in general. In the second scenario of the first pair, the male coworker's comment was interpreted as an attack against her personally as a woman but not as an attack against women in general. Here, the female coworker dissociated herself personally as a woman from women in general.

For the group-directed pair of scenarios, the male coworker made a discriminatory comment against women in general. In the first scenario, the female coworker considered his comment against women in general to also be an attack against her personally as a woman. Thus, she associated women in general with herself personally as woman. In the second scenario, she did not interpret his comment against women in general as an attack against her personally, thereby dissociating women in general from herself personally as a woman.

Following each pair of scenarios, subjects were asked to choose which of the two scenarios in the pair best represented how they interpreted the discriminatory act perpetrated by the male coworker; in effect, subjects chose to associate or dissociate personal and social identity. Therefore, for each of the pairs, subjects could choose to associate or dissociate, thus yielding one of four possible profiles per subject: (a) associate person with group and group with person (bidirectional association), (b) associate person with group but dissociate group from person,

(c) dissociate person from group but associate group with person, or (d) dissociate person from group and group from person (bidirectional dissociation).

In addition, at a time prior to or after responding to the scenarios, women were asked, in the context of a number of filler items, the usual questions about their perceptions of personal and group discrimination. Neither the ratings of personal and group discrimination nor the ratings for each scenario were affected by the order of presentation.

An examination of the frequencies with which subjects endorsed the association and dissociation scenarios reveals that the majority of women (70.1%) made a bidirectional association between personal and group discrimination. Hence, most subjects perceived an attack at the personal level as an attack against women in general, and an attack against women in general as an attack against the subject personally as a woman. This endorsement of both associative scenarios is not surprising, given that the sample was comprised of young women attending university, where women's issues are generally very salient. However, it is important to note that there was also a substantial number of women (the remaining 29.9%) who endorsed at least one of the dissociation scenarios. In fact, a small but not insignificant number of subjects (7.3%) dissociated both person from group discrimination and group from person discrimination.

In order to explore the potential range of individual differences in association among women, the association/dissociation profile for young university women was compared to the profile for older, nonuniversity women. For the older, nonuniversity women, most of whom were homemakers, the frequencies of endorsement for the various association/dissociation scenarios were predictably different from those of the younger, university women: Only 52.5% of the older women (as compared to 70.1% of the younger women) bidirectionally associated person and group discrimination. In addition, 27.5% of the older women (compared to 7.3% of the younger women) bidirectionally dissociated person and group discrimination. The remaining 20% of the older women endorsed at least one dissociation scenario.

It is clear, therefore, that older, nonuniversity women endorsed dissociation scenarios more frequently than younger, university women. However, even within the younger sample, where one would expect the majority to endorse the association scenarios, substantial numbers of subjects endorsed at least one dissociation scenario. Thus, there are individual differences among women in terms of the extent to which they associate their personal and social identity. These individual differences permit a direct test of the hypothesis that women who associate their personal identity and social identity, do not evidence the usual personal/group discrimination discrepancy.

Surprisingly, no evidence was found for this basic hypothesis. Higher ratings for group discrimination compared to personal discrimination were found for women in each of the four association/dissociation profiles. Indeed, the discrepancy between personal and group ratings remains surprising consistent across the four profiles. In comparing even the most disparate profiles, those who bidirectionally associate versus those who bidirectionally dissociate, the discrepancy is essentially the same: 3.3 and 3.2 scale points higher for group discrimination. Hence, whether an individual chooses to bidirectionally associate or dissociate person and group or any of the two combinations between these extremes bears no impact on that individual's perceptions of personal and group discrimination.

In order to make a more complete test of the hypothesis, the relationship between association/dissociation and the personal/group discrepancy was examined from the opposite point of view. Posed from this reversed perspective, the question became: Do subjects displaying little or no personal/group discrepancy evidence any systematic differences in association/dissociation patterns from those subjects who have comparatively larger personal/group discrimination discrepancies?

The overall ratings of personal and group discrimination by the 164 university women replicate the usual personal/group discrimination discrepancy. On a 10-point scale, mean ratings for group discrimination are 6.3 compared to 3.1 for ratings of personal discrimination. From this sample of university women, two subgroups were created in a manner similar to that used for the study involving Haitian and South Asian women (see Fig. 10.2). The first was a small-discrepancy group comprised of women whose group and personal ratings were identical or differed by two scale points or less. A large-discrepancy group was made up of women whose ratings of group discrimination were at least three scale points higher than their ratings for personal discrimination. The results of this arbitrary classification are presented in Fig. 10.4a.

In order to test the hypothesized relationship between perceived discrimination and identity pattern, it was necessary to devise a measure of the extent to

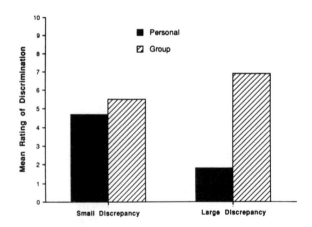

FIG. 10.4a.   Ratings of personal and group discrimination for subjects classified into small and large discrepancy categories.

which a subject associates her personal identity with her social identity and vice versa. This was accomplished by creating a net association score for each woman in the sample. This score was constructed by first calculating the extent to which a subject endorses an associative response (rating from 1 to 10) minus the extent to which that subject endorses the complementary dissociative response (rating from 1 to 10). Such calculations were performed for both person-to-group and group-to-person scenarios. The net association score for each subject was then calculated by averaging the person-to-group and group-to-person scores. This score ranges from minus 10 to 10, where a high score in a positive direction indicates strong association. The net association scores for the small discrepancy and large discrepancy subsamples of women are presented in Fig. 10.4b.

Our original rationale was based on the assumption that women for whom the "I" and "we" are interchangeable would not show evidence for the personal/group discrimination discrepancy. In terms of the present study, this would lead to the hypothesis that net association scores would be higher for those in the small-discrepancy group, than net association scores for those in the large-discrepancy group. Once again, the hypothesis was not confirmed. More importantly, the results in Fig. 10.4a and Fig. 10.4b not only disconfirm the hypothesis, but they are opposite to the hypothesis. That is, women with a smaller personal/group discrimination discrepancy have significantly weaker, not stronger, associations between person and group, and between group and person (see Fig. 10.4b).

On the surface, this result seems counterintuitive. Why is it that individuals who associate more with their group actually demonstrate more of a discrepancy between personal and group ratings of discrimination? A possible answer to this puzzle presents itself on reexamination of the proposals by Brewer (1991) and

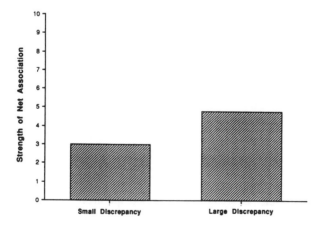

FIG. 10.4b.   Ratings of net association for subjects divided into small and large discrepancy categories.

Turner et al. (1987) on which the original hypothesis was based. Consider Brewer's (1991) definition of social identities as "categorizations of the self into more inclusive social units that depersonalize the self-concept, where 'I' becomes 'WE'" (p. 476). Implied in this definition is that the very characteristics that differentiate the self from others, one's personal identity, are no longer salient when the focus switches to one's social identity as a frame of reference for comparison. Therefore, an increase in the saliency of one's group identity is at the expense of one's personal identity.

This sacrifice of one level of identity while the other is activated is made even more explicit by Turner et al. (1987) who argues that, when one's social identity is activated, one must "shift towards the perception of self as an interchangeable exemplar of some social category and away from the perception of self as a unique person" (p. 50). Therefore, in considering the subjects surveyed in the present study, it may be that those individuals who maintain a strong social identity in terms of "I identify myself with the category of women as a group," do so at the expense of their personal identity, those characteristics that define "me personally as a woman." The original hypothesis is not supported, because it is assumed that if people identified themselves strongly with the group, then the "I" and the "we" would be synonymous such that there would be little distinction between ratings of discrimination at the personal and group levels. The data are consistent with our closer examination of Brewer's (1991) and Turner et al.'s (1987) notion that one level of identity is at the expense of the other level; in short, the "I" and the "we" are not synonymous with increases in social identity. Rather, the prominence of the "we" is at the expense of the "I." It appears that as attention is focused on one level of identity, there is an accompanying reduction in attention to the other level. The implications for perceived discrimination are clear: The more social identity is salient leading to vigilance in the perception of group discrimination, the less salient is personal identity and thus the lower the perception of personal discrimination.

Support for this hydraulic view of identity is found in Fig. 10.4a and in the data presented earlier in Fig. 10.2. If it is true that the more one identifies with one's group, the less salient one's personal identity, then higher ratings for group discrimination should be accompanied by lower ratings for personal discrimination. This is precisely the pattern that emerges in Fig. 10.4a. The more a woman associates herself with women as a group the more pronounced is her personal/group discrimination discrepancy. Moreover, the increased discrepancy does not arise because of increases in group discrimination or decreases in personal discrimination alone but rather because of the simultaneous increase in group discrimination and decrease in personal discrimination.

Precisely the same pattern emerged for perceptions of discrimination by Haitian and South Asian women (See Fig. 10.2). These data were interpreted earlier as evidence for the notion that exaggeration of group discrimination is as viable an explanation for the personal/group discrimination discrepancy as is the more popular denial-of-personal-discrimination explanation. In light of the present discussion, the results also support the notion that having a strong social identity is necessarily depersonalizing in the sense that personal identity is weakened. Naturally then, perceptions of discrimination are affected such that increases in perceptions of group discrimination coincide with decreases in the perception of personal discrimination.

Perhaps a more definitive investigation of the link between personal and social identity and the personal/group discrepancy would be to experimentally manipulate the salience of an individual's personal and social identities and then examine the effects on the personal/group discrepancy.

The present interpretation of our nonintuitive results is tentative at best, and two important disclaimers are necessary:

1. The results for university women show a pattern that directly links net association or degree of social identity with the magnitude of the personal/group discrimination discrepancy. The data for Haitian and South Asian women are far less convincing, because there was no independent measure of degree of social identity to relate to perceptions of discrimination.

2. In conceptualizing identity as lying along a continuum ranging from social to personal, both Brewer (1991) and Turner et al. (1987) had a different definition of personal from the one used here. They defined *personal identity* in terms of those unique attributes that a person does not share with others who are members of the same social category. In the present context, the personal end of the identity continuum is defined as "you personally as a woman." Although emphasizing personal attributes, the present definition nevertheless alludes to the person as a woman.

These disclaimers notwithstanding, the possibility of a link between the structure of self-identity and perceptions of discrimination points to new theoretical challenges. It suggests, for example, that just as theory dealing with personal and social identity provides insights into perceptions of discrimination, so too might research into the personal/group discrimination discrepancy shed light on the structure and process of identity.

SUMMARY AND CONCLUSIONS

From our review of the personal/group discrimination discrepancy phenomenon, it is clear that major theoretical challenges lie ahead. Yet, there is at least some basis for believing that the phenomenon is an important one that may offer some insights into other important psychological processes. In terms of the phenomenon itself, our review suggests that the personal/group discrimination discrepancy is a robust phenomenon and that it is not the result of some obvious artifact.

Thus, differential perceptions of discrimination at the personal and group level represent a psychologically important phenomenon that may help us understand how such a devastating experience is interpreted and felt by people. It may also help in our understanding of people's behavioral reactions to discrimination. The conditions under which disadvantaged group members take individual as opposed to collective action emerge as a central issue in the social psychology of intergroup relations (e.g., Wright, Taylor, & Moghaddam, 1990). There may well be a parallel between perceptions of personal and group discrimination and taking individual or collective action.

In terms of understanding the personal/group discrimination discrepancy, there is some evidence to suggest that denial or minimization of personal discrimination is not the only viable explanation, as has been suggested to date. There is also some indication that perceptions of discrimination have their roots in real experience, and how that experience becomes internalized needs to be addressed fully.

Finally, there is initial evidence to suggest a link between perceptions of discrimination and the nature of personal and social identity. This link needs to be explored not only for what it can tell us about perceptions of discrimination but also for the insights it provides into the very nature of self-identity.

ACKNOWLEDGMENTS

The research described in this chapter was supported by a grant from the Social Sciences and Humanities Research Council. The authors are indebted to Jim Olson, Mark Zanna, and Steven Neuberg for their insightful comments on an earlier version of the chapter.

REFERENCES

Bem, S. L. (1974). The measurement of psychological androgyny. *Journal of Consulting and Clinical Psychology, 42,* 155–162.

Birt, C. M., & Dion, K. L. (1987). Relative deprivation theory and responses to discrimination in a gay male and lesbian sample. *British Journal of Social Psychology, 26,* 139–145.

Brewer, M. B. (1991). The social self: On being the same and different at the same time. *Personality and Social Psychology Bulletin, 17*(5), 475–482.

Crocker, J., & Major, B. (1989). Social stigma and self-esteem: The self-protective properties of stigma. *Psychological Review, 96,* 608–630.

Crosby, F. (1982). *Relative deprivation and working women.* New York: Oxford University Press.

Crosby, F. (1984a). The denial of personal discrimination. *American Behavioral Scientist, 27,* 371–386.

Crosby, F. (1984b). Relative deprivation in organizational settings. In B. M. Staw & L. L. Cummings (Eds.), *Research in organizational behaviour: An annual series of analytic essays and critical reviews* (pp. 51–93). Greenwich, CT.: JAI Press.

Crosby, F., Muehrer, P., & Loewenstein, G. (1986). Relative deprivation and explanation: Models and concepts. In J. M. Olson, C. P. Herman, & M. P. Zanna (Eds.), *Relative deprivation and social comparison: The Ontario Symposium* (Vol. 4, pp. 17–32). Hillsdale, NJ: Lawrence Erlbaum Associates.

Dibble, U. (1981). Socially shared deprivation and the approval of violence: Another look at the experience of American Blacks during the 1960s. *Ethnicity, 8,* 149–168.

Dion, K. L. (1986). Responses to perceived discrimination and relative deprivation. In J. M. Olson, C. P. Herman, & M. P. Zanna, (Eds.), *Relative deprivation and social comparison: The Ontario Symposium,* (Vol. 4, pp. 159–179). Hillsdale, NJ: Lawrence Erlbaum Associates.

Dion, K. L., & Earn, B. M. (1975). The phenomenology of being a target of prejudice. *Journal of Personality and Social Psychology, 32,* 944–950.

Dubé-Simard, L., & Abbondanza, M. (1985). *A personal and collective look at the situation between the sexes: Differences, justice and causal attribution.* Unpublished manuscript. Université de Montreal.

Gelman, D., Springen, K., Brailsford, K., & Miller, M. (1988, March). Black and White in America. *Newsweek,* pp. 18–23.

Guimond, S., & Dubé-Simard, L. (1983). Relative deprivation theory and the Quebec nationalist movement: The cognitive-emotion distinction and personal-group deprivation issue. *Journal of Personality and Social Psychology, 44*(3), 526–535.

Major, B., Carrington, P. I., & Carnevale, P. (1984). Physical attractiveness and self-esteem: Attributions for praise from an other-sex evaluator. *Personality and Social Psychology Bulletin, 10,* 43–50.

Porter, L. E., & Taylor, D. M. (1992). The personal/group discrimination discrepancy: The role of social identity. Unpublished manuscript, McGill University.

Spence, J. T., & Helmreich, R. L. (1978). *Masculinity and femininity: Their psychological dimensions, correlates, and antecedents.* Austin: University of Texas Press.

Taylor, D. M., & Dubé, L. (1986). Two faces of identity: The "I" and the "We". *Journal of Social Issues, 72,* 81–98.

Taylor, D. M., Wong-Reiger, D., McKirnan, D. J., & Bercusson, T. (1982). Interpreting and coping with threat in the context of intergroup relations. *Journal of Social Psychology, 117,* 257–269.

Taylor, D. M., Wright, S. C., Moghaddam, F. M., & Lalonde, R. N. (1990). The personal/group discrimination discrepancy: Perceiving my group, but not myself, to be a target for discrimination. *Personality and Social Psychology Bulletin, 16,* 254–262.

Taylor, D. M., Wright, S. C., & Ruggiero K. (1991). The personal/group discrimination discrepancy: Responses to experimentally induced personal and group discrimination. *Journal of Social Psychology, 131*(6), 847–858.

Turner, J. C., Hogg, M., Oakes, P., Reicher, S., & Wetherell, M. (1987). *Rediscovering the social group: A self-categorization theory.* Oxford: Blackwell.

Wright, S. C., Taylor, D. M., & Moghaddam, F. M. (1990). Responding to membership in a disadvantaged group: From acceptance to collective protest. *Journal of Personality and Social Psychology, 58,* 994–1003.

Zanna, M. P., Crosby, F., & Loewenstein, G. (1986). Male reference groups and discontent among female professionals. In B. A. Gutek & L. Larwood (Eds.), *Women's Career Development* (pp. 28–41). Newbury Park, CA: Sage.

11 Behavioral Responses to Discrimination: A Focus on Action

Richard N. Lalonde
James E. Cameron
York University

In this chapter, we focus on what many social psychologists studying prejudice consider to be its behavioral component—discrimination. Our emphasis is not on the behavior of the discriminator, however, but on the individuals for whom the consequences of discrimination are devastating. These are the victims of discrimination. In addition, we focus on overt behaviors (i.e., actions) that are taken in response to discrimination rather than covert behaviors (i.e., affect and cognition), because it is the actions taken by victims of discrimination that are most likely to bring about a change in the status of the disadvantaged groups of which they are members.

The first part of this chapter examines social psychological approaches that bear on the responses of victims of discrimination. It is argued that theories of intergroup relations hold considerable promise for the study of responses to discrimination (e.g., social identity theory). Although these theories are not formulated explicitly for the study of discrimination, they are formulated from the perspective of disadvantaged group members, they involve a consideration of overt behaviors that can lead to change, and they can be used to guide future research on the subject of discrimination. The behaviors discussed within these theories are contrasted with behaviors of victims of discrimination presented in seminal work on prejudice (e.g., Allport, 1954). Finally, examples of research that focus on the behavior of disadvantaged and discriminated individuals are described, along with a brief presentation of Tajfel's (1978) interpersonal–intergroup behavior continuum as a framework for understanding the interpretation of different situations of discrimination. The second part of this chapter focuses on research we conducted that explores the range of responses that can be taken in different situations of discrimination and the behavioral dimensions underlying these responses. The results of these studies illustrate the limitations that exist within current theoretical models and suggest some directions for future research.

SOCIAL-PSYCHOLOGICAL PERSPECTIVES ON RESPONDING TO DISCRIMINATION

Most discussions of prejudice usually elicit some reference to the notion of discrimination. Despite its clear prominence as a social problem and its common lay usage, however, it often appears in social psychological discourse in a somewhat sterilized form. For this reason, we begin by contrasting a definition exemplifying the view of social psychologists with a classic example of discrimination. Dovidio and Gaertner (1986) provide a typical definition of discrimination that is framed within the context of prejudice: "Whereas prejudice is an attitude, discrimination is a selectively unjustified negative behaviour toward members of the target group. . . . It is important to note that prejudice does not always lead to discrimination and that discrimination may have causes other than prejudice" (p. 3). Several questions come to mind that are both raised and neglected by this definition. For example, how may discrimination occur in the absence of prejudice? More central to this chapter are questions that are not addressed in the definition. What happens to the individual in the target group after the occurrence of this negative behavior? What might he or she do? In order to answer these questions, we offer an example of discrimination that is familiar to readers acquainted with the history of the Civil Rights Movement.

On Thursday, December 1, 1955, after a hard day's work as a seamstress in a department store in Montgomery, Alabama, Rosa Parks boarded a bus to take her home. Rosa Parks had corns and bunions and "she sat in the first seat behind the white section—that is to say the first Negro seat" (Lomax, 1963, p. 17). The bus filled rapidly, and some White people were left standing. The White bus driver ordered Mrs. Parks and three other Blacks to move back so the White people could have their seats. The Montgomery bus system was segregated with Whites at the front of the bus and Blacks at the back, and Whites were given priority over Blacks in terms of seating. Rosa Parks refused to comply with the bus driver's demands, and she was subsequently arrested and taken away by the police (Lomax, 1963). This event in itself represents a dramatic example of discrimination, but the story is not complete.

Although Rosa Parks was not the first person who refused to give up her seat to a White person, word of her arrest spread quickly in the Black community. It was decided that action should be taken, and as part of the strategy, a young Baptist minister, Martin Luther King, Jr., helped organize a bus boycott. The following Monday, 4 days after the arrest of Rosa Parks, 99% of Black commuters started walking or using car pools. This boycott, which continued for over 12 months, is referred to as the Montgomery Walk to Freedom. It led to a Federal District Court ruling on June 4, 1956, against the segregated policy for bus seating in Montgomery, and this ruling was upheld by the United States Supreme Court 4 months later (Lomax, 1963).

The example of Rosa Parks can be used to understand the definition of discrimination taken from Dovidio and Gaertner (1986). An important element of that definition is that discrimination is not necessarily related to a prejudicial attitude. The arrest of Rosa Parks may have had little to do with the underlying attitude of the bus driver who asked her to move or even with the attitude of the police who arrested her. The discrimination that Rosa Parks experienced was institutional; it was built into and buttressed by an entire social system.

A definition of discrimination is correct, therefore, when it states that individual prejudice is not a necessary precondition for acts of discrimination. Why then is there an inherent tendency to view discrimination solely as the behavioral component of prejudice? One reason for this link is historical. Early research on prejudice, which proved to be very influential (e.g., Adorno, Frenkel-Brunswik, Levinson, & Sanford, 1950), viewed discrimination as stemming from the individual. Another contributing reason is that if the source of discrimination lies within the prejudiced individual, it is easier to study and remedy the problem than when discrimination is rooted within an entire social system (see Fairchild & Gurin, 1978). Unfortunately, we must agree with Pettigrew (1986), who stated that "institutionalized discrimination is the core of the problem; prejudice both supports and is derived from these institutionally restrictive arrangements" (p. 172).

When we further contrast Dovidio and Gaertner's (1986) definition of discrimination with the situation of Rosa Parks, we note a limitation in its perspective. The emphasis is on the behavior of the discriminator who is the actor; although the definition does not inherently exclude the discriminated, the latter is put into the more passive role of target. This definitional limitation is not raised as a critique of the excellent work of Dovidio and Gaertner but rather as a means for highlighting the fact that researchers have generally not studied the behavioral reactions exhibited by victims of discrimination. The focus of most research on discrimination has been on the behavior of the discriminator as a function of his or her prejudice.

This unidirectional perspective has profound implications for the study of discrimination. Importantly, it fails to accentuate the need for understanding the phenomenology of being a victim of discrimination. Furthermore, if the goal is to eliminate acts of discrimination, this unidirectional focus (along with a belief in the prejudice–discrimination link) leads to strategies directed at changing the attitude of the discriminator by focusing on that individual. Such strategies, however, are largely ineffectual, and change must come by altering the institutional arrangements that provide a dominant position and special privileges to certain groups (Pettigrew, 1986). Historical examples suggest that most systemic change derives from the actions that are taken by the victims of discrimination and not from the individuals who are in the advantaged position. The Civil Rights Movement in the United States received much of its impetus from the actions taken by individuals like Rosa Parks.[1] In a similar vein, the growing support for native rights and Indian self-government in Canada is the result of a sensitization to native issues that was brought about by actions such as those taken by a group of Mohawk warriors in Oka, Québec, in the summer of 1990. If one is to study discrimination with an eye on social change, one has much to learn by studying the responses of the victims of discrimination.

Three points can be drawn from this exercise in contrast between a social psychological definition of discrimination and Rosa Parks' experience of discrimination:

1. When one studies the phenomenon of discrimination, one must include the thoughts, feelings, and behavior of the victims of discriminatory actions. Unfortunately, little research addresses the phenomenology of the victims of discrimination (Dion & Earn, 1975; Harrison, 1974). One purpose of this chapter is to demonstrate how certain social psychological theories of intergroup relations offer a theoretical framework for understanding and predicting the behavior of victims of discrimination.

2. If one of the goals of social psychological inquiry is the reduction of discrimination through social change, then constructive solutions may be found by studying the actions taken by victims of discrimination. These actions have the potential of bringing about change that has positive consequences for the individual, for the group, and for society. Unfortunately, the research that examines the effects of discrimination on its victims focuses mainly on its affective and cognitive consequences.[2]

3. Victim responses to discrimination are a function of the situations in which they occur. In the case of Rosa Parks, a strictly interpersonal interpretation of her situation does not explain how her behavior became the catalyst for opposition to a systemic form of discrimination. Rather, her situation demands an interpretation from a larger social perspective. In this chapter, the

---

[1] In an invited address to the Society for the Psychological Study of Social Issues in 1967, Martin Luther King, Jr. (1968) stated that, "It was the Negro who educated the nation by dramatizing the evils through nonviolent protest. The social scientist played little or no role in disclosing truth. The Negro action movement with raw courage did it virtually alone" (p. 180). On the other hand, Condor (1989), criticized the "assumption that *all* current efforts for social change come from subordinate social groups" (p. 32) and provided examples in which the activity of high-status groups is also implicated.

[2] All social psychologists agree that discrimination has very negative consequences for its victims. Although some affective and cognitive consequences may be characterized as positive (see Crocker & Major, 1989), these positive consequences are compensatory in nature and they should not have to exist.

problem of discrimination is viewed as an intergroup problem and not an interpersonal one. Later, we introduce the interpersonal–intergroup continuum, discussed by Tajfel (1978), in order to provide a key to understanding both the interpretations of situations of discrimination and the behavioral responses to those situations.

Theories of Intergroup Relations and Responses to Discrimination

Given the assumption that most cases of discrimination are systemically rooted and thus best understood in terms of the imbalance of power between advantaged and disadvantaged social groups, theories of intergroup relations are appropriate for understanding discrimination and its related effects. From an intergroup-relations perspective, discrimination represents a situation where an individual is unjustly treated on the basis of membership in a disadvantaged group. This definition, which clearly puts the focus on the victim and not on the perpetrator, has been forwarded by others such as Jones (1986) who stated that "discrimination refers simply to differential treatment of individuals on the basis of their social category by people or the institutional policies they create and enforce" (p. 289).

Three social psychological theories of intergroup relations that are particularly relevant for understanding behavioral responses to discrimination are: (a) relative deprivation theory (Crosby, 1976; Davis, 1959; Gurr, 1970; Runciman 1966),[3] (b) social identity theory (Tajfel & Turner, 1979), and (c) the five-stage model of intergroup relations (Taylor & McKirnan, 1984). These theories are quite broad in their scope and are not examined in any detail in this chapter (for a review of these theories, see Taylor & Moghaddam, 1987). The question to be addressed at this juncture is, why are these theories useful for understanding the behavior of victims of discrimination? Although they are not explicitly conceived for understanding or predicting the behavior of victims of discrimination, they are formulated from the perspective of individuals who are in a disadvantaged position on the basis of their group membership, a perspective congruent with our conceptualization of discrimination. Moreover, these theories attempt to predict the behavior of those who feel relatively deprived compared to others (relative deprivation theory), of those who have a negative social identity when they compare themselves to members of another group (social identity theory), and of those

---

[3]Relative deprivation has a more complex history of development than the other two theories and has appeared in a number of forms. In the original model, the dependent variable of interest is the feeling of deprivation (an attitude), and the addition of behavior as a dependent variable is a relatively recent development (Martin & Murray, 1984). The more relevant component of the theory with regard to discrimination pertains to fraternal deprivation (Runciman, 1966). The link between fraternal deprivation and discrimination has been described in detail by Dion (1986).

who recognize that they are in a position of social disadvantage (five-stage model). Clearly, these interrelated feelings and experiences can be present within individuals who are victims of discrimination. Instead of using the term *discrimination,* however, researchers working with these theories used terms such as *injustice* (e.g., Crosby & Gonzalez-Intal, 1984), *disadvantage* (e.g., Wright, Taylor, & Moghaddam, 1990), *inequality* (e.g., Martin, Brickman, & Murray, 1984), and *deprivation* (e.g., Smith & Gaskell, 1990). All of these terms reflect the experience of discrimination.

These theories are important because they make predictions concerning the behaviors that will be taken by members of a disadvantaged group. From an experimental perspective, the independent variables are found in the structural characteristics of the intergroup situation (e.g., open or closed intergroup boundaries) and the personal characteristics of disadvantaged group members (e.g., belief in individual social mobility). Of particular interest in this chapter are the dependent variables that are central in these theories, namely, the behaviors that can be taken by disadvantaged group members. Table 11.1 provides a summary of the more detailed typologies of behavioral responses that have been offered by researchers working within the frameworks offered by theories of intergroup relations. This list is meant to be representative rather than exhaustive. The typologies reveal the range and multidimensionality of responses that can be taken, at least theoretically, by individuals who experience social injustice.

An examination of the typologies in Table 11.1 reveals dimensions of behavior that are common to the different theories. These dimensions, which have been identified by some of the researchers listed in Table 11.1, are overlapping and should not be seen as independent from each other. An *active vs. passive* dimension, which has been previously highlighted by others (e.g., Dion, 1986), distinguishes behaviors in terms of whether or not they are directed at bringing about a change for the disadvantaged individual or group. Examples of passive behaviors are stress symptoms, attitudes toward the self/object/system, political apathy, and acceptance. Examples of active behaviors include self-improvement, object-directed behavior, militancy, and social competition. A *normative vs. nonnormative* distinction was explicitly identified by Wright et al. (1990) as well as Dion (1986) in terms of constructive versus destructive behaviors. Along this dimension, behaviors are differentiated in terms of whether or not they are conducted with the approval of the existing social system. Normative behaviors include self-improvement, constructive social change, political participation, and individual mobility. Nonnormative behaviors are exemplified by violence against society, drug abuse, militancy and violence, and terrorism. A third dimension of behavior, which has received considerable attention in many areas of psychology, is the *individual vs. collective* distinction. Although research within personality and cross-cultural psychology recognizes the individual–collective distinction as complex (e.g., Triandis, McCusker, & Hui, 1990), a simple distinction between behaviors that are engaged in alone and behaviors that are engaged in

TABLE 11.1
Typologies of Behaviors That May Result From Relative Deprivation, Social Injustice,
or Social Disadvantage

Relative Deprivation Theory

Crosby (1976)	Stress symptoms
	Self-improvement
	Violence against society
	Constructive change of society

Mark and Folger (1984)

Attitude toward the Self:	self-deprecation, mental-health problems, enhancement of self-image
Self-directed behavior:	self-enhancement through education, self-diminishment with drug abuse
Attitude toward the object:	affective and cognitive upward or downward reappraisal of object that was not attained
Object-directed behavior:	increase or decrease in achievement behavior related to the object
Attitude toward the system:	affective and cognitive reappraisal of system that has denied the object
System-directed behavior:	aggressive behavior, riots, revolution, constructive social change

Dion (1986)	Direct political participation
	Militancy and violence
	Indirect political support
	Political apathy and resignation

Social Identity Theory

Hogg and Abrams (1988)

Individual mobility:	exit, passing, assimilation
Social change:	seek new dimensions of social comparison, redefine the value of existing dimensions of social comparison, use different outgroups for social comparison
Social competition:	civil-rights activity, political lobbying, revolution, terrorism, war

---

Five-Stage Model

Wright, Taylor, and Moghaddam (1990)

Acceptance	
Individual - normative:	individual upward mobility within system
Individual - nonnormative	individual action outside system
Collective - normative:	collective behavior that preserves status quo
Collective - nonnormative:	collective behavior that threatens social order

---

with others can be applied to many of the behaviors that are discussed within intergroup theories (e.g., Wright et al., 1990). Examples of individual behaviors include stress symptoms, self-oriented attitudes or behavior, and, in many instances, assimilation. Collective behaviors are found in riots, revolution, civil rights activity, and some forms of political participation. A fourth distinction underlying many of the behaviors in Table 11.1 is that of *self-directed vs. system-directed* behaviors (e.g., Mark & Folger, 1984). Self-directed behaviors include self-improvement and self-deprecation, whereas system-directed behaviors include violence against society and political participation and lobbying.

The behavior typologies of intergroup theories and their underlying dimensions have their shortcomings regarding their applicability to the experience of discrimination. Because they refer to broadly defined behaviors, it is sometimes difficult to determine how these behaviors can be applied to specific instances of discrimination occurring, for example, in situations involving employment or housing. Furthermore, it should be recalled that these typologies are not explicitly formulated for an understanding of the behavior of victims of discrimination. We now review some of the literature that directly addresses the consequent responses of victims of discrimination in order to determine if intergroup theories are sufficiently comprehensive in their behavioral typologies to be of use in the study of discrimination.

Traditional Psychological Perspectives on Responding to Discrimination

Different perspectives are applied to understanding the range of responses to discrimination. Personality theory, for example, is used to explain the development of a "Black personality" and its relation to racism and discrimination. Early psychoanalytic work by Kardiner and Oversey (1951) provides a very bleak perspective by concluding that oppression leads Blacks to having self-hatred, low self-esteem, and hostility towards Whites. This view, fortunately, is countered by more recent developmental models of Black psychologists who see the potential for a strong personality that is related to a positive social identity (see Jones, 1991, for a brief review). Although the personality perspective on discrimination is important, it is primarily centered on the self-directed behaviors in the typologies that were presented earlier. A number of classic works within social psychology and sociology provide the most comprehensive views on the responses of victims of discrimination. Here, we briefly examine those of Allport (1954), Pettigrew (1964), and Simpson and Yinger (1985).

In his seminal treatise on prejudice, Allport (1954) devoted a chapter to "Traits Due to Victimization" in which he presented 15 responses to discrimination representing different types of ego defenses. In his analysis, Allport distinguished between responses more likely to be used by extropunitive victims, those who attribute their situation to outer causes, and responses more likely to be used by intropunitive victims, those who blame themselves. In his list of behaviors, intropunitive responses include withdrawal and passivity, clowning, aggression against ingroup, and symbolic status striving, whereas extropunitive types use the strengthening of ingroup ties, slyness and cunning, fighting back, and enhanced striving. Allport's intropunitive–extropunitive distinction can be recast in terms of the self- versus system-directed distinction that is identified in the intergroup theory typologies. It should also be noted that most of the behaviors discussed by Allport could be identified along the active–passive, individual–collective, and normative–nonnormative dimensions of behavior.

Pettigrew (1964) presented a behavioral typology that is quite different from Allport's, in a chapter entitled "Reactions to Oppression." He described three general classes of response: (a) moving towards the oppressor (seeking acceptance through integration), (b) moving against the oppressor (fighting back), and (c) moving away from the oppressor (flight or avoidance). A comparison of the classification schemes of Allport and Pettigrew reveals a clear shift from an individual level of analysis (the intro/extropunitive dimension) to an intergroup level of analysis (responses of oppressed in relation to oppressor), yet the specific behaviors and exemplars that are used by both authors are quite similar.

In order to provide a more sociologically oriented perspective, we refer to the more recent edition of Simpson and Yinger (1985), who presented four general classes of behavior in their chapter on "Types of Response to Prejudice and Discrimination." These classes are: (a) avoidance (e.g., passing, separation, escape), (b) aggression or striking back (e.g., protest, hostile aggression, boycotts), (c) reformism (i.e., actions directed at social change within the existing system), and (d) acceptance. Once again, the classes of behaviors put forward by social psychologists interested in the experience of discrimination are found within the response typologies suggested by researchers working within relative deprivation theory, social identity theory, and the five-stage model.

Why are intergroup theories important to the understanding of responses to discrimination when many of these responses have already been discussed in early social psychological analyses of discrimination? These theories offer frameworks from which testable predictions can be made concerning the types of behaviors that will be taken by individuals in a disadvantaged position. More specifically, they deal with the prediction of behaviors that can be taken to bring about social change. A few examples of how these theories are applied to the prediction of behavior of disadvantaged individuals are offered in the following discussion.

Empirical Investigations of Responses to Discrimination

Most of the research addressing the phenomenology of being a victim of discrimination focuses on behaviors that are self-directed and relatively passive in terms of the dimensions of behavior that were identified earlier. Much of this work demonstrates the cognitive and emotional coping strategies that are elicited when an individual must deal with the stigma of belonging to a disadvantaged group (see Crocker & Major, 1989, chapter 12, this volume). The comprehensive research program of Dion serves as a good example of this type of research

(Dion, 1975; Dion & Earn, 1975; Dion, Earn, & Yee, 1978). Dion and his colleagues used an experimental attribution paradigm, in which single members of a minority group (e.g., Jews, women) are led to believe they are competing in a task against either three members of a majority group (e.g., Christians, men) or three nondescript individuals. All minority group members experience failure in the task, and the assumption underlying the paradigm is that subjects who interact with outgroup members can attribute their failure to discrimination. In their study of Jewish subjects, Dion and Earn (1975) found support for this assumption, as well as some interesting effects with regard to the cognitive and emotional consequences of discrimination. Subjects who attributed their failure to discrimination rated themselves more strongly on the positive aspects of their ingroup stereotype compared to subjects who did not make this attribution. In addition, subjects who perceived discrimination reported feeling more aggression, sadness, anxiety, and egotism than subjects who did not perceive discrimination. These emotional responses have been interpreted as indicative of a stress reaction (Dion, 1986).

Experimental studies conducted within the framework of relative deprivation theory also focus on the affective or cognitive consequences of deprivation (Bernstein & Crosby, 1980; Folger & Martin, 1986; Folger, Rosenfield, Rheaume, & Martin, 1983; Folger, Rosenfield, & Robinson, 1983; Guimond & Dubé-Simard, 1983; Mark, 1985). For example, Bernstein and Crosby (1980) looked at the effects of the hypothesized preconditions of relative deprivation (e.g., the perception of entitlement to a desired outcome) on a number of affective responses such as resentment, dissatisfaction, disappointment, anger, and unhappiness.

In fact, much of the research examines behavior that falls on the self-directed end of a self-directed versus system-directed dimension of behavior. More recently, however, some experimental studies framed within the context of relative deprivation theory (Crosby, 1976), social identity theory (Tajfel & Turner, 1979), and the five-stage model (Taylor & McKirnan, 1984), have focused on responses that characterize the active–passive, individual–collective, and normative–nonnormative dimensions of behavior (Ellemers, van Knippenberg, & Wilke, 1990; Inglis, 1990; Martin et al., 1984; Lalonde & Silverman, 1992; Taylor, Moghaddam, Gamble, & Zellerer, 1987; Wright et al., 1990).

Martin et al. (1984) examined the relationship between the severity of fraternal deprivation and the willingness to participate in legitimate or illegitimate forms of collective action. In their role-playing study, the magnitude of fraternal deprivation was manipulated by varying the degree of financial inequity between male and female managers in a fictitious company. Female subjects, who were asked to think of themselves as employees of the company, had stronger feelings of deprivation when faced with greater financial inequities. The severity of the deprivation, however, had no effect on their willingness to engage in collective forms of behavior. Martin et al. concluded that the feelings of injustice associated with fraternal deprivation play only a secondary role in evoking collective action and that other variables such as the availability of mobilization resources are much more important in the prediction of collective behavior. In short, resource mobilization theory (McCarthy & Zald, 1979) posits that an individual's willingness to participate in collective action is influenced by the perception of opportunities for participation (i.e., resources). Mobilization resources were manipulated by Martin et al. by including factors such as the presence of an organized female management group. They found that subjects were more willing to engage in illegitimate forms of collective behavior when resources were present than when they were absent.

The study by Wright et al. (1990) serves as a good example of research addressing individual and collective behaviors within an intergroup theory framework. According to social identity theory (Tajfel & Turner, 1979) and the five-stage model (Taylor & McKirnan, 1984), collective action is more likely to be associated with a completely closed, advantaged group (i.e., impermeable group boundaries), whereas individual action is linked to more open, advantaged groups. In order to test this prediction, Wright et al. (1990) used an experimental paradigm that was first developed by Taylor et al. (1987). In this paradigm, all subjects begin as members of an unsophisticated decision-making group and are told that promotion to a higher status, sophisticated decision-making group will be based on their performance on a decision-making task. All subjects are subsequently rejected by a group of members of the advantaged group. Wright et al. manipulated the degree of group openness so that subjects believed that the advantaged group was either open, partially open, or completely closed to all members of their group. In accordance with social identity theory and the five-stage model, impermeable group boundaries were associated with the willingness to engage in a nonnormative collective action (i.e., to write a message of protest that urged other members of the disadvantaged group to ignore the final decision of the advantaged group and to take action that would allow their entry). This particular finding also received support in a study by Lalonde and Silverman (1992), who additionally found that the salience of an individual's social identity facilitated the propensity to take collective action when group boundaries were closed.

The studies described previously are presented to demonstrate the usefulness of intergroup theories for predicting the behavior of disadvantaged individuals in situations of social injustice. The behaviors under investigation in these studies, however, are constrained by the experimental paradigms selected by the researchers and by the particular dimensions of behavior suggested by the theoretical models that are being tested (i.e., individual vs. collective, passive vs. active, normative vs. nonnormative, self-directed vs. system-directed).

In order to gain insight into the phenomenology of being a victim of discrimination, other types of methodologies have proved to be useful. Adams and Dressler (1988), for example, used an ethnographic approach (i.e., open-ended interviews) to identify the different areas of life in which members of a Black community experience discrimination (e.g., general service, city government, school system, police service). Of particular relevance to this chapter is a study by Lykes (1983) that focuses on the responses that a sample of older Black women had made in situations of discrimination experienced over the course of their lives. Lykes analyzed the oral histories obtained in open-ended interviews of 52 women who had contributed to the improvement of the lives of Black people, particularly in the 1940s and 1950s. Their accounts were content analyzed with regard to the types of situations of discrimination they encountered (personal prejudice vs. institutional discrimination) and the types of coping strategies they used in these situations. These coping strategies were categorized as a function of their instrumentality, such that behaviors were rated as passive, indirect (nonconfrontational), or direct (action directed at the source of the problem). These women were also compared as a function of the predominant culture of their employment setting; some women worked in predominantly Black organizations and some in predominantly White organizations. Lykes' analysis reveals two findings of note. She found that strategies of coping were more direct when discrimination was of a personal nature than when discrimination was institutional. There was also an interaction between the employment setting of the women (Black vs. White) and the type of discrimination experienced (personal vs. institutional) on the types of responses that were taken. Lykes found that women who worked in Black settings were likely to take more direct approaches in cases of institutional discrimination compared to cases of personal prejudice, whereas women working in White organizations were more likely to take direct approaches in cases of personal prejudice than in cases of institutional discrimination.

Another strategy for studying discrimination is found in the work of Mikula (1986; Mikula & Schlamberger, 1985) who used retrospective and role-playing techniques to explore responses to perceived social injustice. In a first study, Mikula (1986) had university students provide a report of an unjust event they had experienced. Their responses were coded according to a number of criteria, including their reactions to the event. The active responses that were identified included a confrontation of the perpetrator, insulting or taking revenge on the perpetrator, avoiding future contact with the perpetrator, and seeking advice, support, or consolation. It should be noted that most of the unjust events that were elicited involved interpersonal situations with the opportunity of continued contact between perpetrator and victim. In a second study by Mikula (1986), high school students participated in school-related scenarios of injustice involving a student and teacher. He found that the most frequent types of action-related thoughts reported by students were (a) attempts at restoring justice, (b) punishment of the perpetrator, (c) passive resistance, (d) opposition, (e) seeking advice or information, and (f) the encouragement of others to take action.

When the behavioral responses identified by Mikula (1986) are contrasted with the dimensions underlying the behaviors discussed in intergroup theories, there is some communality. None of the behaviors found by Mikula, however, qualify as system-directed and very few qualify as collective. Furthermore, some of the behaviors are not considered as potential responses within intergroup theories (e.g., seeking advice). The difference in behaviors raised by his participants and those raised by intergroup theories can be partially attributed to different types of situations of discrimination that Lykes (1983) recognized in her analysis, namely personal versus institutional settings of discrimination. These variations in context may be clarified by placing these situations at different positions on an interpersonal–intergroup continuum.

Discrimination and the Interpersonal–Intergroup Continuum

Tajfel (1978) suggested a behavioral continuum bounded by poles describing interpersonal and intergroup forms of behavior. At the interpersonal end, interactions between people take place on the basis of their individual characteristics, whereas at the intergroup end, interactions are guided primarily by group membership. When interactions between people occur more towards the intergroup end of the continuum, the behavior of ingroup members towards outgroup members is more uniform, and outgroup members are perceived as an undifferentiated mass. When the boundaries between social groups are clear and impermeable, extreme forms of intergroup behavior are more likely to occur. When the boundaries between social groups are more fuzzy and permeable (i.e., individual mobility is seen as possible), interpersonal forms of behavior are more likely to occur (Tajfel, 1978).

Tajfel noted that discrimination is a behavior that falls closer to the intergroup end of his continuum. Some situations of discrimination, however, are closer to the intergroup pole than others. We believe that instances of discrimination that are experienced with a single individual are interpreted at the interpersonal end of Tajfel's behavior continuum, especially when indices of systemic discrimination are not available. With regard to the work of Mikula (1986), individuals recalling their own experiences of injustice were likely to recall events of an interpersonal nature that did not necessarily tie into some type of group membership. In the case of discrimination experienced by Rosa Parks and many of the women interviewed by Lykes (1983), however, behavior clearly occurred at the intergroup extreme of Tajfel's continuum. In our own research, we identify the types of behaviors elicited in situations of discrimination that are perceived as falling at different points on the interpersonal–intergroup continuum.

EXPLORING THE ACTIONS OF VICTIMS OF DISCRIMINATION

In this section, we report some preliminary work that attempts to identify the range of responses that individuals perceive as being at their disposal in different situations of discrimination. This research has two general purposes:

1. We want to compare the responses of lay people to the behaviors that are identified as important in social psychological theories of intergroup relations. By identifying behavioral responses in relation to specific instances of discrimination, it is possible to determine if the behaviors identified in these theories are comprehensive enough in scope.

2. Another purpose is to compare the types of responses that are elicited by instances of discrimination interpreted as falling at different points on the interpersonal–intergroup behavior continuum. The study by Lykes (1983) indicated that Black women differentiated between personal and institutional instances of discrimination and adopted different response strategies as a function of this distinction. Feagin and Eckberg (1980) proposed a typology of situations of discrimination that includes at least four types (isolate, small group, direct institutional, and indirect institutional). It was expected that different situations of discrimination would evoke different types of responses.

Two studies are reported. In the first study, participants imagined themselves in a situation that would eventually lead to an act of discrimination directed at them on the basis of their membership in a particular group. This study identifies the behavioral responses that seem reasonable in different situations of discrimination. In the second study, a new group of participants sorted the behaviors that were generated in the first study. Its purpose was to identify the dimensionality of behaviors that are deemed important by lay people when interpreting behaviors within the context of discrimination. The only manipulated variable in these studies was the type of situation in which discrimination occurred.

Study 1

Before describing the situations of discrimination, it is beneficial to describe some of the primary features of our methodology:

1. Participants were engaged in scenarios of discrimination by means of an interactive role-playing strategy using verbally guided imagery. They chose the category on the basis of which they had been victimized.
2. It was explicitly stated in the scenarios that discrimination had taken place, and it did not have to be inferred as in many experimental studies of social injustice.
3. The questioning of participants and the subsequent analysis of their responses were explicitly focused on the actions that they perceived as possible in their situation and not on affective and cognitive responses.
4. Scenarios were selected to represent situations of discrimination falling at different points on the interpersonal–intergroup continuum.

The first two scenarios involved discrimination in employment and housing situations.[4] For the third scenario, a situation of discrimination was created in which individuals were denied the right to vote in an imaginary "new world."[5] Although any situation of discrimination is fundamentally intergroup when it is based on membership in a social category, the job and apartment scenarios were more interpersonal than the new world scenario, because they described a situation involving a direct personal encounter with the perpetrator.[6]

Method

Respondents.   The interviews took place at the Ontario Science Centre in Toronto. Interested visitors approached a booth that announced a psychology study was in progress. Seventy-four interviews were conducted with 43 women and 31 men with a mean age of 36 years. More than 80% of the participants were Canadian or American (48.6% and 35.1%, respectively), and 10.8% were from the United Kingdom. Participants were not asked to indicate their racial identification, but the majority of respondents did not belong to visible minority groups.

Procedure.   Participants were recruited for a study of Strategies for Dealing With Social Dilemmas and were assigned to one of three interviewers (two male and one female). They were presented with one of the three scenarios that was read aloud and a guided imagery technique was used to elicit the thoughts and feelings that they would experience in the described situation. Each session was tape recorded. The three scenarios are briefly described as follows:

---

[4]These two situations of discrimination were selected on the basis of a search in our university library system. When discrimination was entered as the key word for a subject search, there were 300 general headings. When these headings were broken down into particular areas, the most popular were employment (99 of 300) and housing (63 of 300). None of these latter headings were related to psychological references, thus suggesting that these areas were in need of psychological study.

[5]Although one may conjure images of South Africa for this scenario, it was not so long ago that natives in Canada were in the same situation. In fact, they did not have the right to vote in federal elections until 1960. It is also worthy to note that like South African Blacks, natives living on reserves were restricted in their freedom of movement. According to the Indian act, natives on a reservation needed a special permit or they could be arrested. This restriction was in effect until the 1950s.

[6]Our method has the advantage of exercising control over the situation in which discrimination is experienced, while permitting respondents to choose the basis of the discriminatory action and the responses that they perceived as being appropriate. Such a role-playing method, however, has obvious limitations. Many respondents have no experience with the situations in which they are placed, and many may not have experienced discrimination in their lives. As a result, some of their responses are seen as reflecting strategies that are stereotypically associated with these situations, and respondents may not consider the full consequences of their actions. A central purpose of the study is to identify a range of perceived behavioral options, however, and subjects were not asked for the single response in which they would actually engage.

The Job Application. Respondents were situated in an interview for a specific job that they could realistically get and would like. They were asked to imagine the job and describe it, as well as the interviewer and the setting. Later, they were informed that although they had the necessary qualifications, a better candidate was selected. According to a reliable source (someone working at the same place), however, the job was not filled, and confidentially they were the victim of some type of discrimination in hiring. Participants were also informed that none of their references was contacted. They were asked to think about why they might have been discriminated against (i.e., membership in a particular social group or some defining characteristic).

The Apartment. This scenario was similar to the job situation, except that the primary interaction took place with a building owner for the purpose of renting a desirable apartment. In this story, the participants were told they were called and informed that the apartment had been given to someone else. A good source (someone living in the same building), however, informed them that the apartment was not rented and that, confidentially, they were the victim of some type of discrimination. They also found out that their bank and present landlord were not contacted as references.

A Sad New World. This scenario most clearly represented an intergroup situation, because participants imagined themselves living in a future society in which they are identified as members of a social group that is denied basic human rights (e.g., the right to vote) by a group in power. Participants were asked to imagine that this group is one with which they presently identify.

After selecting the reason for which they may have been discriminated against, participants in all three conditions were asked a number of questions dealing with what they might do in response to their situation. Prior to these questions, the following was read to individuals receiving the job (or apartment) scenarios:

> You are now in a position where you can ignore the situation or you can take some type of action. Remember that it was important for you to get this job [apartment]. Try to imagine how you feel knowing that you probably didn't get the position [apartment] because you were discriminated against. Think about all the different things you might do knowing you have been unjustly refused a job [a place to live].

Participants receiving the sad new world scenario were read:

> You are now in a position where you can ignore the situation or you can take some type of action. Are you going to do something about the discrimination that exists simply because you happen to belong to a particular group? Think about all the different things you might do knowing you are being unjustly treated.

Following these prompts, participants responded to the question that was of central importance in this study: What are all of the possible actions that you might take?

Results and Discussion

Perceived Reason for Discrimination.   Gender was the most frequently imagined reason for the described discrimination, reported by 23% of the respondents (all of these were women). The two other most typical responses were age (both young and old; 13.6%) and ethnicity/nationality or race (12.2%). None of the respondents used the most frequent category of discrimination reported to the Ontario Human Rights Commission in 1990–1991—handicap. The frequencies associated with the reported categories are shown in Table 11.2 as a function of scenario and gender of respondent.

Possible Actions in Response to Discrimination.   In order to determine if the scenarios elicited behaviors that differ from behavior dimensions that are identified as central to intergroup theories, responses were coded as (a) passive (e.g., do nothing about the situation) or active (e.g., take legal action), (b) individual (e.g., gather evidence proving I was a victim) or collective (e.g., demonstrate with others), and (c) normative (e.g., be involved in rallies) versus nonnormative (e.g., plant bombs), which was operationalized as a function of the legality of the behavior in North America. Agreement between two coders was over 92% for each category. Responses were not coded to determine if they were self-directed or system–directed, because the question under investigation precludes self-directed behaviors. There were no significant relationships between gender, nationality, or educational level and the types of actions selected by respondents.

TABLE 11.2
Suggested Basis of Discrimination for Females and Males

Category	Scenario			Totals
	Job	Apartment	Sad New World	
Gender	8F 0M	6F 0M	3F 0M	17F 0M
Age	2F 0M	2F 2M	3F 1M	7F 3M
Ethnicity/Race	3F 1M	0F 1M	1F 3M	4F 5M
Religion	0F 1M	–	2F 3M	2F 4M
Student	–	3F 1M	1F 0M	4F 1M
Politics	1F 1M	–	0F 2M	1F 3M
Parent	1F 0M	1F 1M	–	2F 1M
Educated	–	–	0F 3M	0F 3M
Appearance	2F 1M	–	–	2F 1M
Other	1F 0M	0F 2M	0F 4M	1F 4M
None	0F 3M	3F 3M	–	3F 6M

Approximately 75% of the respondents indicated that they would take some type of action, and no relationship was found between scenario type and the passive versus active distinction. This is not surprising, given that prompts were formulated to evoke active behaviors. There was a significant relationship, however, between the likelihood of an active or passive response and the typicality of the discrimination category, χ^2 (1, $N = 72$) = 13.51, $p < .001$. Respondents attributing the discrimination to gender, age, or ethnicity/race were more likely to engage in some type of action (33 out of 35) than those suggesting less typical reasons (e.g., level of education, appearance) for the discrimination (21 out of 37). One interpretation of this finding is that membership in a more typical social group is more central to one's self-concept, and people are more likely to take an active response when such a membership is threatened by discrimination.

There also was a significant relation between scenario type and endorsement of individual versus collective behaviors, χ^2 (2, $N = 72$) = 36.71, $p < .001$. This relationship is attributable to the collectively oriented responses of most people (75%) imagining themselves in the new world scenario. Only 3 of the 48 respondents in the job and apartment scenarios suggested taking action with others. These results probably reflect the impact of different contexts of discrimination. When respondents were victims of institutionalized discrimination (new world), collective actions came readily to mind. The discrimination here was clearly presented as the product of intergroup power differentials, and most people responded by formulating actions in group terms. In contrast, the job and apartment scenarios depicted discrimination in situations that were more interpersonal, and people were far less likely to spontaneously suggest collective forms of behavior.

The endorsement of normative versus nonnormative behavior was also significantly related to scenario type, χ^2 (2, $N = 72$) = 18.00, $p < .001$. All of the respondents who suggested norm-violating actions (11%) were in the sad new world scenario. This finding is congruent with some research indicating that nonnormative behavioral strategies may be used in extreme situations of discrimination in which there is little or no chance of otherwise escaping the disadvantaged position (Wright et al., 1990).

Study 2

Although the behaviors identified in Study 1 can be coded according to the behavior dimensions implicated by intergroup theories, lay respondents may not conceptualize these behaviors along the same lines. Theories offer overarching dimensions of behavior, but when individuals are placed within the constraints of a particular situation of discrimination, more subtle behavioral distinctions may apply. In addition, there is evidence in the first study indicating that contextual variations across situations of discrimination are reflected by quite different dimensions of behavior (i.e., nonnormative behaviors were found only for the new world scenarios). The purpose of this study, then, is to identify the categories and dimensions that lay people see as representative of behaviors in certain situations of discrimination.

In order to identify the specific behaviors that were accessed by the lay sample in Study 1, all of the discrete behaviors that could be identified from the transcripts of the taped interviews were extracted. This process was achieved in several stages.[7] The end result was the identification of 27 discrete behaviors for the job scenario, 30 for the apartment scenario, and 38 for the new world scenario. These behaviors provided the stimuli for the second study. Given the similarity of behaviors that were elicited in the job and apartment scenarios and a clearer pattern of results for the apartment scenario, the data for the job scenario are not presented here.

Method

Respondents.   Seventy-six undergraduate psychology students were recruited from classes and paid for their participation. There were 55 females and 21 males with a mean age of 21 years.

Procedure.   Each participant received a written version of two of the three scenarios that were used in Study 1 on the basis of a fixed random order, thus providing 52 respondents per scenario. After reading a scenario, the respondent was given the following written instructions:

There are a number of things that a person in your situation may do. We will provide you with a number of actions or behaviors that other people in your situation have thought of. Each of these behaviors is presented separately on a card. Please read all of the cards a few times, so that you become familiar with them. Think about what each behavior involves, and the implications it has.

---

[7]First, the transcripts of 17 randomly selected interviews were examined separately by three raters to determine if they used similar extraction strategies for discrete behaviors. Second, the remaining interviews were divided randomly and evenly between two of the raters. The extraction of ambiguously presented behaviors was resolved by a discussion between the two raters who came to an agreement. Third, the extracted behaviors were retranscribed to follow a similar format. Redundant, ambiguous, or apparently nonsensical items were then eliminated. The result is the generation of a list of discrete behaviors expressed in sentence form for each scenario. These sentences were again rephrased in order to be presented suitably in the next phase of the study. A final examination of the items resulted in the elimination of those that were too general, those that could be collapsed into others, and those that were geared towards seeking the reason for the discrimination. A constant attempt was made to retain the integrity of the participants' responses by using their wording and erring in the direction of overinclusiveness.

The respondent was then given a shuffled set of cards associated with the scenario and a standard set of instructions for card sorting.[8]

Results and Discussion

Similarity matrices were constructed for each scenario on the basis of the frequency of appearance of pairs of behaviors in the card-sorting task. A multidimensional scaling procedure was used to analyze the matrices using an ALSCAL procedure. A three-dimensional solution provided a satisfactory fit for the apartment data (RSQ = .89, Stress = .13), and a two-dimensional solution provided the best fit for the new world data (RSQ = .88, Stress = .19). The list of behaviors for the apartment and new world scenarios is in the appendix at the end of this chapter, along with the symbols used to identify each of them.

Apartment Scenario. In order to facilitate the presentation of the three-dimensional space of behaviors obtained for the apartment scenario, the results are collapsed into 2 two-dimensional views. Figure 11.1 shows how behaviors cluster along Dimensions 1 and 2 when collapsing Dimension 3, and Fig. 11.2 shows behaviors along Dimensions 1 and 3 when collapsing Dimension 2. In Fig. 11.1 and Fig. 11.2, the behaviors that are grouped within circles always clustered together regardless of the perspective that was taken when behaviors were examined in their complete three-dimensional space. These clusters of behaviors are given abbreviated names to facilitate their presentation and aid in the interpretation of dimensions. Examples of the behavior clusters include: (a) resignation (e.g., forget about the apartment and search for another one elsewhere), (b) collective organization (e.g., work to organize others who were similarly discriminated against), (c) government agents (e.g., contact my city councilor), (d) legal action (e.g., take the owner to court), (e) collect evidence (e.g., record all conversations with the owner, and (f) confront perpetrator (e.g., confront the owner and demand to know why I was refused the apartment).

In terms of the identification of the dimensions underlying the spatial organization of the behaviors, Dimension 1 is a *Private versus Public* dimension, because behaviors on the private end primarily focused on interpersonal interactions with the perpetrator, and behaviors on the public end focused on social agencies, government agents, and the media. Dimension 2 is a *Passive versus Active* dimension, where behaviors on the passive end were resignation, talking

---

[8]The instructions were as follows:

"Your task is to sort these behaviors into groups in terms of how similar they are to each other. Cards that you see as similar should be put into the same group. You form a group by putting cards into the same pile. You can form as many groups (piles) as you like, and you can have a different number of cards in each group. You can even have a card by itself, but try to create no more than 10 groups. A card can belong to only one group, but you may change your assignment of behaviors to groups until you are happy with your sorting."

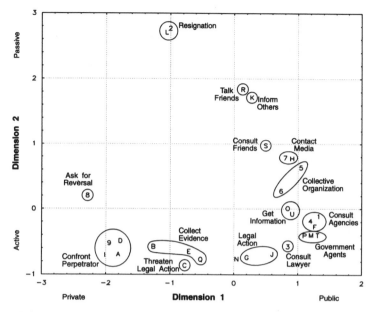

FIG. 11.1.   Two-dimensional view of Dimensions 1 and 2 for the apartment scenario.

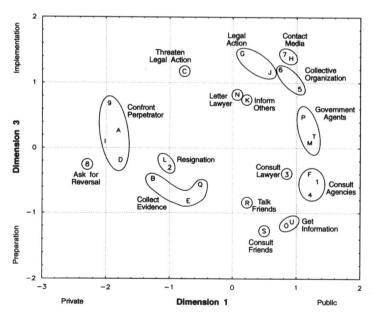

FIG. 11.2.   Two-dimensional view of Dimensions 1 and 3 for the apartment scenario.

with or consulting friends and family, and informing others about the discrimination. More active behaviors included engaging in legal action, collecting evidence, and confronting the perpetrator. Dimension 3 reflects a *Preparation versus Implementation* dimension. Preparation behaviors included consulting family and friends or agencies, getting information, and collecting evidence. Implementation behaviors included taking legal action, contacting the media, and collective organization.

New-World Scenario. The two-dimensional solution for the new world behaviors is seen in Fig. 11.3. Behaviors in this scenario tended to group closely together and only a few distinct clusters were identified to facilitate the interpretation of the underlying dimensions. These clusters are: (a) resignation/exit (e.g., leave or dissociate myself from the group that is being discriminated against), (b) sabotage (e.g., plant or throw bombs), (c) social protest (e.g., demonstrate with others in public places), and (d) group consciousness raising (e.g., write letters to the press describing my experiences of discrimination). Other interesting behaviors included trying to convince those in power that the situation of discrimination is unfair, withdrawing labor as a form of protest, and looking for a leader who could unite people to oppose the discrimination.

The underlying dimensions of behavior for the new world scenario are quite clear and easier to label than in the case of the apartment scenario. Dimension 1 is labeled *Normative versus Nonnormative.* Behaviors on the normative end included group consciousness raising, as well as an active concern for the avoid-

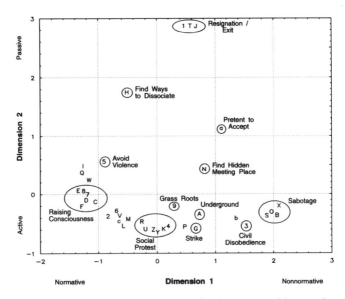

FIG. 11.3. Two-dimensional solution for the new-world scenario.

ance of violence. Behaviors on the nonnormative end included acts of sabotage and civil disobedience. Social protest behaviors fell between these two extremes. Dimension 2 reflects a *Passive versus Active* dimension, with resignation and exit behaviors at the passive end of the dimension, and social protest behaviors at the active end.

Earlier in this chapter, four dimensions of behavior were seen as underlying the behaviors that are available to individuals who are in a position of social disadvantage: (a) active versus passive, (b) normative versus nonnormative, (c) individual versus collective, and (d) self-directed versus system-directed. These dimensions are also applicable to the traditional social psychological analyses of the responses of victims of discrimination (e.g., Allport, 1954). It is of considerable interest, therefore, to compare the dimensions identified by social psychological theorists to those identified by lay people who were asked to classify the behaviors of their peers (note that self-directed behaviors are precluded in this study). We limit ourselves to four observations that can be drawn from this comparative exercise.

A first observation is that the individual–collective distinction in behavior did not surface in the apartment or new world scenarios. As seen in Study 1, the apartment scenario elicited behaviors that were almost exclusively individual, and the new-world scenario elicited behaviors that were largely collective in nature, thus making it difficult for this dimension to appear. A plausible explanation for this pattern in behaviors is that entire classes of response strategies (i.e., individual or collective) may be evoked as a function of where the discrimination situation falls on the interpersonal–intergroup continuum. It is also possible, however, that the individual–collective distinction is not as clear as social psychologists would like it to be. Kağitçibaşi (1987) questioned the validity of the individual–collective distinction within cross-cultural psychology and suggested that they are not incompatible orientations even within the same individual. With regard to social action, the individual response of Rosa Parks (saying no) led to the collective action of her group (bus boycott). Another example of individual behaviors having implications for the status of the group comes from a study by Abel (1981), who found that the pursuit of sex-discrimination grievances by individual women within universities is related to an improved overall status of women on a campus.

These latter examples highlight a second point of the present results. It is more appropriate in some cases to view responses to discrimination in terms of process rather than in terms of discrete acts. As reflected by the preparation versus implementation dimension for the apartment scenario, the exploration of potential responses was an important aspect of the aftermath of discrimination. The role-playing studies of Mikula (1986) also reveal preparatory behaviors, such as seeking advice from others. The conceptualization of responses to discrimination, therefore, should extend backwards from the final action(s). Of course, this must take place along with a consideration of the resources and system structures available to the individual. Social psychological theories of intergroup relations, as well as resource mobilization theory (McCarthy & Zald, 1979), offer insight as to how these resources and structures impact the decisions that are made by individuals and/or their groups in selecting their actions.

A third observation taken from our second study is the potential importance of a private–public dimension in behavior. This is a distinction that merits attention in future theory and research. An important difference between private and public behaviors is in the cost involved in engaging in these types of behaviors. Although on the surface, confronting the perpetrator of the discrimination may seem costly, the victims have nothing to lose, because they have already been refused the apartment. There are significant psychological costs, however, associated with publicly acknowledging the experience of being discriminated against (see Abel, 1981). Both Martin et al. (1984) and Inglis (1990) indicated that this cost factor must be considered in research on social action in response to injustice, and the private–public distinction is one key in unraveling its complex relationship.

A final point to be drawn from the role-playing scenario studies is that they reveal the salience of a particular class of behaviors worth pursuing in future research on discrimination, namely litigation. More than one third of the behaviors that were examined in the apartment scenario referred to the use of a lawyer, the courts, or government agency. These behaviors, which are normative and system-directed, have the potential for bringing about tremendous social change (e.g., *Brown v. Board of Education of Topeka*, 1954). They represent what Simpson and Yinger (1985) called reformism—actions directed at social change using existing social structures. Yet these behaviors are not explicitly and adequately integrated within the social psychological theories of intergroup behavior that are examined in this chapter. Such a class of behaviors cannot be ignored in the development of theoretical models of intergroup relations and the study of responses to discrimination. Although the study of these responses may seem promising for bringing about social change, however, some legal scholars have questioned the utility of the courts for bringing about lasting social improvements for disadvantaged groups (Shattuck & Norgren, 1979).

The role-playing studies presented here have the advantage of helping to identify possible modes of action under a controlled set of circumstances where a discriminatory act was explicitly labeled, without limiting the participants to a specific set of responses. The studies, however, have their limitations and represent only one step in understanding the representation of actions that individuals have when faced with a situation of discrimination. We are now engaged in some new research where similar scenarios (job and apartment) are being presented to individuals who are at a high risk of experiencing discrimination (South Asians and Caribbean immigrants). In these scenarios, we manipulate variables such as the type of discrimination experienced (individual and institutional) and use the behaviors that are identified in the present studies as our dependent variables.

DIRECTIONS FOR RESEARCH ON RESPONSES
TO DISCRIMINATION

In this final section, we highlight some issues that were raised by the literature and our research, in order to make some suggestions for future inquiry. A first observation is that responses to discrimination, whether they be passive or active, should be recognized as part of a process. There are at least two stages within this process: (a) the acknowledgment that discrimination has indeed occurred, and (b) an analysis of the situation in order to determine which strategy of action, if any, to adopt.

The stage of acknowledgment is a particularly difficult one as suggested by the work of Taylor and colleagues on the personal/group discrimination discrepancy (Taylor, Wright, Moghaddam, and Lalonde, 1990; Taylor, Wright, & Porter, chapter 10, this volume). This involves the perception by individuals that their group is discriminated against to a far greater extent than they are themselves. Although the mechanisms underlying this discrepancy are unclear, it represents a potential cognitive obstacle to considering possibilities for action (particularly if personal experiences of discrimination are denied). One challenge for future research is to identify the conditions that bring about an acknowledgment of personal discrimination when it occurs. One key to this recognition is to have discriminated individuals process information at an intergroup level rather than an interpersonal level of analysis (Tajfel, 1978), meaning that disadvantaged group members need to interpret their experiences in terms of category membership rather than personal attributes (in relative deprivation terms, to shift from an egoistical to a fraternal level of analysis). It should be noted that the process of recognition can be facilitated by consciousness raising, which represents a key stage in Taylor and McKirnan's (1984) five-stage model of intergroup relations.

Once discrimination has been recognized by its victim, the theories of intergroup relations that are mentioned in this chapter are particularly beneficial in predicting what type of action will be taken. Much work remains to be done within these theories, however, in terms of an elaboration of the behavioral responses that they have identified. An example of such an elaboration is the recognition of preparatory responses (e.g., information and social support seeking) prior to a commitment to a line of action. In experimental studies, more attention needs to be paid to the dependent variables in order to move from the prediction of broad classes of behavior, such as system-directed behavior, to the prediction of specific behaviors within these broad classes, such as lodging a grievance with the Human Rights Commission. In addition, research paradigms should focus on common experiences of social injustice such as access to employment and housing.

In order to study the more common manifestations of discrimination, future research should use a plurality of methods and approaches. In the studies that were presented earlier, a number of methods of investigation proved to be useful:

(a) experimental studies (e.g., Dion & Earn, 1975; Wright et al., 1990), (b) the analysis of oral histories (Lykes, 1983), and (c) role playing (Mikula, 1986). Although our own studies have a number of methodological limitations, the results still reveal dimensions of behavior that are not explicitly acknowledged by relevant social psychological theories, and they provide more fine-grained behavioral repertoires to be used in future research.

In terms of alternative approaches, there is an emerging body of work in discourse analysis (e.g., Potter & Wetherell, 1987) that ascribes fundamental importance to language in social psychology. According to discourse analysis, social categories do not simply exist in an objective manner but are used flexibly in speech to perform different functions in different contexts; similarly, an experience such as discrimination exists as it is constructed in discourse. Discourse analytic methods move beyond content analysis (e.g., Lykes, 1983) in that the coding of the discourse is not the endpoint of the analysis but the substrate for the generation of hypotheses regarding the functions of discourse in a particular context. By "listening" to the victims of discrimination, a discourse analytic framework reveals the ways in which instances of discrimination are evaluated before any type of action can be taken. Essed (1991), for example, examined accounts of racism in the everyday lives of Black women in the United States and the Netherlands. Her analysis illuminated the often subtle reproduction of structural racism in everyday social practices and ascribed importance to the knowledge that Black women have gained through their experiences of discrimination. Victims of discrimination may be regarded as "experts" in this domain; clearly, an understanding of their knowledge is essential for predicting when an individual will decide to take (or not to take) action in response to the discrimination. Louw-Potgieter (1989) took this perspective in a study of personal accounts of racism by Black students at a South African university. It was found that most experiences were characterized by resignation due to beliefs that covert racism could not be directly confronted and that the racism was institutional in nature. An interesting aspect of these studies is the description of victims' explanations and evaluations of their experiences. The observations that are made within phenomenologically and discourse-oriented approaches can be usefully employed to elaborate theoretical models that focus on discrimination.

Central to the present chapter is the notion that discrimination is systemically rooted in unequal intergroup power relations. Recent theory and empirical work in intergroup relations reflects a growing concern with the issue of power (e.g., Bourhis, chapter 8, this volume; Condor & Brown, 1988; Sachdev & Bourhis, 1991). There is, however, another facet of the power dynamic that needs to be addressed, concerning the present state of social psychological research. The need for a "minority voice" is acutely felt in the field of prejudice and discrimination. We (the authors, as White, middle-class males), are relatively ill-equipped to conceptualize the very experiences of many of the disadvantaged groups we attempt to study (e.g., visible immigrants, Blacks, women). Thus, along with our suggestion that the focus of research shift from the discriminator to the discriminated, we advocate minority input into research and policy in this area. Such advocacy is not new (Lewin, 1946) but is still needed. If the social psychology of prejudice and discrimination is to stand for social justice, social change, and social action, then the notion of affirmative action within our own institutions should not be a point of debate (see Blanchard & Crosby, 1989) but a point of priority.

ACKNOWLEDGMENTS

We would like to thank Richard Bourhis, Jim Olson, Regina Schuller, and Mark Zanna for their insightful comments and constructive criticism of an earlier version of this chapter. The work of Robyn Irving in the collection, transcribing, and coding of a challenging data base was invaluable. We also acknowledge the financial assistance of the Social Sciences and Humanities Research Council of Canada in the form of a research grant and a Canada Research Fellowship to the first author.

REFERENCES

Abel, E. (1981). Collective protest and the meritocracy: Faculty women and sex discrimination lawsuits. *Feminist Studies, 7,* 505–538.

Adams, J. P., Jr., & Dressler, W. W. (1988). Perceptions of injustice in a Black community: Dimensions and variations. *Human Relations, 41,* 753–767.

Adorno, T. W., Frenkel-Brunswik, E., Levinson, D. J., & Sanford, R. M. (1950). *The authoritarian personality.* New York: Harper.

Allport, G. W. (1954). *The nature of prejudice.* Cambridge, MA: Addison-Wesley.

Bernstein, M., & Crosby, F. (1980). An empirical examination of relative deprivation theory. *Journal of Experimental Social Psychology, 16,* 442–456.

Blanchard, F. A., & Crosby, F. J. (Eds.). (1989). *Affirmative action in perspective.* New York: Springer-Verlag.

Brown v. Board of Education of Topeka, 347 U.S. 483 (1954).

Condor, S. (1989). 'Biting into the future': Social change and the social identity of women. In S. Skevington & D. Baker (Eds.), *The social identity of women* (pp. 15–39). London: Sage.

Condor, S., & Brown, R. (1988). Psychological processes in intergroup conflict. In W. Stroebe, A. W. Kruglanski, D. Bar-Tal, & M. Hewstone (Eds.), *The social psychology of intergroup conflict: Theory, research, and applications* (pp. 3–26). New York: Springer-Verlag.

Crocker, J., & Major, B. (1989). Social stigma and self-esteem: The self-protective properties of stigma. *Psychological Bulletin, 96,* 608–630.

Crosby, F. (1976). A model of egoistical relative deprivation. *Psychological Review, 83,* 85–113.

Crosby, F., & Gonzalez-Intal, A. M. (1984). Relative deprivation and equity theories: Felt injustice and the undeserved benefits of others. In R. Folger (Ed.), *The sense of injustice: Social psychological perspectives* (pp. 141–166). New York: Plenum.

Davis, J. A. (1959). A formal interpretation of the theory of relative deprivation. *Sociometry, 22,* 280–296.

Dion, K. L. (1975). Women's reactions to discrimination from members of the same or opposite sex. *Journal of Research in Personality, 9,* 294–306.

Dion, K. L. (1986). Responses to perceived discrimination and relative deprivation. In J. M. Olson, C. P. Herman, & M. P. Zanna (Eds.), *Relative deprivation and social comparison: The Ontario Symposium* (Vol. 5, pp. 159–179). Hillsdale, NJ: Lawrence Erlbaum Associates.

Dion, K. L., & Earn, B. M. (1975). The phenomenology of being a target of prejudice. *Journal of Personality and Social Psychology, 32,* 944–950.

Dion, K. L., Earn, B. M., & Yee, P. H. N. (1978). The experience of being a victim of prejudice: An experimental approach. *International Journal of Psychology, 13,* 197–214.

Dovidio, J. F., & Gaertner, S. L. (1986). Prejudice, discrimination, and racism: Historical trends and contemporary approaches. In J. F. Dovidio & S. L. Gaertner (Eds.), *Prejudice, discrimination, and racism* (pp. 1–34). Orlando: Academic Press.

Ellemers, N., van Knippenberg, A., & Wilke, H. (1990). The influence of permeability of group boundaries and stability of group status on strategies of individual mobility and social change. *British Journal of Social Psychology, 29,* 233–246.

Essed, P. (1991). *Understanding everyday racism: An interdisciplinary theory.* Newbury Park, CA: Sage.

Fairchild, H. H., & Gurin, P. (1978). Traditions in the social-psychological analysis of race relations. *American Behavioral Scientist, 21,* 757–778.

Feagin, J. R., & Eckberg, D. L. (1980). Discrimination: Motivation, action, effects, and context. *Annual Review of Sociology, 6,* 1–20.

Folger, R., & Martin, C. (1986). Relative deprivation and referent cognitions: Distributive and procedural justice effects. *Journal of Experimental Social Psychology, 22,* 531–546.

Folger, R., Rosenfield, D., Rheaume, K., & Martin, C. (1983). Relative deprivation and referent cognitions. *Journal of Experimental Social Psychology, 19,* 172–184.

Folger, R., Rosenfield, D., & Robinson, T. (1983). Relative deprivation and procedural justifications. *Journal of Personality and Social Psychology, 45,* 268–273.

Guimond, S., & Dubé-Simard, L. (1983). Relative deprivation theory and the Quebec nationalist movement: The cognition–emotion distinction and the personal–group deprivation issue. *Journal of Personality and Social Psychology, 44,* 526–535.

Gurr, T. R. (1970). *Why men rebel.* Princeton, NJ: Princeton University Press.

Harrison, G. (1974). A bias in the social psychology of prejudice. In N. Armistead (Ed.), *Reconstructing social psychology* (pp. 189–203). Harmondsworth, England: Penguin.

Hogg, M. A., & Abrams, D. (1988). *Social identifications: A social psychology of intergroup relations and group processes.* New York: Routledge.

Inglis, A. (1990). Social disadvantage and protest action: An intergroup perspective. Unpublished master's thesis, York University, Toronto, Ontario.

Jones, J. M. (1986). Racism: A cultural analysis of the problem. In J. F. Dovidio & S. L. Gaertner (Eds.), *Prejudice, discrimination, and racism* (pp. 279–314). Toronto: Academic Press.

Jones, J. M. (1991). The politics of personality: Being Black in America. In R. L. Jones (Ed.), *Black psychology* (3rd ed., pp. 305–318). Berkeley, CA: Cobb & Henry.

Kağitçibaşi, C. (1987). Individual and group loyalties: Are they compatible? In C. Kağitçibaşi (Ed.), *Growth and progress in cross-cultural psychology* (pp. 94–103). Lisse: Swets & Zeitlinger.

Kardiner, A., & Oversey, L. (1951). *The mark of oppression.* New York: Norton.

King, M. L., Jr. (1968). The role of the behavioral scientist in the Civil Rights Movement. *American Psychologist, 23,* 180–186.

Lalonde, R. N., & Silverman, R. A. (1992). *Behavioural preferences in response to social injustice: The effects of group permeability and social identity salience.* Unpublished manuscript, York University, Toronto, Ontario.

Lewin, K. (1946). Action research and minority problems. *Journal of Social Issues, 2,* 34–46.

Lomax, L. E. (1963). *The Negro revolt.* New York: Harper & Row.

Louw-Potgieter, J. (1989). Covert racism: An application of Essed's analysis in a South African context. *Journal of Language and Social Psychology, 8,* 307–319.

Lykes, M. B. (1983). Discrimination and coping in the lives of black women: Analyses of oral history data. *Journal of Social Issues, 39*(3), 79–100.

Mark, M. M. (1985). Expectations, procedural justice, and alternative reactions to being deprived of a desired outcome. *Journal of Experimental Social Psychology, 21,* 114–137.

Mark, M. M., & Folger, R. (1984). Responses to relative deprivation: A conceptual framework. In P. Shaver (Ed.), *Review of personality ad social psychology* (Vol. 5, pp. 192–218). Beverly Hills, CA: Sage.

Martin, J., Brickman, P., & Murray, A. (1984). Moral outrage and pragmatism: Explanations for collective action. *Journal of Experimental Social Psychology, 20,* 484–496.

Martin, J., & Murray, A. (1984). Catalysts for collective violence: The importance of a psychological approach. In R. Folger (Ed.), *The sense of injustice: Social psychological perspectives* (pp. 95–139). New York: Plenum.

McCarthy, J. D., & Zald, M. N. (1979). Resource mobilization and social movements: A partial theory. *American Journal of Sociology, 82,* 1212–1241.

Mikula, G. (1986). The experience of injustice: Toward a better understanding of its phenomenology. In H. W. Bierhoff, R. L. Cohen, & J. Greenberg (Eds.), *Justice in social relations* (pp. 103–123). New York: Plenum.

Mikula, G., & Schlamberger, K. (1985). What people think about an unjust event: Toward a better understanding of the phenomenology of experiences of injustice. *European Journal of Social Psychology, 15,* 37–49.

Pettigrew, T. F. (1964). *A profile of the American Negro.* Princeton, NJ: D. Van Nostrand.

Pettigrew, T. F. (1986). The intergroup contact hypothesis reconsidered. In M. Hewstone & R. Brown (Eds.), *Contact and conflict in intergroup encounters* (pp. 169–195). Oxford: Blackwell.

Potter, J., & Wetherell, M. (1987). *Discourse and social psychology: Beyond attitudes and behaviour.* London: Sage.

Runciman, W. (1966). *Relative deprivation and social justice.* Berkeley: University of California Press.

Sachdev, I., & Bourhis, R. Y. (1991). Power and status differentials in minority and majority group relations. *European Journal of Social Psychology, 21,* 1–24.

Shattuck, P. S., & Norgren, J. (1979). Political use of the legal process by Black and American Indian minorities. *Howard Law Journal, 22,* 1–26.

Simpson, G. E., & Yinger, J. M. (1985). *Racial and cultural minorities: An analysis of prejudice and discrimination* (5th ed.). New York: Plenum.

Smith, P., & Gaskell, G. (1990). The social dimension in relative deprivation theory. In C. Fraser & G. Gaskell (Eds.), *The social psychological study of widespread beliefs* (pp. 179–191). New York: Oxford University Press.

Tajfel, H. (1978). Interindividual behaviour and intergroup behaviour. In H. Tajfel (Ed.), *Differentiation between social groups: Studies in the social psychology of intergroup relations* (pp. 27–60). New York: Academic Press.

Tajfel, H., & Turner, J. C. (1979). An integrative theory of intergroup conflict. In W. G. Austin & S. Worchel (Eds.), *The social psychology of intergroup relations* (pp. 33–47). Monterey, CA: Brooks/Cole.

Taylor, D. M., & McKirnan, D. J. (1984). A five-stage model of intergroup relations. *British Journal of Social Psychology, 23,* 291–300.

Taylor, D. M., & Moghaddam, F. M. (1987). *Theories of intergroup relations.* New York: Praeger.

Taylor, D. M., Moghaddam, F. M., Gamble, I., & Zellerer, E. (1987). Disadvantaged group responses to perceived inequality: From passive acceptance to collective action. *Journal of Social Psychology, 127,* 259–272.

Taylor, D. M., Wright, S. C., Moghaddam, F. M., & Lalonde, R. N. (1990). The personal–group discrimination discrepancy: Perceiving my group, but not myself, to be a target for discrimination. *Personality and Social Psychology Bulletin, 16*, 254–262.

Triandis, H. C., McCusker, C., & Hui, C. H. (1990). Multimethod probes of individualism and collectivism. *Journal of Personality and Social Psychology, 59*, 1006–1020.

Wright, S. C., Taylor, D. M., & Moghaddam, F. M. (1990). Responding to membership in a disadvantaged group: From acceptance to collective protest. *Journal of Personality and Social Psychology, 58*, 994–1003.

APPENDIX: BEHAVIOR ITEMS FOR THE APARTMENT AND NEW-WORLD SCENARIOS

Apartment Scenario Behaviors

1. Go to the Human Rights Commission to find out what I can do about the discrimination.
2. Not do anything about it.
3. Consult with a lawyer for advice about what to do.
4. Consult with the various social agencies that deal with discrimination.
5. Work to organize others who were similarly discriminated against.
6. Get together with others in the same situation to contact a lawyer.
7. Get together with others in the same situation to contact a newspaper.
8. Try to coax the owner into reversing his or her decision.
9. Demand a written explanation from the owner concerning his or her decision.
A. Demand proof from the owner that his or her decision was not an act of discrimination.
B. Record all conversations with the owner.
C. Threaten the owner with legal action.
D. Set up an appointment with the owner to discuss his or her decision.
E. Gather as much information as possible about the discriminator.
F. Call a tenant association or agency for help.
G. Take the owner to court.
H. Inform the media about the situation.
I. Confront the owner and demand to know why I was refused the apartment.
J. Take legal action against the owner.
K. Inform others by word of mouth about the discrimination.
L. Forget about the apartment and search for another one elsewhere.
M. Contact my city counselor.
N. Ask a lawyer to write a letter to the owner asking about his or her decision.
O. Find out whom I would have to contact about this type of situation.
P. File a formal complaint against the owner with a political agency such as the Human Rights Commission.

Q. Gather evidence proving that I was a victim of discrimination.
R. Express to my friends and family my anger about the situation.
S. Ask my friends and family for their ideas about possible actions I could take.
T. Contact an ombudsman within a government agency.
U. Look into the possible actions I could take in response to the discrimination.

New-World Scenario Behaviors

1. Not do anything.
2. Try to convince those in power that this situation of discrimination is unfair.
3. Become involved in acts of civil disobedience.
4. Become an activist.
5. Avoid using violent actions.
6. Get organized with others who are in the same situation.
7. Seek out others who are in the same situation as myself.
8. Discuss with others in my situation the implications of this discrimination for our future.
9. Oppose those who are ruling by working with others at the grass-roots level.
A. Secretly work with others in an underground operation opposing the ruling group.
B. Work with others in acts of sabotage against the current government.
C. Get ideas together with others who are victims of this discrimination.
D. Try to make people aware of the discrimination that is occurring.
E. Write letters to people describing my experiences of discrimination.
F. Write letters to the press describing my experiences of discrimination.
G. Withdraw labor (i.e., stop working) as a form of protest.
H. Explore ways in which I or others can get out of the group that is being discriminated against.
I. Quietly make people conscious of what is occurring.
J. Move elsewhere to escape discrimination.
K. Demonstrate with others in public places
L. Write letters of protest to members of government.
M. Look for a leader who could unite people to oppose the discrimination.
N. Find a hidden place to hold meetings to discuss the situation.
O. Try to sabotage the ruling group's communication network.
P. Exercise with others what I see to be my rights even if my actions are in violation of the existing rules or laws.
Q. Tell others not to ignore the discrimination.
R. Organize people into some type of protest group.

S. Be involved in violent group uprisings.
T. Leave or dissociate myself, if possible, from the group that is being discriminated against.
U. Be involved in rallies with others in my situation.
V. Sign or circulate petitions requesting social change.
W. Find out what type of actions were already being taken in my community.
X. Plant or throw bombs.
Y. Try to take political action wherever possible.
Z. Lobby against the governing group.
    a. Secretly fight back while I pretend to accept the situation.
    b. Engage in subversive actions in order to overthrow the ruling group.
    c. Use the media to inform others about what is happening.

12 Reactions to Stigma: The Moderating Role of Justifications

Jennifer Crocker
Brenda Major
State University of New York at Buffalo

Social stigma is a pervasive aspect of social existence. Goffman (1963) suggested that there are three major types of stigmatizing conditions: (a) *tribal stigmas,* such as membership in disadvantaged or despised racial, ethnic, or religious groups, (b) *abominations of the body,* including physical handicaps and disfiguring conditions, and (c) *blemishes of individual character,* such as substance abuse, juvenile delinquency, and homosexuality. As Goffman's analysis suggests, a wide variety of conditions are considered stigmatizing; people with those stigmas are the targets of negative stereotypes, are generally devalued in the larger society, and receive disproportionately negative interpersonal and economic outcomes (Crocker & Major, 1989). In Goffman's (1963) terms, the stigmatized have a *spoiled identity* in the eyes of the nonstigmatized.

Empirical research on attitudes and behavior toward members of a wide variety of stigmatized groups supports the idea that the stigmatized are both regarded unfavorably by others and receive more negative outcomes in life than the nonstigmatized (see Crocker & Major, 1989, for a discussion). For example, a number of studies show that people hold generally negative stereotypes about African-Americans (Brigham, 1974; Hartsough & Fontana, 1970; Karlins, Coffman, & Walters, 1969; Samuels, 1973). Although survey studies indicate that the level of expressed racism has declined in the United States over the past 30 years (Crosby, Bromley, & Saxe, 1980; Dovidio & Gaertner, 1986), the work of Gaertner and Dovidio (1986), Devine (1989), and others suggests that negative attitudes about Blacks may have become more subtle or disguised but are still pervasive, even among people who consider themselves nonprejudiced. Furthermore, it is well documented that African-Americans are relatively disadvantaged, both in terms of economic opportunities and outcomes and in terms of interpersonal outcomes (Braddock & McPartland, 1987; Dovidio & Gaertner, 1986; Gaertner & Dovidio, 1986; Pettigrew & Martin, 1987; U.S. Government, 1978).

Individuals with physical stigmas, or what Goffman called abominations of the body, are also the targets of negative stereotypes (Crocker & Major, 1989). For example, the obese are frequently stereotyped as esthetically displeasing, morally and emotionally impaired, and socially handicapped (Allon, 1982; Crandall & Biernat, 1990). The obese also experience negative economic and interpersonal outcomes; obese children are not chosen by others as friends (Richardson, Hastorf, Goodman, & Dornbusch, 1961), employers are unwilling to hire obese individuals (Larkin & Pines, 1979), and members of the health professions rate the obese as the least likable of a variety of handicapped groups (Goodman, Richardson, Dornbusch, & Hastorf, 1963).

What are the consequences of these negative attitudes and negative life outcomes in life for the affect and self-esteem of stigmatized individuals? Interestingly, empirical research indicates that members of many stigmatized groups have self-esteem that is equal to and in some cases higher than that of the nonstigmatized. For example, a host of studies have concluded that Blacks have self-esteem that is equal to or higher than that of Whites (for reviews of the literature, see Hoelter, 1983; Porter & Washington, 1979; Rosenberg, 1979; Wylie, 1979). Research also fails to find consistently lower self-esteem in a number of other stigmatized groups, including the facially disfigured (Clifford & Clifford, 1986), the physically handicapped (Burden & Parish, 1983), and the developmentally disabled (Gibbons, 1985; for a review, see Crocker & Major, 1989).

Studies of other groups, however, indicate that at least some stigmatized individuals are vulnerable to low self-esteem. Several researchers, for example, have found that the obese suffer from low self-esteem (Maddox, Back, & Leiderman, 1968; Wadden, Foster, Brownell, & Finley, 1984). Self-esteem is also lowered by such stigmatizing events as going on welfare (Briar, 1966), developing a malignancy (Abrams & Finesinger, 1953), and being raped (Burgess & Holmstrom, 1979).

How can one account for these divergent findings on the consequences of social stigma for self-esteem? We suggest that the stigmatized often exist in a state of ambiguity with regard to the causes of the negative feedback, rejection, and negative outcomes they experience. On the one hand, negative outcomes might be caused by one's (lack of) personal deservingness. Alternatively, they might be caused by the stigma (Crocker & Major, 1989; Crocker, Voelkl, Testa, & Major, 1991; Major & Crocker, 1993). In this chapter, we argue that attributing negative outcomes to one's stigma sometimes, but not always, protects self-esteem and affect. We suggest that the stigmatized sometimes believe that negative outcomes they receive based on their stigma are unjust, and sometimes believe that those negative outcomes are justified by the stigma. The justifiability of receiving negative outcomes because one has a stigmatizing condition plays a crucial moderating role in cognitive, affective, and motivational reactions to stigma.

THE ATTRIBUTIONAL AMBIGUITY OF STIGMA

A stigma assumes a central role in the way a stigmatized individual construes his or her social world. The stigmatized often take it for granted that their stigma affects all behaviors of those who interact with them. In an ingenious experiment, Kleck and Strenta (1980) demonstrated that this perception may persist even when the stigma has no effect on the treatment the stigmatized receive. In their experiment, makeup was applied to subjects' faces to create a facially disfiguring scar. After subjects had examined the scar in a mirror, the experimenter applied moisturizer, which unbeknownst to the subjects, removed the scar. Subjects then interacted with another individual, who was unaware of these previous events. Subjects who (falsely) believed that they possessed a physically deviant characteristic thought this characteristic affected how they were treated by their interaction partner, even though the partners were unaware of the stigma. Apparently, people with stigmatizing conditions believe that even ordinary social interactions are tainted by their stigmas.

A stigma especially influences the way that the stigmatized construe negative outcomes such as being rejected for a job, receiving negative feedback from a teacher or employer, or being rejected in social relationships. These negative outcomes are particularly ambiguous for the stigmatized, because any negative outcome might be due to one's lack of personal deservingness or to the other person's reaction to the stigma. People who are stigmatized are frequently aware that others hold negative stereotypes about them, which could influence the outcomes they receive. African-Americans past the age of 14, for example, are generally aware that many people are prejudiced against them (Rosenberg, 1979); most women believe that women are discriminated against in employment (Crosby, 1982); mentally retarded persons are aware of the negative connotations of their label (Gibbons, 1981), as are the blind (Scott, 1969), the obese (Jarvie, Lahey, Graziano, & Framer, 1983), and members of many other stigmatized groups. Thus, the stigmatized recognize that negative outcomes they experience might be due to their stigma. In light of evidence that the stigmatized do, indeed, receive more negative evaluations and reactions from the nonstigmatized, attributing negative outcomes to the stigma or to prejudice and discrimination is not only plausible, it is often accurate.

THE SELF-PROTECTIVE CONSEQUENCES
OF ATTRIBUTIONAL AMBIGUITY

According to cognitive theories of emotion, attributing negative outcomes to prejudice and discrimination instead of to one's personal inadequacies protects self-esteem from the potential negative implications of the feedback. Both the reformulated helplessness theory of depression (Abramson, Seligman, & Teasdale, 1978) and Weiner's (1985, 1986) attributional theory of emotion posit that attributing negative events to causes external to the self protects self-esteem, whereas attributing negative outcomes to causes internal to the self, such as one's lack of deservingness, leads to low self-esteem. A study by McFarland and Ross (1982) shows that failure that is attributed to external causes leads to no more negative affect than does success. Because prejudice and discrimination are external factors, attributing one's failure to them protects self-esteem for the stigmatized.

Empirical research is generally consistent with this view. In one study (Dion, 1975; see also Dion, 1986; Dion & Earn, 1975), females received negative feedback from a male evaluator. Following receipt of this feedback, those women who believed that they had been discriminated against were higher in self-esteem than were those who did not believe that they had been discriminated against. The results of this study are consistent with the notion that attributing negative outcomes to prejudice against one's group protects self-esteem. They are also consistent, however, with the hypothesis that people who are initially high in self-esteem are more likely to attribute negative outcomes to prejudice against their group. More direct evidence is provided in two recent studies by Crocker, Voelkl, Testa, and Major (1991).

In our first study, female students were asked to write an essay that ostensibly was subsequently evaluated by a male peer. Prior to writing the essay, the subjects exchanged opinion questionnaires with the evaluator. For some students, the evaluator's answers to several items in the questionnaire indicated that he had negative attitudes toward women, whereas for other students, he indicated positive attitudes. For example, in the prejudiced condition, the evaluator indicated agreement with statements such as "women should avoid fields like engineering because they lack mathematical ability." The nonprejudiced evaluator disagreed with these statements.

Women later heard the evaluator give either a positive or a negative evaluation of their essay over an audio system. Later, they indicated how much they thought the feedback they had received was due to the evaluator's attitudes toward women, and completed the Rosenberg (1965) self-esteem scale and a short form the the Multiple Affect Adjective Checklist (Zuckerman & Lubin, 1965). Consistent with our predictions, a negative essay evaluation was more likely to be attributed to the evaluator's attitudes toward women if he had expressed negative attitudes toward women ($M = 4.15$ on a 7-point scale) than if he had expressed positive attitudes toward women ($M = 2.33, p < .05$). Furthermore, consistent with the discounting hypothesis, women who received negative feedback experienced less depressed affect if the evaluator had unfavorable attitudes toward women ($M = 8.54$ on a 21-point scale) than if he had favorable attitudes ($M = 11.53, p < .05$). Self-esteem also dropped when negative feedback was received from a nonprejudiced evaluator but not when received from a prejudiced evaluator, although these means did not differ significantly.

Our second study provides a conceptual replication and extension of this study. Black and White students were led to believe they were participating in a study on friendship development with a White same-sex evaluator, who either could see them (blinds on the one-way mirror were up) or could not see them (the blinds were down). After exchanging self-description forms with their partner, subjects received either a very favorable or a very unfavorable response to their essay from the other subject. We reasoned that when they received negative feedback and could be seen by the evaluator, the Black students would attribute the feedback to prejudice, and their self-esteem would not suffer, compared to when they could not be seen by the evaluator and hence could not attribute the negative feedback to prejudice.

The results generally support our hypothesis. As the means in Table 12.1 show, among Black students, the feedback was more likely to be attributed to prejudice when it was negative rather than positive and when the blinds were up (and the evaluator could see them) than when the blinds were down. (Both effects were significant for Black students but not for Whites.) Furthermore, Black students were more likely to attribute the feedback (both positive and negative) to their personality when they could not be seen then when they could be seen,

TABLE 12.1
Attributions to Prejudice and Changes in Self-Esteem as a Function of Race of Subject, Valence of Feedback, and Visibility

	Race			
	Black		White	
	Visibility			
Feedback	Seen	Unseen	Seen	Unseen
Positive				
Attributions	5.62	3.40	4.70	4.40
Self-esteem	-0.50	0.40	0.38	0.04
Negative				
Attributions	9.58	7.70	5.63	4.81
Self-esteem	0.06	-0.47	0.07	-0.03

Note. Means for the attributions fall on a scale ranging from 3 (not at all due to prejudice) to 15 (very much due to prejudice). Means for self-esteem were standardized at pretest and posttest, and reported means represent differences in these standardized means.

whereas this effect was nonsignificant and in the opposite direction for White students. Thus, these data suggest that Black students tend to discount interpersonal feedback from White evaluators when they know that the evaluator is aware of their race and are especially likely to do so if the feedback is negative. Furthermore, analysis of changes in self-esteem indicates that for Black students who received negative feedback, self-esteem decreased if they could not be seen by the evaluator, but did not decrease when they could be seen by the evaluator.

Together, these studies indicate that the stigmatized believe that their stigma plays an important role in their social interactions and influences their outcomes, at least under certain circumstances. Furthermore, they show that a stigma can be self-protective, because it provides an explanation for negative outcomes, feedback, and reactions from others. However, we believe that not all stigmas provide this self-protective function.

WHEN ATTRIBUTIONS TO STIGMA ARE NOT SELF-PROTECTIVE

Evidence that attributing negative outcomes to one's stigma is not always self-protective comes from a study of overweight women's reactions to rejection from an attractive, unattached male (Crocker, Cornwell, & Major, 1993). Of all of the conditions for which a person may be stigmatized in our culture, including racial or ethnic group membership, religious affiliation, physical handicaps, and sexual preference, the stigma of being overweight may be the most debilitating (Allon, 1982). In Goffman's (1963) terms, being overweight carries with it the burdens associated with two types of stigmas: It is both an abomination of the body, that elicits immediate negative affective responses from others on the basis of its aesthetically displeasing qualities (Jones et al., 1984) and a character stigma that carries with it the shame and guilt of self-blame for a moral failure (Allon, 1982; Lyman, 1978).

The stigma of overweight is especially problematic for females, from adolescence onward (Allon, 1982). Appearance in general and weight in particular are emphasized more for women than for men in our culture (Millman, 1980; Polivy, Garner, & Garfinkel, 1986; Polivy, Herman, & Pliner, 1990). The negative consequences of being overweight are not confined to those who are medically classified as obese (i.e., at least 20% overweight). According to Allon (1982), dieters who are as little as 10 to 15 pounds over their ideal weight goal feel, and in fact are, just as stigmatized by certain reference groups as those who are 50 pounds or more overweight. Adolescent girls, for example, are stigmatized by their peers for being only slightly overweight. Many adult women and as many as 60% of adolescent women consider themselves to be overweight (Fallon & Rozin, 1985). Thus, a relatively large proportion of women feel stigmatized by virtue of their weight.

In our experiment, overweight and normal weight women were recruited for a study of dating relationships. Specifically, they were told that the study concerned how people start relationships, problems people may have in relationships, and which things people look for in choosing a dating partner. The women were told that another student, who was male, would also participate in the study and was already seated in an adjacent room. The women were then brought into the lab, and their height and weight were measured. The women then exchanged background information forms with the other subject. His form indicated that he was 5' 11" tall, weighed 170 pounds, was a junior in college, a premed major, and was not currently involved in a romantic relationship with anyone. This information was intended to make him attractive to our female subjects. Subjects were not informed about the man's attitudes toward weight. The women completed their form with the same types of information, including their height and weight, and their form was then shown to the other subject.

Subjects then completed a self-description questionnaire on which they answered questions about their personal likes, dislikes, and so forth, which was then ostensibly shown to the male subject. He responded by indicating on a sociometric distance scale how interested he was in dating her. His response indicated either very strong interest in establishing a dating relationship or very little interest in doing so. The women were shown his response and were then asked to complete a number of measures, including measures of their causal attributions for his reaction to them and measures of their current mood. We predicted, based on our previous studies, that the overweight women would attribute rejection to their weight and to his negative attitudes toward their weight and that this would protect their mood and self-esteem. Overweight women therefore should experience less negative mood than normal weight women who received the same rejection but who could not attribute that rejection to a stigmatizing condition.

Analysis of attributions to weight reveals a significant interaction between the weight status of the subjects (i.e., whether they were normal weight or overweight) and the type of feedback they received from the other subject (positive or negative). Overweight and normal weight women did not differ in the extent to which they thought that a positive reaction was due to their weight (Ms = 2.27 and 2.33, respectively), but overweight women were significantly more likely to attribute rejection to their weight (M = 3.82) than were normal weight women (M = 2.60, p < .003).

Although overweight women attributed the rejection to their weight, they did not blame the other student for his reaction any more than did normal weight women. Analysis of ratings of the extent to which the reaction they received was due to the other student's concern with physical appearance and ratings of the extent to which subjects thought the reaction was due to the other student's personality reveals neither a main effect of weight status nor an interaction between feedback and weight status. Thus, overweight women attributed the negative reaction to their weight but did not blame the other person for his reaction. Overweight women also did not blame the rejection on their internal attributes more than normal weight women. Analysis of the extent to which subjects thought the feedback was due to their personality reveals no main effect of weight status nor an interaction between weight status and feedback.

Analysis of covariance on the mood measures indicates that, controlling for initial self-esteem, attributing rejection to one's weight without blaming the other student for his reaction was not self-protective for overweight women. Analysis of the depression subscale reveals an interaction between subjects' weight status and the type of feedback they received on their reports of depressed mood. Overweight women who received negative feedback were more depressed ($M = 17.69$) than normal weight women who received the same feedback ($M = 13.23$, $p < .01$) or women who received positive feedback, whether overweight ($M = 10.08$) or not ($M = 12.04$). Thus, attributing negative feedback to the stigma did not buffer overweight women's mood from the negative implications of the feedback they received, and if anything, made matters worse.

To examine whether attributing negative outcomes to one's weight explains the negative mood that overweight women reported, we computed correlations between attributions to weight and depression within positive and negative feedback conditions. Among subjects who received negative feedback, the more subjects attributed the feedback to their weight, the more depressed they were ($r = .49, p < .05$). Among subjects who received positive feedback, attributing the feedback to weight was uncorrelated with depression ($r = .09$, ns). The attribution that best predicts positive affect (or the absence of depressed affect) for subjects who received negative feedback was attributions to the other student's personality ($r = -.46$, $p < .05$). The more subjects attributed the negative feedback to the other's personality, the less depressed they were. Among subjects who received positive feedback, the correlation between attributions to the other's personality and depression was nonsignificant ($r = .08$, ns). The best predictor of positive mood (i.e., the absence of depressed affect) for these subjects was attributions to one's own personality ($r = -.34, p < .05$). In other words, the more subjects believed that the positive feedback was due to their own personality, the less depressed they were. Attributions to the subject's personality were unrelated to mood for subjects who received negative feedback ($r < .13$, ns).

How can one account for the different affective reactions that African-Americans, women, and overweight women show to rejection from others? A critical difference between the overweight women's responses and those of Blacks or women that we described earlier is that although the overweight women attributed their negative outcomes to their stigma, they did not blame the other person for his negative reaction to them, that is, they did not feel that prejudice and discrimination were at issue. In fact, we suggest that these women felt that they deserved the reaction they received. That is, they believed the male student's negative reaction to them was justified by their weight. This sense that rejection was deserved or justified made them more rather than less emotionally vulnerable to the rejection.

Indeed, prior to the women's movement in the 1960s, it was more common for women to believe that they deserved to be denied jobs or equal pay on the basis of their gender. Similarly, before the Civil Rights and Black Power Movements of the 1950s and 1960s, some African-Americans may also have felt that discrimination against them was justifiable. This is an issue we return to in the last section of the chapter.

THE JUSTIFIABILITY OF NEGATIVE OUTCOMES BASED ON STIGMA

Why are negative outcomes based on a stigmatizing condition sometimes considered justifiable? We identify three reasons:

1. Theories of justice such as social exchange and equity theory suggest that outcome distributions are perceived to be fair if outcomes are proportional to inputs or contributions (Adams, 1965; Walster, Walster, & Berscheid, 1978). Therefore, these theories suggest that if a stigma is judged to be a relevant input that somehow detracts from one's contributions or interferes with one's ability to do a job or fulfill a role, then it may appropriately influence one's outcomes. Negative outcomes or rejection based on the stigma are consequently judged to be fair, just, reasonable, and even predictable if the stigma is considered a negative input.

2. Negative outcomes based on a stigma are considered justifiable if the stigma is perceived as controllable (Weiner, Perry, & Magnusson, 1988). Stigmas that are judged to be potentially controllable are ones that the stigmatized person is believed, at some level, to have chosen. For example, stigmatizing conditions such as obesity, being a rape victim, being on welfare, and in some cases, being a cancer victim are considered to be under the control of the stigmatized person, whereas race and gender are seen as uncontrollable. When stigmatized individuals are judged to have chosen their stigma, it is considered fair and justifiable that they live with the negative repercussions of the stigma.

3. Negative outcomes based on a stigma are perceived as justifiable when believing they are unjustified threatens important and central beliefs, such as the belief in personal control or the belief in a just world. That is, people are sometimes motivated to believe that the stigmatized deserve negative outcomes because believing otherwise is threatening or uncomfortable. Of course, the perception of justifiability depends on whether the stigmatized themselves or disinterested observers are making the judgment. We first con-

sider evidence on this point from the perspective of observers and then consider evidence regarding the perceptions of the stigmatized themselves.

Observers' Judgments of the Justifiability of Negative Outcomes Based on Stigma

Is there evidence that observers feel that negative outcomes based on a stigma are sometimes justified? In a study conducted in our laboratory, a group of undergraduate subjects read a description of a job applicant who was either wheelchair bound or was facially disfigured due to a car accident (Crocker & Major, in prep.). Depending on which description was read, the applicant had applied for a job either as a receptionist, as a mover and stacker of large boxes, or as a data processor. In all cases, the applicant was rejected for the job because of her stigma. Subjects were asked to indicate how fair, legitimate, and justifiable they thought the rejection was. We reasoned that the facial scars might be seen as interfering with doing the receptionist job, which involves greeting the public, but should not interfere with doing either the data-processing job or the moving job. Being wheelchair bound, on the other hand, might be seen as interfering with doing the moving job but should not interfere with doing the data-processing job or the receptionist job. According to equity theory, rejecting a person on the basis of a stigma should be considered more legitimate, fair, and justifiable when the stigma actually interferes with doing the job, because the stigma is considered a relevant (negative) input.

Analysis of judgments of the extent to which the stigma interfered with job performance reveals the predicted interaction between the type of stigma and type of job [$F(2, 34) = 21.57, p < .0001$]. As the means in Table 12.2 indicate, subjects thought that facial scarring would interfere more with doing the receptionist job than with moving boxes or data processing. They thought that being confined to a wheelchair, on the other hand, would interfere more with lifting and moving boxes than with doing the receptionist job or the data processing job.

Analysis of the judgments of the fairness, legitimacy, and justifiability of not hiring the target because of her stigma also reveals significant interactions between the type of job and the type of stigma for all three measures (all Fs > 14.0, all ps < .0001). Subjects considered not hiring the target with facial scars to be more fair, legitimate, and justifiable when she applied for the receptionist job than when she applied for the job moving boxes or the data-processing job. However, they considered not hiring the target who was wheelchair bound to be more fair, legitimate, and justifiable to the target when she applied for a job moving boxes then when she applied for a job as a receptionist or as a data processor.

In a similar study, we explored whether perceivers ever think that it is justifiable for a woman to be denied a job on the basis of her sex (Major & Crocker, in prep.). In this study, subjects again read about a woman who applied for one of

TABLE 12.2
Ratings of the Extent to Which a Stigma Interferes With Job Performance and the Fairness,
Justifiability, and Legitimacy of Not Hiring a Person With the Stigma for the Job, as a Function of
Type of Job and Type of Stigma

	Job		
Stigma	Receptionist	Moving Boxes	Data Processing
Facial scarring			
Interference	2.37a	1.00b	1.00b
Fair	2.62a	1.11b	1.27b
Justifiable	3.75a	1.00b	1.72b
Letitimate	4.00a	1.44b	1.91b
Wheelchair bound			
Interference	2.00b	5.75a	2/57b
Fair	1.25b	4.12a	2/28b
Justifiable	1.75b	4.50a	2/28b
Legitimate	2.00b	4.62a	2/71b

Note. All ratings are on 7-point scales. Within rows, means not sharing a common subscript differ at $p <$ .50.

three jobs. In this case, the jobs were either a data processor, a manager of a team of 15 salespeople who were all men, or a job moving and stacking boxes. In all cases, the woman was denied the job because of her sex. As in the previous study, subjects rated on 7-point scales how much the applicant's sex would interfere with her ability to do the job, and how fair, justifiable, and legitimate it was that she was not hired. Analysis of the ratings of whether sex would interfere with doing the job reveals a main effect of the type of job ($p < .01$). Subjects of both sexes thought being female interfered more with doing the moving job ($M = 3.11$) than performing either the data processor ($M = 1.57$) or salesmanager ($M = 1.35$) job. Similarly, both male and female subjects thought that it was more justifiable for the woman to be denied the moving job on the basis of her sex ($M = 2.90$) than to be denied either the data processor job ($M = 1.39$) or the salesmanager job ($M = 1.73$) on the basis of sex ($p < .01$). Thus, these studies support the hypothesis that observers feel that negative outcomes for the stigmatized are justified if the stigma constitutes a negative input, because it interferes with performing a job or fulfilling a role.

A series of studies by Rodin and her colleagues (Rodin, Price, Sanchez, & McElligot, 1989) suggests that observers also believe that negative outcomes based on a stigma are justifiable if the stigma is controllable. In these studies, subjects read scenarios about a stigmatized person who was the target of negative reactions from others. For example, in one study the target was derogated, in another he or she was excluded from a social event, and in other studies the target was not hired for a job on the basis of a stigmatizing condition. The controllability of the stigmatizing condition was varied, either by manipulating the perceived controllability of a single stigma (e.g., the target was overweight due to overeating or overweight due to a hormonal imbalance) or by varying the type of stigma, so that it was controllable (e.g., the target used a lot of slang in his speech) or uncontrollable (e.g., the target was a stutterer). Subjects read the scenarios and indicated whether the rejection of the target was reasonable or prejudiced. The results of all five studies indicated that rejection of a target with a controllable stigma was judged as more reasonable and less prejudiced than the rejection of a target with an uncontrollable stigma. Apparently, when individuals can potentially control their stigma, it is perceived as legitimate or justifiable to discriminate against them.

Weiner and his colleagues (Weiner, Perry, & Magnusson, 1988) analyzed the perceived controllability of a number of stigmas. They found that physical stigmas, such as blindness, cancer, heart disease, and paraplegia, are perceived as much less controllable than are behavioral and mental stigmas, such as obesity, AIDS, and drug abuse. Consistent with the notion that negative reactions to stigma are perceived as more justifiable if the stigma is controllable, individuals with controllable stigmas are less likely to be liked and elicit more anger, less pity, and less assistance than individuals with controllable stigmas.

Although not specifically directed at stigmatizing conditions, a third line of research also suggests that observers sometimes believe that people who are stigmatized deserve their fate. Specifically, research on the need to believe in a just world indicates that observers often derogate innocent victims in an effort to maintain their belief that the world is just and a place where people get the outcomes that they deserve (Lerner, 1980; Lerner & Miller, 1978). For example, observers often hold rape victims responsible for their rape, by blaming either their character or their behavior (Janoff-Bulman, 1979). Similarly, the poor are often held responsible for their condition by people who believe that the poor are lazy, unmotivated, and do not want to work (for a review, see Morris & Williamson, 1982). According to the just world theory, this process of blaming the victim protects observers from the threatening implication that such victimizing events could happen to them as well.

Stigmatized Persons' Judgments of the Justifiability of Negative Outcomes Based on Stigma

These studies indicate that perceivers who are not themselves the targets of rejection or discrimination consider it justified to reject stigmatized individuals for some stigmas and under some circumstances. But do the stigmatized themselves ever consider rejection or negative outcomes based on their stigma to be fair? Our study, described earlier, of the justifiability of denying a woman a job based on her gender partially addresses this issue. Recall that in that study, subjects read a description of a woman who was rejected for a job as a sales-manager, box mover, or data processor. In addition to the main effects observed for type of job, several main effects were also observed for gender of subject.

Female subjects thought that being female interfered less with doing each of the jobs than did male subjects. Furthermore, female subjects also believed that it was less justifiable ($p < .06$) and less legitimate ($p < .03$) to deny the applicant any of the jobs on the basis of her gender than male subjects did. In addition, females felt sorrier for the applicant ($M = 5.85$) than males did ($M = 4.40, p < .02$). These findings suggest that the stigmatized are less likely than the nonstigmatized to regard negative outcomes based on stigma as justifiable. It is important to note, however, that despite these gender differences, all subjects thought that being female interfered with doing the moving job more than the other two jobs and thought it was more justifiable to not hire a woman for that job because of her gender. Thus, it appears that under some circumstances the stigmatized themselves believe that discrimination based on the stigma is justifiable.

Unfortunately, the role-playing nature of this study leaves open the question of whether stigmatized individuals who actually receive negative outcomes sometimes feel that those outcomes are justified. A more definitive answer to this question is provided by a follow-up of our study of overweight women (Crocker & Major, in prep.). Similar to the previous study, overweight and normal weight women were rejected by an attractive male. However, in this study, the women were either rejected as a potential dating partner or were rejected as a potential work partner. Half of the women inadvertently learned that they had been rejected because of their weight, and the others were given no reason why they were rejected. We then measured attributions for the rejection and the degree to which subjects felt the rejection was justified. We reasoned that overweight women were more likely to attribute the rejection to their weight than normal weight women. Furthermore, we reasoned that because of the emphasis placed on physical attractiveness as a criterion for romantic attraction in this culture, rejection as a dating partner would be perceived as more justified than rejection as a work partner, particularly among overweight women.

Analysis of the attributions reveals that the overweight women did, in fact, attribute their rejection to their weight ($M = 3.9$) to a greater extent than did normal weight women [$M = 3.0, F(1, 71) = 16.02, p < .0002$] Furthermore, the overweight women were just as likely to attribute the rejection to their weight, whether they had been rejected as a work partner ($M = 3.86$) or a dating partner ($M = 3.98$, ns). Analysis of the judgments of the justifibility of the rejection reveals a significant interaction between subjects' weight status (overweight vs. normal weight) and the domain for which they were rejected (work vs. dating partner). As predicted, regardless of whether or not they were explicitly told that they had been rejected because of their weight, overweight women thought that the rejection was less unjustified (or more justified) when they were rejected as a potential dating partner ($M = 2.60$) than when they were rejected as a potential work partner ($M = 3.85, p < .01$). Normal weight women, however, thought it was equally unjustified whether they were rejected as a potential dating partner ($M = 3.43$) or as a potential work partner ($M = 3.53$, ns). Apparently, even the stigmatized themselves consider rejection based on their stigma to be justifiable, depending on the domain in which the rejection occurs.

A number of factors cause those who are disadvantaged to believe they deserve their lower outcomes, including a tendency to compare themselves with similar others who are also disadvantaged (Zanna, Crosby, & Loewenstein, 1987) and a tendency for the disadvantaged to undervalue their own inputs (Major & Forcey, 1987). The belief that the procedures that produce their own (or their group's) lower outcomes are fair or just may also lead the disadvantaged to believe they deserve their lower outcomes (Major, 1987). According to research on procedural justice, people are more satisfied with their outcomes, even relatively poor outcomes, when they believe that the procedures by which those outcomes are determined are fair (Folger, Rosenfield, Grove, & Corkran, 1979; Lind & Tyler, 1988). This was demonstrated in a recent study by Bylsma, Major & Cozzarelli (1991) on the effects of ingroup and outgroup comparisons on perceived entitlement. Women in this study worked on a task for a set amount of time and were then asked to indicate what they felt they deserved to be paid for their work. Half of the women were exposed to comparison information indicating that women who had participated in the study previously had been paid substantially less than men who had participated. The other half of the women were exposed to comparison information indicating that women had been paid substantially more than men in the past. In addition, half of the women were told that pay was based on objective performance on the task. The other half of the women were told that pay was based on subjective factors as well as objective performance. In addition, in this condition a confederate spoke up while the experimenter was out of the room, commenting that she had heard that the experimenter was unfair. We reasoned that women would estimate their own deservingness based more on the outcomes received by other women than by other men, unless they believed the procedures that produced those outcomes were unfair.

Women in the objective condition thought that the experimenter was significantly less biased ($M = 1.94$) than did women in the biased condition ($M = 3.85$). In addition, women in the objective condition thought they deserved significantly less money if they had seen that other women were underpaid relative to men ($M = \$2.59$) than if they had seen that other women were overpaid relative to men ($M = \$3.70$, $p < .01$). In contrast, women in the biased condition did not feel they deserved less if other women had been underpaid ($M = \$3.56$) than if other women had been overpaid ($M = \$4.09$) relative to men (ns). Thus, when women believed that women had earned less than men in the past because of justifiable wage-allocation procedures, they too believed they deserved less. However, if they believed that women had earned less than men in the past because of unfair procedures, they did not feel they deserved lower pay. Thus, the stigmatized feel satisfied or content when their outcomes are objectively poor if they believe that the procedures used to determine those outcomes are fair. We suggest that procedures that are perceived to be influenced by prejudice and discrimination are perceived as unfair, and outcomes determined through those procedures are seen as unjustifiable.

Is there any evidence that people who are stigmatized ever prefer to believe that they deserve the negative outcomes they receive rather than believe that they are victims of prejudice and discrimination? Three lines of research suggest that believing one deserves one's fate is sometimes preferable to concluding that one is the victim of prejudice and discrimination:

1. People who are victimized by random and unpredictable events often blame themselves for the event. For example, rape victims often blame themselves for the rape (Janoff-Bulman, 1979), and victims of freak accidents sometimes blame themselves for what appears to observers to be completely random events (Bulman & Wortman, 1977). Even people who are obviously randomly assigned to their outcomes, such as those who were randomly assigned a number in the 1971 United States draft lottery (Rubin & Peplau, 1975) appear to restore justice by regarding themselves as deserving of their fate. This apparently unrealistic self-blame may stem from the need to believe that the world is just or that one has personal control over events (Bulman & Wortman, 1977; Wortman, 1976).

2. Research has shown that women who are underpaid relative to men often believe that they deserve their lower pay and do not believe that they personally are discriminated against (Major, 1987, 1989; Crosby, 1982, 1984; see Taylor, Wright, & Porter, chapter 10, this volume, for a review and discussion). The belief that one deserves the outcomes one receives may be motivated by the need to believe that the world is just (Lerner & Miller, 1978). Indeed, there is suggestive evidence that people who are treated unjustly but who cannot change their situation may come to believe that they are entitled to less or that they deserved their fate, rather than believe that they are victims of injustice (Crosby, 1982; Kanter, 1977; Wortman, 1976).

3. More direct evidence that victims of injustice are sometimes motivated to believe that their outcomes are fair is provided by two studies by Hafer & Olson (1989). In their studies, subjects performed a computer task to earn points toward a goal that had desirable consequences. All subjects received bogus feedback indicating that they had not earned any points. The results indicate that the more strongly subjects endorsed a belief in a just world, the more likely they were to perceive that their own failure to earn points was fair. This relationship was particularly strong when the subjects decided not to practice the task (in Experiment 1) and when the experimenter made an error (in Experiment 2). In these conditions, the fairness of subjects' outcomes was particularly ambiguous, permitting the motivation to believe in a just world to affect judgments.

These findings suggest that the stigmatized sometimes believe that they deserve their fate in an effort to maintain important beliefs. These include the belief in personal control, the belief that the world is just, and the belief that the system in which they work and the relationships in which they are involved are fair. Disrupting these beliefs has implications and costs that the stigmatized person simply doesn't want to confront. For example, acknowledging that one is discriminated against at work suggests that one should take some action, such as confronting one's employer with the inequity or finding another job. However, such actions are risky, especially if one is vulnerable to discrimination from other potential employers. Alternatively, one can stay in the job and take no action, but that may compromise not only one's pride but also one's faith in the justice of the system. Consequently, to avoid these costs individuals sometimes prefer to believe that they deserve negative outcomes based on their stigma.

THE CONSEQUENCES OF PERCEIVED JUSTIFIABILITY

We propose that the perceived justifiability of negative treatment based on a stigma has a number of consequences for affect, self-esteem, and motivation. These consequences are summarized in Table 12.3. In the following paragraphs, the basis for our predictions is explained.

Affect. According to recent cognitive theories of emotion (Shaver, Schwartz, Kirsen, & O'Connor, 1987; Smith & Ellsworth, 1985, 1987), emotions follow from one's appraisals or construals of events. According to these theories,

TABLE 12.3
Consequences of Negative Outcomes Based on a Stigmatizing Condition for Affect, Self-Esteem, and Motivation as a Function of the Perceived Justifiability of the Negative Outcomes and the Controllability of the Stigma

		Controlability of Stigma	
	Consequence	Controllabile	Uncontrollable
Justifiable negative outcomes	Affect	No anger, satisfaction	No anger, satisfaction
	Self-esteem	Lower self-esteem	???
	Motivation	Personal change	Acceptance/ learned helplessness
Unjustifiable negative outcomes	Affect	Anger dissatisfaction	Anger dissatisfaction
	Self-esteem	No loss of self-esteem	No loss of self-esteem
	Motivation	Personal change or protest	Protest (personal or collective)

anger results from appraisals that one's goals are unjustly blocked by another. Thus, we predict from these theories that stigmatized individuals who receive negative outcomes based on their stigma would feel anger if they perceived those outcomes to be unjustified but not if they believed they were justified. Similarly, theories of justice, such as equity and relative-deprivation theories, suggest that it is subjective evaluation of outcomes rather than their objective status that determines whether people feel satisfied or discontent. Outcomes that are perceived to be just or fair lead to relatively high levels of satisfaction, whereas outcomes that are perceived to be unjust lead to feelings of dissatisfaction and discontent (Adams, 1965; Crosby, 1976; Walster et al., 1978).

The fact that individuals who are disadvantaged often believe their lower outcomes are justifiable or deserved helps to explain the paradoxical contentment frequently observed among those who are objectively disadvantaged. For example, a number of authors have found that women who are objectively paid less than comparable men are no less satisfied with their pay than men (e.g., Crosby, 1982). Major (1987, 1989) suggested that this finding occurs in part because women believe the pay they receive is what they deserve.

Self-Esteem.   The perceived justifiability of negative outcomes based on one's stigma also has implications for self-esteem, a few of which we speculate on here. We have already noted that attributional theories of emotion (Weiner, 1985, 1986) predict that low self-esteem results from making internal attributions for negative events, and high self-esteem results from making external attributions for negative events. We suggest that when negative outcomes based on a stigma are perceived as justifiable, the stigmatized individual blames the outcome on the stigma. Attributions to a stigma are internal attributions, because they explain outcomes in terms of the characteristics of the person (e.g., race, physical handicap, or weight). However, stigmatizing attributes such as race or a physical handicap are often relatively superficial characteristics of a person, revealing little about the bearer's personality or character. Thus, the consequences for self-esteem of attributing negative outcomes to one's stigma are unclear.

Although we are aware of no data on this point, we suggest that attributing negative outcomes to a controllable stigma should have damaging consequences for self-esteem, because the stigmatized individual not only blames the negative outcomes on the stigma but also blames the stigma on the self. For example, an overweight woman who is rejected for a date because of her weight not only blames the rejection on her weight but also blames her weight on her lack of self-control. This characterological self-blame should be associated with low self-esteem (Janoff-Bulman, 1979).

The implications for self-esteem of justifiable negative outcomes based on an uncontrollable stigma are less clear. If the stigmatized individual does not feel responsible for the stigma, then even justifiable negative outcomes based on the stigma may not lower self-esteem. For example, someone with a physical hand-icap that is completely outside his or her control who is rejected for a job that requires physical agility may feel frustrated and disappointed but is unlikely to experience low self-esteem.

Alternatively, if the negative outcomes based on the stigma are perceived as unjustifiable, then the other person, rather than the stigma itself, is blamed. That is, when the negative outcomes are perceived as unjustifiable, the cause of the outcomes should be located in the other person's prejudice, insensitivity, or unfairness rather than in the stigma. Thus, we suggest that when negative out-comes based on a stigma are perceived as unjustifiable, those outcomes are attributed to an external cause (the other's prejudice) and consequently self-esteem should be protected. As we noted in the previous section, although believing that negative outcomes based on a stigma are unjustified may protect self-esteem, it may threaten other important beliefs such as the belief in personal control and the belief that the world is just. Thus, the perceived justifiability of negative outcomes based on stigma may be a critical moderator of the effects of those outcomes on self-esteem.

We expect that stigmatized people who accept negative stereotypes about their group are lower in self-esteem than those who do not accept these stereotypes. This relationship may happen for two reasons: (a) because of the direct effects on self-esteem of accepting negative attitudes about the self, and (b) because inter-nalizing negative stereotypes also leads one to believe that specific negative outcomes one receives are justifiable, which in turn lowers self-esteem.

Research on a number of stigmatized groups indicates that the stigmatized frequently do accept stereotypes, both positive and negative, about their group. For example, research on gender stereotypes has generally found those stereo-types to be as pervasive among women as they are among men (Broverman, Vogel, Broverman, Clarkson, & Rosenkrantz, 1972). Similarly, research on stereotypes about weight has shown that the overweight are just as likely as the normal weight to endorse negative attitudes toward fatness (Crandall & Biernat, 1990). This acceptance of stereotypes about one's stigma or group membership should be associated with believing that certain types of negative outcomes for one's group are sometimes justified. For example, Martin (1986) found that feminist secretaries were more distressed by gender-based occupational segrega-tion and job discrimination than secretaries with a more traditional orientation. This latter group presumably felt that their treatment was justifiable, given the differences they perceived between themselves and their (relatively advantaged) male coworkers.

The effects of justifiability on self-esteem also depend on the importance of the stigmatizing attribute to one's self-concept. Consistent with this view, Cran-dall & Biernat (1990) found that self-esteem was lowest among overweight women who endorsed negative attitudes about overweight people (and, we would argue, presumably thought that negative reactions to them were justified). This same relationship was not found for overweight men. The authors interpreted this gender difference as a function of the differential importance of weight to the self-concepts of women and men.

Motivation.   Finally, we speculate that the perceived justifiability of negative outcomes based on stigma should have consequences for motivation, in particular for efforts at both personal and social change. The type of motivational effect, however, may depend on whether the stigma is considered controllable or uncontrollable. If the discrimination is perceived as justifiable and the stigma is controllable, negative outcomes perceived as justified should lead to attempts at personal change, including attempts to remove or ameliorate the stigma. For example, overweight women who feel that social rejection of them is justified should be especially likely to attempt to lose weight. If discrimination is perceived as justifiable and the stigma is not controllable, then negative outcomes may simply be accepted. In this case, the individual may become hopeless with regard to the stigma and its associated outcomes, and clinical depression may ensue (Abramson et al., 1978; Abramson, Metalsky, & Alloy, 1989).

When negative outcomes are perceived as unjustifiable, the stigmatized individual should also be more likely to seek change. The nature of the change depends on whether the person feels that the injustice is directed at themselves personally or at their group. Wright and his colleagues, for example, found that people who have been denied entry into a high-status group endorse disruptive forms of collective action only when they believe that membership in the high-status group is completely closed to members of their own group (Wright, Taylor, & Moghaddam, 1990). We interpret this as due to the perceived justifiability of the exclusion. That is, exclusion of all members of one's group, regardless of personal attributes or qualifications, is perceived to be discriminatory and unjustifiable.

Again, the perceived controllability of the stigma moderates protest reactions to unjustifiable negative outcomes. When the stigma is uncontrollable and attempts at personal change are impossible, then protest should be especially likely. Collective protest is more likely when the problem is seen as collective rather than personal (i.e., when one believes that others with one's stigma are also discriminated against). When others with one's stigma are not discriminated against, personal protest is is more likely (Dube & Guimond, 1986; Martin, 1986; Vanneman & Pettigrew, 1972). When the stigma is potentially controllable, the stigmatized individual has the choice of protesting the unjustifiable negative outcomes or attempting to change the stigma. Thus, a stigmatized group such as obese women may act collectively only when they believe that their treatment is unjustifiable, their stigma is uncontrollable, and other obese women are also discriminated against.

CHANGES IN JUSTIFIABILITY OVER TIME

The perceived justifiability of negative outcomes is not a fixed quality of a stigma or of the particular combination of stigma and circumstances. Although we are unaware of data that address this issue directly, we think it is clear that the perceived justifiability of negative outcomes based on stigma has changed dramatically over the past 30 years for members of several stigmatized groups. For example, it was only a few decades ago when exclusion of Blacks from public facilities, schools, and jobs was both legal and considered justifiable by many Americans. Similar if less dramatic changes have occurred for women, the physically handicapped, and to a lesser extent, lesbians and gay men. The rights movements associated with these groups have dramatically altered the degree to which negative outcomes based on stigmatized status are considered justifiable.

Although this is an issue that social psychologists have largely ignored, it is interesting to speculate about how these political and social changes take place. To some extent, these changes reflect changes in the degree to which certain stigmatizing conditions are perceived as controllable. For example, in this century cultural views of alcoholism have shifted from a moral model to a medical model. Weiner and his colleagues (Weiner et al., 1988, Study 2) attempted to manipulate the perceived controllability of stigmas by providing subjects with information about responsibility for the onset of the stigmas. For example, a person with AIDS was said to have contracted the disease through a blood transfusion (uncontrollable onset) or through leading a promiscuous sex life (controllable onset). They found that providing subjects with information that the onset of the stigma was controllable led to increased judgments of responsibility and blame and increased anger and led to decreased liking, pity, desire to give personal assistance, and charity. Thus, it appears that the perceived controllability—and presumably the perceived justifiability of negative outcomes based on the stigma—are alterable through information. These data further suggest that a shift to perceiving stigmas as uncontrollable results in more positive evaluations of the stigmatized. Weiner et al. (1988) also found, however, that the controllability information was differentially effective for different stigmas. For example, controllability information had little effect on responses to a child abuser but had a dramatic effect on responses to a person with AIDS. Thus, there appear to be limits to the degree to which the perceived controllability of a stigma and the perceived justifiability of negative outcomes based on the stigma can be altered.

In addition, the degree to which some stigmatizing conditions are seen as relevant inputs may change over time. Beliefs that the stigmatized group actually contribute lower inputs (e.g., have less ability) may change. Independent of this, beliefs about whether an individual's group membership (or stigma) is a relevant factor to consider may change. For example, although it used to be commonplace to justify lower pay for women in terms of their lower need, greater home responsibilities, and so on, most Americans now overwhelmingly support the notion of equal pay for equal work, regardless of need. It is unclear whether this is because most people now believe that men and women have equal abilities and skills or because they believe that men and women should be treated equally, in spite of differences in their contributions.

Sidanius (in press; Sidanius, Pratto, & Govender, 1990) recently argued that oppression of low-status groups is maintained through what he calls *legitimizing myths,* which justify the oppression. These legitimizing myths often make reference to the lower inputs of oppressed groups. For example, the argument that slavery was actually benevolent and in the interests of Blacks because they were simply incapable of attending to their own affairs suggests that slavery was not only economically advantageous but morally compelling. Although this legitimizing myth is rejected by virtually all segments of the American population today, other beliefs that are more widely endorsed may also be considered legitimizing myths. For example, the belief that women are too emotional to hold jobs of great responsibility, such as president of the United States, legitimizes denying women positions of power. According to Sidanius and Pratto (in press), a very robust legitimizing myth in our culture is the American belief in meritocracy and individual achievement. According to this myth, the higher status and outcomes of White males relative to other groups in the society is prima facie evidence of their greater inputs. This legitimizing myth is so ingrained in our culture, according to Sidanius, that it takes on the appearance of self-evident truth. Although it may be difficult to recognize legitimizing myths in one's own culture, it is clear from a historical perspective that these legitimizing myths exist and that they can change over time.

SUMMARY AND CONCLUSIONS

The perceived justifiability of negative outcomes based on a stigma has important consequences for how individuals react to those outcomes. Negative outcomes based on a stigma may be perceived as justifiable (a) when the stigma is judged to be a relevant negative input, (b) when the stigma is controllable, (c) when perceiving negative outcomes based on stigma as unjustifiable threatens other important beliefs or (d) when legitimizing myths support the low status of stigmatized groups.

Stigmatized individuals who believe that negative outcomes based on their (controllable) stigma are justifiable should react with depressed mood and low self-esteem, should be relatively satisfied with their outcomes, and should respond with either hopelessness or attempts at personal change. On the other hand, stigmatized individuals who believe that negative outcomes based on their stigma are unjustifiable should react with anger and with high self-esteem, should be discontent with their outcomes, and should respond with personal protest or attempts at collective action.

The stigmatized and the nonstigmatized may disagree about the justifiability of negative outcomes based on stigma. Our own research (Major & Crocker, in prep.), for example, has shown that women think that being female interferes less with doing a number of jobs than do males. The women also believe it is less justifiable and less legitimate to deny a woman a job on the basis of her gender than male subjects do. These disagreements about the justifiability of negative outcomes based on stigma may be an important contributor to social conflict between the stigmatized and the nonstigmatized.

Finally, our analysis also has implications for the justifiability of positive outcomes based on a stigma. We argue elsewhere (Crocker et al., 1991; Major & Crocker, in press) that members of stigmatized groups sometimes receive positive outcomes because of their group membership. For example, some social programs and policies, such as affirmative action, are designed to overcome past histories of discrimination against certain groups. We suggest that reactions to those programs, by both the beneficiaries of those programs and other disinterested individuals, depends heavily on their perceived justifiability. A growing literature on responses to preferential selection suggests that both the beneficiaries of affirmative-action programs and observers have strong negative reactions to these programs, presumably because they believe such treatment is not justified by membership in a social category (Taylor & Dube, 1986). We argue that responses to a variety of programs intended to benefit members of stigmatized groups could be better understood by considering the conditions under which such programs are considered justifiable.

ACKNOWLEDGMENT

Preparation of this chapter was supported by NSF grant BNS 9010487.

REFERENCES

Abrams, R. D., & Finesinger, J. E. (1953). Guilt reactions in patients with cancer. *Cancer, 6,* 474–482.

Abramson, L. Y., Metalsky, G., & Alloy, L. B. (1989). Hopelessness depression: A theory-based subtype of depression. *Psychological Review, 96,* 358–372.

Abramson, L. Y., Seligman, M. E. P., & Teasdale, J. (1978). Learned helplessness in humans: Critique and reformulation. *Journal of Abnormal Psychology, 87,* 49–74.

Adams, J. S. (1965). Inequity is social exchange. In L. Berkowitz (Ed.), *Advances in experimental social psychology* (Vol. 2, pp. 267–299). New York: Academic.

Allon, N. (1982). The stigma of overweight in everyday life. In B. B. Woldman (Ed.), *Psychological aspects of obesity* (pp. 130–174). New York: Van Nostrand Reinhold.

Braddock, J. H., II, & McPartland, J. M. (1987). How minorities continue to be excluded from equal employment opportunities: research on labor market and institutional barriers. *Journal of Social Issues, 43,* 5–40.

Briar, S. (1966). Welfare from below: Recipients' views of the public welfare system. *California Law Review, 54*, 370–385.

Brigham, J. C. (1974). Views of black and white children concerning the distribution of personality characteristics. *Journal of Personality, 42*, 144–158.

Broverman, I. K., Vogel, S. R., Broverman, D. M., Clarkson, F. E., & Rosenkrantz, P. S. (1972). Sex stereotypes: A current appraisal. *Journal of Social Issues, 28*, 59–79.

Bulman, R. J., & Wortman, C. B. (1977). Attributions of blame and coping in the "real world": Severe accident victims react to their lot. *Journal of Personality and Social Psychology, 35*, 351–363.

Burden, P. R., & Parish, T. S. (1983). Exceptional and normal children's descriptions of themselves. *Education, 104*, 204–205.

Burgess, A. W., & Holmstrom, L. (1979). *Rape: Crisis and recovery.* Bowie, MD: Brady.

Bylsma, W., Major, B., & Cozzarelli, C. (1991). *The role of social comparisons and procedural fairness in the perpetuation of disadvantage.* Manuscript submitted for publication.

Clifford, E., & Clifford, M. (1986). Social and psychological problems associated with clefts: Motivations for cleft palate treatment. *International Dental Journal, 36*, 115–119.

Crandall, C., & Biernat, M. (1990). The ideology of anti-fat attitudes. *Journal of Applied Social Psychology, 20*, 227–243.

Crocker, J., Cornwell, B., & Major, B. (1993). The stigma of overweight: Affective consequences of attributional ambiguity. *Journal of Personality and Social Psychology, 64*, 60–70.

Crocker, J., & Major, B. (1989). Social stigma and self-esteem: The self-protective properties of stigma. *Psychological Review, 96*, 608–630.

Crocker, J., & Major, B. (manuscript in prep.). *When bad things happen to bad people: The perceived justifiability of negative outcomes based on stigma.*

Crocker, J., Voelkl, K., Testa, M., & Major, B. (1991). Social stigma: The affective consequences of attributional ambiguity. *Journal of Personality and Social Psychology, 60*, 218–228.

Crosby, F. (1976). A model of egotistical relative deprivation. *Psychological Review, 83*, 85–113.

Crosby, F. (1982). *Relative deprivation and working women.* New York: Oxford University Press.

Crosby, F. (1984). The denial of personal discrimination. *American Behavioral Scientist, 27*, 371–386.

Crosby, F., Bromley, S., & Saxe L. (1980). Recent unobtrusive studies of Black-and-White discrimination and prejudice: A literature review. *Psychological Bulletin, 87*, 546–563.

Devine, P. (1989). Stereotypes and prejudice: Their automatic and controlled components. *Journal of Personality and Social Psychology, 56*, 5–18.

Dion, K. L. (1975). Women's reactions to discrimination from members of the same or opposite sex. *Journal of Research in Personality, 9*, 294–306.

Dion, K. L. (1986). Responses to perceived discrimination and relative deprivation. In J. M. Olson, C. P. Herman, & M. P. Zanna (Eds.), *Relative deprivation and social comparison: The Ontario Symposium* (Vol. 4, pp. 159–179). Hillsdale, NJ: Lawrence Erlbaum Associates.

Dion, K. L., & Earn, B. M. (1975). The phenomenology of being a target of prejudice. *Journal of Personality and Social Psychology, 32*, 944–950.

Dovidio, J. F., & Gaertner, S. L. (1986). Prejudice, discrimination, and racism: Historical trends and contemporary approaches. In J. F. Dovidio & S. L. Gaertner (Eds.), *Prejudice, discrimination, and racism* (pp. 1–34). New York: Academic.

Dube, L., & Guimond, S. (1986). Relative deprivation and social protest: The personal–group issue. In J. M. Olson, C. P. Herman, & M. P. Zanna (Eds.), *Relative deprivation and social comparison: The Ontario Symposium* (Vol. 4, pp. 201–216). Hillsdale, NJ: Lawrence Erlbaum Associates.

Fallon, A. E., & Rozin, P. (1985). Sex differences in perceptions of desirable body shape. *Journal of Abnormal Psychology, 94*, 102–105.

Folger, R., Rosenfield, D., Grove, J., & Corkran, L. (1979). Effects of "voice" and peer opinions on responses to inequity. *Journal of Personality and Social Psychology, 37*, 2253–2261.

Gaertner, S. L., & Dovidio, J. F. (1986). The aversive form of racism. In J. F. Dovidio & S. L. Gaertner (Eds.), *Prejudice, discrimination, and racism* (pp. 61–90). Orlando, FL: Academic Press.

Gibbons, F. X. (1981). The social psychology of mental retardation: What's in a label? In S. S. Brehm, S. M. Kassin, & F. X. Gibbons (Eds.), *Developmental Social Psychology* (pp. 249–270). New York: Oxford University Press.

Gibbons, F. X. (1985). A social-psychological perspective on developmental disabilities. *Journal of Social and Clinical Psychology, 3,* 391–404.

Goffman, E. (1963). *Stigma: Notes on the management of spoiled identity.* Englewood Cliffs, NJ: Prentice-Hall.

Goodman, N., Richardson, S. A., Dornbusch, S. M., & Hastorf, A. H. (1963). Variant reactions to physical disabilities. *American Sociological Review, 28,* 429–435.

Hafer, C. L., & Olson, J. M. (1989). Beliefs in a just world and reactions to personal deprivation. *Journal of Personality, 57,* 799–823.

Hartsough, W. R., & Fontana, A. F. (1970). Persistence of ethnic stereotypes and the relative importance of positive and negative stereotyping for association preferences. *Psychological Reports, 27,* 723–731.

Hoelter, J. W. (1983). Factorial invariance and self-esteem: Reassessing race and sex differences. *Social Forces, 61,* 834–846.

Janoff-Bulman, R. (1979). Characterological versus behavioral self-blame: Inquiries into depression and rape. *Journal of Personality and Social Psychology 37,* 1798–1809.

Jarvie, G. J., Lahey, B., Graziano, W., & Framer, E. (1983). Childhood obesity and social stigma: What we know and what we don't know. *Developmental Review, 3,* 237–273.

Jones, E. E., Farina, A., Hastorf, A. H., Markus, H., Miller, D. T., & Scott, R. A. (1984). *Social stigma: The psychology of marked relationships.* New York: Freeman.

Kanter, R. M. (1977). *Men and women of the corporation.* New York: Basic Books.

Karlins, M., Coffman, T. L., & Walters, G. (1969). On the fading of social stereotypes: Studies in three generations of college students. *Journal of Personality and Social Psychology, 13,* 1–16.

Kleck, R. E., & Strenta, A. (1980). Perceptions of the impact of negatively valued physical characteristics on social interaction. *Journal of Personality and Social Psychology, 39,* 861–873.

Larkin, J. C., & Pines, H. A. (1979). No fat persons need apply. *Sociology of Work and Occupations, 6,* 312–327.

Lerner, M. J. (1980). *The belief in a just world: A fundamental delusion.* New York: Plenum.

Lerner, M. J., & Miller, D. T. (1978). Just world research and the attribution process: Looking back and ahead. *Psychological Bulletin, 85,* 1030–1051.

Lind, E. A., & Tyler, T. R. (1988). *The social psychology of procedural justice.* New York: Plenum.

Lyman, S. (1978). *The seven deadly sins: Society and evil.* New York: St. Martins Press.

Maddox, G. L., Back, K. W., & Liederman, V. (1968). Overweight as a social disability with medical implications. *Journal of Medical Education, 44,* 214–220.

Major, B. (1987). Gender, justice, and the psychology of entitlement. In P. Shaver & C. Hendrick (Eds.), *Review of personality and social psychology* (Vol. 7, pp. 124–148). Beverly Hills, CA: Sage.

Major, B. (1989). Gender differences in comparisons and entitlement: Implications for comparable worth. *Journal of Social Issues, 45,* 99–116.

Major, B., & Crocker, J. (1993). Social stigma: The consequences of attributional ambiguity. In D. M. Mackie & D. L. Hamilton (Eds.), *Affect, cognition and stereotyping: Interactive processes in group perception.* (pp. 345–370). New York: Academic.

Major, B., & Crocker, J. (in prep.). *When sex discrimination is justifiable.*

Major, B., & Forcey, B. (1987). Social comparisons and pay evaluations: Preferences for same-sex and same-job wage comparisons. *Journal of Experimental Social Psychology, 21,* 393–405.

Martin, J. (1986). The tolerance of injustice. In J. M. Olson, C. P. Herman, & M. P. Zanna (Eds.), *Relative deprivation and social comparison: The Ontario Symposium* (Vol. 4, pp. 217–242). Hillsdale, NJ: Lawrence Erlbaum Associates.

McFarland, C., & Ross, M. (1982). Impact of causal attributions on affective reactions to success and failure. *Journal of Personality and Social Psychology, 43,* 937–946.

Millman, M. (1980). *Such a pretty face: Being fat in America.* New York: Norton.

Morris, M., & Williamson, J. B. (1982). Stereotypes and social class: A focus on poverty. In A. G. Miller (Ed.), *In the eye of the beholder: Contemporary issues in stereotyping* (pp. 411–465). New York: Praeger.

Pettigrew, T. F., & Martin, J. (1987). Shaping the organizational context for Black American inclusion. *Journal of Social Issues, 43,* 41–78.

Polivy, J., Garner, D. M., & Garfinkel, P. E. (1986). Causes and consequences of the current preference for thin female physiques. In C. P. Herman, M. P. Zanna, & E. T. Higgins (Eds.), *Physical appearance, stigma, and social behavior: The Ontario Symposium* (Vol. 3, pp. 89–112). Hillsdale, NJ: Lawrence Erlbaum Associates.

Polivy, J., Herman, C. P., & Pliner, P. (1990). Perception and evaluation of body image: The meaning of body shape and size. In J. M. Olson & M. P. Zanna (Eds.), *Self-inference processes: The Ontario Symposium* (Vol. 6, pp. 87–114). Hillsdale, NJ: Lawrence Erlbaum Associates.

Porter, J. R., & Washington, R. E. (1979). Black identity and self-esteem: A review of studies of Black self-concept, 1968–1978. *Annual Review of Sociology, 5,* 53–74.

Richardson, S. A., Hastorf, A. H., Goodman, N., & Dornbusch, S. M. (1961). Cultural uniformity in reaction to physical disabilities. *American Sociological Review, 26,* 241–247.

Rodin, M., Price, J., Sanchez, F., & McElligot, S. (1989). Derogation, exclusion, and unfair treatment of persons with social flaws: Controllability of stigma and the attribution of prejudice. *Personality and Social Psychology Bulletin, 15,* 439–451.

Rosenberg, M. (1965). *Society and the adolescent self-image.* Princeton, NJ: Princeton University Press.

Rosenberg, M. (1979). *Conceiving the self.* New York: Basic Books.

Rubin, Z., & Peplau, L. A. (1975). Who believes in a just world? *Journal of Social Issues, 31,* 65–90.

Samuels, F. (1973). *Group images.* New Haven, CT: College and University Press.

Scott, R. A. (1969). *The making of blind men: A study of adult socialization.* New York: Sage.

Shaver, P., & Schwartz, J., Kirsen, D., & O'Connor, C. (1987). Emotion knowledge: Further explorations of a prototype approach. *Journal of Personality and Social Psychology, 52,* 1061–1086.

Sidanius, J., & Pratto, F. (in press). The inevitability of oppression and the dynamics of social dominance. In P. Sniderman & P. E. Tetlock (Eds.), *Prejudice, politics, and race in America today.* Stanford, CA: Stanford University Press.

Sidanius, J., Pratto, F., & Govender, R. (1990). *Social dominance, social attitudes, and legitimizing myths: An application to the American dilemma.* Manuscript submitted for publication.

Smith, C., & Ellsworth, P. (1985). Patterns of cognitive appraisal in emotion. *Journal of Personality and Social Psychology, 48,* 813–838.

Smith, C., & Ellsworth, P. (1987). Patterns of appraisal and emotion related to taking an exam. *Journal of Personality and Social Psychology, 52,* 475–488.

Taylor, D. M., & Dube, L. (1986). Two faces of identity: The "I" and the "we." *Journal of Social Issues, 42,* 81–98.

U.S. Government. (1978). *Income and earnings differentials between Black and White Americans* (Document No. TF-6-95-0). Washington, DC: U. S. Government Printing Office.

Vanneman, R. D., & Pettigrew, T. F. (1972). Race and relative deprivation in the urban United States. *Race, 13,* 461–486.

Wadden, T. A., Foster, G. D., Brownell, K. D., & Finley, E. (1984). Self-concept in obese and normal-weight children. *Journal of Consulting and Clinical Psychology, 52,* 1104–1105.

Walster, E., Walster, G. W., & Berscheid, E. (1978). *Equity: Theory and research.* Boston: Allyn & Bacon.

Weiner, B. (1985). An attributional theory of achievement motivation and emotion. *Psychological Review, 92,* 548–573.

Weiner, B. (1986). Attribution, emotion, and action. In R. M. Sorrentino & E. T. Higgins (Eds.), *Handbook of motivation and cognition* (pp. 281–312). New York: Guilford.

Weiner, B., Perry, R. P., & Magnusson, J. (1988). An attributional analysis of reactions to stigmas. *Journal of Personality and Social Psychology, 55,* 738–748.

Wortman, C. B. (1976). Causal attributions and personal control. In J. H. Harvey, W. J. Ickes, & R. F. Kidd (Eds.), *New directions in attribution research* (Vol. 1, pp. 23–52). Hillsdale, NJ: Lawrence Erlbaum Associates.

Wright, S. C., Taylor, D. M., & Moghaddam, F. M. (1990). Responding to membership in a disadvantaged group: From acceptance to collective protest. *Journal of Personality and Social Psychology, 58,* 994–1003.

Wylie, R. (1979). *The self-concept* (Vol. 2). Lincoln: University of Nebraska Press.

Zanna, M. P., Crosby, F., & Loewenstein, G. (1987). Male reference groups and discontent among female professionals. In B. Gutek, & L. Lorwood (Eds.), *Women's career development* (pp. 28–41). Newbury Park, CA: Sage.

Zuckerman, M., & Lubin, B. (1965). *Manual for the Multiple Affect Adjective Checklist.* San Diego, CA: Educational and Industrial Testing Service.

13

The Social Psychology of Prejudice: Getting It All Together

Marilynn B. Brewer
University of California, Los Angeles

It was three men of Indostan
  To learning much inclined
Who went to see the elephant
  Though each of them was blind.

The first no sooner had begun
  About the beast to grope
Than, seizing on the swinging tail
  That fell within his scope
'I see,' quoth he, 'the elephant
  Is very like a rope!'

The second, feeling of the tusk,
  Cried: 'Ho! What have we here
So very round and smooth and sharp?
  To me 'tis very clear,
This wonder of an elephant
  Is very like a spear!'

The third approached the animal,
  And, happening to take
The squirming trunk within his hands
  Thus boldly up he spake:
'I see,' quoth he, 'the elephant
  Is very like a snake!'

—John G. Saxe (source unknown)

As the 1991 Ontario Symposium was convening in Waterloo, Ontario, the city of Dubuque, Iowa, was receiving considerable media attention in the United States for a controversial experiment in intergroup relations. A city of 58,000 in the heart of America's Midwest, Dubuque had a tiny racial minority of 331 Black residents scattered among its neighborhoods. In that environment, a White resident could go for years without even seeing a Black, and issues of prejudice and racism were viewed as remote problems afflicting the Deep South or large urban centers but not Dubuque. That was until a cross burning in 1989 ignited a Black family's garage and shattered the city's complacence.

In response to the cross-burning incident, Dubuque's city council established a task force of business leaders and school and city officials to review the situation and make recommendations for preventing future incidents of racial conflict in the city. Based on the idea that greater exposure to minority groups promotes tolerance, members of the task force concluded that Dubuque needed more minority citizens. In May, 1991, the city council adopted a plan involving a system of incentives for local businesses to hire minorities, particularly Blacks, with the goal of recruiting to Dubuque 20 new Black families a year over the next 5 years.

Even before the plan could be implemented in any meaningful way, the idea of an influx of Black residents produced widespread reactance. Racial fights in the local high school and additional cross burnings ensued. Rumors about the recruitment plan and its effect on local jobs, housing, and safety in the streets spread rapidly. Graffiti containing racial epithets appeared, and a group of young males organized a local chapter of the National Association for the Advancement of White People. As one resident put it, "We won't be able to open our windows, sit on our porches, stroll in our neighborhoods" (Wilkerson, 1991).

As the turmoil in Dubuque reached the news, I was contacted by a journalist who wanted to know what social psychologists had to say about the causes of racial tension in Dubuque and the probable outcomes of the city council plan to increase minority presence. I found trying to answer her insightful questions one of the most challenging experiences of my career—not because social psychology has little to say about this situation but because, in a sense, it has too much to say! Understanding prejudice and intergroup conflict invokes virtually every area of social psychological inquiry, including the study of person perception, social attitudes, aggression, self-esteem, social comparison, equity, cooperation and competition, and conformity and compliance. Further, the study of prejudice crosses all levels of analysis, from intra-individual to interpersonal to intergroup processes.

From research in all of these areas, there is a wealth of relevant information about: (a) the cognitive and motivational underpinnings of stereotypes and attitudes toward social groups, (b) ingroup bias in intergroup perception, (c) effects of category-based expectancies on interpersonal encounters, and (d) the consequences of intergroup contact. Unfortunately, much of this knowledge is encapsulated in isolated—sometimes competing—research traditions. The lack of integration of social psychological research and theory relevant to the understanding of prejudice and discrimination makes it difficult to tell the story to the world. Whereas psychodynamic explanations on the one hand and Marxist theory on the other are widely represented in public debates on issues of intergroup hostility, social psychological perspectives are less accessible than they should be.

The organizers of the 1991 Ontario Symposium took a significant step in providing a forum where social psychologists representing different programs of research in the study of intergroup attitudes and behavior could engage in discussion and exploration of mutual interests. I take it as my challenge in this concluding chapter to press that integrative effort just a but further.

A HISTORY OF ISOLATIONISM

Although prejudice, stereotypes, and discrimination traditionally appear as topics in the same chapter in introductory social psychology texts, the three terms actually represent at least three discrete research traditions. The study of category *stereotypes* is associated most closely with research on person perception and social cognition. Within this tradition, stereotypes are conceived as category-based expectancies that influence attention, interpretation, and memory for information about social category members (Hamilton, Sherman, & Ruvolo, 1990). Category stereotypes originate in the service of cognitive economy, and biases in information processing, storage, and retrieval are understood as consequences of normal cognitive functioning. In this framework, the evaluative implications of stereotypes and stereotypic beliefs are secondary to the structural and functional determinants of their formation and activation.

The evaluative and affective aspects of intergroup perception are embodied in the study of *prejudice,* associated (within social psychology) most closely with research on social attitudes and attitude change. In this perspective, prejudice is a personal disposition or response orientation toward a particular social group or its symbolic representation, and the focus of research in this tradition is on assessment of individual differences and of the interrelationships among evaluative beliefs, affect, and values as components of prejudice at the individual level (Esses, Haddock, & Zanna, in press). Prejudice is viewed as having its origins in individual socialization (Sears, 1988), sustained by the functions that prejudicial beliefs serve for the protection of individual self-esteem and the maintenance of social regulations (Snyder & Meine, chapter 2, this volume).

Although there have been efforts to incorporate behavioral measures in research on prejudice and intergroup attitudes (e.g., Crosby, Bromley, & Saxe, 1980), the study of *discrimination* (differential behavior directed towards individuals or groups as a function of category membership) represents yet a different research tradition. Much of it derives from the field studies of Sherif and his colleagues (e.g., Sherif, Harvey, White, Hood, & Sherif, 1961; Sherif & Sherif, 1953). Research on intergroup relations has focused on the nature of the structural relationships between social groups and their consequences for intergroup contact, conflict, and cooperation (e.g., Miller & Brewer, 1984). Whereas the study of stereotypes and prejudice is undertaken primarily with the individual as the unit of analysis, research on discrimination and intergroup relations is more likely to be concerned with aggregate behaviors, with the interdependent group as the unit of analysis.

These research traditions associated with the study of stereotypes, prejudice, and discrimination have a common ancestry, best represented by Allport's comprehensive book, *On the nature of prejudice,* published in 1954. In the years since Allport's opus appeared, however, lines of research on different aspects of the social psychology of intergroup phenomena have become more and more isolated. Much like the adage of the blind men and the elephant—each draws its own conclusions about the nature of the beast without much cross-referencing to work done in the other traditions. Different research agendas, methodological paradigms, and intellectual heritage make cross-communication among programs of research difficult, if not impossible. As a consequence, the bodies of knowledge regarding these different aspects of intergroup perception and behavior bear a relationship more analogous to that of distant cousins than of immediate family.

LEVELS OF ANALYSIS

To complicate matters further, stereotypes, prejudice, and discrimination can each be conceptualized at two different levels of analysis: (a) the individual/interpersonal level, and (b) the societal/intergroup level (Tajfel, 1978; Tajfel & Turner, 1986). As Gardner (chapter 1, this volume) points out, personal stereotypes or beliefs about particular social groups can and should be distinguished from social stereotypes, which are beliefs shared among members of a community. Individual community members may have knowledge of shared social stereotypes that they do not personally endorse (Devine, 1989) or, conversely, may hold idiosyncratic beliefs that are not part of the social stereotype. Further, stereotypes about groups as a whole may or may not be represented in interpersonal perceptions between individual members of different social categories.

Although prejudice is most often represented in social psychological research as an individual disposition or social attitude, it is also conceptualized in terms of social norms characteristic of particular communities, cultures, or regions. Further, prejudicial attitudes can be expressed in interpersonal relationships or in the form of social policies directed toward the group as a whole. Thus, both the source and the target of prejudice can be defined at either the individual or the group level.

Similarly, discrimination can be manifest in interpersonal behavior or as institutional discrimination. At the interpersonal level, discrimination is the behavioral component of individual prejudice and category-based expectancies (Neuberg, chapter 5, this volume). At the intergroup level, discrimination is reflected in differential access to resources, status, and power as a function of group membership (Bourhis, chapter 8, this volume). Further, discrimination can be experienced at the personal level, with consequences for individual self-concept and aspirations (Crocker & Major, chapter 12, this volume) or at the collective level, with consequences for collective action and the rise of social movements (Lalonde & Cameron, chapter 11; Taylor, Wright, & Porter, chapter 10, this volume).

Considering stereotypes, prejudice, and discrimination as three separate manifestations of intergroup orientations, each of which can be defined at the individual/interpersonal or societal/intergroup level, provides a framework for representing the current status of social psychological research in this area. This analysis gives rise to a 3 × 2 taxonomy, depicted in Fig. 13.1. Each cell in this classification scheme represents a distinct perspective on the social psychology of prejudice.

Collectively, the chapters in the present volume represent all six of the research orientations depicted in Fig. 13.1. What is of most interest, however, is the fact that several of the chapters defy simple classification and instead overlap two or more cells of the taxonomy. For instance, the experiments reported by Esses, Haddock, and Zanna (chapter 4, this volume) are part of a larger research program assessing the relationships between the evaluative content of stereotypes (cell 1) and prejudice (cell 2), thus forging links between social cognition research methods and traditional approaches to the study of social attitudes. Similarly, Neuberg's (chapter 5, this volume) analysis of the social-cognition mediators of interpersonal behavior links stereotypes (1) and discrimination (3) in a reciprocal-causal system at the individual/interpersonal level.

Several of the chapters also cross levels of analysis between individual and group. Gardner (chapter 1, this volume) explicitly compares and contrasts personal and social stereotypes (cells 1 and 4), whereas Taylor, Wright, and Porter

	Individual/ Interpersonal	Societal/ Intergroup
Stereotype	1	4
Prejudice	2	5
Discrimination	3	6

FIG. 13.1.   Six distinct research perspectives.

(chapter 10, this volume) provide a similar comparison between the experience of discrimination at the personal (cell 3) or collective levels (cell 6) of identity. Batson and Burris' (chapter 7, this volume) work deals with the link between group norms (5) and personal prejudice (2). The program of research by Crocker and Major (chapter 12, this volume) demonstrates how collective beliefs or group stereotypes (cell 4) impact the attributions and self-concept of individual group members (cell 3), whereas Lalonde and Cameron's (chapter 11, this volume) research illustrates how individual experiences of prejudice and discrimination (3) can become linked to system change (6).

It is these linkages between rows and columns of the basic research taxonomy that provide the basis for some integrative themes among the symposium presentations. In the sections that follow, I highlight some of these common themes and consider their implications for future research on the social psychology of prejudice.

Linking Affect and Cognition: The Role of the Unconscious

Currently, one of the most challenging areas of research and theory in social psychology concerns the relationship between cognition and affect. Theories of emotion are characterized by controversy over the role of cognitive appraisal as a determinant of emotional experience (Lazarus, 1982; Roseman, 1984; Weiner, 1982; Zajonc, 1984). In general researchers are divided as to whether affect drives cognition, cognition drives affect, or cognition and affect are essentially independent, dissociated response systems.

The study of social attitudes in general, and prejudice in particular, is also marked by conflicting perspectives on the nature of the relationship between cognitive and affective components of attitudes. Traditionally, evaluative beliefs and affective reactions have been conceived as different manifestations of a single underlying response disposition toward a social object or issue (Ajzen, 1988; Campbell, 1963). Empirical evidence for strong intercorrelations among affective and cognitive measures, however, is mixed (Breckler, 1984), and calls into question the single-disposition conceptualization of attitudes. Recently, a number of theorists have endorsed the idea of distinguishing between attitudes that are primarily *affect-based* from those that are primarily *cognition-based*, depending on which measures best predict overall evaluative ratings of or behaviors toward the attitude object (Esses et al., in press; Wilson & Dunn, 1986).

At its most virulent point, prejudice is more like a strong emotional reaction than a cognitive assessment of a social group. Hence, the role of the evaluative content of group stereotypes in prejudice and discrimination is always somewhat problematic. The notion that cognitive biases associated with stereotype-based expectancies account for intergroup prejudice is challenged by evidence that the evaluative content of personal stereotypes often bears little relationship to affective ratings of the stereotyped group (e.g., Brigham, 1971; Esses et al., in press). Further, although there is some evidence that group stereotypes change in response to dramatic shifts in the nature of intergroup relationships, research on social stereotypes generally indicates that the content of stereotypic beliefs is remarkably robust in the face of changes in affect and affiliation between groups (Hewstone, 1989; Rothbart, 1991). All of this contributes to a view that cognitive, affective, and behavioral orientations toward individuals and social groups represent different, independent response systems whose interrelationships are more complex than previously recognized (Carlston, in press).

One promising avenue for better understanding the link between affective and cognitive response systems lies in research on the differences between conscious (controlled) and unconscious (automatic) processing (Bargh, 1984). Research reported in several chapters in this volume suggests that direct, bicausal relationships between affect and cognition are operative at unconscious or preconscious stages of information processing, even when not manifest at the level of conscious self-representation.

The clearest evidence for such effects is represented in Banaji and Greenwald's (chapter 3, this volume) research on implicit stereotyping. Using priming techniques, these authors demonstrated that the unconscious association between familiarity and affect is a powerful determinant of judgments of fame and credibility but one that is moderated by the fit between such judgments and preexisting group stereotypes. In other words, the priming effect associated with conscious or unconscious exposure to affect-laden stimuli is not a simple main effect of affect on cognition but one that interacts with cognitive content to produce stereotype-consistent processing of ambiguous information when affect and cognitive content converge.

The subtle, interactive effects of affect and cognition at the preconscious level are further reinforced by results of the research reported by Esses, Haddock, and Zanna (chapter 4, this volume) and by Neuberg (chapter 5, this volume). Unexpectedly, Esses et al. found that direct manipulation of individual mood (temporary affect) did not have the anticipated effects on differential accessibility of stereotypic beliefs with positive or negative content. Instead, mood effects were evident in the evaluative connotation assigned to the same stereotypic traits. Given that many traits and behaviors are ambiguous with respect to their evaluative meaning, these results converge with those of Banaji and Greenwald (chapter 3, this volume) in demonstrating that conscious interpretation of information about a particular person or group is influenced by the intersection of affective and cognitive associations at the unconscious level.

The effects of preconscious assessment of fit between stereotypic beliefs and affective and behavioral response dispositions are also represented in Neuberg's (chapter 5, this volume) model of expectancy–confirmation processes in interpersonal contact situations. Again, this model does not assume that expectancy confirmation is a simple, automatic outcome of prior expectancies imposed on selection and interpretation of incoming information. Rather, expectancies interact with perceiver goals and target behaviors to determine the fit between category-based expectancies and perceptions of individual category members.

Research on implicit stereotyping and affective priming suggest that the traditional methods of assessing prejudice in the form of conscious self-report measures obtained under neutral mood conditions is ill-suited to a complete understanding of the strong bidirectional relationships between affect and cognition in intergroup perception. Divorced from actual intergroup contact, individuals report beliefs about social groups as objective appraisals, independent of current affective reactions to those groups. Conversely, individuals interpret their emotional reactions to group members as direct responses to that person's behavior or characteristics, without recognition of the stereotypic beliefs that contributed to the interpretation and appraisal of that behavior. In either case, the conscious representation belies the actual mutual influence between affect and cognition and their joint role in intergroup behavior.

The Discontinuity Between Personal and Collective Representations: Some of My Best Friends Are . . .

The apparent dissociation between affective and cognitive manifestations of intergroup prejudice is paralleled by even more dramatic evidence of discontinuities between personal and collective (group based) representations of social categories and category members. Social identity theorists (Tajfel, 1978; Tajfel & Turner, 1986) consistently call attention to the distinction between *interpersonal* and *intergroup* orientations, largely in response to what they regard as the excessive individualistic reductionism of North American social-psychological theories of intergroup relations. The contention is that intergroup behavior cannot be understood simply as an extension of processes operative at the individual/ interpersonal level. Instead, social identity theorists expect qualitative differences between affective, cognitive, and behavioral reactions toward other persons depending on whether the individual is responding in terms of *personal identity* (interpersonal mode) or *social identity* (intergroup mode). The same target individual may be evaluated quite differently depending on whether he or she is personalized or perceived as a representative of a social group (Brewer, 1988). There is a general person positivity bias in that persons are evaluated more favorably as individuals than in the aggregate (Sears, 1983), but the inconsistency operates in both directions. It is possible to dislike particular individuals personally but still treat them positively as members of a favored ingroup, just as it is possible to find other individuals personally likeable while rejecting them as members of a despised outgroup.

The discontinuity between personal and collective experience is explicitly represented in Taylor, Wright, and Porter's (chapter 10, this volume) analysis of perceived discrimination. Across a wide range of social groups and intergroup settings, they observed a consistent pattern of differentiation between individuals' ratings of the degree to which their social group is discriminated against and their ratings of personal experience of discrimination. Overall, for members of disadvantaged groups, ratings of collective discrimination are higher than ratings of personal discrimination, and there is little correlation between measures of discrimination at the two levels. As these authors recognized, their findings are compatible with social identity theory which holds that personal and social identity are mutually exclusive (rather than derivative) forms of self-categorization (Brewer, 1991; Turner, Hogg, Oakes, Reicher, & Wetherell, 1987), such that the more salient one's membership in a social category, the less relevant one's personal experience becomes as a determinant of intergroup attitudes or beliefs.

The discontinuity between personal and collective orientations shows up across much of the research reported in this volume. Gardner's (chapter 1) research, for instance, demonstrates that personal stereotypes and social (shared) stereotypes may differ not only in content but in structure and function as well. His finding that shared stereotypes (but not personal beliefs) facilitate reaction time to stereotype-consistent associations is consistent with other experimental research, indicating that reaction time for evaluative judgments is significantly faster for stimuli that elicit high agreement (consensus) in evaluative connotation than for stimuli that are associated with interpersonal variability (this independent of the extremity of the individual's own evaluative response) (Bargh, Chaiken, Govender, & Pratto, 1992). Gardner's work is also consistent with Devine's research indicating that collective stereotypes have strong unconscious priming effects on individual information processing even when those stereotypes are rejected as personal beliefs (Devine, 1989).

Yet another perspective on the relationship between individual and collective orientations is provided by Batson and Burris's (chapter 7, this volume) program of research on religiosity and prejudice. Their results clearly indicate that the direction of correlation between religion and prejudice is moderated by whether prejudice/tolerance is embedded in group norms or in personal beliefs. When prejudice is controlled by normative proscriptions, there is evidence of inconsistency between public (overt) and private (covert) expressions of prejudice. Under conditions where social identity is salient, the expression or inhibition of prejudice is a joint function of group identification and perceived group norms. On the other hand, when social identity is not salient, expression of prejudice is unrelated to group norms and predicted instead by personal values.

The distinction between personal and collective orientations has parallels in functional analyses of the origins of prejudice (see Snyder & Meine, chapter 2, this volume). Some forms of prejudice are expressions of personal needs and values or generalizations of personal experiences with group members. Other forms of prejudice are expressions of shared beliefs and symbols of collective identity. The dissociation between individual and collective orientations has implications for the effectiveness of interventions designed to reduce prejudice, depending on whether they are aimed at personal or group-based perceptions. Interventions designed to change the motivational bases of prejudice at the individual level have little impact on prejudicial attitudes that are embedded in group norms and social identity or vice versa.

Altemeyer's (chapter 6, this volume) research on right-wing authoritarianism (RWA) indicates that Rokeach's value-confrontation intervention is most effective when it is directed at personal value systems. Feedback on discrepancies between the value placed on personal freedom and equality at the collective (aggregate) level had little or no impact on high RWA respondents, perhaps because it reinforced their beliefs that their own values are normative. Only personalized feedback produced significant effects on endorsement of authoritarian beliefs. Altemeyer is cautious about the long-term significance of these findings, in part because it is unclear whether changes in personal beliefs (in the college classroom setting) will generalize to conditions where social identity and group norms favoring ingroup discrimination are more salient. Similar reservations may be directed to results of Snyder and Meine's intervention research. The relative effectiveness of attitude-change strategies directed toward ego-defensive functions or social regulatory functions may well be context specific. Reducing the personal threat associated with an outgroup category may well be effective in decreasing negative beliefs about that social group when personal identity concerns are particularly salient, but it remains an open question whether the same methods are effective when group identity is threatened.

Recognizing the distinction between interpersonal and intergroup processes raises interesting issues about the interrelationships between them. One possible interpretation of social identity theory is that the two levels of orientation are essentially independent of one another, so that changes in interpersonal relationships have no direct implications for change at the intergroup level and vice versa (Hewstone & Brown, 1986). Much of the research reported in the present volume, however, suggests that the boundaries between interpersonal and intergroup orientations are permeable and that there are pathways of mutual influence between processes at the two levels.

For instance, the research by Crocker and Major (chapter 12, this volume) documents mechanisms by which collective stereotypes and institutional discrimination impact the personal self-concept of individual members of a stigmatized group. Contrary to earlier theorizing, there is no simple, direct relationship between collective stigmatization and individual self-esteem. Instead, the relationship is mediated by shared attributions about the causes of personal outcomes. If negative outcomes (such as social rejection or academic or economic failure) can be attributed to unjustified discrimination directed toward the group as a whole, then the self-esteem of individual group members may be shielded from effects of personal failure or negative intergroup comparisons. On the other hand, if members of stigmatized groups accept negative stereotypes and discrimination as legitimate or justified, there is a direct relationship between identification with the stigmatized group and low self-esteem at the individual level.

Attributions of legitimacy and stability also mediate the relationship between experiences of discrimination at the individual level and active involvement in social change at the group level. The dissociation between personal and collective discrimination documented by Taylor, Wright, and Porter (chapter 10, this volume) means that experiencing discrimination based on one's social group membership is neither necessary nor sufficient to motivate social change at the intergroup level. In fact, the results from Lalonde and Cameron's (chapter 11, this volume) experimental simulations suggest that the most likely responses to personal discrimination occur at the interpersonal level, directed against the perpetrator of the discriminatory behavior rather than against the system as a whole. On the other hand, these studies indicate that some individuals equate personal discrimination experiences with unjustified collective discrimination and endorse collective action as the appropriate solution. There is also evidence from the sociological literature on social activism that those individuals who experience directly the discrepancy between personal aspirations and discriminatory limitations (e.g., upper-class Blacks) are most likely to be active participants in social-change movements (Gurin, Hatchett, & Jackson, 1990). Thus, it may be the perceived convergence between discrimination at personal and collective levels that motivates social change rather than either factor alone. Again, understanding the mechanisms that link experiences at the two levels of representation should provide a more complete social psychology than traditional approaches that isolate levels of explanation.

The Locus of Prejudice: Perpetrators and Victims?

Many of the chapters in this volume share the implicit assumption that prejudice is a unilateral phenomenon. That is, some groups are represented as the sources or perpetrators of prejudice and discrimination whereas other groups are designated as targets or recipients of prejudicial attitudes and discriminatory practices. This assumption is reflected in distinctions between unstigmatized and stigmatized groups, majorities and minorities, advantaged and disadvantaged, dominant and subordinate. When one's goal is to understand the origins of prejudice, one studies groups of the first type; when one seeks to understand the consequences of prejudice and discrimination, one studies groups of the second type.

This separation between perpetrators and victims of prejudice conflates, perhaps unnecessarily, the social psychology of prejudice and the social psychology of power and dominance. Although some theories explicitly equate prejudice with social dominance motives (Sidanius, in press), most functional analyses suggest that the need for power is only one among many of the cognitive and motivational underpinnings of intergroup prejudice.

The presence of power and status differentials in many intergroup contexts raises interesting issues about the role of structural relationships between groups at the societal level and intergroup attitudes at the individual level. The fundamental question is whether structural factors play a causal role in determining affective and evaluative biases or whether intergroup structure simply provides the context within which psychological forces underlying ingroup favoritism and/or outgroup hostility are played out.

Within social psychology, research on intergroup relations initiated by Sherif and his colleagues (Sherif & Sherif, 1953; Sherif et al., 1961) best represents the structural determinist position. But the early experiments using the *minimal intergroup paradigm* (Tajfel, 1970; Tajfel, Billig, Bundy, & Flament, 1971) clearly demonstrated that intergroup competition and status differentials are not necessary prior conditions for the expression of ingroup bias and discrimination. One extreme position holds that power and status differences between groups are relevant only to the extent that they affect the salience of particular social categories and intergroup distinctions (Brewer, 1979). But Tajfel clearly went beyond a purely cognitive explanatory model and recognized the functional significance of stereotypes as justifications for existing status and power relationships between groups (Tajfel, 1981), as well as the motivational significance of threats to status relationships as a factor in intergroup discrimination (Tajfel & Turner, 1986).

The results of the program of experimental studies reported by Bourhis (chapter 8, this volume) illustrate the complex bidirectional relationships between structural and psychological determinants of prejudice and discrimination. On the one hand, these studies clearly demonstrate that power provides the means for expression of ingroup favoritism in allocation of resources rather than its motivational base. Previously low-power groups readily reveal ingroup bias when power differentials are reversed. Further, affective attachment to and positive evaluation of the ingroup are equally strong for high- and low-power groups. Motivations for group identification and preferential treatment of ingroup members do not depend on power or status advantages of the ingroup (Brewer, 1991).

On the other hand, research by Bourhis and others also indicates that power and status differentials do play some role in motivating intergroup discrimination. Members of high-power groups exhibit less discrimination and ingroup bias when status differences are secure and stable than when they are insecure or threatened. Members of low-status or disadvantaged groups exhibit greatest ingroup bias under conditions where intergroup power differentials are in flux. In either case, social change at the societal level is associated with increases in prejudice and intergroup discrimination.

Power and status relationships between groups are particularly important when ingroup evaluation is defined in terms of relative position of ingroup and outgroups. Under these conditions, positive distinctiveness is a zero-sum game, where ingroup advantage is achieved at the expense of outgroup derogation. Relative gain orientation is characteristic of many sociopolitical contexts in which intergroup attitudes are developed and expressed, but it is not the only context in which prejudice is manifest. Positive distinctiveness can be achieved in arenas that are independent of outgroup status (Mummendey & Simon, 1989), and ingroup favoritism does not necessarily imply negative attitudes toward specific outgroups.

Ingroup preference in the absence of outgroup derogation is not necessarily socially benign. Indeed, many discriminatory practices are probably motivated more by positive attitudes toward the ingroup than by the need to establish superiority over outgroups. Territorial battles over the maintenance of existing group boundaries can be quite volatile, in the absence of struggles involving dominance of one group by another. (Relationships among academic disciplines provide an interesting case in point here.) Although competitive orientations may fuel intergroup hostilities, competition is not a necessary condition for prejudice and discrimination.

Prospects for an Integrated Theory: Is There an Elephant?

To return to Fig. 13.1, the distinctions among the six conceptualizations of prejudice have some empirical basis. Affect, cognition, and behavior do seem to represent independent response systems that operate differently at interpersonal and intergroup levels. To the extent that is true, there is some justification for studying each in its own right. But, like the proverbial elephant, prejudice is a complex creature that is more than the sum of its parts. Learning that the trunk is "very like a snake," and the tusk "very like a spear" tells little about how the organism functions as a whole. To fully understand what is going on in Dubuque, one needs to know more about the mechanisms that link shared beliefs with individual information processing, how affective states such as fear and uncertainty influence the accessibility of social stereotypes, and why the forging of distinctive social identities becomes tied to intergroup conflict and hostility. This volume holds promise for how an integrated theory might emerge from the convergence of research traditions.

REFERENCES

Ajzen, I. (1988). *Attitudes, personality, and behavior.* Pacific Grove, CA: Brooks/Cole.

Allport, G. W. (1954). *On the nature of prejudice.* New York: Addison-Wesley.

Bargh, J. A. (1984). Automatic and conscious processing of social information. In R. S. Wyer and T. K. Srull (Eds.), *The handbook of social cognition* (Vol. 3, pp. 1–43). Hillsdale, NJ: Lawrence Erlbaum Associates.

Bargh, J. A., Chaiken, S., Govender, R., & Pratto, F. (1992). The generality of the automatic attitude activation effect. *Journal of Personality and Social Psychology, 62,* 893–912.

Breckler, S. J. (1984). Empirical validation of affect, behavior, and cognition as distinct components of attitude. *Journal of Personality and Social Psychology, 47,* 1191–1205.

Brewer, M. B. (1979). In-group bias in the minimal intergroup situation: A cognitive–motivational analysis. *Psychological Bulletin, 86*, 307–324.

Brewer, M. B. (1988). A dual process model of impression formation. In R. S. Wyer & T. K. Srull (Eds.), *Advances in social cognition* (Vol. 1, pp. 1–36). Hillsdale, NJ: Lawrence Erlbaum Associates.

Brewer, M. B. (1991). The social self: On being the same and different at the same time. *Personality and Social Psychology Bulletin, 17*, 475–482.

Brigham, J. C. (1971). Ethnic stereotypes. *Psychological Bulletin, 76*, 15–38.

Campbell, D. T. (1963). Social attitudes and other acquired behavioral dispositions. In S. Koch (Ed.), *Psychology: A study of a science* (Vol. 6, pp. 94–172). New York: McGraw-Hill.

Carlston, D. (in press). Impression formation and the modular mind: The associated systems theory. In L. Martin & A. Tesser (Eds.), *The construction of social judgment*. Hillsdale, NJ: Lawrence Erlbaum Associates.

Crosby, F., Bromley, S., & Saxe, L. (1980). Recent unobtrusive studies of Black-and-White discrimination and prejudice: A literature review. *Psychological Bulletin, 87*, 546–563.

Devine, P. (1989). Stereotypes and prejudice: Their automatic and controlled components. *Journal of Personality and Social Psychology, 56*, 5–18.

Esses, V. M., Haddock, G., & Zanna, M. P. (in press). Values, stereotypes, and emotions as determinants of intergroup attitudes. In D. Mackie & D. Hamilton (Eds.), *Affect, cognition, and stereotyping: Interactive processes in group perception*. New York: Academic.

Gurin, P., Hatchett, S., & Jackson, J. S. (1990). *Hope and independence: Blacks' response to electoral and party politics*. New York: Sage.

Hamilton, D. L., Sherman, S. J., & Ruvolo, C. M. (1990). Stereotype-based expectancies: Effects in information processing and social behavior. *Journal of Social Issues, 46*(2), 35–60.

Hewstone, M. (1989). Changing stereotypes with disconfirming information. In D. Bar-Tal, C. Graumann, A. Kruglanski, & W. Stroebe (Eds.), *Stereotypes and prejudice: Changing conceptions* (pp. 207–223). New York: Springer-Verlag.

Hewstone, M., & Brown, R. (1986). Contact is not enough: An intergroup perspective on the "contact hypothesis." In M. Hewstone & R. Brown (Eds.), *Contact and conflict in intergroup encounters* (pp. 1–44). Oxford, England: Basil Blackwell.

Lazarus, R. S. (1982). Thoughts on the relations between emotion and cognition. *American Psychologist, 37*, 1019–1024.

Miller, N., & Brewer, M. B. (1984). *Groups in contact: The psychology of desegregation*. Orlando, FL: Academic.

Mummendey, A., & Simon, B. (1989). Better or different? III: The impact of importance of comparison dimension and relative in-group size upon intergroup discrimination. *British Journal of Social Psychology, 28*, 1–16.

Roseman, I. J. (1984). Cognitive determinants of emotions: A structural theory. In P. Shaver (Ed.), *Review of personality and social psychology* (Vol. 5, pp. 11–36). Beverly Hills, CA: Sage.

Rothbart, M. (1991). *Stability and change in stereotypic beliefs*. Paper presented at the Annual Convention of the American Psychological Association, San Francisco.

Sears, D. O. (1983). The person-positivity bias. *Journal of Personality and Social Psychology, 44*, 233–250.

Sears, D. O. (1988). Symbolic racism. In P. A. Katz & D. A. Taylor (Eds.), *Eliminating racism: Means and controversies* (pp. 53–84). New York: Plenum.

Sherif, M., Harvey, O. J., White, B., Hood, W., & Sherif, C. W. (1961). *Intergroup conflict and cooperation: The Robbers Cave experiment*. Norman, OK: University of Oklahoma Book Exchange.

Sherif, M., & Sherif, C. W. (1953). *Groups in harmony and tension*. New York: Harper.

Sidanius, J. (in press). The psychology of group conflict and the dynamics of oppression: A social dominance perspective. In S. Iyengar & W. McGuire (Eds.), *Current approaches to political psychology*, Durham, NC: Duke University Press.

Tajfel, H. (1970). Experiments in intergroup discrimination. *Scientific American, 223,* 96–102.

Tajfel, H. (1978). *Differentiation between social groups: Studies in the social psychology of inter-group relations.* London: Academic.

Tajfel, H. (1981). *Human groups and social categories: Studies in social psychology.* Cambridge, England: Cambridge University Press.

Tajfel, H., Billig, M., Bundy, R., & Flament, C. (1971). Social categorization and intergroup behaviour. *European Journal of Social Psychology, 1,* 149–177.

Tajfel, H., & Turner, J. C. (1986). An integrative theory of intergroup behavior. In S. Worchel & W. Austin (Eds.), *The social psychology of intergroup relations* (pp. 7–24). Chicago: Nelson-Hall.

Turner, J. C., Hogg, M., Oakes, P., Reicher, S., & Wetherell, M. (1987). *Rediscovering the social group: A self-categorization theory.* Oxford: Basil Blackwell.

Weiner, B. (1982). The emotional consequences of causal ascriptions. In M. Clark & S. Fiske (Eds.), *Affect and cognition: The 17th annual Carnegie Symposium on cognition* (pp. 185–210). Hillsdale, NJ: Lawrence Erlbaum Associates.

Wilkerson, I. (1991, November 3). Seeking a racial mix, Dubuque finds tension. *The New York Times,* p. 30.

Wilson, T. D., & Dunn, D. S. (1986). Effects of introspection on attitude–behavior consistency: Analyzing reasons versus focusing on feelings. *Journal of Experimental Social Psychology, 22,* 249–263.

Zajonc, R. B. (1984). On the primacy of affect. *American Psychologist, 39,* 117–123.

Author Index

Subject Index